D1561458

The Lytle-Tate Letters

The Lytle-Tate Letters

The Correspondence of Andrew Lytle and Allen Tate

Edited by
THOMAS DANIEL YOUNG
and ELIZABETH SARCONE

University Press of Mississippi
Jackson & London

The paper in this book meets the guidelines for permanence and durability of the Committee on Production Guidelines for Book Longevity of the Council on Library Resources.

British Library Cataloguing in Publication data is available.

Library of Congress Cataloging-in-Publication Data

Lytle, Andrew Nelson, 1902–
The Lytle-Tate letters: the correspondence of Andrew Lytle and Allen Tate/edited by Thomas Daniel Young and Elizabeth Sarcone.
p. cm.
Includes index.
ISBN 0–87805–326–3 (alk. paper)
1. Lytle, Andrew Nelson, 1902– —Correspondence. 2. Tate, Allen, 1899– —Correspondence. 3. Authors, American—20th century—Correspondence. I. Tate, Allen, 1899– . II. Young. Thomas Daniel, 1919– . III. Sarcone, Elizabeth, 1947– . IV. Title.
PS3523.Y88Z497 1987
816′.52′08—dc19 87-16014
CIP

Contents

Introduction

These letters reveal that a closer, more personal relationship existed between Andrew Lytle and Allen Tate than that between any of the other Nashville writers. In fact one would have to search carefully through literary history to find two other writers who confided so completely in each other. Tate wrote many letters to other poets, critics, and novelists. In fact after searching through the collections of letters at Princeton and Vanderbilt—and there are many to and from him elsewhere—one begins to wonder how Tate had time to produce nearly fifty books,—which included more than two hundred poems and nearly as many essays. In every genre in which he worked, furthermore, including fiction, he is one of the most original and influential artists in modern American literature.

In a closely printed volume of more than four-hundred pages of *The Selected Letters of John Crowe Ransom,* about half of the letters are to Tate, and there is sufficient evidence to support the supposition that Tate answered every letter he received. Few of these letters, however, were personal letters. Many of them were devoted to developing a theory of the nature and function of poetry or to discussing ways in which one could best employ an influential literary quarterly. The correspondence between Tate and Donald Davidson makes a book of more than four-hundred pages. Although there is some discussion of personal matters, particularly to poems, essays, and books that both men had written, the most interesting and informative of the letters are those devoted to the activities of the Fugitives and the Agrarians. For nearly thirty years Tate corresponded with John Peale Bishop, and it is true that some of the letters were devoted to quasi-personal matters, but most of them were concerned with close and helpful readings of each other's poems or to the state of the vocation of letters in America. This is not to say that there was not a feeling of admiration and respect between the two men. Bishop admitted more than once that had it not been for Tate, he probably would have given up the writing of poetry while he was a young man. Tate's admiration for Bishop, as man and poet, is obvious, not only in his letters but in the essays he wrote about Bishop, and the edition of his friend's poetry he edited after Bishop's death.

These three men are not the only ones to whom Tate wrote. There were also T. S. Eliot, Fitzgerald, Harriet Monroe, Marianne Moore, and many, many others. The letters to Lytle, however, are different. Not only did these two discuss in minute details the poems, stories, essays, novels, or plays that the other was writing, they wrote about *I'll Take My Stand, Who Owns America?* and Southern art, culture and social institutions. They discussed frankly, and not always uncritically, their mutual friends: Davidson, Ransom, and Robert Penn Warren.

The correspondence gets off to a slow start. There is no evidence to indicate that Lytle and Tate were close friends at Vanderbilt. Lytle was never a member of the Fugitives, though he did attend one or two meetings of the group and he published an undistinguished poem, "Edward Graves," in *The Fugitive* as well as one or two in *Driftwood Flames,* the undergraduate literary magazine. At Vanderbilt Lytle's primary literary interest was drama, and immediately after graduation he enrolled in George Pierce Baker's school of drama at Yale. About the same time Tate went to New York to try to earn his living at free-lance journalism. Lytle appeared as an actor a few times in Off-Broadway Theaters, Tate attended as many of the performances as he could, and wrote Lytle complimentary letters about his presentation of his roles, although he always protested that he knew nothing about drama and surely could not offer any helpful criticism. Then Tate, apparently lonely and wanting some reminder of his Nashville days, began writing Lytle to visit him and his wife, Caroline Gordon, so there are many notes of invitation and acceptance or regrets. There are also many apologies because promises were not kept.

Tate and Lytle began to realize that they were kindred spirits, however, after Lytle moved back to Tennessee and was living either in Murfreesboro or at Cornsilk, the family plantation near Guntersville,

Alabama. Although Tate was in France on a Guggenheim Fellowship, he and Lytle began to exchange views about the proposed symposium defending the South and its culture. They agreed from the first in their opposition to the emphasis that modern society has placed on technology and consumer economics. They believed such emphasis had tended to dehumanize man so that he could no longer create an intellectual climate in which Christian values could exist. They did not believe that the problems of modern man could be solved by science or the planned society of some social scientists. Man should not accept change in the name of progress. He should be convinced that that which he was accepting was superior to that which he was rejecting. All of these things and more, both agreed on completely, but they discovered how close their agreement was only after their detailed discussion of these matters in their letters. Along with Robert Penn Warren, they strongly opposed calling the symposium *I'll Take My Stand* because they thought a phrase from a popular song was little more than a Madison Avenue advertising slogan, intended to attract attention, and did little to suggest the nature and intensity of their protests. Although it must be said that the title suggested by the dissenters—*Tracts Against Communism*—was little more appropriate than the one used. The agreement between Tate and Lytle on the essential purpose of the dissent was firmly established, however; therefore when Tate and Herbert Agar were planning *Who Owns America?* (1936), Lytle was Tate's principal advisor.

Lytle and Tate were not in complete agreement, however, on the means by which one could acquire the good life. Lytle was convinced that being firmly settled on a piece of land and practicing subsistence farming was the only way one could be sure of avoiding the dehumanizing effects of uncontrolled acquisitive materialism. In his young and middle years, therefore, he was searching for a small farm on which he could raise most of his food and have sufficient time left for writing. Tate, on the other hand, agreed with Thoreau, who insisted that once one became thoroughly convinced that he should be sure that any material possession was worth no more than the amount of that which we call life we must exchange for it, he could find the good life almost anywhere. Tate was content, therefore, after his experience at Benfolly, a farm near Clarksville, Tennessee, to teach during the year and either spend the summer in Monteagle, Tennessee, or travel abroad. After Lytle was married and had the responsibilities of a wife and family, he came nearer Tate's attitude.

Both Tate and Lytle sent their poems, essays, and novels to the other for comment and suggestions for improvement. Tate sent Lytle several drafts of the poem that would eventually become "The Mediterranean" with questions for Lytle's comments on specific lines or images. (At the same time he was sending copies to John Peale Bishop requesting the same information.) It is interesting to examine the final draft and note which of the suggestions from Lytle and which from Bishop went into the final version of the poem. (Although Lytle was not a poet, and freely admitted it, he had definite ideas about how a line or an image was supposed to affect the reader, and he was not at all reluctant to express his opinions.)

When Tate was writing *The Fathers* (1938) he was having trouble with transition. He immediately sent a draft to Lytle and asked his advice. Lytle reassured him that his use of an involved angle of narration was handled very well—he wanted the reader to see most events from two points of view: how the event impressed a fourteen-year-old as he experienced it and how it impressed the narrator, the fourteen-year-old who is now a retired doctor and has had fifty years to think about it. The greatest difficulty in the novel, Lytle wrote Tate (and most readers have agreed with Lytle), is that the reader is not well enough aware of the protagonist's condition to accept his falling into a trance and conversing with his dead grandfather. Although Tate altered the passage to indicate the boy's illness, he was never able to establish the illusion of reality he desired.

Lytle followed Tate's pattern and sent his books to Tate as he completed them—he sent *The Velvet Horn* (1957) many times before he finished it—and Tate's remarks were always candid, incisive and usually helpful. *Bedford Forrest and His Critter Company* (1931) is the "best biographical study available" of the man Lee thought was the outstanding soldier on the Southern side in the Civil War. *The Long Night* (1936): The reader has to go through too many seemingly unnecessary details before he is made aware of their function or is involved in any significant action. Although Lytle worked hard on the first part of the novel, many readers still react to it as Tate did. *At the Moon's Inn* (1941): The introductory section is too long and really not essential to the story Lytle is telling; furthermore it is complete within itself. Lytle took Tate's advice and published it as a novella in the *Kenyon Review* (1942), as "Alchemy," where it consumed fifty-four pages, one of the longest works of fiction Ransom ever printed in the *Review. A Name for Evil* (1947): Too obviously an imitation of James's *A Turn of the Screw,* Tate wrote, "I am always so vividly aware of James's story that I lose the thread of yours." Lytle even uses, Tate pointed out, some of James's language. Besides, the point of view or angle of narration destroys the illusion of reality. James, Tate claimed, never allows his narrator to *see* the apparition; he made her aware of his presence by other means. Lytle admits that he deliberately imitates, but he tries to defend himself on Tate's final points by saying that he was trying to differentiate between different grades of evil.

The greatest artistic difficulty Lytle ever encountered in his work apparently was trying to find an appropriate angle of narration from which to tell *The Velvet Horn* (1957), surely one of the most original and compelling works of fiction in twentieth-century America. He was literally stuck on this point, how to present his narrative, for years. After Tate had read and thought about a draft of *The Velvet Horn* for a week, he wrote, "You have two wonderful episodes—the waterwitching and the hunt-seduction-knifing episodes." But, he continued, "The continuity is tough. You would lose nothing and you would attract your reader's attention by making all the complicated family relationships perfectly plain at the outset." In this novel, Tate continued, you are extending the method used by Faulkner in *As I Lay Dying,* but your narrative is much more complicated than Faulkner's. His story is very simple, really concentrated on and concerned with getting Addie Bundren to the place where she wishes to be buried. The consciousness of the characters is very narrow and their soliloquies are very narrow, but in your novel the action reaches such "magnitude that it is severed from the narrator" and the reader is hopelessly lost.

Lytle's response to this astute reading by Tate is one of the important essays on the creative process in fiction written in the twentieth century. "I had not realized how confusing the family relationship is," he wrote on 11 December 1954; "I think one reason for it is that I had so much trouble recreating the physical world, and even learning about the people, that I had to plunge in where I could in an exploratory way, to involve them, to see who they were." He had started out, he wrote, with an incestuous theme, "which I feel is pretty strong in our society," but then he realized he had to explain what incest is. Then he became aware that he wanted to set the novel between 1880 and 1910 "which I take to be the last moment of equilibrium in the western world." He proceeds to relate how in the process of writing who the protagonist of the novel is and in five pages to justify his method of creating the novel. His argument is very convincing, but he uses as many of Tate's suggestions as he can.

More than anything else, however, this is a personal correspondence. In some of the early letters each man begins to call the other "brother"—though half-facetiously, as in "Brer Tate" or "Brer Lytle"—but it soon becomes evident that the relationship between the two is that of two brothers with the deepest affection for each other. Lytle spent a greal deal of time and effort trying to find a place so that they could live near each other, but it was not until both retired that he could arrange that they live within easy visiting distance, one in Monteagle and one in Sewanee, just a few miles apart. Even during the time they lived thousands of miles from each other, however, they made every attempt to arrange travel schedules and vacations so that they could spend as much time as possible together.

It was this enduring affection that sustained Lytle through the excruciatingly slow and painful death of his beloved wife, Edna, and through two serious and incapacitating operations. Tate relied on Lytle, too, as he attempted to fill the emptiness left in his life when Caroline Gordon divorced him after thirty-six years of marriage. Lytle was also the person from whom he expected to receive the strength, sympathy, and resourcefulness to cope with the many complications of his marriage to Isabella Gardner. Along with Tate's wife Helen, Lytle supported Tate as he mourned for his son Michael, who died so unfortunately before he was a year old.

Few other writers in American literature have had a relationship similar to that which existed between Allen Tate and Andrew Lytle. But to know this fact, the best plan, it would seem, is to let him read the letters and discover it for himself.

Thomas Daniel Young
Elizabeth Sarcone

Chronologies

JOHN ORLEY ALLEN TATE

1899 Born in Winchester, Clark County, Kentucky, to John Orley and Eleanor Varnell Tate.

1906–8 Lives in Nashville at intervals while brothers Ben and Varnell are in Vanderbilt; enters Tarbox School in Nashville; remains only three months.

1909–12 Attends Cross School, a private academy emphasizing Latin and rhetoric, in Louisville, Kentucky.

1912–14 Public high school in Ashland, Kentucky.

1915 Half-year in public high school, Evansville, Indiana.

1916–17 October 1916 to April 1917 in Cincinnati Conservatory of Music; studies violin under Jean Ten Have and Eugene Ysayë; enters Georgetown Preparatory School to prepare for Vanderbilt admission.

1918 Admitted to Vanderbilt for fall with provision that he pass a third-year Latin examination; taught English by W. C. Curry and John Crowe Ransom, philosophy by Herbert Sanborn, Greek by Herbert Cushing Tolman.

1919–20 First published poems, "Impossible" and "Red Stains," appear in *American Poetry Magazine;* joins Calumet Club in which fellow members are Ransom, Curry, Davidson, and Alec B. Stevenson.

1921 Publishes "A Ballade of the Lugubrious Wench" in *Jade,* humor magazine of Calumet Club, of which he is president; invited by Davidson to informal discussions with group that later published *The Fugitive*.

1922 In April, in first issue of *The Fugitive,* publishes under Henry Feathertop pseudonym "To Intellectual Detachment" and "Sinbad"; from June to September in Valle Crucis, North Carolina, for reasons of health; in fall and winter works in family coal business in Ashland, Kentucky.

1923 Returns in February to Vanderbilt to complete degree; meets Robert Penn Warren and rooms with him and Ridley Wills; places "Calidus Juventa," "Euthanasia," "William Blake," and other poems in *Double Dealer;* with Ridley Wills writes *The Golden Mean,* privately printed in a two-hundred-copy edition; is graduated in August; exchanges letters with Ransom in the *Literary Review* on *The Waste Land;* assistant editor of *The Fugitive;* remains in Nashville during fall expecting scholarship for master's degree in classical studies.

1924 In February accepts position as English teacher in Lumberport, West Virginia, high school; meets Laura Riding Gottschalk in Louisville; in New York meets Hart Crane, Gorham Munson, Slater Brown, Edmund Wilson, and others; returns in July to Guthrie, Kentucky, to visit Warren; there meets Caroline Gordon, whom he marries in the fall; returns to New York and rents apartment at 30 Jones Street; begins career of free-lance writing with the *Nation,* the *New Republic,* the *Herald Tribune,* and other periodicals.

1925 Accepts position with Climax Publishing Company, publisher of *Ranch Romance* and *Telling Tales;* Nancy Tate born September 23; Tate moves to larger flat on Morton Street; meets John Peale Bishop; rents part of rural house in Patterson, New York; Crane lives with the Tates.

1926 Tate working on "Ode to the Confederate Dead"; moves to 27 Bank Street, New York City, where he does janitorial work in building to assist with expenses.

1927 "Poetry and the Absolute," first important critical essay, appears; helps find publisher for *Fugitive* anthology; meets Ford Madox Ford.

1928 Contributes to *Fugitives: An Anthology of Verse;* publishes *Mr. Pope and Other Poems* and *Stonewall Jackson: The Good Soldier;* receives Guggenheim fellowship; in London from September to November; meets T. S. Eliot, Herbert Read, and, in Oxford, L. A. G. Strong; in Paris on Thanksgiving Day; meets Julian Green, Morley Callaghan, Sylvia Beach, Ernest Hemingway, Gertrude Stein, and others; lives rent-free for six months in Ford's apartment at 32 rue de Vangirard; Warren, then a Rhodes scholar, visits him; establishes friendship with John Peale Bishop; writes "Mother and Son."

1929 Publishes *Jefferson Davis: His Rise and Fall;* writes "Message from Abroad."

1930 Sails for New York, January 1; leaves for Tennessee in February; in April is given by his brother Ben an antebellum farm house near Clarksville, Tennessee, about forty-five miles from Nashville; Caroline and Allen christen home "Benfolly"; contributes "Remarks on Southern Religion" to *I'll Take My Stand.*

1931 "Sonnets of the Blood" appears; begins work on a biography of Lee, never completed.

1932 Becomes southern editor for *Hound and Horn;* publishes *Poems: 1928–31;* writes "To the Lacedemonians" for the Confederate soldiers' June reunion in Richmond; edits southern number for *Poetry;* in France from June 1932 to February 1933 (Caroline Gordon has Guggenheim award); writes "Picnic at Cassis" (later entitled "The Mediterranean").

1933 Becomes friends with Herbert Agar and invites him to submit articles to the *American Review;* receives Midland Author's Prize from *Poetry;* "The Immortal Woman," a short story Davidson found "repulsively Jamesian," appears.

1934 With Herbert Agar explores possibilities of establishing a midwest-southern political weekly; "Sonnets at Christmas" appears; becomes lecturer in English at Southwestern, replacing Warren, and moves to 2374 Forrest Avenue in Memphis.

1935 In July makes first appearance at a writers' conference, at Olivet College, Michigan; "The Profession of Letters in the South" is published.

1936 Edits, with Agar, *Who Owns America?* to which he contributes essay "Notes on Liberty and Property"; publishes *The Mediter-*

ranean and Other Poems and *Reactionary Essays on Poetry and Ideas;* resigns from Southwestern and returns to Benfolly; takes summer job as lecturer in English at Columbia University; "Narcissus as Narcissus" published; with Anne Goodwin Winslow does dramatic version of *The Turn of the Screw* entitled "The Governess."

1937 Publishes *Selected Poems;* Ford Madox Ford spends summer with Tate at Benfolly; Robert Lowell visits; becomes involved in the controversy over Ransom's leaving Vanderbilt for Kenyon; participates in writers' conference at Olivet College.

1938 Accepts position as professor of English at the Woman's College of North Carolina and moves to 112 Arden Place, Greensboro; spends summer at Scoville Cottage, West Cornwall, Connecticut; completes *The Fathers* there on July 21; novel appears in early fall; "Tension in Poetry" appears; becomes advisory editor of *Kenyon Review.*

1939 Lectures at St. John's College, Annapolis, Maryland, and considers position there; participates in a writers' conference at Savannah, Georgia; becomes resident poet in Creative Arts Program at Princeton; spends summer at "Westwood Cottage," Monteagle, Tennessee, where he finishes "The Trout Map," in September and moves to 16 Linden Lane, Princeton; impressed with professionalism at Princeton and the fact that the creative writing program is separate from the English department; begins work on "Miss Emily and the Bibliographer."

1940 Begins to appear as panelist on CBS program "Invitation to Learning"; declines offer to become consultant in poetry to the Library of Congress; "Understanding Modern Poetry" appears.

1941 Publishes "Literature as Knowledge: Comment and Comparison" and *Reason in Madness, Critical Essays.*

1942 Submits unsuccessful application for commission in U.S. Naval Reserve; with John Peale Bishop edits *American Harvest;* edits *The Language of Poetry* and *Princeton Verse Between Two Wars;* publishes "*The Fugitive,* 1922–25, A Personal Recollection"; resigns at Princeton and returns to Monteagle, where he writes "More Sonnets at Christmas." Robert Lowell and his wife, Jean Stafford, join Tates there.

1943 Completes draft of "Jubilo" on January 20 and "Winter Mask" in February; begins "Seasons of the Soul"; translates *Pervergilium Veneris* and writes "More Sonnets at Christmas"; in September moves to Washington to accept position as consultant in poetry at the Library of Congress; edits, with the assistance of Frances Cheney, *Sixty American Poets, 1896–1944, A Checklist;* becomes involved in the activities to save the life of Ezra Pound.

1944 John Peale Bishop dies April 4; begins work on Bishop's manuscripts to prepare the collected edition of his poems, not completed until 1948; in July moves to Sewanee, Tennessee, to become editor of *Sewanee Review.*

1945 On January 23 consults with Archibald Macleish about position of cultural attache to the American embassy in Paris; resigns from the *Sewanee Review* October 15; publishes "The New Provincialism, with an Epilogue on the Southern Novel."

1946 In January receives divorce from Caroline Gordon; visits her in New York in February and in March they agree to remarry in April; sells Benfolly; moves to apartment at 108 Perry Street, New York; becomes editor of belles letters for Henry Holt and Company; T. S. Eliot visits Tates in May.

1948 Publishes *Poems, 1922–1947,* "Longinus and the New Criticism," and *On the Limits of Poetry, Selected Essays 1928–1948;* leaves Henry Holt to become lecturer at New York University; becomes a fellow of the Kenyon School of English; serves on jury which awards Bollingen prize to Pound and states reasons for voting for Pound in *Partisan Review.*

1949 Publishes *The Hovering Fly and Other Essays;* serves year as visiting professor of humanities at University of Chicago; buys home from Louis O. Coxe on Nassau Street in Princeton; for Ben Tate, who had paid for it, house is called "Benbrackets."

1950 Joins Roman Catholic Church.

1951 With Caroline Gordon publishes *The House of Fiction;* publishes "To Whom is the Poet Responsible?"; accepts appointment as professor of English at the University of Minnesota and in September moves to Joseph Warren Beach's old house at 1409 University Avenue, Minneapolis.

1952 Delivers "The Man of Letters in the Modern World" as Phi Beta Kappa lecture at Minnesota; delegate to the Congress for

Cultural Freedom in Paris, where he delivers a shortened version of "The Man of Letters in the Modern World"; in August delegate to the UNESCO conference in Venice; granted audience by Pope Pius XII; publishes "The Angelic Imagination: Poe and the Power of Words," "Is Literary Criticism Possible?" and "The Symbolic Imagination: A Meditation on Dante's Three Mirrors."

1953 In summer, lectures in the American Studies Program in Oxford under auspices of Fulbright program; during fall and winter is Fulbright professor at the University of Rome; publishes *The Forlorn Demon: Didactic and Critical Essays.*

1955 Tate and Caroline Gordon separate.

1956 Arranges lecture for T. S. Eliot at University of Minnesota; Fugitive reunion at Vanderbilt May 3–5; lectures in India during fall for Fulbright program; returns by way of Europe and lectures in Turin, Rome, Milan, Florence, Paris, London, and Nottingham; receives Bollingen Prize.

1958 Fulbright lecturer at Oxford University, from which he receives honorary master of arts degree; lectures at the University of Leeds in spring and Harvard University during summer.

1959 Is divorced by Caroline Gordon and on August 27 marries Isabella Gardner; autumn issue of *Sewanee Review* is devoted to a celebration of his sixtieth birthday; Ransom, Davidson, Eliot, and Read are among those offering tributes; publishes *Collected Essays*.

1960 Publishes *Poems;* publishes "A Southern Mode of the Imagination."

1961 Receives the Brandeis University Medal for Poetry.

1962 Receives *Medaglia d'Oro di Società Italiana di Dante Alighieri* at Florence, Italy.

1963 Receives $5,000 Fellowship Award from the Academy of American Poets.

1964 Elected to American Academy of Arts and Letters.

1965 Elected to American Academy of Arts and Sciences.

1966 Isabella Gardner is granted a divorce on March 28; made Regents' Professor of English; marries Helen Heinz on July 30; teaches at University of North Carolina at Greensboro during fall semester.

1967 Teaches spring term at Vanderbilt; twin sons, John Allen and Michael Paul, born August 30.

1968 Serves as president of the National Institute of Arts and Letters; retires from University of Minnesota in June and moves to Sewanee; Michael dies in July.

1969 A third son, Benjamin Lewis Bogan, born December 18. *Essays of Four Decades* is published by Swallow.

1971 *The Swimmers and Other Selected Poems* is published by Scribners and Oxford University Press.

1974 Delivers principal address on centenary of Robert Frost's birth, March 26, Library of Congress.

1976 Publishes *Memoirs and Opinions* by the *Swallow Press.*

1977 Publishes Collected Poems by Farrar, Straus and Giroux.

1979 Dies in Nashville on February 9.

1983 *The Poetry Reviews of Allen Tate, 1924–1944,* ed. by Ashley Brown and Frances Cheney, published by Louisiana State University Press.

ANDREW NELSON LYTLE

1902 Born on December 26, in Murfreesboro, Tennessee, to Robert Logan and Lillie Belle Nelson Lytle.

1907 Father buys the Log Cabin at Monteagle, Tennessee.

1916–20 Enrolls in Sewanee Military Academy as a day student in fall of 1916; attends as boarding student after fall of 1917 when mother buys house in Sewanee; wins the Golden Medal for Scholarship; upon graduation is offered but refuses an appointment to West Point; travels in France with mother and sister, Polly; writes a letter from France to Sewanee's headmaster, Major Henry Gass, which is printed in *The Little Tiger,* the student publication; prepares for admission to Oxford while at the home of Mademoiselle Durieux on the Left Bank in Paris with an English tutor; studies fencing.

1921 Enters Exeter College, Oxford; called home after three weeks because of death of grandfather, John Nelson; enrolls in Vanderbilt in fall to be near grandmother, Molly Nelson, in Murfreesboro.

1922 Takes sophomore literature under Donald Davidson.

1923 Publishes two poems in Vanderbilt's undergraduate review, *Driftwood Flames,* "Hill Cattle" and "Une Réflexion."

1924 Becomes a student of John Crowe Ransom and a classmate of Robert Penn Warren during Vanderbilt career; writes *Journal of European Tour: 1 July–6 September 1924;* attends Fugitive meetings during senior year.

1925 Publishes "Edward Graves" in March issue of *The Fugitive;* Vanderbilt's Calumet Club produces his one-act play, *The Gold Tooth;* graduates from Vanderbilt with B.A. degree; goes to Guntersville, Alabama, where he runs his father's farm, Cornsilk, for a year.

1926 Begins a long play entitled *New Ground;* raises strawberries; becomes a student of George Pierce Baker at the 47 Workshop at Yale in the fall; wins several acting roles.

1927 Receives an invitation from Tate in March to visit him at 27 Bank Street, New York City; their friendship begins.

1928 Baker's Experimental Theatre produces his one-act play, *The Lost Sheep;* earns role in a twelve-week Broadway production of *The Grey Fox.*

1929 Does research for a biography of Nathan Bedford Forrest; plans a biography of J. C. Calhoun; lives with a paralytic boy as a paid housekeeper; returns to South in May to continue Forrest research; spends June in New York trying out for *The Patriarch* which opens in fall; becomes involved in plans for an Agrarian offensive.

1930 Contributes "The Hind Tit" to Agrarian symposium; argues against title, *I'll Take My Stand;* continues work on *Forrest.*

1931 Oversees strawberry crop in Huntsville, Alabama; publishes *Bedford Forrest and His Critter Company;* reviews Stribling's *The Forge* in "Life in the Cotton Belt" for *New Republic;* is reported in July in Huntsville's *The Times* to advocate erecting a Forrest statue; returns to Southampton on Long Island in summer where, with George Haight as director and treasurer, he and others start the Hampton Players; in July performs in *The Immodest Violet;* reviews four Lincoln books for *Virginia Quarterly Review* in "The Lincoln Myth."

1932 Publishes first piece of fiction, "Old Scratch in the Valley," in *Virginia Quarterly Review;* decides against Calhoun biography; reviews book on Robert Barnwell Rhett and one on Edmund Ruffin for *Hound and Horn* in "Principles of Secession"; visits Albemarle, Virginia; there becomes engaged to a daughter of the Pattons who, in September, breaks the engagement; gets involved in a legal battle over mortgage rights to Cornsilk; continues work on long play; begins "Mr. MacGregor." His mother dies.

1933 Reviews book on Sherman for *Virginia Quarterly Review* in "A Tactical Blunder"; contributes "A Confederate General" to *New Republic;* finishes revision of "The Backwoods Progression" and publishes it in *American Review.*

1934 Receives Owsley's narrative of his Uncle Dink in June; attends Alabama's Writers' Conference; completes "John Taylor and the Political Economy," a three-part essay published in *American Review;* spends Christmas in New Orleans with Tates.

1935 Publishes "The Passion of Aleck Maury," a review of Caroline Gordon's novel in *New Republic;* attends the Mercantile Library Association meeting in Cincinnati with Tate; "Mr. MacGregor" appears in *Virginia Quarterly Review* in April; works on a play, possibly *The Gold Dust Family,* while at Cornsilk; reviews Chilton's *Follow the Furies* and, later, Freeman's *R. E. Lee* in *The Southern Review;* begins paper for second agrarian symposium.

1936 Becomes professor of American History at Southwestern College in Memphis; "Jericho, Jericho, Jericho" appears in *The Southern Review;* contributes "The Small Farm Secures the State" to *Who Owns America?;* by August the Alabama Supreme Court decides in favor of his father in farm lawsuit; "The Approach of the Southern Writer to His Material" appears in *The Atlanta Constitution.*

1937 Goes to New Orleans in February then on to Hollywood; visits George Haight and investigates movie possibilities; helps wage campaign to retain Ransom at Vanderbilt; begins work on *At the Moon's Inn.*

1938 Reviews Styron's *The Cast Iron Man* in "John C. Calhoun" for *The Southern Review;* continues research on De Soto in

Nashville and Little Rock; marries Edna Langdon Barker in June; spends three months in California working on novel; moves to Monteagle in fall.

1939 Attends Writers' Conference in Savannah; continues work on De Soto and publishes excerpt, "A Fragment: How Nuno Tovar Came to Cross the Ocean Sea," in June; remains at Monteagle but buys a 330-acre farm in Robertson County, Tennessee.

1940 Receives Guggenheim Fellowship; spends part of summer with Tates at Princeton; in December, secures 627 Dumaine Street in New Orleans for three months and works on De Soto.

1941 Gets a three-month extension of Guggenehim; returns to Monteagle around June first; accepts offer of a rent-free house at Sewanee in exchange for public lectures; *At the Moon's Inn* appears November 16, the day his first daughter, Pamela, is born.

1942 Accepts a teaching position at Sewanee Military Academy; later becomes professor of history at the University of the South and managing editor of *Sewanee Review;* "Alchemy" comes out in *Kenyon Review.*

1943 Reviews Freeman's *Lee's Lieutenants* for *Sewanee Review;* father dies on Valentine's Day in Gunterville; sells what remains of Cornsilk after TVA flooding; spends summer at farm in Portland in Robertson County; publishes a review of Warren's *At Heaven's Gate* in *Sewanee Review,* declines job in war department.

1944 Raises turkeys and tobacco in Portland; continues to edit *Review* through spring issue; goes on duck hunt to Reelfoot Lake which contributes to the creation of "The Guide."

1945 "The Guide" (later "The Mahogany Frame") appears in *Sewanee Review* and wins Lytle a cash prize from Prentice-Hall.

1946 Remains in Portland and begins work on *A Name for Evil;* a second daughter, Katherine Anne, is born on May 12.

1947 Goes on University of Iowa for spring semester to take over fiction classes and work on novella; makes a three-day trip to California in April; spends summer in Portland finishing *A Name for Evil* which comes out in August; returns to Iowa in fall as Acting Head of the Iowa University School of Writing; Flannery O'Connor is in his writing class.

1948 Takes over household chores while Edna recuperates from an operation; attends a ten-day workshop in Missouri in June; returns to Portland; publishes "Note on a Traditional Sensibility," a tribute to Ransom in *Sewanee Review;* in fall accepts position of Lecturer in Creative Writing at the University of Florida in Gainesville.

1949 Publishes "Regeneration for Man," an essay on Faulkner's *Intruder in the Dust* in *Sewanee Review;* starts work on what will become *The Velvet Horn;* sells the Log Cabin to the Woman's Association; begins building a house in Gainesville; assesses Gordon's fiction in a *Sewanee Review* essay entitled "Caroline Gordon and the Historic Image."

1950 Moves into newly finished house at 1822 North West 8th Ave. in May.

1951 Continues work on *The Velvet Horn.*

1952 Contributes to "The Agrarians Today," a symposium published in *Shenandoah;* leases Portland farm.

1953 Submits "How Many Miles to Babylon" to the Hopkins symposium; "Image as the Guide to Meaning in the Historical Novel" appears in *Sewanee Review;* the third daughter, Lillie Langdon is born November 15.

1954 Heads the humanities division of the International Seminar of the Harvard Summer School; visits the Allen Tates in Princeton; works five weeks on a Faulkner paper; reviews Gerald Carson's *The Old Country Store* for *The Southern Folklore Quarterly;* goes to New York in December to summarize three papers given at the MLA symposium, "The Southern Literary Renascence."

1955 Publishes Faulkner essay, "The Son of Man: He Will Prevail," in *Sewanee Review;* continues work on *The Velvet Horn;* his "A Summing Up," along with the three other papers from the MLA symposium, is published in *Shenandoah.*

1956 Participates in the Fugitives' Reunion held at Vanderbilt, May 3–5; "What Quarter of the Night," an excerpt from *The Velvet Horn,* still in progress, appears in *Sewanee Review;* publishes "A

Hero and the Doctrinaires of Defeat" in *The Georgia Review* and an essay on Gordon's collection of short stories, *The Forest of the South,* in *Critique.*

1957 Leaves Bobbs-Merrill for McDowell, Obolensky; sells Portland farm in April; publishes an essay on Faulkner, "*The Town:* Helen's Last Stand" in *Sewanee Review; The Velvet Horn* comes out in August; goes to New York to promote sales.

1958 Reviews works by Walter Sullivan, Howard Nemerov, and Peter Taylor in "The Displaced Family" in *Sewanee Review;* reviews *The Lasting South,* ed. by Kilpatrick and Rubin, in "The Quality of the South" for *National Review; A Novel, Novella and Four Stories* comes out with a new "Foreword"; reviews Cheney's *This Is Adam* and Wright's *The Long Dream* in "Man or Symbol" for *National Review.*

1959 "The Working Novelist and the Mythmaking Process" appears in *Daedalus;* has a serious operation in June which forces him to cancel a summer lectureship at Harvard; attends McDowell, Obolensky anniversary party in New York in August; visits Tate and Isabella at Princeton; publishes "Allen Tate: Upon the Occasion of His Sixtieth Birthday" in *Sewanee Review;* writes an introduction for a new printing of *Forrest;* spends Christmas with Tates in Florida.

1960 Funding from Guggenheim Fellowship begins; makes plans to write memoir; travels to Mexico, but Edna becomes ill there; returns to Florida then Memphis where she is diagnosed as having lung cancer; buys back the Log Cabin from the Woman's Association; the new printing of *Forrest* appears.

1961 Takes leave of absence from Gainesville in May to edit *Sewanee Review* and becomes lecturer in English at the University of the South; winterizes the Log Cabin; begins editing *Review* with Autumn number.

1962 Attends Literary Festival in Spartanburg and ALMA in New York; works on essay on impressionism.

1963 Learns that Edna's cancer has returned; publishes "Agee's Letters to Father Flye" in *Sewanee Review* and "Impressionism, the Ego and the First Person" in *Daedalus;* is called back to hospital during Vanderbilt's annual symposium; Edna dies April 26; invites Pamela and her husband, Jim Law, to move in the Log

Cabin; fulfills engagements at Richmond, Kentucky, and Tryon, North Carolina, before attending the William Elliott celebration in Cambridge in July.

1964 Undergoes another serious operation in spring; daughter Kate marries in August; delivers Founders' Day Address, "A Christian University and the Word," at Sewanee in October; publishes a tribute to Flannery O'Connor in *Esprit,* the literary magazine of the University of Scranton.

1965 Plans a special issue of the *Review* devoted to Eliot and guest edited by Tate; is accorded an honorary Doctor of Letters degree from Kenyon; publishes an essay on Hemingway, "*A Moveable Feast:* The Going To and Fro" and one on *Bovary,* "In Defense of a Passionate and Incorruptible Heart" in *Sewanee Review.*

1966 Brings out Eliot issue; participates in a discussion published in *Alabama Alumni News* as "And Like All Good Conversations It Never Ends; adds " 'The Open Boat': A Pagan Tale" to the essays collected and published as *The Hero with the Private Parts;* receives the National Foundation for the Arts and Humanities Award.

1967 "A Wake for the Living" appears in *Sewanee Review* as an excerpt from a memoir by that name, still in progress.

1968 Attends Dallas Literary Festival honoring Nashville Agrarians and presents paper on Joyce; promoted to rank of Professor of English at University of the South.

1969 *A Name for Evil* appears as unauthorized Avon Paperback; "A Reading of Joyce's 'The Dead' " printed in *Sewanee Review;* adds "Foreword" to a collection of Owsley's essays, *The South: Old and New Frontiers.*

1970 Accorded honorary Doctor of Letters degree by University of Florida during Florida's Writers' Conference; "Jericho, Jericho, Jericho" is dramatized at Vanderbilt.

1971 "The Garden of Innocence," a second excerpt from *The Wake* and "The State of Letters in a Time of Disorder" appear in *Sewanee Review;* edits and prepares "Foreword" to *Craft and Vision: The Best Fiction from "The Sewanee Review."*

1972 "The Old Neighborhood," a third excerpt from the memoir in progress, appears in *The Southern Review.*

1973 A surreptitious Avon Paperback of *The Long Night* comes out in March; retires as editor of *Sewanee Review* with the Autumn issue; accorded honorary Doctor of Letters degree from University of the South.

1974 Serves as Vanderbilt's Visiting Professor during spring semester.

1975 Moves to a 75-acre farm in Kentucky in April; *A Wake for the Living* appears in July; a response to questions is recorded in *South Dakota Review* as "The Writer's Sense of Place."

1977 Composes a tribute to Peter Taylor, "On a Birthday," for *Shenandoah*. Sells the Kentucky farm and moves back to the Log Cabin.

1978 Writes "A Ploughman's Politics" on the republication of John Taylor of Caroline's *Arator* for *Modern Age*.

1979 Prepares an "Introduction" for the Palaemon Press's limited edition of *Alchemy;* contributes "The Momentary Man" to *The Hillsdale Review,* a publication of Hillsdale College, Michigan.

1980 Publishes "They Took Their Stand: The Agrarian View After Fifty Years" in *Modern Age* and, separately, as *Reflections of a Ghost;* contributes an untitled response to the question "Is Regional Writing Dead?" for *The Student,* a publication of Wake Forest University; publishes a reminiscence, "A Journey South," in *Kentucky Review;* attends Vanderbilt's Fiftieth Anniversary of the Agrarian Manifesto; participates in a discussion published as "The Agrarian-Industrial Metaphor" in *A Band of Prophets,* ed. by Harvard and Sullivan; writes "A Tribute" for the Katherine Anne Porter entry in the 1980 Yearbook of *Dictionary of Literary Biography*.

1981 Publishes "The Artist in a Time of Disorder" in *The Chattahoochee Review;* "A Partial Reading of *Parade's End* or the Hero as an Old Furniture Dealer" in *The Presence of Ford Madox Ford;* "The Search for Order in American Society: The Southern Response" in *The Southern Partisan;* the "Afterword to *Why the South Will Survive;* and "A Tribute" for the Caroline Gordon entry in the 1981 Yearbook of *Dictionary of Literary Biography*.

1982 Nominated for the Presidential Medal of Freedom; honored at a celebration of his eightieth birthday at Sewanee; *The Velvet*

Horn is reprinted; "Allen Tate and John Peale Bishop" appears in *Grand Street;* "Recollection and Reflection" appears in *Mountain Voices: The Centennial History of the Monteagle Sunday School Assembly.*

1983 Adds a personal perspective on Frances Cheney in *Reference Services and Library Education: Essays in Honor of Frances Neel Cheney.*

1984 *Alchemy and Other Stories* published; *Bedford Forrest* reprinted; "Three Ways of Making a Saint: A Reading of 'Three Tales' by Flaubert" appears in *Southern Review;* Katherine Anne Liggett, Lytle's daughter, dies in Pensacola.

1985 Writes "Foreword" to *Shakespeare's Insistent Theme,* a volume in honor of Charles Harrison. Wins the Lynhurst Foundation grant.

1986 Awarded the Ingersoll Foundation prize, the Richard M. Weaver Award for Scholarly Letters given in Chicago in November. Continues to live in the Log Cabin at Monteagle.

The Lytle-Tate Letters

I

1927–1939

The letters of Allen Tate and Andrew Lytle open with an invitation. Tate, who was in New York, had learned from Ransom that Lytle was at the Yale Drama School. So, with a short note expressing his new-felt warmth toward the South, Tate invites Lytle, whom he as yet barely knows, to visit him at 27 Bank Street. Although Lytle's response is missing, it must have been prompt and positive; in a week Tate writes back glad to learn Lytle is coming soon.

Considering the difference in their interests, that this exchange would mark the beginning of a lifelong friendship and a significant correspondence seems unlikely. During this time Tate is doing free-lance journalism and working on his biography of Stonewall Jackson and Lytle is concentrating on the theater where he sees his future as actor and playwright. But if the letters in the early part of the sequence mostly concern trips and meetings, they are indicative of a growing relationship. And quickly the real bond between them and the theme of this section emerges, for this is the period of the waxing and waning of the Agrarian movement.

Although this portion of the file includes analyses of poems Lytle receives from Tate while he is in France—one year on his Guggenheim, another on Caroline's—and alludes to Lytle's plays and short stories, the majority of letters attend to the South's tradition more directly. Many letters discuss the writing of the Southern biographies—after Tate's *Jackson* (1928), his *Davis* (1929), and his abandoned start on Lee; Warren's *John Brown* (1929); Lytle's *Forrest* (1931) and his unfulfilled plans for a Calhoun. These letters also reveal the planning and politics that lie behind the two symposia which highlight the Agrarian effort and Tate as the causal factor of their publication. The first of these, *I'll Take My Stand* (1930), brings to focus ideas which had been circulating among the Nashville group for several years while the second, *Who Owns America?* (1936), results in their culmination.

For after 1936 a change sets in. Already what Lytle planned as a fictionalized biography, *The Long Night* (1936), had turned predominately fiction. Similarly, what he planned to be his family's genealogy, Tate rejected as such and began using as material for his novel, *The Fathers*. But, as the letters suggest, if with Tate and Lytle's failed attempt to prevent Ransom's leaving Vanderbilt for Kenyon in 1937, the agrarian theme plays out, the narrative of their friendship nevertheless continues.

In the summer of 1937, Tate is at Benfolly describing Robert Lowell and the Fords; Lytle, meanwhile, reports on his DeSoto research. The next year Tate writes from Greensboro where he is teaching, and Lytle announces his marriage, his subsequent stay in California, and his return to Monteagle. When Tate publishes *The Fathers* (1938), Lytle offers congratulations and a keen appraisal. The last year in the section finds the Tates situated at Princeton and the Lytles at Monteagle buying a farm.

27 Bank Street
New York
March 15, 1927

Dear Lytle: [New Haven, Conn.]

John Ransom happened to say in a letter the other day that you are at Yale.[1] I was extremely glad to have some news of you, for after I left Nashville some years ago I lost track of you altogether. I should be very happy to have you call upon us here the next time you are in New York, if you have an hour or two to spare. Interesting things are, I believe, at last stirring in the South, and in that part of the South which we cannot help taking about with us forever, wherever we may go.

Sincerely yours, Allen Tate

AL[2]

1. Lytle spent two years studying with George Pierce Baker at his famous 47 Workshop at the Yale University School of Drama.

2. The abbreviations beneath each signature indicate whether the original manuscript is an autographed letter (AL) or a typed letter signed (TLS).

27 Bank Street
New York
March 22, 1927

Dear Lytle: [New Haven]

I'm glad to hear from you, that you're coming down soon. I'd like to see the play, but you must excuse me from any criticism! I know nothing about plays, never having been in a theatre more than a dozen times in my life. But I'd like to see what significance you give your theme—that would interest me greatly.

I wish you could have been here this week. We have a kind of Southern horde here this week. My wife has cousins visiting from Staunton [Virginia]. Catherine Michal, who I believe is your cousin, is here. And of course Lyle Lanier is here all the time. Red,[1] I hope, will be up this summer—if he can elude the San Francisco police.

Yours sincerely, Allen Tate

AL

1. Robert Penn Warren—Warren is completing his master's degree in English from the University of California.

27 Bank Street
New York
June 27, 1927

Dear Andrew: [University Players, N.Y.]

I am glad to hear from you; I thought you must be at Southampton by this time. Our plans for the summer have matured, so far as the mere planning goes; yet there may be some changes that we can't foresee. We intend to camp out on James Rorty's[1] farm near Westport, Conn. The uncertainty is in the time we shall go, but we hope to get there by July 10th.

Red's plans to some extent depended on ours. He will come up here in

August. He intends to come to our camp for the rest of that month. Beyond that I have no real idea of what he will do. He hasn't mentioned Yale in his recent letters; though I imagine he has it in mind. I should add that secrecy seems to be his watchword, and that his summer plans are like Jackson's at Second Manassas. The space between San Francisco and Guthrie[2] being the "front," he intends to march on Pope's rear in New York. Speed and secrecy are indispensable to the march.

The more I read the less I know how I am going to do the book. I only know I have got to decide damn soon! Our Southern brethren have the literary gift of mummifying everybody they write about, and Jackson, except his military record, has long been extinct.[3] If I were Jesus, I should not be afraid of this new Lazarus, but now I can see him meeting the public in his winding-sheet.

You will surely be in town soon. Be certain to come to see us here, or come to our camp. It is only an hour from Grand Central.

Yours in esteem, Allen Tate

AL

1. Author of *Children of the Sun* (1926) and other works. 2. Warren's family home is in Guthrie, Kentucky. 3. Tate is working on *Stonewall Jackson, The Good Soldier* (1928).

The University Players
Friday [Summer, 1927]

Dear Allen:

This is dated Friday, but it happens to be Sunday at this moment. I was so exhausted after the performance Friday that I couldn't construct the simplest sentence, my exhaustion resulting from the concatenation of labors. Besides being an actor, I had to take charge of ten thousand projects, assist at constructing and painting the set, and entertain, or rather stand on exhibition at teas and luncheons. So that we might loosen a few silver pieces from society's money bags. We have been fairly successful so far—but I gather from the present tune of the receipts that I will carry away much more experience than gold. Expenses are wicked. It costs $2.50 to have a suit cleaned and pressed. Everything else is in proportion. It is gouge or be gouged.

I want to discuss further with you Jackson and the general situation before I completely rewrite *New Ground*,[1] but with rehearsals for the next play I don't see how I can get to New York if you leave the 10th of July. I am going up to see [George Pierce] Baker for a few days after I leave here, and if your camp is on my way home to Alabama,[2] I'd like to drop by for a day, that is if it would be without any embarrassment to you. Otherwise I'll wait until the fall. I'd like to get a glimpse of Red. I'm afraid that he like Jackson, if he is not careful, may be done in by his own people, falling with a trap which his "speed" and "secrecy" have laid for the enemy. Jackson forgot what a good disciplinarian he was, and carelessness grows from godship. I'm supposed to have my play in good condition by the first week in August and turn it into Baker. It doesn't look at present as if I am going to be very busy on it.

If you assume the role of Joseph of Arimathea, you might be able to unravel the winding sheet so much better than Jesus, who, I fear, ripped it, and in his zeal mutilated poor Lazarus. At least let me hear from you.

Comme Toujours, Aff-

AL

1. Unpublished play by Lytle, written under pseudonym K. L. Alexander. 2. Lytle is returning to Cornsilk, his family's plantation near Guntersville, Alabama.

27 Bank Street
New York
July 17, 1927

Dear Andrew: [University Players, Southampton, N.Y.]

Your letter reached me a few days ago in Staunton, Virginia, and I hasten to reply immediately on our return lest you misunderstand my failure to urge you to come to see us in the country. As plans have turned out, we shall not be in the country at all; but I do hope you come to see us here the very first chance you have.

We seemed to have a choice between going to the country and motoring to Virginia; and a good secondhand Ford suddenly appearing on the market, we chose the latter. We left July 4th and got back today—thirteen days, 1150 miles, not a single puncture, not a single repair of any kind! We have named the Ford General Jackson.

I am torn between the desire to tell you everything we saw, and my laziness. Let it suffice that I saw all the battlefields and Manassas, and all Carolyn's[1] relatives and all mine, the two together totalling the existing population of Virginia.

If you haven't already gone home, be sure to come here on the way. Red seems to be in Guthrie, but God knows where he really is!

Yours as always, Allen Tate

AL

1. Caroline Gordon, the novelist and Tate's wife. She was christened Carolyn Gordon.

27 Bank St.
New York
Aug. 11, 1927

Dear Andrew:

Your arrival here Sunday, or even Monday, will be most satisfactory in many ways. First, I will be extremely glad to see you—and I will produce witnesses of "Jackson's" miraculous march through Virginia; and, secondly, Red will most probably be here to greet you. He is due to arrive tonight or tomorrow some time.

I have written three chapters of the biography, but so far mere chronology is my form rather than character; but it may improve some.

Telephone Chelsea 4975. We are sure to be here.

In haste, Allen

AL

April 2, 1928
New York

Dear Andrew: [New Haven]

I am very much moved by your fine letter, and I wish you were here so that I could really acknowledge it. When you come down to see Alexander,[1] you must be over here a good deal of the time.

I wish we *could* have a prolonged holiday together this summer. I am afraid, though, that we are stuck in New York. There's no rest for the wicked, for I must finish up my Davis book[2] by September. However, we shall see.

The Caravan rejected Carolyn's stories—for much the same reason as they rejected your plays. I am in a fury about it; but it is obvious that I am even more powerless to act in her case than in yours. You can cut off a man's ears; you can hang him; but you can't give him what he hasn't got.

Yours ever, Allen

AL

1. Henry C. Alexander, from Murfreesboro, for years a New York broker and a member of the Vanderbilt Board of Trust. 2. *Jefferson Davis, His Rise and Fall: A Biographical Narrative* (1929).

561 Haden St.
May 23, 1928
N.Y.

Dear Andrew: [New Haven]

I thought it best to ask Red his plans—we had suggested last winter that he drive down with us, before we knew your plans—but it seems he is going to California, and now the way is clear. I fear, though, that the trip to Alabama is out of the picture. We are terribly disappointed. I'll explain when I see you Saturday. I am coming to New Haven.

For this reason: Rorty says Old Jack[1] is about to fall to pieces, and I want to get another Ford, before it is too late to trade this old one in for a substantial sum. I'm driving to New Haven from Rorty's on Saturday morning in Old Jack. Meanwhile, could you look around for a sturdy second hand car, costing not more than $100.00? I hope to get $25.00 to 35.00 on the old one. (I struck [Earle] Balch[2] a mighty blow.)

If we get a satisfactory car, could I leave it with you, and you drive down to N.Y. in it next Thursday, so that we could get an early start from Caligari[3] on Friday morning?

The trip, as planned, will be wonderful; though, of course, we'll have to say goodby to you in Richmond. I hope you won't object to a sort of dawdling pace. We expect to spend one night at Erwinna, Pa. (with Josephine Herbst and John Hermann),[4] one (the next) at Bryn Mawr with Col. & Mrs. Radford (C's cousins) where there son (aet. 22) will join us with his car. Then Gettysburg, Antietam, Shenandoah Valley, and Richmond.

If you agree to all this, or if you don't be sure to write me by return mail, so that I'll get your letter by Friday morning.

Love from us all, Allen

AL

1. Tate's old car, which he called General Jackson. 2. Of Minton, Balch and Co., Tate's publishers. 3. A Revolutionary Inn on Hudson Street where the Tates lived for a time. 4. Two writer friends of the Tates.

Bryan Park
Richmond, Va.
June 25th, 1928

Dear Andrew: [University Players, Southampton, L.I., N.Y.]

Your letter came this morning, and I was for every reason glad to get it. I can't be certain how long I shall be able to write, as the usual daily storm is coming up from the usual direction, and I may have to seek shelter. The weather has been alternately hot and rainy. It has rained every afternoon since you left. I have not yet got any work done. Between fighting nature and our anxiety for Nancy,[1] who is now quite sick, our once idyllic camp life is broken with alarms and excursions.

The doctor says Nancy has acidosis, which I take to mean an old-fashioned upset stomach. Stubborn little mule that she is, she would stay out in the broiling sun until she said she was dizzy; and I think it went to her stomach. She can't even retain water. We are worried. But I am not sure she would be better off amid the stinks and stenches of Caligari. We shall see what develops. We took her to a doctor yesterday in Ashland, who prescribed some treatment; we shall let that have a chance for a day or two.

A letter from Red this morning. I won't detail its contents, because I forwarded one to you that came in the same mail. Calamities still pursue him. He tells me that Fleming has much Davis[2] material, which he is willing to show me. Yet Mr. Gordon says that it would be better not to come to Guthrie; so we may not get to Nashville, near as it is to Guntersville. As you see, we are still set towards Alabama, and will remain so unless Nancy develops a real illness.

Old 97 has been acting up pretty badly. Got so she burns up oil at a terrific rate. Had to put in a new battery today, the generator quit generating, and the battery went dead. I was told by three garages that it wasn't worth recharging: it would have cost seven dollars to rebuild it, and the new one cost only three more. I am told, however, that she has a great deal of life still, and will take us many more miles.

Please come back as soon as possible. All we have done since you left is combat the elements, look after Nancy and visit Aunt Bessie in Ashland.

I simply can't write a real letter! Forgive this incoherent gurgle. Hurry back. Love from us all,

Allen

TLS

Next morning! Nancy better this morning! Yesterday the best she could do was rub noses, now she bounces and fusses; so we know she is about normal again! She has just said, I love Uncle Andrew."

1. The Tates' daughter, born September 23, 1925. 2. Jefferson Davis; Walter L. Fleming, the Vanderbilt historian to whom *I'll Take My Stand* (1930) is dedicated.

July 2nd, 1928

Dear Andrew:

Your salvation came yesterday at 1 P.M. and much relieved was I. I trust you received the cheque this morning, as it was mailed Saturday. I'm certainly much obliged. And you must charge the cost of wiring against me. At this late hour I recall my failure to reimburse you for getting the license plates. Please put that down with the new item.

Letter from Bill Clark today; says that Cinina[1] continues to write him and gives the impression that she and Red are hunky-dory. I hope not, if I may put it in black and white. I guess my motive in the opposition is personal. We'll lose Red if he marries that girl.

A routine at last progresses here. I'm getting something done. But Carolyn[2] is just a punching bag for Nancy all day, and she will not be sorry, I believe, to change the scene. Nancy continues well.

We look for you two weeks from today at the latest. Make it a day sooner if you can. Love from us all.

Allen [Tate]

AL

1. Warren's first wife. 2. Mrs. Tate

Bryan Park
July 5, 1928
Richmond, Va.

Dear Andrew: [University Players
Southampton, Long Island, N.Y.]

We have enjoyed your letter a great deal. We shall be delighted to visit Miss Veteran Mollie[1] and look forward to the visit. Time is passing, and we shall be on the road again in about ten days. I am doing some work here, but I could do it elsewhere. I think probably Fleming has as much material on Davis as anybody in the country; so the trip to the Lower South has ethical motivation. Red reported Fleming's possession of these documents and his willingness to share them. I have written him.

I can't write you at length. I can only record my belief that you are doing your part of the play beautifully, and will carry off the honors of the season. Flushed with triumph, you will come to Richmond, mount old 97, and with three cheers for Jefferson Davis, who is the moral excuse for our good time, we shall all depart for the land of cotton.

Old 97, by the way, runs like a sewing machine. She hasn't been in such good condition since we started. All doubts of her capacity are dissipated.

Love from us all, Allen

P.S. I'm sending a letter for Red via you. I lost his letter and his address, which is Cinina's.

1. Lytle's grandmother, Molly Greaves Nelson, to whom he dedicated Bedford Forrest.

26 West 9th St.
New York, N.Y.
Wednesday Eve [1928 ?]

Dear Andrew:

Instructions received. Will move battalion by easy stages. Official visit to Washington first. Plan of campaign is to move out of New York

Saturday or Sunday. If Saturday, will by forced marches make Washington Saturday night. Will send postcards in military code en route to advise you of advance. Sunday night Charlottesville. Monday and Tuesday nights in secret camps along line of march. Wednesday, Chattanooga. Guntersville either Wednesday or Thursday. If we break camp here Sunday will be one day later on all stops.

Trunk will be shipped Friday. Enclosed find check for five dollars to pay charges. If we prepay we have to take trunk up to station and weigh it.

Don't bother to post scouts. We will enquire at Guntersville Pharmacy and attack Cornsilk[1] suddenly. This way we will be able to break down, without bloodshed, your agrarian community. In two weeks, factories will be built. In three, the railroad and airport.

In four, the now wasted agricultural territory will be a booming metropolis, everyone will be wearing store clothes and attending movies. In one year—the South will lose its identity—in two it will lose its shirt. Then we pack up and attack some other section.

EXPECT US!

X 42 [Tate]
TLS

1. Lytle's family plantation.

S.S. America
Oct. 2nd, 1928
3:30 P.M.

Dear Andrew:

The fifth day out.[1] First two days the sea was like a mirror. I told an officer that I'd like to see a storm—magnificent sight, etc. The officer was kind. On the third day a swell which I took to be a gale and which frightened Nancy and made her father and mother uneasy came down from Labrador. It was nothing, said the kind officer. So yesterday and today he granted my wish. At this moment, waves like mountains lash the stern of the ship, and break upon the deck. I am constantly ascending and descending in an elevator, and it is my constant hope that each latest descent will not be the last. The ship groans and heaves, and all the time a brilliant sun covers the sea. Where the gale comes from is a mystery that no officer will clear up. They will never tell you what to expect—neither life nor death.

None of us has been seasick. None of us feels normal. My head feels constricted, but my stomach is orderly: the same for Carolyn & Nancy.

Ah, dear Andrew, would that you were here and immune to seasickness. There's no company and I grow morbid thinking of the perils of the sea.

I am afraid Uncle Penn[2] is very ill about a hundred miles away. This gale covers the whole North Atlantic. But I'd like his company even if I had to nurse him.

Nancy sends Uncle Andrew her love, and says to tell him she is trying to get to Europe. Much love from her parents, too.

Allen

ALS

1. The Tates are on their way to Europe on a Guggenheim Fellowship. 2. Warren.

American Express Co.
6 Haymarket
London
Oct. 28, 1928 (Saturday)

Dear Andrew:

Your letter is here, and we are much pleased to get it. Carolyn wrote you the other day, and I fear her letter must do the honors of correspondence for the moment. I have been laid up with "flu" exactly a week today; I put on my clothes this morning for the first time. We went to Oxford last Saturday, and the miasmal airs of the place, the moment we got off the train, struck me down. What a God-smitten climate fair Albion is! I have found another reason for the migration of our ancestors to our own happier shores.

Gloom, as you see, fills my eyes and dampens my spirit. The way you speak of missing us, Andrew, conveys some irony, for it seems to imply that you alone are forlorn while we are having the good time. Nothing could be remoter from the truth. We have missed you more than ever before. I am sure I have never been so lonesome. We spend our time pointing out (to each other) how inferior the English are. Their physical background is impressive, but they don't appear to be equal to it or to deserve it.

Red looked disconsolate but stoical. I don't think he likes Oxford, but he will as time goes on.[1] He is already instructing the innocent Britons in the manly art of poker, and I infer that their living will shortly be his.

I promise to be brighter next time. As to the essay on the Negro theatre—why not extend it to about 3,000 words, and send it to [James Southall] Wilson of the *Virginia Quarterly Review?* The letter you forwarded was from him; he suggested an essay on the Old South; so I believe he would be interested in your views of the modern negro and the drama.

I am so weak that I'll have to rest. Love from us all, dear Andrew, and please write at length now that Machiavelli[2] is settled into routine.

Allen

AL

P.S. If you espy any reviews of my poems, please send them.

The enclosed scrawl is a letter from Nancy to Uncle Andrew. It says, "love and a kiss to Uncle Andrew."

Postage to England is the same as domestic—it only takes 2 cents for a letter. I see that you put 5 on yours.

Have met [T. S.] Eliot, [Herbert] Read and other English writers. About them later.

1. Warren is a Rhodes scholar. 2. A reference to the Broadway play Lytle was performing in, *The Grey Fox*.

3 rue de Fleurus
VIe
Paris, le 21 Decembre 1928

Dear Andrew:

After writing twenty-five lines on my poem since breakfast[1] I felt that as a Roman I was entitled to all the pleasures of that citizenship, which Greece in her contempt and poverty, provides. I am therefore as you see seated in the Café du Dôme, with an amer picon avec citron before me and a serviceable escretoire supplied by the waiter. The historical situation of the present moment (I incline to view nearly everything I do historically for the drama it gives to quiet conduct) this moment is amusing, to a high degree, for its long and complicated connections, for the moral it gives the best laid plans of history. Was it ever intended that Allen Tate should represent himself to New York capitol as Literature, get the money on that pretense to go abroad, enter the Dôme at four in the afternoon, and write a letter to his sad and sympathetic friend Andrew Lytle? Was it intended besides that their friend Warren should be crucified by the necessity to make a living? For such, when I last saw Red a week ago, here in Paris on his way South, was the lugubrious cast of his mind. Was it ever intended that our friend Warren should make virtue of necessity, and bring to the fore the vices of his ancient friend Tate? I hope this is not the plan of history. Red is, in short, about to toss the sponge high in the air and become a professor. I didn't know the date of the first edition of Fuller's Worthies;[2] this is my vice. I should be sad for Red's sake were it not for the reflection that his dedication to the Academy has been inspired by the culture of the Far West; I am delighted to have my convictions of its barbarisms controverted.

On the strength of these melancholy views I have ordered a second amer picon avec citron.

We have been in Paris three weeks. We like it so much better than

London that I sometimes forget, and think I am in New York. You will doubtless observe with a [illegible] you seldom show that I speak with affection of the place I used to curse. It is really a question of relative distance. Yet I often feel that New York is as far back as I dare to go.

We are living in two rooms at present, but [Ford Madox] Ford is leaving for New York in two weeks; he is giving us his apartment till May. He is really one of the best men I have ever known. Not for that alone, but because he has a simple heart and hates the English. He is like our own people in the old time, doing pleasant things over and over again just for the things; if there is any interest in it it is the aesthetic one of seeing a gracious thing performed. We shall all be sorry to see him leave; he is the best company we have here. Perhaps I had better analyze "we." We are Carolyn, Nancy, Léonie [Adams], and myself. Did I tell you that Léonie joined us in London? If I would have three wives, and were privileged to *take* them, they would be Carolyn, Katherine Anne [Porter], and Léonie; but since Carolyn is all three, I have them already.

I have ordered a third amer picon avec citron.

I am sending you a few lines from the Induction to the long poem.[3] The framework is the flimsy scaffolding (that of the *Inductions*) derived from [François] Villon's reflections upon reaching his thirtieth year; the rhetoric of the poem is based upon the fact that I haven't reached mine but look forward to the benefits of that age. I review a little of our history and describe the birth of the new Messiah (son of Pasiphaë and the Bull) born in Los Angeles. I enclose one of the historical passages.

I will write you again in a few days, but don't wait to write me. What has happened since Machiavelli[4] began? And tell Katherine Anne, if she hasn't written that review, not to write it; I have countless books that I never reviewed (the ones that most interested me) and foolishly kept awake over. Love from us all,

Allen

Nancy saw a pipe in a tobacco store and said, "It's dear Uncle Andrew's." Nancy further said that she is the virtuous Mary and her doll is Lord Jesus.

I haven't even said Merry Christmas. Here our life is timeless, without reason. The apotheosis of New York.

[Allen]

AL

1. "Message from Abroad." 2. A reference to Thomas Fuller's *The History of the Worthies of England* (1662), a lively encyclopedia which deals separately with each county. 3. "Fragment of a Meditation," (1935). 4. Another reference to *The Grey Fox,* the play Lytle was performing in.

246 Sullivan Street
New York City
Jan. 31, 1929

Ami De Mon Coeur:—

Your letter is just at hand, and I am so enthused about its contents that I am sitting down at once to answer it. And now that I am here I don't know where to begin, so many things want to crowd onto the sheet. If I gave full vent to my excitement, my keys would get a hotbox. Really, the idea of the history of the South[1] is beyond words. And just at this time, before the final concentration of the empire, it will be a crying protest against that short-sighted greed which killed the goose that laid the egg. Were I ever to doubt that Biblical axiom about the sins of the fathers, New England's condition today would force a wholehearted acceptance. The hardest thing we've had to bear is that, after the murder of the South, we've had to submit to our enemies in the presentation of our case to the world. The half-baked unseasoned victual has so disturbed the digestion of history that its thwarted appetite will devour a properly prepared, and what is most important, a tasty seasoned dish. Strange to say, I've vaguely felt for some time that it ought to be done, and done by you, but I hesitated to mention the fact, as I know you were pretty well occupied for the time being. But with Davis to press, your long poem completed,[2] you can give your undivided attention to this matter. You know, I feel we ought to devote the next three to five years to a lucid and forceful restatement of our philosophy, for when the industrial powers completely dictate, there will never again be the chance. It is also more desirable since out of The Reconstruction came certain feeble movements that denoted the possibility of life, but the way of the good life was dead, not only in its concrete manifestations, but abstractly as well. I don't know why I say these things which you know perfectly well, unless it is that I can despise the evil the more by stating it the more. I can see no reason at all why Calhoun[3] and the History shouldn't dovetail. Even better than that, they can dovetail their bills, as lovebirds do. The whole thing seems to work so well together. Now, if Caroline[4] would only get her novel published, and by that time she should have another ready, all coming out about the same time, we can hit the enemy, front, flank, and rear, all at once, just like Old Forrest. It never failed to the discomfiture of the West Pointers opposed to him. It's great if you can get Harper's to publish the Calhoun. I'm afraid [Earle] Balch will want it to join the series, and to my mind at the moment, it should be a little stiffer stuff. I will keep your secret like the grave itself, for I think you are perfectly justified. It's true he has been decent, but as well it is a business proposition. You can't raise corn to give away.

By no means let them persuade you to write the Lee first.[5] I can appreciate their desire that it should precede the other, from the money standpoint; but with the more comprehensive work as a background, it is bound to clear up some points which will make it easier to write the Lee book. Not that you couldn't do a good piece of work now, but in the light of your added knowledge, a later handling is bound to be more complete. I may be wrong in this, but such considerations come to mind at once.

And now I have an idea for us to make a lot of money. My Scotch ancestry will never down. I noticed where [David W.] Griffith, the guy who did the *Birth of A Nation,* is contemplating a movie called, *The Rise and Fall of the Confederacy*. Does it click? It will probably be a talkie. You with a history, Davis, and Jackson, to your credit, I with Forrest and Calhoun, and a certain dramatic knowledge to my fewer books (says he with none as yet written) together we ought to become Mr. Griffith's right-hand men. If he doesn't do it, I am working for an introduction to Fox, probably the largest organization of its kind in the country. The difficulty at the moment is that Griffith is out of money, I hear. That might work to our advantage. He might get it just when we would be able to render him assistance. We ought to make a hundred thousand apiece out of this; then we can go the happy isles together. It's worth pondering, don't you think. As an interlude, it should be interesting, if it is profitable, and I don't see how it can help being. Then in eight years, or maybe ten, with sufficient money for a start, we can get us a large island somewhere and experiment on the Venezuelan lines. How does this sound to you?

This brings to mind a very sad thing. Eliza Dallet[6] has been sent to the asylum. She got worse and worse, tried to kill herself on their plantation, accused her father and step-mother of not, or rather, of refusing her food as they passed through Washington, and on her return, the doctor forced the decision. K. A.[7] had to persuade her to go peacefully. It gave K. A. an attack of flu. She will write the details. I only know the bare outlines. She began to feel the appearance of leprosy, syphilis, etc. It's really horrible, and so useless, it seems. There is insanity in the family, however, and as it is due to the disintegration of the brain cells, I don't suppose it can be helped. The disease is, of course, progressive. K. A. will write you the details. I've been closely confined at home here. Mother has had a bad case of flu herself; so I've been close-put and don't get about much. She is up today, however, and practically well. I perhaps shouldn't have told you about Liza. It is bound to be so depressing, away from home, but you should have known.

I must say I rejoice at the [Emma] Brescia letters, although it is bound to be hard on Red at the moment. Red will graze and grow stronger on fresher pastures. Let us see if we can't find one with a cool spring running through it. Then everything will be to the heart's desire. In his infrequent letters to me I've noticed that his spirits were dulled. That must not happen to him. He will pick up now, and like you I shall bear this music in my heart, long after it was heard no more. That wench that is after Bill [Clark?] is still on his trail. It has upset him again. I made some very poignant suggestions which he will not heed, as they may have appeared to him to be a trifle violent. Our friends' women have certainly caused us concern. Let's hope the end will find itself more cheerful.

Tell Nancy her tender sentiments touch me very deeply, and that Uncle Andrew finds his affection and respect for her grow when he learns what a ready stroke she answers insult with. Tell her I am coming to see her sure, over there. Just when I can't at the moment say. Not until Forrest is off my mind,[8] but I'm on the way. Yes, brother, I'm on the way. Sweet Jesus, Bless his name. Balch wants it to come out this Fall. I'm bending my efforts toward that end. Whether it comes out so quickly I don't know. I begin writing the first of Feb., and as soon as I begin, I doubt not but the old boy will not let me rest until he is done with me.

My love to ye all, and write me often. I will some day drink amer picons with ye.

Andrew

TLS

1. This project later became *I'll Take My Stand* (1930). 2. "Ode To The Confederate Dead," (1928). 3. Lytle had tentatively planned a book on Calhoun which he never completed. 4. *Penhally* (1931). 5. Tate began a biography of Lee but abandoned it in 1932. 6. Wife of John Dallet whose grandfather owned the Red D. Shipping Line between the U.S. and South America. 7. Katherine Anne Porter. 8. Lytle is working on *Bedford Forrest and His Critter Company* (1931).

Parie, Vie, France
March 14, 1929

Dear Andrew: [N.Y.]

Yours of the 1st is just here. Things do happen and get over with before the news reaches the other side; and I only hope you and your mother are, by the receipt of this, entirely out of the flu. I am very much worried about you; this is the time for you, it seems to me, when calamities can best be dispensed with. They seem to have struck us all with particular fury this winter. I am certainly glad you kept after K. A. She is one of the bright spots in a dingy world, and we must keep her shining. . . *The Paris Times* carried the story of the young man's suicide, but I am pleased to hear some further detail. There must have been behind it something besides John

Coffey's failure to pay him. I suppose I need not ask how the wood business is getting along.

Your remarks on the progress of Forrest fill me with the liveliest anticipation (I have read so much of Davis that I begin to write like him) for the finished product. Your distinction between the imperial motive and the mere desire to better oneself is particularly original, and it ought to throw a new light on the western South. In fact without such an idea, it would be hard to explain the high degree of culture that existed, for example, in Middle Tennessee after two generations. This fact has often been observed, but never explained. It really deserves more amplification than you will probably be able to give it in your narrative, and I hope you will make at least a separate essay out of it; it would easily support a book. Davis is going ahead. I have been compelled to make my terms with Harper's on the Lee book, but I am forcing certain concessions. First, they agree to publish a book of literary criticism before the Lee volume appears; and they agree to finance the general Southern history after these two books are issued. You were quite right: it would be better to prepare the soil, to fertilize it in its whole extent, before attempting Lee, for he is a mighty difficult crop to grow. But expediency is the god who rules all things; I am willing to sacrifice to him for the promise of my way in the end. It goes without saying that the need for secrecy is still pressing.

Our little tempest in a teapot, which I let loose upon you not long ago, will doubtless subside by next week; but meanwhile we have had a hard time. Work has been doubly hard, and it is all that patience can do to remain a virtue. Perhaps I have never quite lived up to the convention that calamity must be covered with a smile, but at least I have covered it with a frown; and I am not prepared to sympathize with people who cover it with hysteria. We have both decided that a vaporish woman is confusion's masterpiece.

I think you overpraise the poems, but you're quite right about the loss of the word "tired."[1] I am trying to get it back in again, without losing the better rhythm of the second version. It is astonishing how most Americans know nothing of their own history. I showed the poem to some well-educated Yankees here in Paris, and they hadn't the slightest idea what it is about. They live in a kind of vacuum. I prefer to be more suffocatingly surrounded.

Paris is beginning to crawl out of its hibernation, and I go every afternoon at four to sit in front of the Deux Magots. It is not quite what it will be, but give it another three weeks. I know you are working your utmost on Forrest, but remember that his completion will bring you to

Paris; that the pleasure of others besides yourself is involved in it. I intend to keep after you till you come.

Red is due here in two weeks. He has had the flu—as you probably know. We are all well. I hope to heaven you all are too. Love from us all,

Allen

TLS

P.S. Nancy is fully expecting you to appear here in the summer. You must come to forestall her already developed tendency to live in the past. It runs in her family, and I don't want to encourage it.

1. Probably "Historical Epitaphs."

VIe, France
April 1, 1929

Mon Cher ami:

Yours of the 21st came this morning, beautifully synchronized with the arrival of a long letter from Katherine Anne. She seems to be better, thank God, trying to work at her book.[1] Doubtless you have heard from her and have had her description of the machineless paradise of Bermuda. I would we were all there.

You have probably seen Léonie[2] by this time, and are wondering how such a modest little girl could have set us all by the ears. Well, she doesn't know to this hour that she did it, and I am willing to let her ignorance be bliss. She is one of the most complex characters I have ever seen. Also the most perfect example of the Puritan mind. This, in spite of her Maryland mother. It all goes back to her remarkable father who, on his deathbed and delirious, imagined that he turned into money: he had all his life lived a high-minded and insanely noble existence, believing it was ignoble [to] touch money at all, but in the end the true Puritan traits came out. The right hand doesn't know what the left hand does: that's my present definition of Puritanism. The trouble is, they all have to establish their moral superiority over their whole environment, and in the end you wonder in what the superiority consists. Our little friend is a very superior character, but in spite of her reasons for thinking so.

The other day I re-read Eckenrode's Jefferson Davis,[3] and I had to revise my original opinion of the book. It suffers from a belief in the Nordic myth, but aside from that it is a brilliant performance. It is positively the best correlation of the military and political history of the Confederacy. One wouldn't expect to find much in it to illuminate the career of Forrest, but it contains a great deal. Eckenrode is the first critic to point out that the West was the main theatre of war, as it actually was, and that the Confederate failure there meant total failure. It is a complex situation: Davis' capitulation to the Virginia viewpoint after he went to Richmond, and his neglect of the West; Lee's state rights provincialism, which led him to prefer doing his duty to winning the war—his duty being to Virginia alone. But the point that Eckenrode brings out—perhaps excessively but with great interest—is that Bragg was the villain of the plot. Even after Davis removed him from command, as you know, he took him to Richmond as his chief adviser, in which role he seems to have got a complete ascendancy over Davis. He exaggerated to Davis the size of Johnston's army and minimized Sherman's, so that Johnston (his hated successor) would be made out a coward for not taking the offensive. The point for you is this: Johnston was constantly urging that Forrest be called up from Mississippi and given a large force with which to fall upon Sherman's communications—the only way, in Johnston's opinion, which was at least not disproved by the facts, that Sherman could be turned back. Bragg thwarted all this—because, in Eckenrode's opinion, he wanted Johnston to fail where he had himself failed. Hood turns out to be the tool of Bragg: Bragg knew that Hood would fail under any circumstances; he was afraid that Johnston might succeed if given a fair chance. All this seems a little exaggerated—as if Eckenrode had to find a villain, but I think it is fundamentally sound. Davis' fundamental weakness of character made it possible for Bragg's plot to succeed: Davis had an enormous vanity which Bragg constantly flattered. Eckenrode's narrative of these events is almost a masterpiece, and his whole book would be too if he had not swallowed Madison Grant's Nordic moonshine. I hope you will read it, and let me know what you think: I know less about the Western campaigns than I ought to, and you will be able better than I to judge whether Eckenrode's theory is sound.

You are quite right about Forrest and Lee. Lee was a European to the last, and Forrest was a Southern American. I say this in a whisper and at present for your ears alone: Lee had a kind of egoism that yielded to no influence—not even to the independence of his country. It was the egoism of self-righteousness, and it was absolutely unassailable. Eckenrode almost says this when he points out that Lee's life belonged to his State, but his honor was his own. I believe that Lee was in the sole position in which even personal honor becomes secondary; he valued his own honor more than the independence of the South. If he had taken matters in his own hands, he might have saved the situation; he was not willing to do this. It would have violated his Sunday School morality. Here we have an example of a man whose character was greater than his creed, but the creed won.

Davis is at last taking wing, and I do hope that he and his misused subordinate will make their autumnal bows together. Alas, Andrew, that we are not together; but you must come over at the earliest possible time. Red will not appear until April 16th; the reason for the delay seems to be, in his own words, "one of the daughters of Britain"—which is not so bad under the circumstances as it might be. Bill Bandy[4] is here at this moment and sends regards. Love from us all, and kisses from the ladies.

Allen

TLS

P.S. Many thanks for the enclosures. The *Virginia Quarterly* took the ms. with my name on it. Don sent me his review of my poems[5]—a noble effort because he neither understood nor liked them. I've come to believe Don enjoys his martyrdom; he could have got a Guggenheim for the asking but he wouldn't ask. Did I tell you that mine has been renewed for six months.

I sent some time ago, to [Minton] Balch [and Company], an old "New Guide to the Conversation in Portuguese and English" with the suggestion that he republish it. The book is a scream; everything in it is wrong and extremely funny. Balch turned it down, but I still think that it would make money. My suggestion is that you get the book from him and take it to Coward of Coward-McCann. We could split the proceeds, if any. If Coward rejects it, the next attempt should be Simon & Schuster—Clifton P. Fadiman—unless you know of some one better. I would be willing to write a Preface if the publisher wanted one. After you see the book you will see its virtues. It has one great drawback; it is too long. We might pick up a little easy money.

One more thing: We've heard from Donald Clark,[6] but he has not said what happened to our trunk and boxes, if anything. I'd hate to lose the family pictures. The next time you're in that neighborhood, would you drop in and ask about the stuff? And tell the landlord we will gladly pay him storage if he wants it. We should certainly be obliged to you.

1. Porter worked on a biography of Cotton Mather, but never completed it. 2. Léonie Adams, the poet. 3. Hamilton James Eckenrode's *Jefferson Davis: President of the South* (1923). 4. William O. Bandy, a classmate of Tate's, who later had a distinguished career as Professor of French at the University of Wisconsin, Vanderbilt, and elsewhere. 5. *Mr. Pope and Other Poems* (1928); Davidson's review appeared in the Nashville *Tennessean,* February 10, 1929. 6. A friend of Mark Van Doren's who lived for a time in Greenwich Village.

246 Sullivan Street
New York City
April 20, 1929

Dear Allen: —

Your girl, Léonie, never called me up to help her get a rooming place. She evidently found the friend you spoke of; she may, of course, have tried to get me here while I was at the Library. I am sorry, for I wanted very much to see her. You had aroused my curiosity. I'll go by Clark's place and see if your stuff is still there, and I will deliver your message, that you will pay the janitor for storage. As I remember it, Clark had us tell her it was stuff of his to be stored. Do I understand that he is no longer there? I've never seen him again. He is very repulsive. In case I'm not able to find the right house, send me its number. I know about where it is, though.

Your suggestions that I read about the political-military situation in Eckenrode's Forrest [in *Davis*] was a splendid tip, and I'm very obleeged for it. I already know most of the facts of the case, and I was wondering where I could find the dope on Bragg. I'm sure that Bragg had a double motive: Forrest was added as well in his revenge. After I quote you an interview they had after the battle of Chicamauga, you will understand what pleasure Bragg must have got in seeing two enemies go down under the same blow. I don't believe Eckenrode when he tires to make the case so studied on Bragg's part. Like you, I think it fundamentally sound. You knew after Chicamauga, when the defeated Yankee army was allowed a month to recuperate, Davis came out to look into the matter of Bragg's removal. Eckenrode makes that very clear. I have found a Diary which strengthens his case. It goes so far as to say that Davis held a meeting of the general officers in Bragg's presence (I think at Bragg's insistence, thinking perhaps that frankness would be inhibited by his presence) for the purpose of ascertaining their opinion as to his continuing in command. Longstreet spoke first. He told Davis he had not been on the field a half an hour before he saw that Bragg was incapable of commanding an army, and for fifteen minutes enumerated all his mistakes in a gentle but crushing manner. The others agreed. Why, after this, Davis still kept him in command when corps and division commanders told him to his face he was no leader is amazing. Eckenrode's explanation is the only satisfactory one. When Forrest rode into Chattanooga and saw the confusion of the enemy after the battle, he urged, begged, and did every thing to make Bragg follow up immediately with a crushing blow. When he didn't, it was hard for a man like Forrest, who understood so perfectly the art of war, to keep his tongue. He immediately gave open voice to his sentiments. Bragg removed him from command, and in an obnoxious manner. He knew that Forrest had sworn never to fight under General [Joseph] Wheeler. He ordered him to turn over his command to Wheeler. Forrest lost control, wrote him a fiery letter, and followed it up with a personal visit, taking only Dr. Cowan, his medical director, with him. This is Cowan's account of the interview:

"I observed as we rode along that the general was silent, which was unusual with him when we were alone. Knowing him so well, I was convinced that something that displeased him greatly had transpired. He wore an expression which I had seen before on some occasions when a storm was brewing. I had known nothing of the letter he had written General Bragg, and was in utter ignorance not only of what was passing in Forrest's mind at this time, but of the object of his visit to the general-in-chief. As we passed the guard in front of General Bragg's tent, I observed that [the] General did not acknowledge the salute of the sentry, which was so contrary to his custom that I could not but notice it. When we entered the tent where Bragg was alone, this officer rose from his seat, spoke to Forrest, and advancing, offered him his hand. Refusing to take the proffered hand, and standing stiff and erect before Bragg, Forrest said: 'I am not here to pass civilities or compliments with you, but on other business. You commenced your cowardly and contemptible persecution of me soon after the battle of Shiloh, and you have kept it up ever since. You did it because I reported to Richmond facts, while you reported damned lies. You robbed me of my command in Kentucky, and gave it to one of your favorites . . . men that I armed and equipped from the enemies of our country. In a spirit of revenge and spite, because I would not fawn upon you as others did, you drove me into west Tennessee in the winter of 1862, with a second brigade I had organized, with improper arms and without sufficient ammunition, although I had made repeated applications for the same. You did it to ruin me and my career. When in spite of all this I returned with my command, well-equipped by captures you began again your work of spite and persecution, and have kept it up; and now this second brigade, organized and equipped without thanks to you or the government, a brigade which has won a reputation for successful fighting second to none in the army, taking advantage of your position as the commanding general in order to further humiliate me, you have taken these brave men from me. I have stood your meanness as long as I intend to. You have played the part of a damned scoundrel, and are a coward, and if you were any part of a man I would slap your jaws and force you to resent it. You may as well not issue any more orders to me, for I will not obey them, and I will hold you personally responsible for any further indignities you endeavor to inflict on me. You have threatened to arrest me for disobeying your orders promptly. I dare you to do it, and I say to you that if you ever again try to interfere with me or cross my path it will be at the peril of your life." The press all through the west, and the populations began to feel he was invincible, just as the obverse was true of Bragg. There can be no worse feeling for an army to have at its head a general whom they consider a blunderer. When an advantage was gained, they never gave him credit for it. An army that marches with the feeling they are going into a trap is almost whipped before the battle. With it all the Army of Tennessee fought through the entire war with a desperation and a valor which is misunderstood. What they could have done under Jackson and Forrest!

It is interesting to compare the two governments in relation to the advisability of sending Forrest on Sherman's communications. Grant and Sherman were keeping the wires hot about Forrest. Three distinct armies were sent to keep him in Mississippi, and the Union Headquarters congratulated itself that their strategy had succeeded. Forrest had been kept in Mississippi. It is hard to be charitable to Davis when this is known. Davis finally let him go, but [not] until after Sherman had reached Atlanta. It was too late, then, Sherman could feed on Ga. Have you noticed how many things Davis reversed his stand on, only to do it too late?

Well, Goodbye. My love to you all. I want to see you, but God knows when.

Andrew
TLS

32 rue de Vaugirard
Parie VIe
May 4, 1929

Dear Andrew: [New York]

You already have my letter of about a week ago. I thought there I was well, but next day I had a relapse, and I am up again today for the first time—three weeks having been sliced out of a period when I could least afford it. I hope never to have such a winter again. I am at last sending Balch the front matter for the dummy,[1] but it's like pulling my eye-tooth to let it go. The book seems to me to be a series of fragments. Nevertheless the Louisa project has given me one of those legitimately ulterior motives which rouse waning enthusiasms and carry work to an ecstatic end. I have never been able to get excited about the making of a mere living—I've been contented to let it be *mere*—but now that the vision of something central, and constructive is before me, I feel that no labor is too great.

Where *did* you find that Cowan diary? I am greatly tempted to insert that speech of Forrest's in my chapter entitled "General Bragg and the West: 1864." You are turning up some great stuff, and I can depend on you to get out of it all its dramatic possibilities.

By the way, if you are in N.Y. in July and August, could you do me a great and priceless favor—*provided* Forrest is finished?[2] I mean, read the proof of Davis, and make all suitable corrections—style, punctuation, and even minor amplifications, to say nothing of inaccuracies you may find. I shouldn't consider having you do this unless Forrest is off your mind.

I read about a third of John Brown[3] while Red was here (I was too sick to read more) and I am all applause. It's a great piece of work—very deceptive at first glance. The first few pages give you the idea that the book will be a dull accumulation of facts; the style seems utterly undistinguished if competent; but very soon you are simply amazed at the subtlety of the presentation—at the way small facts connect with other small facts further on, and at the quiet, dawning case that is being built up against the pseudomartyr. It's going to be a great book.

The more I think of Louisa,[4] the more sold I am. Here we are all working at the same idea, and think of the encouragement and support we could feel if we worked as neighbors. I should prefer to be farther South, but some compromise with N.Y. is necessary. Carolyn is already planning a vast partnership in the chicken business, for which your expert knowledge is indispensable. When Carolyn, of her own will proposes the chicken business, I know that the plan is not only desirable but eminently practicable. When I want to test the reality of an idea, I outline it to Carolyn, who is the best judge of actuality I have ever known. This is the first time my imagination and her sense of the actual have coincided, and I for once feel secure. You must come with us because this is the most immediately realizable version of Brazil. I know you will have trouble thinking about it while Forrest is in your mind. There's plenty of time. If not Hawkwood, then some other place in the neighborhood. Red will spend a few days in Louisa in July, and will find out other available places. As to Hawkwood: remember that the building alone would now cost about $40,000 to replace. At $10,000 the land would be $6.25 an acre, not excessive price for fairly good land! You get the buildings free. . . .

A long letter this moment from K. A. [Porter] and a picture of [a] thin lady in a bathing suit tugging at the bow-line of a sail boat! She seems to be in great spirits. We have decided to present her with five acres as soon as we sign the deed to Oakleigh!

Must stop now, and give the first chapter its 57th reading before I send it to Balch.

Love from us all, Allen

AL

P.S. When Red was here and we were discussing Louisa, Nancy said, "Where is Uncle Andrew going to live?"—this, plaintively. You can't resist this.

We'll write the melodrama the first summer.

I saw a review in the *Herald Tribune* by Emily Clark of Hergesheimer's

Swords or Roses[5] (a book which is historically unsound to the core—if it have a core). The review annoyed me. Emily Clark, who is from Richmond, asserts that Forrest was less Southern than "American." This view always annoys me. It is absurd to suppose that only the quality people were Southern. In my view the poor whites and the negroes were as Southern as any other people. I fear that Davis was intimidated by this Virginian belief (a belief not peculiarly Virginian, however) and became convinced that Forrest, for example, was negligible because his grammar was imperfect. All people in a society are as much a part of it as any group. Statements like Emily Clark's are a slap in the face of the valor and devotion of the poor people in the Southern Armies. That sort of snobbery is utterly offensive.

The pictures & trunks are at 144 West 11th. We just want to be assured they are there. Clark has been in Santa Fe since November—tuberculosis of the kidneys, one of which was taken out. Very little chance to recover.

1. *Jefferson Davis: His Rise and Fall* (1929). 2. *Bedford Forrest and His Critter Company* (1931). 3. Warren's *John Brown: The Making of a Martyr* (1929). 4. The Tates are planning to establish an agrarian community in Louisa County, Virginia, where Caroline's father, James Morris Gordon, was born. 5. Joseph Hergesheimer, *Swords or Roses* (1929).

May 13, 1929
par Leviathan
Cherbourg

Dear Andrew: [N.Y. City]

I am about to ask of you what may be an impossible favor. I desperately need some books that I just can't get here. They are in the British Museum, but I can't afford a trip to England—either money or time. They are not at Oxford or Red would send them to me.

The main thing left to be done is to fill in local color and scenes: I thought there was already too much of that, but now it seems very thin. The books I need are:

A Diary from Dixie, Mary Boykin Chestnut.
A Rebel War Clerk's Diary, J. B. Jones.
Four Years in Rebel Capitals, De Leon.
Memoirs of Mrs. C. C. Clay.
Richmond During the War (I can't find author's name in my notes).
Jefferson Davis, William E. Dodd.
Jefferson Davis, Armistead C. Gordon.

The two last are not indispensable; the others almost are. If these books could be bought, I would reimburse you by return mail. Possibly you could get them at the library; I could get what I want in less than a week, and shoot them back. It may not be possible to get them at all. You may have worries of your own. In any case, use your own discretion.

In much haste, Allen

Cherbourg
[May ?] 16, 1929

Cher Andrew: [Murfreesboro]

I thanks-ee kindly fer these yere letters and sich like that come to me hyar in this derned furrin town. The pitcher of that there fetchin leetle sister o'yourn[1] shore is a sight fer sore eyes. You better keep a eye peeled in the next year er so, cause she's a-goin to start settin' that country a-fire, so's people 'll say Sherman's done broke loose again. I seed by your unclosure that the Phi Beta Kappa sassiety has done gone and dunned me fer $1. I ain't got no use fer them folks nohow, so's if ye want to buy out my seat in the meetin' fer $1, I'll give it to 'em, like a honest man ought to, so's they can't say I never paid 'em nothin'. Hopin' your folks is all well and enjoyin' your Ma's nice letter what come yesterday, and awaitin' your reply.

Yours truly, (X) his mark A. Tate

1. Polly Lytle.

Huntsville, Alabama
503 Franklin Street
May 23, 1929

Ami De Mon Coeur:—

Your two letters followed me here. I wanted to answer them at once but I had to rush off to Montgomery in search of material, and I have just today returned. Montgomery is a beautiful old town, and the capitol a fine dignified place. There is just enough of the tropics that far South to have made it the ideal capitol of the Confederacy, without consideration of the other strategical and political advantages.

I am disgusted with this flu that has dogged your steps. Mother is just recovering. In fact, I hurried up my journey South because she was not doing any good. At the moment, though, she is rapidly recovering, and is in Murfreesboro with Polly,[1] who is growing into a young woman mighty fast. Boys swim in her head both night and day. She is very stern with them, and stands out in strong contrast to the other little girls in town.

My enthusiasm finds no limits concerning the Louisa projects. I can think of nothing so good, or so practicable; and of course, I want to jine the settlemint. The Hawkwood deals seems too good. . . .there must be something the matter with the place. If I remember correctly it had passed through hands several times. Nobody seemed to make a go of it. It is just old enough to be hanted. Perhaps some of the Morris spirits[2] came from Purgatory to dog the steps of those who presume to squat on their land. If anything can bring an old landowner back to this earth, that can do it. I believe there is no passion so strong or so persistent, or none that grows more dominant with age. We'll talk it over when you all get back. It's going to be hard to convince my family that we need more land when there are two or three thousand fine acres here. I'll try to persuade Dad to go over and look it over some time. I might trick him. I imagine one trouble about handling so large a place in Virginia is a lack of labor. Most of the land, too, is exhausted. There are some soils which never can be rebuilt. Tell Caroline I've a fine plan about a combination of chickens, turkeys, and dairy. The skimmed and buttermilk can go to feed the fowls. If we can ever afford to fence properly, there is good money in sheep. The wool will pay for the upkeep, and the lambs are pure profit. Bees work for nothing. A hive, always if properly cared for, can make twenty-five dollars a year. There are numerous things we could do. There is only one serious difficulty that comes to my mind. How can a Tennessean and Kentuckian return to Virginia? I have a suspicion that a Virginian doesn't differentiate much between one who comes from the North and one who comes from behind the blue ridge, and if he does, he will favor the carpetbagger to, shall I say, the scalawag. You remember we ran across several unpleasant occurrences. Tell Nancy her devotion touches me deeply. I have always been her slave; now my fetters are irrevocably fixed. Such constancy is a rare find these uncertain days, but she comes by it proper. Uncle Andrew will do his best to find some sort of house, tell her. It does look like we ought to be able to settle somewhere together. I certainly can't stand that city another winter. It nearly broke my spirit. Two or three months a year is all I can go of it. I don't see why we can't all three keep up one room there so that we'll have some sort of headquarters in the city. I don't believe it will cost too much, and we'll be running in enough to justify it.

Balch doesn't want Forrest to come out until next spring. It's just as well, because I couldn't have got it ready on time for him. It's taking me longer than I thought it would. Although he is a violent man of action, and seemingly is simple to handle, yet the job grows difficult when I try to redefine certain terms so that the casual reader will understand them. Then I am using Forrest as the type Emily Clark would like to call "American." As a matter of fact that good yeomanry was more Southern than the Quality, certainly they were more numerous, and certainly their bravery and devotion to the cause, seasoned with a salty humor, can demand the finest sort of admiration. I am going to show how the Jeffersonian Democracy leavened the whole, making it possible for a man like Forrest to become a rich planter, and Davis's people for that matter, as well as Calhoun's. There was this interplay between all the classes, a mutual esteem, that made it a solid thing. The Southerner should always remember that the negro in those last years of the war remained faithful. I don't believe there was a single case where they abused the women and old men at home. When they were led away and misbehaved, it wasn't their fault. I am very anxious to see Davis. I'll be mighty glad to go over the proofs if you want me to. I don't know whether I can do it satisfactorily. There is the difficulty that I won't be in New York, but perhaps they can send it here. My plans have changed slightly. I must return East in the middle of June to try out for *The Patriarch*[3] which will open in the fall, I hope. I ought to get good money out of it, if I get the job and if it runs. It is embarrassing because it will take a month out of the summer. I haven't done the work on Forrest this last month I should. Write Balch to send them here, or I can see him as I go through. I think he'll be in the city then.

I ran across the Blackford Diary by accident. I spent the week-end in the country and found it in somebody's house. The Forrest speech wasn't in it. It, the diary, was written by the wife of a colonel who came West with Longstreet. There are several priceless things about Lee in it for you. I could only hastily scan it, and there may be more. I don't think libraries have a copy. It was printed only for the family. I have at hand a few quotations: "General Lee, you will remember, told Mrs. Page that it took three rounds of the enemy's cannon on the battlefield to arouse him (Longstreet) to action, but that then he was terrible." Again, "Everybody wants to go back to Virginia, including Gen'l Longstreet, who told Sorrel that while it was more honorable, possibly, to have a separate command, he preferred being under Lee, as it relieved him of responsibility and gave him assured confidence." It's a pity he didn't find this out before Gettysburg.

Kiss Caroline and Nancy. Lee was asked at the surrender which officer under him was the best, and he replied: "A man I never saw, sir. His name is Forrest."

My love to you all, Andrew.

TLS

1. Lytle's sister. 2. Gordon's relatives on her father's side. 3. The opening play at Yale written by Boyd Smith, one of Baker's students, set in the Blue Ridge Mountains. Lytle played the part of the girl's father.

Parie, VIe, France
June 16, 1929

My dear Andrew:

Yours of June first is just here. It was certainly nice of you to go to all that trouble to get me the books, and I only hope that the trip to Nashville involved only an incidental search for them. I am having no luck here. I should have taken fuller notes; but you really can't see just when that kind of material will be effective until the last moment. It is most useful in filling in and in toning up scenes, and it is impossible to take the right kind of notes for that purpose.

The book, thank God, is almost done and ought to be in Balch's hands by the tenth of July. (I will simply have to leave out much of the diary material.) I am verily afraid it is an incoherent mess. It has become increasingly harder to hang upon Davis what I want to say and make it a publisher's book at the same time; so I fear it represents a defeat of both purposes, Balch's and mine. I think there are a few well-written parts, even chapters, but it is very uneven, and I doubt if I could make it better with six months more of work, without writing another book entirely—which, as you may imagine, I am hardly willing to do. I fear I must face the truth—that a military subject gives me more pleasure because it permits me to indulge my preadolescent hero-worship of the great generals. From whipping imaginary Yankees in the back yard with a wooden sword is but a step to an imaginary whipping of real Yankees with a steel sabre . . . either that or a purely philosophical rendering of the situation. Davis, involving both elements, turns out to be neither. I have discovered that [Robert Barnwell] Rhett is the best figure for a purely speculative book, and I may do him some day.

Which reminds me that I recently wrote to Colonel Harry Rhett asking for a portrait of his grandfather for my book. I suspect that he isn't much interested in restoring his ancestor's fame, and I have no idea that he will give me the picture—if he has it. I gather that he isn't subject to appeals of any sort; so I made none. However, I did say that the portrait of the most distinguished statesman in the Confederate Congress is indispensable. This was no more than the truth. Rhett interests me more and more. If the fact that I am sympathetic to his grandfather might move Colonel Rhett, I shouldn't mind the fact being known. A certain obloquy fell upon all the extremists after the war, and I guess their descendants still feel it in their bones. If I had lived in that time I should probably have been a moderate, but looking back it is easy to see that the extremists were right; they were the only men who really understood the situation and knew their own minds. Davis never knew his; Davis never knew fundamentally what the war was all about. He really thought it was about political abstractions and civil liberties; it was fought (largely unconsciously) for that irrational good known as national independence. It was less principle than sheer desire. Rhett and [William Lowndes] Yancey understood this.

There is already a damper on the Louisa project. It has been cast by no other a person that the Rev. J. M. Gordon, who vows that he will never go back to the house where his father read Plato and put the Bride of Lammermoor into verse while the family didn't have enough to eat. He didn't phrase the vow this way; but I suspect it comes to that. We have to get a place where he will eventually jine us. Of course, he may be won over; but the place isn't worth the preliminary anxiety it would cause the old gentleman. I still think that section is the right place, all things considered; so we propose to find a house the same distance from Charlottesville, but on the other side—nearer the Blue Ridge, in fact, possibly to keep the symbol in mind. Of course, Hawkwood is no place for a man who must make his capital pay; it is sheer luxury. Mr. Gordon, by the way, points out that the grandchildren of the master of that place are now croppers. It is possible that the grandchildren of a new owner would come to the same end.

If we get back early enough in the fall we intend to take a flying trip down there, and look round. We've got to act quickly, or our money will be frittered away on bad living in New York. Red commissions us to look out for a place for him, and we shall look out for one for you. Perhaps you could take the tour of inspection with us; it would last only about a week. The atmosphere of Virginia is rather stuffy; its most appropriate symbol for me is Uncle Van standing at the door and seeing no one; but what I want is a temperate climate far enough from New York to give me the feeling that I am independent of it, even if I'm not. The only place having that advantage and the indispensable library is Charlottesville. I shrink from the project unless you and Red can manage to join us.

Red says he is not going to America this summer, but he may change his mind. It would certainly be a waste of money; but the rational move is not invariably the economical move, although as a rule it is.

You have Carolyn's letter. I hope we can fix up some plan together for New York next year. That arrangement for a permanent communal place there after we get away is just what we need. I prefer to live in the country and camp in New York, instead of the other way round.

Have you seen John Ransom's essay in *Harper's*?[1] It is a great piece of work. The whole thing is so brilliant and profound that the editor had to put it in the back of the magazine; I am amazed that he ever accepted it. I am sending you a piece that I wrote last winter, now in *The Criterion.*[2] It is nowhere so fine as John's, and it doesn't touch the political and social question, but it argues for much the same views from a more general position.

Nancy sends love to Uncle Andrew—as we all do—and says to tell you that she speaks only French. She does do remarkably well; better than her parents. We miss you extremely, Andrew, more and more the longer we are away. The reunion will be a great occasion which I am eager to improve. Love from all.

Allen

TLS

1. "The South Defends Its Heritage," 99 (June 1929), 108–118. 2. "The Fallacy of Humanism," 8 (July 1929), 661–681.

Guaranty Trust Co.
4 Place de la Concorde, Paris
July 31, 1929

My dear Andrew: [Monteagle]

I have been at the point of writing to you for several weeks, but always something got in the way—moving to this place for one thing, and then the sudden death of my mother on the 17th. We had just got here (the 18th) and the cablegram bringing this news lay in Paris unforwarded until the 22nd. Even now I know only the bare fact; though a letter from Ben[1] is on the way. It has just about flattened me out, and not the least part of it all is the anxiety in the lack of precise information. I am left to infer that Mama died at Monteagle—at least she was there by the last of June—but where they took her I haven't the slightest idea. I know that Mama always wished to be cremated for the idea of being buried near any of her people filled her with horror because of the calamities that fell upon her family in the last forty years; but I doubt if my brother carried out her wish. I imagine Ben took her to her father's burial ground in Washington, but it is possible that cousin Frank Bogan (who loves to lead funerals) took her to Illinois to lie by Uncle Johnny's children. In my ignorance of what happened, I am left to speculate upon the most morbid part of it. If you are at home, it is likely that you heard the news before I did.

I planned for a day or two to come home, but I should have been too late to help anybody. My absence at the last fills me with rather bitter feelings, but in as much as I couldn't be there in Mama's last hours, there is no use coming now.

I finished Davis on July 1st, and it is now being set up. Balch writes me that he likes it extremely, and I can see that he likes it better than Jackson. In some ways it is a better book, but the treatment isn't nearly so original: perhaps that's why he likes it. Balch sees only what I have done, but I see what I failed to do, and my opinion of the work remains very low. I hope Forrest will be done by the time we arrive in New York: we have passage for October 5th.

I have just got a letter from Red in Guthrie. I imagine you saw him either in New York or in Nashville. He is, I believe, on his way to California. You see the news I had was wrong.

I understand that the Fugitives are planning a Southern offensive. In reply to Red's letter, I outlined a program of action which, in my opinion, is indispensable to success. It is the formation of a society, something like the *Action Française* group, composed of 15 active members (critics, poets, dramatists, publicists) and 10 inactive (politicians, lawyers, private citizens). All writings should be signed "John Doe of ______________," or whatever the society is called. Such a society should announce a whole religious, philosophical, literary, and social program, anti-industrial on the negative side, and all that implies, and, on the positive, authoritarian, agrarian, classical, aristocratic. Without the group the Southern movement will fail, for it will lack a rallying point. It will be dissipated over too many shades of opinion none of which could be crystallized. The group would create powerful opposition in the South which would clarify the issues, and create an *independent internal problem to be solved.* I ask you to ponder this last point, for on it everything depends. The group alone can bring it about. Some of us may hesitate to subscribe to a sort of philosophical constitution, but minor differences should be put aside in view of the ends. For example, Red would demur at religious authority which is absolutely necessary for the kind of society we want: that was the great lack of the old South.[2] I would have other reservations. But we should suppress these. I will write more at length later. Meanwhile I'd like your opinion. There's no use taking half measures. We must go the whole hog, or we shall end by merely brooding over the past. Instead, we must *use* the past for daring and *positive* ends.

Please let me know your plans. We shall be here about two weeks longer and then go back to Paris till we sail. We're all in fine health. Nancy's French is too expert for us: she really speaks it better than English. Love from us all.

Affectionately, Allen

AL

1. Tate's brother. 2. Tate is giving his initial reaction to the formation of the Agrarians.

c/o Guaranty Trust Company
4 Place de la Concorde
Paris, Nov. 3, 1929

Mon cher ami: [Hunstville]

I am sending you a poem that you have already seen, but it is much revised and added to—in fact, a new poem, or at least what the poem should have been in the first place.[1] While I was re-writing it, I kept thinking of it as in some sense a special communication to you,and I have presumed to dedicate the piece to you as a summary of all the ideas we have talked about over a number of years.

There is no news here, and I am beginning to think of letters, after this time, as very unsatisfactory—that is, letters written by me, not you—for we shall be with you in a couple of months. I will therefore not make this letter topical. But I hope you will write me an extremely topical letter, about yourself and everything. We've been through a preliminary skirmish with the flu, but all are well now. Nancy never forgets you. You should hear her speak French: she corrects every word we speak; her accent is perfect, and she never puts a pronoun in the wrong place! We expect to see Red at Christmas: you know all the news there. Lyle [Lanier] writes me that Bill Clark at last has put the noose round his neck, and that morning coats will be worn. I've had no word from Bill direct. Bill Bandy is to be married, day after tomorrow, to a nice sensible girl from Jersey City. Precedent notwithstanding, a married man is to be his best man—and I am he. I'm working hard at my book of essays[2] and at my Poem[3] and poems. Please let us know where you are and what you're doing. My lack of news is my fault: I haven't felt much like correspondence these last few months. Love from us all,

Allen

TLS

1. "Message from Abroad," in *Three Poems* (1930). See Appendix A. 2. Not published until 1936. 3. "Ode to the Confederate Dead."

Murfreesboro, Tenn
225 East Main Street
Nov. 26, 1929

Dear Allen: —

I didn't think there was anything which would be able to bind us more closely together until your letter, your "Message from Abroad," arrived. You may understand by this how greatly moved I was by it. To have dedicated a poem to me would have flattered me, but just that alone could not have strengthened ties which I had already thought of as tougher than hickory. It is, I believe, because the ideas which we have discussed for so long, and which are the poem, have almost become a part of me, are my raison d'etre, that I feel as I do. You have bound them with so much beauty, with so much austerity, that the stiff-backed liars will never understand how much passion they hide. Only the initiate can understand; so I, like Davis, can be secret and exult as I read. I feel like the priest who alone in the Temple has believed when he suddenly discovers another who also believes, and has seen the god, who promises destruction to the stiff-backed liars the dupes. It is even better than "The Ode to the Confederate Dead," and I believe it will be difficult for you to make another which is better. I have compared it with the other versions and without any technical knowledge to go by I don't see how you could improve on it. I have already, my friend, said too much, and for fear that I will by overstating nullify that which I want to say I shall stop.

I like "The Pit."[1] It doesn't somehow seem that both came from the same hand. I suppose this is a superficial understanding of it, but it is so entirely of another tone that to read them one after the other is like walking out of the Parthenon to step into the Church of Our Lady.

It will certainly be fine if you and Caroline and la mignone come to the country with me. We should all be in this part of the South until the Old South Movement gets organized, and it will be a fine place, as you say, to write Lee; and certainly it ought to be like the balm of Gilead to Caroline. We can get us a cook to do away with those habits a New England housewife likes so well and for which she is so well qualified to maintain. The Nashville group is heartily in favor of your plan. They are only waiting until you return to get it well organized. We have had one discussion, and I am going to take them to Monteagle soon to go into it more thoroughly, but we are holding up any decisive action until you and Caroline get back. You would be surprised at the number of young college men who will be fertile fields for us. The South is coming back to the Democratic party; the issues have recently been raised in the halls of Congress under other names, so that in time I believe some union with the Agricultural west will present a number of fascinating possibilities. Ransom is afraid the issues will be too clearly defined before we can get into it, but I doubt that. We will all have to make a close study of economics to show the people that their so-called prosperity is delusion, to show them for what a mess of pottage they are selling their birth-right. It may be that we can be only John the Baptists unless certain issues define themselves in our life-time. The most important concern is, as you point out, to make the enemy define his stand. This will produce the greatest possible results, but I'm afraid he may beg the question. Hurry on home. Tell Nancy uncle Andrew will hunt her up a pony to ride this spring, and that she must correct her old uncle's accent which by now must be muchly tattered.

The prospect of the tin soldiers is alluring. Certainly I'll go in with you on them. Do they all cost $35 or is that my share. Write me. Tell them to make J[oseph] E. Johnston big in the saddle. He had that appearance, although standing on his short legs he was a small man.

Will you try to find a book written by Marshall Foche, I think it was a series of lectures at Cheumont, in which he deals with Forrest's battle of Brice's cross roads. Let me know what it will cost and I will send you the money. At last Forrest has fallen into the divisions he should have fallen in earlier. I can go ahead much more rapidly now. I don't think I'll have anything but the first draft finished by the time you get back. I want to send you Fort Donelson[2] when I get it polished a little to see what you think of it. By the way, have you seen the editing of Marshall's letters? It throws very important light on Gettysburg, on the Second Bull Run. [General Edward] Fitsmaurice does it.

Bill's [Clark] wedding is this week. I march down the aisle with him in borrowed plumage. I am to blame for you not hearing from him. He has repeatedly asked for your address, and I've always forgotten to send it until the other day. I must go down this afternoon and take part in the festivities and squire his woman around until he gets down from Philadelphia. Incidentally I've become very much interested in a squirrel-eyed gal from Memphis. She's a powerful pert. I somehow ain't able to keep after the women-folks like I ought to. I gits to steadying bout the weather and sich-like and fergits em. As soon as I get this marriage off my mind and hands, I want to write more fully on Davis. I've been under such pressure I wasn't able to write as I wanted to about it.

Write me soon. Kiss Caroline and Nancy for me.

Love. A.

TLS

1. Appeared as "The Cross" in *Saturday Review of Literature,* 6 (18 January 1930), 649. 2. Part Two of *Bedford Forrest,* "Donelson—A Tragedy of Errors."

c/o Mrs. Douglas Meriwether
Route #1, Trenton, Ky.
Mar. 26, 1930

Cher ami: [Murfreesboro]

I hope you got my telegram on Saturday. I got back Friday evening after a pleasant and successful trip. Ben did himself proud. We have found a beautiful place for $6,000, and $2,000 more will make it palatial. It is just the kind of house we all like—a pioneer frame, dog-run hall, chimneys at end, a long ell in rear—eleven rooms; 185 acres.[1] It is in the southeast corner of Christian Co., Ky., at Kennedy depot on the L. & N., 11 miles from Clarksville, 14 from Hopkinsville. Unless Ben's affairs have changed in the past week the deed will be signed on Monday. I'm having the title traced now. If all goes well, we'll move in next week-end, and we hope you'll be on hand to "help" us.

I can't come to Nashville till next week. Let me know your immediate plans. We've found just the place for you here. Come up as soon as you can & I'll show it to you. It's better than the big house on the hill—which by the way was priced to us at $12,500 with 125 acres. $10,000 would get it. We're all in good shape. I'm enclosing a check for $2.60 for those express charges. Love from us all.

Allen

AL

1. Benfolly.

Friday
Clarksville
Mar. 28, 1930

Dear Andrew:

Have you heard of the iron chest salvaged from Ft. Donelson and now owned, with its dozens of mss., by Brice Runyan of Clarksville? He will show it—and it hasn't been looked at by historians. Better come up and look it over. I'll fix up a meeting.

A.

AL

Monteagle, Tenn.
Saturday
[June 1930]

Mon Cher Ami:—

I have neglected you pretty badly, but I have delayed writing notes to send you a letter. I am rather sorry that you did not take up with Harper the change of title. I like the tactical import of *Tracts Against Communism;*[1] the selling value; and the added surprise which the contents would give the reader, expecting a discussion of the Reds and the activities of New York's idle who form the bulk of the supposed Communistic party in this country. I do not think that you should feel that it was attempted dictation on your part, and certainly they didn't take it that way.

I was in Nashville for a day and Don spoke of your disturbance, but he had not in any way got that impression. He is worried now because Harper's has not fussed about the last two essays. He feels that they perhaps are losing interest. I don't [know] much about publishers, but I can't believe they would lose interest so soon. I was there but a few minutes; so I didn't get to talk much with the brothers.

You have chosen the most difficult subject of all;[2] that is why it is so slow to get underway. Don't you worry about it, because you can't do a bad piece of work; and if, in your estimation the performance is not up to your usual, it will be better than most of us can do. I want very much to see what you do. I wish you'd send me a copy when it is done. Religion, certainly, is general; but it is also a very particular matter with us in the South in its own right; it has, rather, been made particular by the enemy. I imagined you would take that as a starting point and proceed from that into its cultural implications.

Has anybody heard from Red? I've a very strong suspicion that he is now in California, moving towards that front by the Northern route. If he comes through this way I certainly want to see him. Your tales of what awaits me in Clarksville are very alluring, and I don't want you to think I ain't thankin ye fer what ye've done fer me. I've got to git me a good woman, but I've got to git my roots in the ground fust. I'll shore God bring her fer yore inspection, fer I don't want no wench what my friends don't like. I can't mess with em much now. I can't work and court too, and I've got work to do. General Kirby-Smith's granddaughter is on the mountain,[3] and as purty a young un as you ever seed. She says she tuck a fancy for me, but I never paid her no mind, but I mought yit. Do ye reckin her grandpap's rank and behavior will pass our inspection? He was a full gineral.

I read Caroline's "A Long Day,"[4] both mother and I read it, and I think it's one of the finest short stories I've ever read. I never saw such careful selection of language, nor words so filled and charged with the exact emotion. If she has any more like that, I want to see them. Mother liked it too. She read it before she knew who it was. I think she suspected it.

I've been wanting to come down to see you all this entire month, but I haven't been able to get off. I can't get off until the plans for this family are arranged for the fall and winter. Would you like for me to come down and stay a month in the fall? Times are mighty hard, and we may stay on the mountain until I get the gineral done. Dad has made some such suggestion.

Supper is ready. I've got to dirty a plate, so I'll rush this off. I'll write again in several days. Kiss both the girls. My love to you all is what it always has been and always will be.

Andrew

TLS

1. Tate, Lytle, and Warren preferred this rather than *I'll Take My Stand* as a title. 2. Tate's contribution to the agrarian symposium was "Religion and the Old South." 3. Monteagle, Tennessee. 4. First appeared in *The Gyroscope*, 2 (February 1930), then in *Scribner's*, 88 (August 1930), 162–66.

Clarksville, Tenn.
[1930]

Dear Andrew: [Monteagle]

We've had to call it off. The furniture isn't here and may not arrive this week: Ben is coming down this week end to see the results of his largess, and will expect me, not unreasonably, to devote my time to him. But the main point is the uncertainty of our being able to offer you all hospitality. Don responded with great spirit just as you did, and I am sorry to have to let you down. We can have it later in the summer. Let's have a ceremony at Franklin as Don has already proposed, and then come here the next day and repeat it, perhaps also at other towns if we make connections there in the meantime. Caroline has the whole thing planned here, and all we shall need to do is to carry the plans out later. You should have heard Caroline berating the preacher after his speech! It would have done you good. She let all the ladies tell him it was wonderful, and then suddenly while they stood around told him that it was an insult to the old veterans, an insult to the South, and a perversion of the Southern character.

Don sent me a copy of Jim Campbell's[1] speech. It is fine stuff. We must get him to speak more.

I got a letter from Red Saturday. He's coming in September. He says that the title "I'll take my stand" is a goddamned outrage, that [John Donald] Wade[2] must be an idiot, that we are idiots too if we let him put it over on us. Amen. (Them was his exact words)

I'll wire you the moment the furniture is in the house, and will expect you to come the earliest possible day after that. I'm trying to get Don here at the same time. More later,

Love from all, Allen

TLS

1. A classmate of Lytle's at Vanderbilt who went on to become a lawyer in Franklin, Tennessee. 2. The title was Wade's invention.

Monteagle, Tennessee
Monday Evening
[Spring 1930]

Dear Allen:—

When I reached Nashville in the cool of the morning, I found it a very hot place. I had a premonition of Don's misinterpretation of the last moment effort to select a better title, but I had no idea he would take it so hard. Don took it almost as a personal attack on his editorship. He is like a woman a few weeks before finding a child, all nervous and a little milk-leggish. Your communication was like a black cat running across the road to mark the baby.

I first found Ransom, as he had asked me to spend the night with him on my way back to the mountain; and he explained Don's troubled state to me. I went into the history of the attempt to change the title with him and discovered what I had thought was the situation. When Don and I were with you and we went over the thing, I understood that when he returned to Nashville he was to write Ransom and inform him of our dislike; then if Ransom had no violent objections, we would change the title. Don wrote him, but left no impression with him that the title would be changed unless he particularly disliked it. He merely told him that *Tracts Against Communism* had been suggested along with many others, to which he replied that he preferred the *I'll Take My Stand*. That is, Don left the impression that it was just another title.

This, of course, was not a deliberate attempt to table the matter, but an unconscious defense of what he all along has preferred. He allowed himself to be overborn at Clarksville, and then recouped in this manner. When I related this bit of history to him, he answered that the Clarksville discussion was no more than that and had not brought anything to an issue. I pointed out that if that were the case he would not with you have re-written the prologue to take care of the attack on Communism. In the course of this Ransom saw the history of [the] case and afterwards said as much, that the delay and all the disagreement had largely come from Don's inability to act. I tried to unfold the whole case, step by step, to clear in their minds that this was not a piece of sabotage on our parts, but particularly not on your part as the center of opposition to the title. Don made what amounted to a confession of guilt when he said the trouble with all of us is that we have been making the mistake of trying to read each other's motives. Poor fellow, dark vapors gather in his mind to plague him. I think I was able to clear the air, and there is peace and calm again in Tennessee. They felt a little badly about the letter they wrote to us and both wrote you personal notes the day I left.

The carelessness you have accused them of is, I believe, this thing that is troubling poor Don, whatever it is. I feared it at the time. That is why I wanted you to write Ransom direct. Ransom told me that as a Southern gentleman you probably thought that it was not necessary to lift your voice, that the mere statement of dislike was sufficient.

This note may add a few links, although I can go further into detail when I come down.

He [Ransom] was very troubled when he discovered for the first time how badly you disliked it. I made the point that as several of the brothers disliked it very much, the others who were luke-warm or indifferent should be brotherly and follow their wishes.

This is a little inchoate, as I've just got off an accidental drunk in M'boro.

Kiss the gals and let me hear from you soon.

Affectionately, A.

TLS

P.S. Brother John made in Nashville the same statement he put in the letter to us, that the issue of communism had not been made the central one of our exhibit, and that therefore it would need a full-length paper elaborating the issue. I made the point that no paper was needed, because the defense of agrarianism was, itself, an attack on Communism that a paper on the subject would expose it only as evil, one among many, which instead of clearing the debris for the attack would further confuse it.

Headquarters Forrest's Calvary
Corps
Army of Tennessee
Six miles north of University Place
July 13, [1930]

General:—

Enemy made feint on Shelbyville, turned left of Army of Tennessee by Matt's Hollow. Now in rapid rereat over mountains to Chattanooga. The General Commanding so taken by surprise this corps at Spring Hill was tardily notified of movement. Barely saved the wagon train. Now struggling with trains over mountain passes; so it will be impossible to reenforce at Clarksville. You will be compelled to hold that front with Marine Brigade and Home Guards from Nashville. Your present position overlooking the Cumberland should control that water-way without difficulty. If pressed hard send your chief of Staff, C. Gordon, to the border of the Meriwether lands with her horn, and all the Fergusons, Barkers, and Meriwethers will come to your assistance.

Keep this headquarters informed of your conditions.

A. Lytle, A.A.G.

TLS

Huntsville, Alabama
503 Franklin St.
May 19, 1931

Dear Bre'r Tate:—

I got the poems just before I left for Alabam. Now who says the Memphis trip was no good. I like all three of them, but I don't believe I like "The Legacy" as well as the first time I read it. I don't remember the first version well enough to make comparisons but I can still feel the rhythm, and my feeling is that the present last stanza's rhythm is not quite as good. I like "Instructions"[1] mighty well; in fact, I think it is swell. It goes with "The Legacy" all right. I don't know but what you need another in between the two. It's a great leap from Alpha to Omega. You always manage to close the poems powerful well; expecially so with these three. I believe "The Wolves"[2] is the best. It's a mighty rich poem—has a majestic flow. You are certainly trying all sorts of forms these days, br'r Tate. How is Robert Edward? Did Memphis help the flow there. Probably the formula for stiff work on that gentleman will be a quick-paced trip; three or four excellent poems; then prose.

Well the strawberries are here. It's a sight. Three hundred people picking in the fields. They put me over the negroes. I've got them doing some better, but the more I deal with them the more I realize what an art it is to work them and get the most out of their hands. Some are stupid; some intelligent; some tricky; a few sullen when corrected. I had to fire two the first day. My cabin is still to be raised, as we had to postpone it on account of the berries. I suppose I'll get it up the last of this month. Dad and I are planning to go to Columbia for the debate,[3] but I am in doubt whether it is Thursday or Friday. Will you drop me a card here? No. I'll get Don to do it. I'm afraid you couldn't reach me in time. You and Miss Carrie aim to come, don't ye?

Whup the princely General onto paper.

My love to ye all, A.

TLS

1. Two of Tate's poems he chose not to collect. 2. "The Wolves" (in the group "The Rooftree"), *Poetry,* 39 (November 1931), 68–69. 3. Donald Davidson debated William S. Knickerbocker on May 21, 1931, in Columbia, Tennessee.

May 31, 1931
Saturday
(Colored Decoration Day)

Dear Sir:

We seen your ad sent out by them book-sellers in the city and we ain't lyin none to say we're plumb pleased with hit. Me an' the old woman will be thar long with Grampa Wilds[1] who fit with the gineral. Yore berries is shore picked by now so they ain't no reason fer not comin up. Be ready to come—June 5th. We'll bring the other boys & r'ar around. Thar's a new raft on the river fer swimmin'. Genl. Lee is a comin' along; the ole woman gets done with hern tomorrow. We're right peart.

Love from all, A. T.

AL

1. The grandfather of Catherine Wilds, a first cousin of Caroline Tate and her Aunt Pidy's daughter.

6/11/31

Dear Bro. Lytle:

The cherries arrived yesterday in fine condition. Half will make wine, the other half preserves. Come up for a share of both. The madam feels right poorly—often being deprived of a job—but works valiantly at the fruit. We're shore obleeged to ye. Ain't heerd nothing from nobody since we seen ye. Bro Warren got away on schedule. Have jist finished givin' Uncle Doc a hair-cut, so I ain't so pert & must close. Give yore folks our love.

A. T.

AL

July 4, 1931
(damn far from 1776)

Dear Br'er Lytle:

I shore will tell Br'er [John Gould] Fletcher about the speakin',[1] only I don't know whar he's a-hidin' out this last month. I'm obleeged to ye for the information when I'm to speak. I'll be thar.

This here Stonewall Place sounds mighty patriotic but I disremembers if I heerd you expressin' any interest in hit when we was a-visiting Br'er Warren a few weeks back. Pears to me like you didn't say nothin' tall. Hope the place ain't standin' like a stone wall, and you kin break thoo without wastin' too much ammynition.

Give my respects to Br'er John, and say I ain't heerd nothin' from him. I knowed these forced marches of Marse Robert[2] was goin' to peter out, so's when they did on yestiddy I jest upped and writ some poems,[3] which the onliest thing about 'em I'm afeered they ain't no good fer golden texts for a feller who's a-cou'tin'. I'm sendin' to ye anyhow but the last thing the gal wants to hear about is how hit all ends with artyficial grass tented up on the grave. Hits got so a feller can't even die no more.

We shore is honin' t see ye, Br'er Lytle, and we shore expects ye to come fore long. Nancy's done named one of the pups Uncle Andrew cause she says he's so tall and got light hair.

The ole 'oman jines me in love from us all, Allen

TSL

1. Tate is probably referring to the round table conference held at the University of Virginia. 2. Tate's work on the Lee biography. 3. "Sonnets of the Blood."

July 14, 1931

Dear Br'er Lytle:

We shore hopes you air a-comin' up this week. I seen Ed Kibble[1] in the city last week, and he 'lowed you was goin' to Monteagle for Satday, or I shore would've pestered the telephone till I got ye here to visit with Br'er Stark Young. Ed make right smart pint of your promisin' him to visit his folks, so I says I ain't got no right to interfere. Miss Carrie's proofs in gallus form is here, and shore does look peart. She's a-saving a set for you to peep at so's she kin profit by you when the page proofs come. How's the Gineral doin'? We seen a good account of him in the *N.Y. Times;*[2] we was mighty proud . . . By the way, I'm havin' to go back on reviewin' them four Lincoln books for [Stringfellow] Barr so I'm sendin' 'em back. Reckon you could do 'em?[3] I'm just *suggestin'* you, but ain't goin' so far as to give him much hope. Come as soon as you can.

Love from us all to you all, Allen

AL

I'm bein prosecuted for stealin' a plow. Mr. Armes let Jesse have hisn, which I never said I'd pay for. So Armes says I did, and he's all swelt up.

1. Edwin Keeble, a distinguished architect in Nashville. He is from a family in Murfreesboro where the name is pronounced Kibble. 2. C. W. Thompson's review of Bedford Forrest appeared in the *New York Book Review,* 5 July 1931, p. 3. 3. Lytle's article "The Lincoln Myth" appeared in *The Virginia Quarterly Review,* (7 October, 1931), 620–26. This essay is a review of Edgar Lee Masters, *Lincoln the Man;* Don C. Seitz, *Lincoln the Politician; New Letters and Papers of Lincoln,* ed. Paul M. Angle; and Donald Jordan and Edward Pratt, *Europe and the American Civil War.*

July 16, 1931

Dear Br'er Lytle:

I almost headed your way yesterday to enlist your services in my behalf when you shall arrive in New York. Of course you will see Balch. Won't you explain to him my situation with regard to Lee?[1] I think you already understand it, but I will go into it briefly. I suppose I am bound to be a little disingenuous with him, but that is none of his business; just as it's none of the land-owner's business if the nigger fools him a little, for the nigger knows that every year he gets in so deep at the master's store that he will never do more than pay out. I mean that I have an instinctive dislike of letting Balch know that the ms. is not complete in some form. For even if it were, I would have the same almost desperate qualms that assail me now. It is simply that at two different times since I began, the job has turned my stomach. For your confidence, you will know that this is because I never got, in the first place, my inner consent to write the book, but was driven by the necessity to make a few thousand dollars; and, in the second place, I have never got my own consent to deal politely with Lee. It is really worse than that: I have hinted at my misgivings, but now I will tell you how deep they are. Call them the glimpse of the "poetic insight" into the Shadows, or what you will. At any rate, the longer I've contemplated the venerable features of Lee, the more I've hated him. It is as if I had married a beautiful girl, perfect in figure, pure in all those physical attributes that seem to clothe purity of character, and then had found when she had undressed that the hidden places were corrupt and diseased. Can any man alive write this way about Lee? No. Nor can I easily get my consent, overwhelmed as I am by this vision, to write a facile discussion of Lee as the exemplar of the Virginia virtues, or to keep my hands off him in order to write a tract for the cause. For somehow the integrity of the cause is one with the integrity of its defenders, and there's no integrity in defending the cause in so shallow a way. You see, my dear old friend, that I'm in a mortal dilemma, and I can't hope to get out of it unscathed. Balch will receive a book on Lee from me, but it will be two months before he does. I've simply got to worry, and contrive, and tone up and tone down, to create one of those productions that, being riddled with compromise, will be dead! In the end, I suppose, I am willing to issue a shallow book, but I guess I've got to suffer over it a little before it can be done. There is a way out—to tell Balch to go to the devil and keep his money—but I can't really do it; and there's no use putting it on high ground. Just let's say that Balch is a good man, and good men don't treat each other that way. For the first time in my life I've wished I were a damned scoundrel, but wishing doesn't make me one, and that's the end of that. Perhaps I have written to you in this vein chiefly because it is one of the privileges of friendship to do so,and one of the benefits. I wanted you to talk to Balch, but mostly I wanted you to see something of this dilemma, since as a friend I am obligated at such crises, which occur maybe once in a lifetime, to expound the truth and keep the record straight. In the case of a man like Davis, there is weakness but a certain purity, but in Lee, who was not weak, there is when we see under the surface an abyss, and it is to this that I do not want to give a name. I don't think any publisher could understand this, but you will, and you will know what to say. . . . We're already awaiting eagerly your return before you're gone. We must get to the play as soon as you get back.

Love from all of us, Allen

AL

Route 6
Clarksville
July 28, 1931

Mr dear Br'er Andrew:

I heard from Balch yesterday and it is evident that you conveyed to him the precise nature of my difficulty. I can't tell you how grateful I am. Friendship should not be called upon for such offices, but if friends can't be called, who can? Who else can bear the strain so beautifully?

I am writing Balch today that September is final. In the next two weeks, by great effort, I *could* give him a ms. but I won't. The real trouble is this: although, even before I began to write, I saw something disagreeable in the *man who could not fail,* how can I be sure that my own disgust has not exaggerated this Pharisee's character? I don't like him, but I've got to do justice to him. And I can't go off half-cocked for the sake of the book-market. This whole situation puts palsy in my hand, and I write with devilish slowness.

Look up the N.R. [*New Republic*] for July 29, for [Edmund] Wilson's article on the "Tennessee Agrarians." He was my guest when he got the "Cousin Charles" material (Mr. John Ferguson); so I can't answer him. I've asked John to take him down. He won't read our book and answer arguments but complacently puts it all down to *ancestor worship.* I can't answer him personally in public, but I can privately.

I've seen two good reviews of *Forrest,* and I hope there'll be more. [Henry Steele] Commager has professorial omniscience, which is often ignorant, when he says that the military part is unoriginal.[1] He ought to read the O.R. [Official Records][2] before he accuses you of libel. It is all there as you put it down. If Bedford's picture would befit Chicago as well as Richmond, the answer is: Why isn't it there?

Miss Carrie's page proofs are done, and we expect the book soon.[3] I read it consecutively for the first time. My God, but it's grand!

Hurry back. I seen in the papers where Monsieur Julien Rochells (I bet he's a fairy) got the job in Nashville.

Love from us all, Allen

AL

1. "The Terror of the Damn Yankees," *The New Republic,* 67 (22 July 1931), 266–67. 2. *The War of the Rebellion: A Compilation of the Official Records of the Union and Confederate Armies,* 130 vols., Washington, 1880–1901. 3. *Penhally* (1931).

Southampton, New York
The Hampton Players
July 29, 1931

Dear Bre'r Tate:—

I went by to see Balch, and did the best I could. I think I convinced him. It was a shock to him as he was expecting to get it out this fall as his leading book. I was handicapped by the fact that I had to argue on the basis of one draft being already completed. He said that with the Davis you had a draft done, got a new idea, which after six months delay you discarded, sending in the original manuscript. This took me by surprise and I had to think fast. The only way out was to say that the Lee dilemma grew upon you gradually and that after it was done, it became suddenly clear and overwhelming—so much so that it made you physically ill. His mind was so taken up with the loss of a strategic place for the book, I don't know how well he listened. There is no way I suppose, for a publisher to regard a piece of work in any other light than a manufactured article to be turned out according to contract. Well, I done the best I could and thare she'll have to rest. Let me know how you come along and how well you feel satisfied with the toning up and down.

Did you see the review of Forrest in the *New Republic?*[1] I thought some of the remarks were a hit at you through me as a medium. It's very amusing to see them refer to the *I'll Take My Stand* [1930] in this indirect way. Well, enough for that. I got the Lincoln books in time to bring them along with me. Much obleege for the quick action.

I am here and now heavy at work. Go down to the beach and swim whenever I can. Al Smith was there Sunday, with a watermelon in his belly to attract the South vote. I talked to a producer about our scenario and I will tell you what he said in detail when I get home. I will be so busy acting, etc. that I won't have time to write much. Let me know how you all are getting along, and take keer of yoreself.

Love to you, the old woman, and the youngun.

Andrew

TLS

1. Edmund Wilson, "Tennessee Agrarians," *New Republic,* 67 (July 29, 1931), 279–81.

July 31, 1931

Dear Andrew: [Hampton Players, Southampton]

I knew you'd fixed it right with Balch. I can't take very seriously his talk about leading books when he can argue over the best biography he has had, for two months, and then hurriedly issue it at the end of the season, in June.[1]

I think he'll be able to get mine out in October after all, not on the 2nd as announced, but by the last of the month. I'm knocking it off at a great rate; your little prevarication for me is now almost literal truth. But the more I write the worse it gets. So I plug away at about 3000 words *per diem,* and don't give a damn.

You've seen Wilson's outburst by this time. I enclose a private reply I sent him.[2] I'm trying to get John to answer him publicly. (In case you *haven't* seen it, get the N.R. for July 29th.) John was here day before yesterday and we talked it over. Not a peep out of Don. I fear the air of the Green Mountains ain't good fer pant'ers, and makes 'em lie down with the lambs. Hurry back. Hear that Red & Cinina arrive in 3 weeks. Maybe he'll speak at Monteagle.

Love from us all,

Allen

AL

Cousin John is simply bursting with praise of *Forrest.*

1. Minton Balch, a division of G. P. Putnam's Sons, brought out *Bedford Forrest* on 29 May 1931. 2. See Appendix B.

The Hampton Players
Southampton, N.Y.
Monday
[Summer 1931]

Dear Sister Carrie:[1]

Your'n come in tother day. I'll be thare about the middle of September or thereabouts. I'm proud I'll git to see the Ransoms before they git off.

I've applied to review your novel to the *Times*.[2] I'll know this Friday whether or not it is to be given to me. If that fails, I'll try the *Herald Tribune* as you suggested. I had already written to [Malcolm] Cowley on the N.R. [*New Republic*]. Gee, gal, I hope it knocks em over. It ought to, and I want to drink to it before it comes out. If I make any money here, I'll buy a little something to toast it with, although I may save the money and get good corn. No new fangled drinks for *Penhally*.

We've worked our pants off on the *Immodest Violet*. I undress on the stage to the tune of an old fashioned Edison vic, vintage 1910. The rehearsals were deadly, but the audiences react properly; so I'm enjoying the performances somewhat. I never leave the stage, though, and it's very exhausting.

I think Forrest is selling tolerably well for these summer months, although I've not had any consecutive report from Balch. How did the Agrarians come out at Monteagle? And how has Lee marched through the hot, dry days that you must have had? Write me everything I want to know. I don't see nothing to keep me from going to New Orleans to see Bill. It's been a long time since we've taken a trip together and I think New Orleans would be swell. I've wanted to see it in good company. Maybe we can run up to bayou LaFourche where papa lived.[3]

Write me Care George Haight, 229 West 45th. Love to all of ye. Kiss the young-un. Have they jailed brother Tate fer stealin the plow?

TL

1. Caroline Gordon Tate. 2. *Penhally*. 3. Lytle's grandfather, John Nelson.

Oct. 1, 1931

Dear Brer Lytle:

I've been trying to write you a note ever since Sat. I suppose you've heard about Mrs. Warren. She's terribly ill. A week ago Monday she had the first operation, and *seemed* to get better; last Sat. she was operated on again, and has been expected to die almost every hour since. It is really remarkable how she hangs on, in view of her condition. The doctors hold out little hope, and I think Mr. Warren has none. We've been at the hospital practically all the time since Sat., and Sat. and Sun. nights none of us went to bed. Yesterday she showed some *slight gain* after another bad relapse, but I fear that only will serve to raise their hopes and torture them; there's a chance, but a small one. I've tried to stay with them as much as possible to try to give them some conversation to support their really pitiful self-control, which would be terrible if it had nothing to fasten to. If she has to die, it would have been better if death had come sooner, and spared them this torture. I've never seen such *character* so uniformly possessed by a whole family. You will be prepared for the worst news, for I fear it will come soon. I'm sending a pamphlet which is the best criticism our position has received.

Love from all, Allen

AL

Red asked me not to inform you—it would only worry you, etc. But I think I'm right in disregarding his suggestion, which was not his real wish. I should have done it before.

Tuesday
Feb. 16, 1932

Dear Andrew: [Nashville]

I am in bed again, but Caroline continues to improve so much each day that we hope she will avoid the operation. But Dr. Ross says she must stay in bed at least a week after all trouble disappears, and that will mean, probably, another ten days. He put me back in bed. Since last Thursday at least I had been running a temperature of 96⅗ to 97, and yesterday I almost fainted going down for the mail; the doctor says it's a definite variety of flu, the worst, and is dangerous for the heart and lungs unless I keep absolutely quiet till I regain strength and a normal temperature. Now we are both wondering if your supervision of the play is about over, and if you could continue any of your present work up here? We needed the cash on hand in this emergency, so I let them take the telephone out, and to this inconvenience must be added the absence of any one to drive in once a day to get things. That's the only attention we require. I know Cinina would gladly come up, but the poor child is so anxious to do the right thing that she keeps our minds on her efforts and makes things difficult. If your work is so that you don't need a library, you might go ahead here without any distraction whatever—for example, your long story,[1] which ought to be finished before it gets cold on you. But if your work would suffer in the least, don't heed this call. Our situation isn't that serious. I must confess that your company tempts me—I am too weak to work but not too weak to escape the boredom of lying in bed. I'm telling Red why we're asking you to come instead of Cinina—that you have no domestic duties at present, while hers are constant and her health must be considered too.

Please remember us to Mr. and Miss Bagley[2] and family.

Love from us both, Allen

AL

1. "Old Scratch in the Valley," *Virginia Quarterly Review,* 8 (April 1932), 237–46. 2. Thomas and Daisy Pitts Bagley, long-time members of the Monteagle community, were friends of both the Lytles and the Tates.

March 29, 1932

Dear Andrew:

Hell's done broke loose in the Cumberland basin. I fear we've given Cinina the works, and it's all over but putting away the maimed bodies. It happened this way. C. had been particularly absurd, but in the face of it Red said to me how well Cinina was "adjusted," that the "understanding" we'd had had done so much good, etc., which riled me to the point of blurting out that she had *not* observed the understanding in good faith, that *after* we'd talked it over she'd been trying to justify herself in the New York difficulty, and had said to you that she had *supported* us there. I'm terribly sorry, Brer Lytle, but I spilled it. Red of course reported it to C., and she called me on the carpet. She said you had lied, that she had never said she supported us, that moreover she had not told you anything about it in Murfreesboro while your mother was ill; the only time she had mentioned it,she said, was Thanksgiving, on the occasion of Mrs. Du Pont's visit, etc. That brought on the Armageddon. I've told Red that he is asking too much of us to bear with her—that it is not immaturity, that it is a fundamental difference in one's feeling for the values of life; that I am willing to go ahead and try to get along with her, but unwilling to pretend that it is a mere conflict of temperament among equals. I told him that the trouble is due to Cinina's need to put upon our social life an inferior interpretation, etc. etc. I suppose this was due to come. I regret like the devil dragging you into it.

Will write more later about other matters. We've got a renter for the house. Let us know what you all are doing and how things are going.

Love from us all, Allen

TLS

Clarksville

Dear Brer Lytle: [Guntersville]

I know how you feel, and I'm mighty proud you don't feel hard towards me. Of course she just told a story about it, and Red, in spite of more violent things since, is still lying about it with her. That being the case, she will let it drop, and never bring it up with you; she can't afford to bring it up. No, she didn't whup us, we whupped her. I finally wrote Red a letter. The dilemma seemed to me to be this: on the one side, the possibility of even deeper falsification of our friendship with Red, until we got to the point where it was virtually impossible to communicate the simplest feeling and thoughts—facing that, I had determined to cease communication at all, without explaining it; on the other hand, there was the possibility of telling him just what I thought about her, what I think of the way her vulgarity, her stupidity, and pretentiousness has corrupted our Community. Not being a hero, I chose the latter. He admits everything we say *in detail,* but of course he could not admit the abstract words with which we describe the situation entire. He will admit that she doesn't understand our kind of folks; he will admit all particulars; and I think it has done him good, as well as our relations, to admit all this. What he asks is that we use jesuitry with her, and lie along with him, in the hope that she can be brought to see some things. He is aware that her difficulties are due to stupidity—though his phrase is failure of perception—and that she will have to make more effort. The curious thing about it all is that he says he cringes at the knowledge that people are gossiping about our conflict; but he doesn't seem to cringe when she makes a fool of herself, or when he admits to us in substance that she is a fool. Well, the whole thing has kept us in a turmoil; but now I think since there's nothing more we can do, that there will be a little peace. Caroline wrote her a long letter cataloguing in detail her faults, but she was evidently so stupid that she didn't get the force of the indictment, and rested her anger on Caroline's statement that she had the wrong attitude towards her father-in-law, and treated him horribly; that is, she resented a purely conventional charge. I think the situation is fundamentally hopeless, but Red will appreciate all the duplicity we all can exercise, and I reckon we've got to exercise it. I just wasn't willing to have Red get to thinking of us in her terms—which was happening every day. For example, even after we'd discussed the thing with blood and thunder, he said that "Cinina in California had gone around entirely with our kind of people" meaning Bohemians, etc., and California literati; but Caroline caught him on that. She pointed out that Cinina would run around with them, but would condescend to them—just as she thinks we aren't gentle folks because we don't do this and that, or rather *have* this and that. Well, he will no longer be allowed such indoctrination from her, and I think our stand will do him good. I'm sure you will never hear again about the Supporting [of] the Tates in [the] New York matter. She has been routed on all fronts. When she didn't break off completely after Caroline's letter, she confessed defeat.

We plan to get down to Cornsilk about June 20th or 25th, and go from there to Monteagle, and all do our lecturing. Miss Carrie is doing one too. We go to Merry Mont April 15th. Address: Care Mrs. D. Meriwether, Route 1, Trenton, Ky. Telephone Clarksville 295-2.

Love from us all, Allen.

TLS

Merry Mont
Trenton, Ky.
April 16, 1932

Dear Brer Lytle: [Guntersville]

I'm shore proud to git yore letter. But fust thing I'll tell ye the bad news, which ain't so bad as hit mought be. Miss Carrie's done had a attack of appendicitis a week yestiddy,and I got to take her to the horspital come this Monday for a operation. But hit ain't serious, she ain't had no misery to amount to nuthin sense the fust time, and the doctor says hit won't be more'n having a tooth pulled. Takin hit by the forelock this-a-way affore hit gits too cantankerous is best and unless you hyar from me you'll know she's doing fine.

We've done moved to Merry Mont, and hit's raht nahce fer a spell anyhow. I been out fixin Old Miss Carrie's chicken coops and hit were more of a job than I thought fer at fust, cause they ain't no nails cept what she picks outen the kindlin' that comes offen the smoke house and the granary and the ice house. All the time I just comparisoned this here farm to Benfolly and says what a shame hit be that a real farm like this here one ain't in better shape, why the ground lays like a flat saucer with cream in hit.

Brer Warren come down by hisself two weeks ago and we talked hit all over, and we say he ain't got no right to do like he's been a doin', naw siree, and what do you think, he upped and said he ain't neither. Then I said I knowed we'd acted mighty common, but I said too we ain't had no choice, sense hit lay between being fightin' common and common like a snake in the grass, which I was plumb tired of being all the time. He knows they ain't nothin fer us but bearin' and forebearin', and that's what he wants. Hits shore done him good, cause when Miss Carrie piped up and said his old woman needed a good whupping, he sorta agreed, and said she was a gittin hit. As you may have heerd he's got a job there again next year,[1] Brer Davidson being of a mind to go away for a rest next year.[2] That's good news, ain't it? No more Californ-i-a.

No, I wouldn't give Balch nuthin, not another shot at nuthin, cept maybe a shot at sunrise. Scribner's have done sent me a check to do this new book on,[3] but [Walter J.] Minton is being a dog in the manger—doesn't want the book himself and don't want anybody else to git it. Hits the only hope of ever finishing Lee. I've got to git money to finish it on, for expenses for further documentation, etc., including travelling expense. In the first place it's all my fault for underestimating the proportions of the job; I found to my grief that I can't sit on Benfolly hill and spit it out of my cocoon. This has nothing to do with your Calhoun, but really Balch's list every season gets worse. Bobbs-Merrill are at least merchants, and not half way between.

We hope to leave Alabama about June 20th. Phelps Putnam was all set to visit us again this spring, but then we decided to give up the house. How about him coming to Alabama about July 5th, and staying till we all go to Monteagle? He's going east with us, and we're stopping off with him at Sandy Spring, Md. There's to be a conference, I think, at Sandy Spring of the *Hound and Horn* staff, if Putnam agrees to it; I had intended to have it here but can't now of course. You ought to attend that conference, and I know you'll want to stop off with us just careless-like at Lindsay, Ole Va., for a day or two. You better drive up with us, and bum your way back some way. Be thinking this over. And if Putman's visit won't crowd you none, won't you write him a letter—Phelps Putnam, Mirival, Sandy Spring, Md.

The Laniers have decided to spend the summer in France with us. Hit do seem like Brer Warren—sense this news got out—will have to spend the summer in Italy, just like Brer Lanier says among all them greasy wops. But ain't nobody goin' to spend no summers that Brer Warren's old woman don't spend. She's going to study in one of them colleges in Italy. Hit shore beats the Jews how a feller that don't have no money to quit techin' on, so's he can write, can spend the summer in Europe. I cain't figger it out at all. I reckin his ole woman's got pore health, so's she's got to *study* about hit.

We're honin' to see both of ye. I'm glad yore pa seems to be feelin' like hisself agin. Thar's a man fer ye, and I don't keer ef I do say hit. Miss Carrie jines me in love to ye both.

Allen

TLS

1. Warren was Assistant Professor of English at Southwestern College, Memphis. 2. Davidson spent 1932–33 at John Donald Wade's place in Marshallville, Georgia. 3. *Poems, 1928–1931* (1932).

Merry Mont, Trenton, Ky.
May 30, 1932

Dear Brer Lytle:

Your cousin Chink[1] and her old man was here yestiddy, and I promised I would write you a line about some business that she spoke of. I was wanting to write you any how. You remember the Scotch lady, Miss

Moonie? Well, she wants a copy of *The Lost Sheep.*[2] She may give it over the radio up in Canady, or arrange to have you read it over the radio in Nashville. Either way you'd make a little money. Chink says to send it to her mother—I reckon you know Mrs. N.'s address, just Belle Meade Boulevard.

Brer Warren came along with your kinfolks and we had a good picnic at Buck Spring. Madam Warren didn't come. But from what Brer Lanier says she put up a fight, as Brer Warren had to go back and argufy with her two hours before he could get started, and they didn't get up here till two o'clock.

Brer Owsley sent in his review of the Jefferson books. I saw it before it went, and I would have held it up, but I thought it was a first draft, it was so bad. I wired [Bernard] Bandler[3] to send it to me without reading it, and I wrote Frank a letter asking him to rework it. I also indicated some changes in diction and construction, but there were so many that I quit before the end. It amazes me that a man who has written two books and innumerable articles can't write at least correctly. Some of the sentences were so bad that they were ludicrous. What Frank has to say is extremely valuable, and needs like hell to be said, but God knows if he will ever learn how to write. It's mighty bad that a fine agrarian like Frank got into the University of Chicago school of history. I believe he thinks it's contemptible to write well—literary and artistic, etc. Well, if a historian is not a writer, like any other writer, I'd like to know what he is. I didn't want that review to be read up there, since I'm trying to put our group over as the leading crowd of contributors to the magazine. Till we get one of our own, we've got to use every organ we can.

As the time to leave approaches we're having qualms about doing much visiting.[4] I've hated to face the thought, but I don't believe we deserve to come to Alabama. Our sickness has made us so trifling that we are hopelessly behind. And after we leave we'll not get down to work again before September. In spite of all this I would make it to Alabama if you were not going to Virginia with us. And we'll get in some visiting at Monteagle. We won't see your father this way, and we're both mighty disappointed, but we'll make it there on the way back. Seems like our visits to Cornsilk are hoodooed.

Love from us all, Allen

TLS

1. Chink Nichol, wife of Lyle Lanier. 2. A one-act play by Lytle produced while he was a student at Yale but never published. 3. An editor of *Hound and Horn*. 4. Caroline Gordon has been awarded a Guggenheim, so the Tates are planning to leave for France in July.

Merry Mont
Trenton, Ky.
June 9, 1932

Dear Brer Lytle: [Guntersville]

Some days ago [Allen] Cleaton asked me to write a poem to be published on the front page of the [Richmond] *Times Dispatch* on the first day of the Confederate Re-union. Here's the poem.[1] I undertook it because I feared if I didn't they would get somebody worse. Now I feel that it turned out much better than I could have hoped. There are two weeks before it will appear, and I want you to tell me what you think of it. I've tried to weave into the old man's mind, brokenly at first, with alternations of flat statement and rhetoric, and then working up to the climax in the regular rhythm at the end.

I'm very much worried about the title. It isn't good. I do need one that gives the reader the idea that it is a soliloquy or revery, and this is the best I can do so far.

Brer Warren and his lady spent the day here yesterday. They were in good form. They leave tomorrow for Californy.

Love from us all, Allen

TLS

1. See Appendix C.

Merry Mont
Trenton, Ky
June 12, 1932

Dear Brer Lytle:

We've done a little more tergiversating, and if you all will let us we want to come down for a week before July 10th. We don't owe it to ourselves on any scale of merit, abut I'd feel that we weren't starting off right for the year if we didn't come. We should have decided to make it a week, instead of a month, in the first place, and then it would't have seemed so self-indulgent. Besides, my father's birthday, his 70th, is June 23rd, and all of his sons plan to go to Ashland to see him on that day. I'll get back here about the 25th, and spend a week getting things in shape. We can get down to Corn Silk by about the 2nd or 3rd of July.

I hope this about-face won't catch you all with changed plans. Just let me know if it does. I'm writing to Putnam that we plan to be with you all for a week, and he can decide whether he wants to make the trip for such a short visit.

Love from us all, Allen

TLS

Guntersville, Alabama
Cornsilk Farm
June 12, 1932

Dear Allen,

I started a letter to you, but was called away to Anniston about directing a play or two next year and also about putting on *The Lost Sheep* there. Of course we are powerful let down about your failure to rest some here before the Europe jaunt; but I seen it coming when you lowed you might put it off until the twenty-fifth. Will you write Marse Phelps about the change in the plans? He wouldn't find it very interesting to visit here without you all.

I had thought about your first title and tried to sketch a new one, but your later draft seems right; and so I won't send them. I never thought "secret" was quite right but I believe it ought to go in the subtitle, a secret he would tell between the four walls of his room. I don't like "speaks." He might be speaking to the young men, and they wouldn't listen. There is an added irony that he is speaking to himself. There are few to hear but the gray dead. The march on the morrow will be through conquered damned country, a last feeble defiant step. Your insertion ending with

. . . Obey them,
what commands.

He has already realized that they will give no commands. If you keep this stanza in, I would suggest that you extend it or change it so that he makes it clear that the "Go tell them . . ." is an ironic offer. I am not sure that I like the insertion. It interrupts the disclosure of the secret, which is important and should not be delayed except by the second stanza. I don't think "sullen" is as specified as "bloodless," particularly since "There's now only wind for breath" follows after it. "Sullen" connotes the period immediately after the war; "bloodless," though not so beautiful a word, more exactly gives the meaning you want. One more thing, I would like a homelier image than ancient tower, that is, I believe the Old Confederate would have used a homelier image. It is so fine, though, that I doubt if it should be tampered with. After all he was familiar with the towers of Medieval Europe. So long as he says, "My secret, gentlemen, is Damnation," why don't you let the secret be between himself and other old veterans, huddled together in this strange land. You could tell this in the sub-title.

Most of these suggestions don't amount to much. It is a very fine poem, one of the best you have written. I am very greatly moved by it, and a perfect sequel to the "Ode." The one to those dead, this to those living but dead. It's really powerful. I am anxious to hear the reaction at Richmond.

The Virginians may be corrupt, but they have preserved a capacity to understand a criticism of the damnation. They, I doubt, will be able to act. The people here could act if they could understand. Polly was mighty pleased by it too. The baby learns right well and is developing her feelings in the right way.

After talking with Red I've about made up my mind to postpone the Calhoun. My desire to do the book almost obscured its difficulties and the terrible drain and interruption to more creative writing. Perhaps in the future I will be able to try it, if nobody else gets ahead of me. I'm trying to get started on a play,[1] but it's slow work.

Well, you all take keer of yoreselves ontell I see ye.

Andrew

TLS

1. Lytle is probably referring to "The Gold Dust Family," a three-act play he wrote while living at Cornsilk. It was never published.

Trenton, Ky.
June 14, 1932

Dear Andrew:

By this time you have my letter saying we can come, and I do hope most devoutly that you hadn't made other plans after we said we couldn't. Miss Carrie will get down for the last two or three days only; since we plan to leave Nancy with Aunt Maragret (Mrs. Campbell)[1] while we're in Europe, she will want to stay with her at the end as much as she can. I've written Marse Phelps to plan on arriving at Chattanooga on the morning of the 2nd or 3rd, so we can get to Cornsilk by sundown at the latest. I'll let you know a week ahead whether it'll be the 2nd or the 3rd, but I think the 2nd.

After much discussion we decided it would be better for Nancy to leave her here; though Miss Carrie may weaken and take her at the last minute. We have so little money that I fear we may run short and Nancy might actually suffer; and she couldn't possibly continue her school as she should.

Your comments on the Confederate poem are extremely valuable and helpful, though I fear your praise is due to two very fine things—friendship and the subject matter of the poem. Your point about the subtitle I am adopting forthwith. I feared the "Go you tell them" passage might not convey all the irony intended. It is really a paraphrase of Simonides' passage where he gives the message of the dead Spartans at Thermopolae. I will try to point it up, and if I can't I may leave it out as you suggest.

I have heard nothing from Cleaton about it. He may consider it too long, or he may be afraid of it. He should have known better than to expect anything like the Noble Veteran but Better Off Defeated theme. Don is frightened by it; so I can't blame Cleaton if he is. I enclose Don's marginal comments on the first draft, and a letter he wrote after he got the second. I send them because they have a certain interest in the history of Don's mind. I think Don expects our poems and plays to be propaganda pure and simple—that is, he wants us to try to control minutely the reactions of the public. But I am content to move them as powerfully as possible, and there is nothing like telling them they're damned for stirring them up.

Well, General, we'll be a-seeing' ye mighty soon now, and it can't be too soon. All send love to your pa and to Polly, and to any others of the ladies who may still be down there. Bless Polly's heart, I'm delighted that she liked the poem.

Allen

TLS

1. Caroline Gordon's aunt.

Trenton, Ky.
June 17, 1932

Dear Micajah's Bro.:[1]

Well, hit'll shore do me good to see ye. Marse Phelps is a comin to Chattanoogy by sunup of the 2nd, so we git down thar by sundown. Have them squirrels cut up to flavor the licker.

I know yore plumb tired of this here poem of mine. But I've changed it right smart, and hit makes me oneasy to know you've got the old one. So here [is] the new one.[2]

I've fixed up the thing to meet our main criticism. I'm sure it's better now.

Love to you all, Allen

TLS

1. Micajah Searcy is one of the main characters in Lytle's first published story, "Old Scratch in the Valley." 2. See Appendix D.

Merry Mont
Thursday, June 30th, 1932

Dear Andrew:

Just back from upper Ky. and busy as a dog's fleas. We ain't goin to git away till Sunday which will throw us at Cornsilk sundown on the 4th, or maybe the 5th. I hate to keep you oncertain like this, but there's so many different people to get arranged at the right times, and all different times, that I can't do no better. Hit'll be the 4th most likely, and the 5th for certain. I'll send you a wire Sunday, so be looking out for it; it will give the exact time.

Love from all, Allen

TLS

The *Times-Dispatch* used the poem handsomely on the front page.[1] I can't tell you how pleased I am that Hoover snubbed the veterans in Washington. It will help make people mad, and that's all to the good. I had a presentiment he'd do it. I had a section in the poem on the "march to Washington," but left it out because it didn't fit. Wish I could have left it in.

1. "To the Lacedemonians."

Guntersville, Ala.
Aug. 18, 1932
Cornsilk Farm

Mes Enfants:—

I would have writ you long before this, but courting is strenuous business; and it mighty nigh requires all a body's time, if he do hit right and proper. I got back the first of the week, and pappy lowed I didn't look as stout as when I left; I told him hit was the bus, but he knowed better. We mighty nigh married, but I lowed we'd better wait ontell this here farm business was settled one way or tother.[1] She got to know me well enough to do a side face of me, and lowed for I left she'd like to do a nude. I told her us holly rollers didn't allow no sich takens on. Besides *everthing* was all right. We even let snakes bite us. I told her, though, if she was obleeged to see how the land lay, I'd send her aunt Tene.[2] Me and her had about the same build, barring one thing. I got to going to bed several nights bout sun, and her mammy got skeered. She set a jar of cayenne pepper by my bed and told me to sprinkle a lettle on me when I got to feeling porish. I lowed to her pepper was dangerous stuff to leave around us Lytles; and if anything happened, she'd have to answer fer it. I told her looks lika I'd sneeze at a picture of pepper. The doctor thought hit was sensible in a man going to bed by sun.

I ast em to let me name the new baby. I been pondering on some Spanish name. Hit's a Spanish fly baby, you know; and it ought to git its race name proper. Sister Patton lowed she'd wire her brother when the other un come; so she said Baby done come. Looks like Mean. Her brother wired bac [back]. And a good thing.

I shore miss you all. Done already begun lookin for the time when you'll git back. They ain't no news back here worth mentionin now. Have you all seen that beautiful, soft-talking tiger-wandering woman, Katherine Anne?

I hear she got a Prize outarn the Scribners? Was it all the first prize? I hope to our Saviour hit was. I'd shore like to see her, Gene [Pressly][3] and all. I read her story and thought hit was a good un, but I didn't like the folks in hit as well as I done in her book,[4] though I'll say it was as good a story as ever I read. Lawd, I fergits you got most of the agrarians along with ye. How's Miss Sally[5] and her ailments? And cousin and her old Dan. Tell her ef she ain't keerful, he git down in the belly and think hit's his back. Tell Miss Marion [Henry] not to pay them fellows what combs the hair on the street and admires theyselfs in the public mirrors no mind. They eats frogs I've heared tell. Eff you run into Major Ford say to him I say to you I sont my howdy do. I called up the Campbells when I come through Chattanoogy,and they lowed Nancy was fine and peart as they make em. I didn't git out, as I was a-passin through. I agoin to Nashville in a week or two. By then Brer John ought to be thare. I'll git some first hand news of ye. But write me a letter soon as you git settled. I don't really know whare to send this. I want to see the short story[6] when hit's done, fer I think it's the best one you've done. You gonna try and publish hit abroad or send hit back here? Ef I take the notion, I might run over for a few weeks this winter. Ketch a boat. Don't guess I will though, fer my belly ain't no good in salt air. I got in a nest of bumble bees at Patton, and was laid up in bed a day with high fever. I vomicked three times. Mighty unromantic. I mought a killed my chances in my puke.

Well, this is all I got to say right now. I'm agoin to New Orleans in two weeks to see about gittin Polly some lernin this winter. Found whare I kin borry the money. Guess I'll start out a-walkin.

My love to ye both, Andrew

TLS

1. Andrewena, a half-sister of Lytle's father, tried to take away Cornsilk from him through foreclosure. But by August, 1936, the Alabama Supreme Court decided in his favor. 2. Lytle's unmarried great-aunt. She was the youngest daughter of Joseph and Mary Nelson. 3. While on a Guggenheim in Mexico, Porter met Eugene Pressly who was with the U.S. Foreign Service. In 1933, they were married in Paris, but the marriage ended in divorce in 1937. 4. *Flowering Judas and Other Stories* (1930). 5. Sally Wood. 6. Tate is working on his first short story, "The Immortal Woman." It was published in *Hound and Horn* 6 (July–September 1933), 592–609.

Pension Mon Reve
La Garonne Plage
par Le Pradet (Var)
August 22, 1932

Dear Brer Lytle:

I ain't been myself or I'd have written to you much sooner; this is the first letter I've attempted to write back home. We've been in Toulon—this beach is six miles from the city—a week today, but only yesterday did we move into our present quarters. Ford has behaved very badly—insisted that we visit him in his villa where it was impossible to sleep or work; but at last I won the battle, and got away. We're in a small pension right on the shore; our front window is not more than fifty feet from the water. I am delighted, but I did want to stay in Paris for a month; I can't get books here for my next article. But I will make out I reckin. The swimming is fine, and I ain't et so well since I left Cornsilk. You may imagine that our long journey was not without its complications. Everybody wanted to do something different, and the newcomers to France couldn't at first resist the notion that the novelties of a foreign country were there as criticism of them. This was very trying. At last I got so that I was afraid to say, "Ain't that a pretty tree?" for fear Brer Lanier would attack me for Francophilism. When we drove into Marseille, he remarked that it was a shoddy looking city. Ain't it queer how a fine fellow can turn into that when he's away from his country. Seems to me like we don't have to be so careful if we know whose legs we're standing on. But I reckin we're all different. Mannie[1] is having a fine time, and Old Sall, who is the real Francophile, has been drunk with her love of it from the first moment she landed. I don't exactly approve of that either. Seems to me like she don't have no country of her own to love; we can have four mistresses but we can have only one country. Miss Mannie don't like the way folks squat in the street, but she is getting over that, and she has a real sense of what the people are in spite of her complete ignorance of the language.

Well, I been thinkin' about you all the time, and a-wishin' you was here. We ain't heard yet how long you stayed in Albemarle, or ef you went back home by yourself. Give our love to the Patton gals, Cousin Jinx, and the Doctor. You must tell me how things is since there ain't no other way I can find out.

We drove to Paris through Normandy, and then down here. I think you saw some of rural France, but we have really seen it. It is the most impressive experience of that kind I've ever had. It is perfect agrarianism. There are now, at this moment, 57% of the population on the land, and what wonderful cultivation there is! In the papers you hear of Le Crise, but I get the notion that this civilization is indestructible and eternal. Toulon, as you know, is a city of 250,000, so it is difficult to believe that civilization is dying when, in a city of that size, a hen can lay an egg on the street-car as it did the other day. This is my first real view of France. I am forced all the time, in spite of my personal dislike of Frenchmen, to believe that they are the most wonderful people in the world, especially here in the south where life is at its best as with our people.

Last week Ford took us to a party at Cassis given by a French friend of his. We got in a sardinier and sailed about five miles out of the harbor back into a calanque, or deep gorge where the water was a like a lake, and perfectly transparent at a depth of thirty feet and where the cliffs, almost perpendicular, rise for three hundred feet.[2] The back of the gorge is an impasse; the only access is from the sea. It must have been the hiding place of Phoenician traders and Carthaginian pirates. We swam all morning, and at eleven began the dinner. The first course, Bouillabaisse, said to have come down from the Phoenicians, was marvellous, or so we thought until each of the seven successive courses arrived, the last coming at four-thirty. This was not a picnic dinner planned by our Parisian host. It was a peasants' feast. The cook was our host's friend, and so was the fisherman whose boat carried us there. Our host says that the cook is the fourteenth recorded generation of his family, who have always been small landowners; he took to cooking because he happened to be an artist. The astonishing thing is the perfect breeding of these people. One of the guests, an old peasant who scaled the cliffs from the landward side so as to investigate the number of game birds this season in that neighborhood, furnished the wine for the feast, his own make and the best in this part of Provence: it is not for sale! Our host said it was impossible for him to give a party; his peasant guests always insist upon bringing their own choice products. This old peasant, just as we were saying goodby, had his right hand engaged when Caroline suddenly turned to shake hands. With the grace of a courtier he extended his left hand, and smiled alternately into the faces of the two ladies, and slightly bowing he withdrew from both at the same time, backing away ten feet or so before he turned around. It was simply perfect. He was like a shepherd in Theocritus, and indeed I felt afterwards that this same feast had been given in that same place since the time of Homer. There has never been a machine age in Southern France and there never will be. It appears that the reason why the peasants are so fine down here is their complete independence. France as a nation and the political organization of Europe may fall, but these people will never change.

And that's why our notion is right—independence on the land. And that's why France is our model for that idea at the present time. I intend to study this subject in order to write about it effectively: their idea here is the same as ours—the land not for profit but for enjoyment of civilized life.

We missed Brer John,[3] but you've already heard about it from him. We were all mighty sorry. I must end this now, but will take it up again in a few days. Love to your father and the ladies, from us both,

Allen

TLS

1. Mrs. Lyle Lanier. 2. The setting of "The Mediterranean." 3. Ransom was spending a year in England but had to return before the Tates and Laniers arrived.

Villa Les Hortensi
Chemin du Fort
Capbrun
Toulon (Var)
September 3, 1932

Dear Brer Lytle:

Hit shore is good to be a hearin' from ye and to larn how the courtin' is. I reckin yore pappy ain't easy fooled when he said it ain't the bus that made ye look puny. Hit ain't the courtin that's so bad, hit's this here titillation that's so weakenin'. Seems like you done found out how they done hit, them chillun I mean. Sister Patton ought to knowed it warn't no use of tryin' the same thing on all men cause they ain't all alike, leastways hit don't seem right to think the Doctor needed red pepper. Maybe they think all men's that way just like them Injuns thought a man and a hoss was one big varmint cause they ain't ever seen it except that way. To tell the truth I been gettin' a little scared of your gallivanting round Virginny that a way. I ain't goin' to have no malice in this here business to keep a body swelled up all the time, and hit shore 'pears to me like them ladies is grindin' a axe all the time for pore Brer Tate. I feel mighty bad about this, cause I feel mighty affectionate towards all them gals. Seems like they ain't nothin a body can do to keep women folks in their place. They's always cookin up something that ain't got nothing in hit but air. Hit ain't human nature to be generous and kind I reckin, that's hit. I'm feelin' mighty down in the mouth about this. We done got enough pizen in our lives, and I ain't honin' for no more, air you? Maybe I'm all mixed up, and I hope you'll tell me how I'm wrong.

Ain't no change here since I writ ye a few days ago. I might as well be in Floridy. Hit's raht purty, but I ain't got time for scenry. I ain't done no work since I got here, but Sister Carrie is finishin' up "Tom Rivers,"[1] and a powerful good tale it is too. Old Sall is abed today with a cold, but she's raht peart most of the time, and workin' on her book about how a New England gal ain't got no choice between bein' a old maid or a fancy woman. Course, she ain't neither, and I reckin that surprises her so she's got to write the book.

I do wish you'd ketch that boat you talk about. Honest to God, Brer Andrew, hit would make a new man outen me. Hit's mighty cheap too, and once ye got here you could stay free at our villa—we kin sleep nine folks. Keep thinkin' about hit. I reckin Brer Warren and Sister Cininy is back from Californy; give 'em our love. Brer Lanier and his ole woman will be thar about the time this letter is. Miss Mannie had a raht nahce tahme, but I declar' she jest couldn't git used to the way folks wet over hyer. Course she didn't say nothin' but I could see she was mighty worried cause they warn't no way to do it except stand straight up or squat clar down. I ain't sartain she knowed what I was talkin't about, but I kept sayin' this here country was made fer men. And ain't that agrarianism, Brer Lytle?

Tell yore pappy I miss him a heap, and give Polly a kiss. Tell me how the ladies at Murfreesboro air. They're all mighty sweet.

Miss Carrie jines in love, Allen

TLS

1. *Yale Review,* 22 (October 1933), 794–815.

Guntersville, Ala.
Cornsilk Farm
Oct. 23, 1932

Dear Bre'r Tate:

I hope to be able to write you a letter, now that I am back here with nothing and nobody to disturb me. I came back from the city, as usual, with a bad cold, with my nose running over my boots and my mouth, meant for a more honorable use, a-popping with sneezes. I raised all the toll-gates on miles of my intestines with little buggies of senna who rant shouting, like uncle Jack used to do when he rode home drunk and wanted to save a quarter, "open the gates, she's a-running away, a-running away." And so again I feel something like myself; in fact I feel more like somebody else in these fall days, so crisp at either end and so mellow in the middle.

I enjoyed your letters and Caroline's to the Laniers. I would have given half the hairs on my head, and you know how precious they are to me, to have seen that scene when the Rhenish lady asked the little boy to bring her some bread. I gather you have moved considerable but should be this time be settled. I got desperate for a while here and thought I would come over with the money I had borrowed from George Haight,[1] as the ladies almost decided not to let Polly go to school on borrowed money. I suppose it was a weakness in me prompting me to run away from mortgages and troubles. We are still undecided what our fate will be but will know in a few weeks, I think. The men of the farm associations were here yesterday looking over the land; they said it was twice as good a farm as they expected to see and the best crops they had seen this year. Mr. Clark is president of the Federal land bank, and he will, naturally, do all he can. We are, however, none too hopeful. I have secured the mountain farm, I think, as a stake: and we will move up there. Dad and I were busy planning the log cabin we would build; and we both got so enthusiastic that we could hardly wait for them to foreclose and put us out. He is that way. I don't know anybody who lives better, for he enjoys with extravagance what he does, whether it's a new cow, or a ditch he's had dug, or some dahlias he grew, or a forest of tall fat trees.

You are wrong about the ladies in Virginia. It seems there was some misunderstanding on the last visit, but all of them were full of praise for you all after you had left. But it looks as if my courtship will come to nothing. We had agreed to get married in the spring;[2] but you know how I am about letters. I failed to answer a thirty page letter she sent me, which was delayed by Dad (He opened it thinking it was a legal document; then was ashamed to send it) and I was moving about the country, and I can't write when I'm on the march. So I got back here and found a military note and a longer letter breaking our engagement. Looks like I can't git me no woman; they's always somethin to break it up. She lowed we would make good superficial mates but not fundamental ones, whatever that means. I'm afeard she's got a lot of her Pappy's words, besides being spoiled by her other lovers. They come flocking down when they found I was there, meaning business, and I whipped em out; but it looks like they done told her she could wear the breeches; and I let her know I meant to. I'm show gonna look for a widdy-woman; they don't rust like these here virgins; the first paint's been wore off, and they'll stay greased in all sorts of weather. But I'm sorter disconsolate. I'm gettin tared a-spittin in the fareplace by myself. I'm ready to buy snuff.

Well, hit's over. Don't name [sic] awhile. I seen the folks in Nashville. We had several poker parties, and I lost as usual, after first heavy winnings. John's tariff sounds pretty reasonable, if an internal policy can be worked out to fit it. Everybody there's spread out. Red and Cinina have moved out on the Birch place; John on the outskirts of town; Don's in Georgy, I'm afeared, to clean out his fester. Write me and let me know if they stole the French money out of my last letter. The French do that often. Lyle is still troubled with insomnia; the trip to Europe did him no good, and they are thinking about taking next year off and make sure he will get a good long rest. John Wade returned with a touch of melancholy and a hardened skepticism. Maristan-Chapman[3] answered Knickerbocker[4] in the Contempto magazine, and people are beginning to feel that Knicky-wicky will hang himself sooner or later; but I'm of the opinion it will be later, for Sewanee has been poor and virtuous so long, she has tried to do a little whoring. Kn. brings a small sum of money with his presence; and I don't believe the authorities will relinquish it. They had rather have a bad fullness rather than empty vacuum. In my stronger moments I have been thinking about a theatre after the Dublin pattern and a press, even if we have to have a hand one. But it looks like I ain't no good this year for nothin. I've been trying to write my long play and have written a scene or two; but I lack the passion Longinus talks about. Maybe I'll get on my feet when winter comes. The North Carolina people turned down my essay on the "The South as Backwoods";[5] they wanted me to write a purely descriptive something about something that no longer exists; and I scared them, I think, when I said a state could no more be founded on private property than a marriage on a bed. I took the thesis that the South was in the eyes of the rest of the country a backwoods, and I tried to define what that meant. They wanted, so they said, to know what kind of window curtains the folks hang up in their cabins five miles from the arterial highway. They ought to have sense enough to know that folks have quit hanging up curtains; they are wearing em.

They killed the calf agin my home-coming, but I was so long on the way it had been all et up or traded except a roast and a few steaks. One fellow said I'd been gone so long he didn't keer nothing about me no more; another'n lowed he'd forgot what I looked like. I did get back in time to help with the sorghummaking, and I wish you and Miss Carrie could taste them syrups this year. They shore eat good. It's one thing common folks eat that's fine-enough-flavored for an epicure. When the juice first runs into the pan; it throws up a fine steam that settles in your head like the aroma of Jasmine tea; then travels to the far end of the pan, gradually thickening until it bubbles up, rich and luxurious, like liquid amber. The yellow jackets swarm in its sweet steam, or plunge to death in its precious craters, to be scalded and boiled for their madness. It fell my job to skim away the green skum that is rolled to the sides of the pan. There are always two large pools of this gorgeous-ambered skimmings on either side of the pan and furnace which lies there to ferment. Three shoats regularly grunt their way down to fill their bellies with it. It tastes so good to them they then roll and wallow in it, giving off the most satisfactory grunt known to a hog's world. They've been drunk a week and wobble up to play snouts with you. This is the syrup that people resign to negroes and those that can't buy the sweet, insipid sugared water the grocers sell in cans.

Well, they ain't much more to say. Dad frequently says, apropos of nothing, what a fine woman Miss Caroline is; so you name it to her.

Write when you got the time. I'm as far off down here as you all are over there from what's going on. I'm afraid Red is gradually growing more like Miss Emma. John noticed he didn't have his old life and spontaneity. Things have come to a pass when you've got to fight to be natural around your friends.

Well, my love to you both. Drink a lot for me and come on home as soon as you kin. I shore miss you.

Andrew [Lytle]

TLS

1. A playwright, producer, and advertising executive who became a friend of Lytle's when they both were attending the Yale University School of Drama. During his most successful years in the theater and in Hollywood, Haight helped out Lytle financially. 2. The Patton daughter Lytle was courting. 3. The pen name of John Stanton Higham Chapman and his wife, Mary Isley Chapman, who wrote novels as a team. 4. William S. Knickerbocker was editor of *The Sewanee Review*. 5. In 1934 W. T. Couch of the University of North Carolina Press brought out a collection of essays entitled *Culture in the South,* but rejected Lytle's contribution.

Villa Les Hortensias
Chemin du Fort
Capbrun
Toulon (Var)
November 2, 1932

Dear Brer Lytle:

When your letter came the other day I was already so depressed that I couldn't answer it. Great God, we surely all have a devil of a time. The more I think of it the worse off we seem over here, but I reckin we'd be still worse off if we had stayed at home. We have enough money coming in to get along on, but it's a long time getting here. I'm glad you were able to get Polly started in school. I hope the mortgage nuisance you told me about has eased up a bit. If we can get along some way for another year I believe we will survive.

Please write me at length now that, I suppose, you are back at Guntersville. I have never wanted news of you all so badly before. We have a very hollow and peculiar kind of life here. We are so harried by our worries that it is hard to sink into the country and enjoy it. Then we must work, so that diversion seems wicked. We have little society. There is Ford, who is not well and seems depressed, deserted by the countless people he has befriended. Then there are some nice English people, the Cecil Wrights, Sally's old friends from her days at Venice some years ago. Wright is a good painter, and is doing a portrait of Caroline now. That ends our society. Wright is a splendid fellow, was raised on a large English farm which he was to inherit from his uncle, but the war came and he couldn't get back to that life. We both like him immensely; but old Sall, bless her soul, thinks we don't admire him enough—you can't get even the best of them New England Yankees to forget that they ought to worship the abstract quality of English. When we first got here Sally was all French; now she's English. It is too much for me, in this atmosphere where, insulated as we are, all trifles take on enormous consequence. The poor child is constantly "explaining" things—the Wrights to us, and us to the Wrights, till I had to say once that there is no art to read the mind's construction in the face American or English. So we go. I am working on my book; Miss Carrie has finished three chapters of hers, and fine it is too.

I have literally had no word from Tennessee but your brief letter from John's office. Everybody owes me a letter. I had heard that the Warrens and the Ransoms were on the same farm, but your letter seems to contradict that. Somehow I didn't think they would do that. Do you mean that Red is at the old Burch farm in East Nashville? Tell me how they are all getting along. I imagine the air is clearer now that the terrible Tates are away. When I undertook the crusade last year I knew I should regret doing it; I do now, extremely. But maybe it did some good, though it did my own soul much harm. I will of course never say anything more.

What are you writing? I hope Bandler is keeping in touch with you. You know I reread your H&H review the other day, and I think it is very fine;[1] the notion I had about it last summer was all wrong. I am glad that Bandler printed Frank's review after all.[2] It isn't good but its viewpoint is right, and it may contribute a little to the spread of the truth. It seems that the impetus of our campaign is spent, for the time, but I have great faith in it in the long run. We must hold on to that notion. An army fights with its stomach, and that's why we aren't fighting now; but we are still ready to fight.

I have written a short story that I will send along when I can make another copy.[3] When we drove through Washington in July, I took Miss Carrie to show her Greatgrandpa Varnell's old house in Georgetown, and the story is about the house; I hadn't seen it since I was a boy. I have written two poems,[4] which I enclose. I have also written some articles for the N.R. I seem to accomplish little, but after a month things accumulate.

Tell me how the ladies are in Virginny, and give them my love. And how the courtin progresses. A letter from K. A. today; she seems right peart, but is going to London, where the fogs did in her kinswoman Pocohontas some years ago. We're trying to get her to come to the Riviera.

Love from us all. Tell your father we want to see him, and want to come down to Corn Silk when we get back. Give him our love too.

Yourn, Allen

TLS

1. "Principles of Secession," *Hound and Horn,* 5 (July–September 1932), 687–93. Review of Laura White's *Robert Barnwell Rhett: Father of Secession* and Avery Craven's *Edmund Ruffin, Southerner.* 2. "Two Agrarian Philosophers: Jefferson and DuPont de Nemours," *Hound and Horn,* 6 (October–December 1932). 3. "The Immortal Woman," in *The Fathers* (Baton Rouge: LSU Press, 1977), 351–370. See Appendix E. 4. The first version of "The Mediterranean," *Yale Review,* 22 (Spring 1933), 474–75; and "The Meaning of Life," *New Verse,* no. 2 (March 1933), 9–10. See Appendix F.

Villa Les Hortensias
Chemin du Fort
Capbrun
Toulon (Var)
November 4, 1932

Dear Brer Lytle:

I just mailed a letter to you day before yesterday, but your fine letter has just come. We're going out in a little while, so I will indite you this brief note. I'm mighty worried about you all down at Cornsilk; I had hoped that the mortgage villain was brought to his senses; but nobody seems to be in his senses just now. And I'm very much distressed to hear that the Virginian episode has become just that—an episode. Patty is a mighty fine gal, but I reckin Providence saw she warn't good enough for you, and saved you in the end. I wish you could get you the right kind of woman; I swear to God I believe you're right about the widow. It takes one marriage to show nine out of ten of 'em what a man ought to be. But whar's the widow? There's plenty of grass widows, but that ain't the same thing; usually they've left some good man. I wish you could get up enough cash to come over here to new air for a while; though I must confess that I myself find it hard to breathe; that's because we lack people to breathe it with.

Somehow I don't like the way things are going with the Brethren in Nashville. John is the only one there who seems able to keep his head up. Fine men haven't any right to muddle their heads and ruin themselves over some tangle in their private lives. I reckin after all, in spite of what you seem to lose, it's better for you to be a little canny about this marriage business.

Manny writes us that Lyle [Lanier] is no better for his trip, and indeed I knew that when he left; he was worse. I've known him for years, or I should have said there was no excuse for his conduct over here. He was consistently and ingeniously rude to everybody, and seemed to think that the whole French nation existed only to criticize him. Unless we can pull our group together in the next year, I fear it will go to pieces. Either external calamity or some fault of temperament has affected us all.

I feared the N.C. people wouldn't take to your essay. You must send it to Bandler right away. He's very much interested in just that kind of thing.

This is Friday; Tuesday we go over to Wright's house to listen to the election returns by radio. From this distance I can't see much in Roosevelt, but he's a Democrat and better than Hoover. I fear that no one is at hand for the crisis, yet it is true that money power is everywhere declining, and the only alternative is land; in that lies our hope. We've got the essence of a real popular movement; but we can't move people by the old direct appeal; propaganda is necessary and that takes money.

I wish you would keep at that notion of an Abbey Theatre[1] and a hand press. Alas, even that requires, if not large capital, at least enough to feed us. For example, I couldn't at present write for any hand press in the world; I have to send off an article to the N.R. [*New Republic*] for fifty dollars, and write a hack book for Balch. That is the trouble with us all. But we've got to overcome this very soon.

I must quit now. By all means send the backwoods article to Bandler. By the way, Cousin Gus, Marion Henry's father, died a few weeks ago. Marion is now running the farm—fought like the devil to keep the place out of the hands of a trust company, and won. It's splendid; I think a great deal more of her than I did. . . . You must go on with your play; we've all got to go on. I wish we had some of them 'lasses you've been making; ain't nothing here as good. Miel de Provence is a beautiful word, but that's about all. I named your pa's compliment to Miss Carrie, and she promptly returns it. They's shore right, both of them. Love from us all to you all.

Allen

TLS

Tell Red I'd like to hear from him.

1. A famous acting company founded in Dublin, Ireland, in 1904 which played a large part in the literary Irish Renaissance in the first two decades of the twentieth-century.

Guntersville, Ala.
Cornsilk Farm
Nov. 16, 1932

Dear Bre'r Tate and Sister Carrie:—

I shore was glad to git yore letter, the poems, and the *Hound and Horn* with Miss Carrie's story in hit.[1] I am writing a short story myself while the plot to a play resolves itself through its various forms before it becomes intellible to the conscious mind.[2] I ought to be finishing it up today; but as you see, I am doing the more pleasant thing. Perhaps I can drive myself to close it after the letter is done; but if I wavered between the letter and the story, I would do neither, would grow irritable (I'm a little that way today anyway, account of an injured foot keeping me too close to the house, where I stifle) and take it out on George,[3] the cats, and Dad. I've already given them several before breakfast lashes of tongue. I suppose it is the strain of a year's suspense and too much recent confinement.

Well, at any rate the news from you all was mighty good to hear, even if it tells you were a little downhearted and forlornish. Don't let your work interfere with the pleasure the country can give you. I believe you'll do better work in the long run if you pleasure yourself a good deal in them furrin parts. A spell of routy liven loosens up the gizzard and shakes down the liver; and, in the end, gets your saliva all loosened up for that fatted calf. I've always thought what a disappointment the prodigal's home-coming would have been if he'd went to the best hotels and boarden houses and filled up on beefsteaks and biscuits and looked around to set himself up in business when he tuck that trip to them furrin lands. Think how good one of them Merrymount muttons is goen to taste and how close it'll settle around your ribs when you git back.

I certainly do like "The Captive." It certainly sustains its dramatic interest for so long a story, making it appear to the reader much shorter than it actually is. Miss Carrie is [hitting] her stride. There is the greatest difference between these last stories of hers and "Summer Dust,"[4] although I don't believe she will ever get another title as good as that one. It is a difference, it seems to me, between episodes strung together in extension, like the spokes of a wheel, where the marrow is reserved in the hub, and the concentration of treatment of the very marrow itself. I feel that the whole structure of pioneeer society is implicit in this story, and the atmosphere that rises is pure, without admixture of extraneous or anachronistic adulteration. There is one detail I am doubtful about. Would the flooded river be muddy, that is, were enough lands cleared at that time to make the rivers run cloudy? The book came while I was away, and Dad read it to George. They both seemed to enjoy it, each after his fashion. Dad wants to know what she gave the baby to quiet it; was it a piece of sugar or what? Another point I am not positive of: but it is my impression that the Cherokees had pretty much wiped out the Shawnees by the time the settlers had come over in any great numbers. I know this is so, but I don't know whether any remnants held on in other places. They were driven pretty early away from their capital at Sewanee. From your description of her stiff legs descending the mountainside Dad felt you could have used string-halt as a more accurate description than stifle. He said the stifles was a glandular trouble. String-halt is a stiff leg. He told me not to mention it as it was a minor point; but I thought I would anyway, since there seems to be some doubt at that point, enough to distract the mind of a reader. I don't understand why Scribner's didn't give it at least one of the prizes. The main character is splendid, of an Aeschalean stamp; and the minor characters properly subdued to a subordinate place but distinct.

In many ways I like it better than "Tom Rivers."[5] In "Tom Rivers," as I remember it, there is a zigzagged rise to the climax, if you have worked that out, of one big scene. This is the general form of a play; at least it is one form of holding suspense; first tricking the reader's attention; feeding it; then gouging it, until he is ready for a catharsis. This story is the treatment of one long scene, or rather state of mind for the episodes resolve themselves into this from the act of the character's narration of past events. It would be a scene in a play.

I do not follow the way a poem is made. The landmarks I should recognize mean so little to me, but I liked both the poems, especially "Picnic at Cassis." It is rich and complete. I think you have told about as well as you have ever told your lament. The fine images binding so well the central emotion a poorer imagination would have been riddled like a flour sifter—make the form equal the content. The analogy of moccasin comes to mind: its outer covering beautiful of itself but flexible enough to show its own strength in the power it suppresses into the long almost round body, which when it does not strike always threatens to strike. "The Meaning of Life" is calmer, more resigned. The introduction presents a philosophical mood as of an old man abstracting experience: but then I discover where it begins. "There's more in killing than mere commentary." A sharp change of released passion; then I know it is not an old man speaking: but that the early restraint could not control the emotion, and it comes tumbling at the end. I like this treatment. It is very concentrated; it must be to be successful. It lets down in a place or two. "As often as one gets the rare chance" if not prose sounds like it. Since this sentence closes the first mood, it ought to close it definitely, and it doesn't. It slops over the change. I don't believe you have done this, and I am anxious to see it completed. This is the way the two poems strike me. You may have meant to leave other effects. And of course there are always effects that never reach definition and that give the greatest pleasure, besides the residual effects of images and tone. For example that stanza, "When you O Trojans . . ." I am led to compare the fall of Ilium with the fall of the Confederacy and think awhile of the connotation this comparison implies. Be sure and send the short story. I'm anxious to see what it is like.

We are still in a state of suspense about the mortgage. There is the chance that we might get something from the Land Bank and another chance. Pretty soon now I expect the pending crisis to reach a head. If we lose this place, we will move out on the mountain farm; and we have planned a fine log cabin. I think Cannon Clark[6] will come up to live with us for a while. He and I will do a little farming and raise chickens. There is money under them thar feathers. We can do things on an intensive scale up there and still have two years to redeem this place. At any rate the dark and fatal nineteen thirty-two draws close to its end. This is a great deal, for there's been little joy to living this year. I expect I will go to Nashville for Thanksgiving; and if you haven't heard from those quarters, I'll relay the news. Red is living in the overseer's house on the Burch place in East Nashville. The rent is free. Red fixed it up to the sum of two fifty and made it habitable. That is the last I've heard. It's possible they didn't go out, as I've not heard from them. I somehow feel a lack of cohesion among the brothers at Nashville this time. I think they lack the Tates as a nucleus to rally on, and Benfolly to meet at. This is a long distance for the crowd to come. Don is away, and that removes the nervous energy spewing about. I somehow feel that the agrarians have let out their air. I wish I could believe it was because an army cannot travel on its stomach. That may be the answer, and it may be passing through its fallow time.

The mail has come; so I'll close this. Dad and I both send love. We'll be looking for you here at Cornsilk or on Sand Mountain. Remember me to Sal and Ford. Why don't you bring him back with you and settle him on the waters of the fair Cumberland.

Yurn, Andrew

TLS

1. "The Captive," *Hound and Horn,* 6 (October–December 1932), 63–107. 2. "Mister MacGregor," *Virginia Quarterly Review,* 11 (January–October 1935), 218–227. 3. George Summerford was the fireman at the Lytle sawmill. Later he watched over Cornsilk and served as a friend and companion to Lytle's father. 4. First appeared in *Gyroscope* (November 1929), a mimeographed magazine edited by Yvor Winters. 5. First appeared in *The Yale Review,* 22 (October 1933), 794–815. 6. Bill Clark's younger brother, later murdered in Mexico.

Murfreesboro, Tenn.
225 E. Main St.
Tuesday [Winter 1932]

Dear Allen:—

Your letter gave me almost as much comfort as your presence here. It came to me here just as we were going to Huntsville to break up the house, pack the furniture and other things for storage and for the farm.

We delayed as long as we did to sell a small farm to care for mother's expenses, or I should have been, as you hoped, at work in Alabama.[1] We decided that the quicker we finished with the house in Huntsville the better it would be, but the ordeal was a little too much for me; and I am ashamed to say I almost gave down in the form of a cold. I have felt as you feel that there must be only a pause, a renewal; and it will be so, but my friend it has taken longer than I thought it should take. I have not been so good a soldier as my mother, and I have tried desperately hard to be. For the first time in my life I have been swept away from a crushed base, and I was slow to find another to rally upon. During this awful timeless pause I have thought repeatedly of you and Caroline and of how desperate you must have felt those thousands of miles away, without knowledge, unable to assist, unable to stand by as the immense silence gathered; and this thought of the courage you were called upon to show has brought me closer to you than you will ever know. I was unwilling to write until I could fight again; but I am now ready, and it will take a great deal to throw me again.

On top of everything the bank closed its doors a week ago, shutting up Tean's burial money and what Mamma and May[2] had saved for taxes and insurance. We don't at the moment know where it will finally lead. Dad owes them some $6,000, and they may call for a settlement. It seems too much for this happen on top of real trouble.

Caroline's family album is at the hotel at Guthrie. A stranger passing through here had seen the pictures while breaking her journey there. I suppose Brother Gordon must have left it sometime. I thought I would return it because it's unlikely that she knows of its whereabouts.

I don't know when we will get up to see you. There is so much work to be done in Alabama, and we have put away the car for the moment. But we will try to make it there sometimes in the spring. I am thinking about doing the Calhoun, and I may use the libraries in Nashville for a look before I go back. If I decide on this now, I'll try to get up for several days, but my available supply of money is so low I can't make any decisions at the moment; especially since the bank's closing. In the past I could always count on the ladies for emergencies.

To tell of our love at a time when we are shaken out of the details of living is the only comfort against the heavy odds we must face. While under ordinary circumstances the mere knowledge is enough, it becomes now the comfort of the Holy Ghost, of what the Holy Ghost was once intended to give. And so, my friend, I tell it back to you and Caroline.

Andrew

AL

1. Lytle's mother died in 1932. 2. Lytle's mother's older sister, also referred to as Mary. She was like a second mother to Lytle.

POST CARD
Paris
Xmas Eve, 1932

Dear Brer Lytle: [Guntersville, Alabama]

We done had our hog fer Xmas but we couldn't find no hominy and corn bread. Hit don't seem right. We hope you are rarin' round with the boys.

Katherine Anne is a plumb flurry of sentiment.
A bas la bourgeoisie! O'l.Crowe
(Katherine Anne's Knight)
[but a 'hind-titter too.]
Greetings to Marse Bob![1]

Old Miss Brer Tate[2]

1. Robert Lytle, Andrew Lytle's father. 2. Caroline Gordon.

Murfreesboro, Tenn.
225 East Main St.
Feb. 23, 1933

Dear General:—

I have had your good letter a couple of weeks. It came shortly after my last despatch to you; so I have waited for gathering news. As you see, I am in Murfreesboro. The girls have been sick with the flu, and I have been lingering around, although I've done very little. They are much better, and May is at last up and about to get on her feet. I am going to direct the Cap and Bells again this year. I have a few debts that must be paid, and so I won't return to Cornsilk until April. It is all surrounded with water. Dad has to go and come in a row boat. You never have seen as much water as the sky has been pouring. For months the ground has been spongy, and every new rain gathers on the surface and flows in great rivers through the pikes and streets. It certainly looks as if the old gentlemen who saw things as all good and all bad saw them naturally. It is we who are abnormal. It doesn't rain with the proper distribution of water, nor does anything else behave with this sensible balance. I believe this point counterpoint which seems so desirable is the first stages of death. But enough of this, sir. I have things strategic to discuss.

I read your letter to John, and it was a fiery declaration of war. For several weeks things have been gathering to a head—they are still gathering—and by your return we will be ready to act. Lyle and I have been working on a program to get five million people back on the land, and this has lead me to ponder about the rehabilitation of those already there, just as necessary to our agrarian program. I believe with you that our job is not to carry out the details of a program. But our next book ought to have several practical ways of obtaining the objective.[1] We must busy ourselves with giving terms, ideas etc; but unless we ourselves consider the ways and means we are likely to make blunders in ideas. There is a great difficulty in uniting the western and southern farmer. They are almost entirely industrial while our farmers are still agrarian, if shabbily so. This last crisis has shown that. They are so well fixed that you can't make them revolt. That is, not enough of their farms are mortgaged and not enough of them have been improvident enough to go without food and clothes. The revolution has already taken place, and the oncoming administration understands the need for union between South and West. We can still give them ideas, which I am sure they will need, if we can only reach them. This other book might open the way. Certainly, if we could revive the *Southern Literary Messenger,* we might be able to press our advantage. As a matter of present knowledge, our first book has done a lot to give certain terms and phrases to editors of papers, etc. and even jack-rabbit politicians. I hope you had luck with [Eugene F.] Saxton,[2] but we will never be able to do much good until we are able to effect a physical break with New York. That immense industrial edifice is already rotten at the bottom. The slightest wind will topple it. If we could make that wind before its leaders rally and prop it. That's what I fear. The whole North and East is afraid of the farmer now. They understand that their greediness has worked against their own interests, for the farmer holds the strategic position of food and needed supplies. It has occurred to me to use the phrase internal balance of trade between the two great forces, agricultural and city-industrial. The balance, as in foreign trade, must be even between them, certainly if the industrialist is to exist. It is apparent to all, I think, that capitalism (in all its senses, good and bad) is dependent upon a stable farming population. The industrialist has destroyed his customer. Since the Civil War the farmer has had an unfavorable balance of trade, the industrialist a too favorable one. The industrialist didn't suffer until he found he couldn't collect for his foreign business. Now he is getting it from both ends and the two-edged sword of retribution is squirming in his belly and bowels. Since 1914 the farmer's dollar has gradually declined in relative purchasing power until now it's worth only fifty-three cents. This is gradual confiscation, and he has not felt it because of his inherently firm position. He can be robbed and robbed and not notice it until he wakes up and discovers his land is going. Then he acts as the western farmers act. Their discovery has come quicker than it will come to the southern farmer, for the reasons mentioned. I will send you a copy of our article when it is done. I want to expand part of it into an essay for the book. This book should deal with the basic matters of an agrarian culture, the farms and farmers themselves. Its different phases can be divided up amongst us, and we can write it off in no time.

Let me know if you want me to go to Richmond about the *Messenger*. I bought a copy of Lanux's book in New Orleans. I skimmed through it. It is behind in that it stresses Virginia too much, but that was to be expected. A foreigner had to take what books were extant. I have also been thinking what could happen if I could get my hands on a lot of money. I have thought how nice it would be if I could find someone who would like to purchase what is left of my virtue. The price I fear wouldn't buy meat for the winter.

I've done a short story called "Mister MacGregor." Sent it to *Scribner's* and it was returned with a note saying it was skillfully written but they had no place for it in their magazine. I thought I'd send it around and try to get Barr to take it if I failed elsewhere. The N.R. asked me to do a review of a new biography of Beauregard. I was long in getting the letter, and they may have given it to somebody else. I have great sympathy with old Johnston. Poverty is the greatest sin. It looks now that we might save the farm. Robertson[3] was too smart for himself, and so we protested the sale and threatened suit for something he did. On a compromise we may be able to cut the timber and pay him. I'll explain when I see you. We've got nine fine pigs. We'll cook one whole when you all git here.

I'm right proud Katherine Anne is in such good spirits and that her man appreciates her. I hope he won't keep her in foreign climes and never let us see her no more, onless we gits our walking shoes on. I'll look for "Tom Rivers," as I am anxious to see the last draft of it. You all have certainly done a powerful lot of work this year. It makes me ashamed of myself. I'm gradually working up to a point where I'll leap off and strike out at something. I can't git easy in my head, though, and all I do is study and try to pleasure myself now and then.

I've just looked for your short story to read it closely, where I have some peace; and I find I left it with Chink[4] to read. I'll write you again as soon as I can get it from her. It's certainly a splendid piece of characterization, and if your book treats of its people in the same way, it will make you a lot of money and fill out your reputation by adding fiction to it. The tone lingers with me now, strong and genuine. A good piece of work must haunt you many days, and the old lady is as clear to me as Aunt Tene is.

Tell Caroline I am waiting for that copy of her new story.[5] If you all keep on working like this, you'll burn out. Better drink a lot of wine, for when you git back, you ain't gonna git it so regular.

With love to you both, and hurry on and git back here.

Andrew

TLS

1. The beginning of a sequel to *I'll Take My Stand.* 2. An editor at *Harper's.* 3. The husband of Lytle's Aunt Andrewena. 4. Lytle's cousin. 5. "Old Red," *The Criterion,* 13 (October 1933), 51–73.

Merry Mont
Trenton, Ky.
May 15, 1933

Dear Brer Lytle:

"Southern Backwoods"[1] is your finest essay. It is certainly the most powerful piece of critical writing you have done. There is no doubt whatever about its availability for [Seward] Collins, or if he refuses it, I know that [Lincoln] Kirstein[2] will print it. Please get to work revising it. I have gone over it indicating some changes that might improve it. There is a long section, which I have marked, that I believe ought to be omitted. Another section, not marked, might be left out too: that on religion; I think you lean a little heavily on John there, which is all right, except that the reader would have to know John's special vocabulary in order to get your meaning. On this point, there is an allusion to the value of myths at the end of a paragraph; but you don't explain the point, and indeed such explanation would be a confusing digression, and I urge you to leave that allusion out. On the whole you might here and there, in the revision, try to curtail the extensions of your main idea: at times in the middle of the essay the reader tends to lose the connection between the general concept of the backwoods and the specific character of the modern South as the industrial backwoods. You bring it all to a head at the close; but a sentence here and there in the middle would help, particularly in the discussion of the planter before the war; it isn't clear there, without some close reflection, in what sense he was of the backwoods. The whole groundwork of the essay is powerful and subtle, and cuts through the entire growth of assumptions on which this industrialism is based. Please get to work on it; and send me a carbon of the new version. I want to show it to Cowley; he might consider it for the NR in two installments. Cowley, by the way, is adjusting himself (so far) beautifully, and is getting surprises every day.[3]

Don is acting up mighty bad. He's written a sassy letter to Collins demanding back his poems and articles—as if Collins had not kept all that stuff we sent him at first. Don tells Collins that he is preoccupied and can't be counted on in the general program; says that it seems that Collins is expecting of him reviews only—and there lies the point. Don feels that he doesn't have importance enough in this thing. I've written him a very moderate letter, and if he replies evasively, I'm a mind to state the whole case against his inability to act and his cantankerousness in general. But I don't think I will. We hope to get down the last of June. Tell your father we both send our love. Nancy is due here day after tomorrow; I'm getting her a small Shetland pony for her homecoming, for $5.00! Rest up and get in good shape. But get the revised essay done as quickly as you can. If it were ready by June first, I'd try to get it in the July *Hound and Horn*. Love from us both,

Allen

TLS

1. This is the one refused by UNC Press for *Culture in the South*. Published as "The Backwoods Progression," *The American Review*, 1 (September 1933), 409–434. 2. Editors of *The American Review* and *Hound and Horn*, respectively. 3. Malcolm Cowley is spending the summer at Merry Mont, finishing his *Exiles' Return* and getting acquainted with Agrarian philosophy.

Guntersville, Ala.
Cornsilk Farm
May 21, 1933

Dear Bre'r Tate:—

It cheers me considerably to know that you think the "Southern Backwoods" is good. I set to work at once and began its revision, and this next draft will be much better, I think. I am compressing it considerably and pointing up the logical progression of ideas. I have taken your suggestions as to the omissions and reduced the religious aspect to the minimum, alluding to it but not making it an integral part of the essay. I was reading the second volume of [Oswald] Spengler at the time,[1] and he influenced me considerably. Spengler and John made such stiff bedfellows that a marriage of their ideas did not take place in the feather-bed of my skull. I thought I had thrown some new aspects on the situation, but I am convinced that this essay is probably not the place to go into it. As you pointed out, it would require too much digression and would only make my position appear confused and my ideas too diffuse. Thank you for your criticism. It gave me the impetus to pull it together. I had about decided to abandon it to the waste basket. I am not sure enough of my own critical apparatus to trust it entirely. Perhaps when the hazy whiteness, which is my dome, becomes completely bare and shiney I will be more sure of myself. The real matter is, I suppose, I need more study and work. I wrote to Collins but as yet I haven't heard from him. I just addressed the letter in care of *The American Review*. Will you send me his address on a card? Do you suppose he intends sending us the review? If not I would like to take it. Has the May issue come out? I am rereading [John C.] Calhoun and [John] Randolph [of Roanoke] material before I rewrite the middle part of the essay; so it will take me at least the rest of the week to finish it. I'll send you a copy. Do you suppose I ought to try Kirstein out on it? If Collins can't get it in the June issue—and I don't see how he can—what do you think about keeping it over until fall? I'm inclined to want an early publication, as it is, in a way, current.

I'll declare, Don's got no business acting up this way. You've put your finger on the real reason. I don't know that it would do any good to point it out to him. I thought he acted right ugly down here; and Dad was considerably puzzled by his early departure and his refusal to let us drink a toast to him. As Dad pointed out, nature makes you put off going to the dentist two or three times. It is putting it mildly to say that he was ungracious not to accept the toast of his friends. It certainly said, to me at least, I am no longer in accord with you. Poor fellow, he probably didn't realize the real cause for his action.

Chink suggested we have a barbecue the Fourth of July down here, and I was mighty pleased to find out you all could get off about that time. You all come down the end of June and stay as long as you can, and you will be here for it. Dad will be powerfully disappointed if you don't get down. Be sure and bring Nancy.

Love to you both, Andrew

TLS

If Nancy has come in, kiss her for her Uncle Andrew.

1. *The Decline of the West.*

Merry Mont
Trenton, Ky.
June 2, 1933

Dear Bre'r Lytle:

I was simply delighted to hear that you were already at work on the revision of the essay. Please send it to me as soon as it is done. I have a suggestion to make since I wrote you about it. We have heard nothing from Collins, none of us, and we hardly know what to make of it, unless the additional fact that he has not paid any of us explains it all. He has not paid Wade and Don for their pieces in the April issue, nor Frank, John, Don, and myself for our work in the May number. (He printed an entirely rewritten version of my unemployment satire, some of the rewriting being done by himself without my authority, in the direction of making it innocuous to club ladies.) My suggestion is this. Send me the original copy of your essay, and I'll push it right on to Kirstein. Collins has become so unreliable (apparently) that I believe if I were you I would try the H&H first, where I'm sure the article will meet with great enthusiasm. Kirstein's new position on the Southern question endures with great heat, and I think we may count on him for some time. At least, more than ever he has got so he asks for my opinion in these matters,[1] which seem to occupy his mind. He wrote out some questions for me to answer on the negro problem; I replied in a long letter which he wants me to expand into an article. What do you think of that? You know the general argument: That the "problem" is insoluble in any absolute sense, and the northern pretense, whether industrial or communist, that it is so soluble, is irresponsible and entails eventually upon the negro an appalling amount of hardship; that the Southern assumption, in politics of all shades of application, is that the state must be ruled in the interest of order out of which justice is administered, and not in the interest of abstract justice which produces anarchy; that the inescapable assumption is the separation of the races, not on a theory but on the results of three centuries of experiment, and this separation implies the rule of one race by another; that within this scheme, if it is not constantly interfered with, so that the Southern desire for betterment of the negro is not betrayed into aims that he cannot achieve, much can be done for the negro, but that outside this scheme nothing can be done, and all agitation outside it tends to sacrifice the real interests of the negro to the chimerical justice of the agitators. What do you think of it?

We had a big picnic here Sunday. The Warrens and the Ransoms were absent, but all the others except you were here. We missed you, but we are counting on the 4th of July in Alabama. We may not get down before that, but we are definitely planning to come then. Chink said you were planning to have the Cabeens[2] down, and she suggested that you have the Owsleys with them, in that separate party. She asked if I would be writing to you, so I said yes, and that I'd name it to you. I think Malcolm [Cowley] would like to come too; I know he would very much. Alas, for the firmness of principle in this world. Malcolm is capitulating steadily, if a little secretly, to his new environment, and we hear almost nothing, in fact really nothing of the Housing Problem or any other problem. He has been confused by Marx, so he still thinks of any property system as a capitalist system; but he admitted to me the other day that evidently the Southern capitalist system had produced the finest class of people in America, and that if he weren't against all capitalism he would be sorry to see that class suffer even more decadence than it already had. He has revealed a sensitiveness to his situation here that astonishes me, and he is a general favorite in the neighborhood. Even old Miss Carrie says that Mr. Cowley is one of the nicest *northern* gentlemen she has met. She is a good judge of character, and I think she sees in him his stolid Pennsylvania Dutch integrity beneath all his doubts and tergiversations. So I want to show him another country region. Most people like him are exposed to the towns and cities, where they see the vices of their own places in the North parodied and exaggerated. He made an extremely acute remark here the other day—that the people on the farms in the neighborhood were not in the least provincial, but that Clarksville was provincial and Nashville very much so. He was of course using the word provincial to mean something bad, but within it he made a perfectly just distinction. He made the point that Nashville people are conscious of being behind what New York does, but that the country people were conscious only of being themselves.

The book is coming along nicely, it progresses so well that I am permitting Balch to announce it for late fall.[3] As soon as he returns the ms. of the second chapter and the Foreword I will pass them on to you. They are in final form.

All of us send love to Mr. Bob; tell him we're mighty pleased with the prospect of seeing him so soon. Write me soon. Love from us all,

Allen

TLS

Nancy is here and weighs 71 lbs., 20 overweight . . . Chink says she has picked you out a woman, and although I thought she was a raht nahce gal, I got to look her over agin. She told Chink she would like to come agin to them "bohemian" parties.

1. From 1932–1934 Tate acted as southern regional editor for the *Hound and Horn*. 2. She was a librarian, he a teacher of French at Vanderbilt. 3. Not published; he might be referring to *Ancestors of Exile*, which, he wrote to John Peale Bishop on 11 February 1932, he was working on and again on 30 October 1933, he had abandoned.

Monday

Dear Andrew:

I think this is fine. What have you done with it? It is now coherent all through, and I feel this is the first essay you've written in which you use a style capable of bringing all the complexities of your ideas to a clear and moving statement. It is really very fine. So far as I can see there is only one inadequate place in it, the passage I have worked on page 12. I think you are right, but this is an immense weight of opinion, even among certain Southerners, to the effect that your yeoman was really crushed by competition with slave-labor both on the farm and in the "mechanic arts." Can't you rephrase that passage to take cognizance of that point?

We've heard nothing from Collins. My last letter came in mid-April. I feel more than ever that you should try the essay on the H&H.

Can't you run up here for a day and a night before you go back to Alabama? The bus goes to Guthrie and is now very cheap; we could meet you there. There are many matters I want to talk to you about. Nashville is a mighty poor place for that. If you decide to come on the spur of the moment, just go to Guthrie, and call Marion Henry (Clarksville exchange) and she will drive over and tell us, so we can meet you.

Anyhow we'll see you on the 4th. Tell Polly we want to see her, and send her our love. And give the sweet ladies there our love too.

Love from us all, Allen

TLS

Merry Mont
Trenton, Ky.
June 15, 1933

Dear Brer Lytle:

Today is Thursday. Expect me at Cornsilk by a week from today. I will wire you the exact time. I will come by bus, as I'm leaving the Ford with Caroline, who would otherwise be marooned here. I expect to go to Nashville Sunday, and stay there till Thursday morning. Caroline will probably come down for the Fourth. I may want to stay a month if you can keep me; there's no doubt about my wanting to stay that long; it's a question whether I can . . . Feed him saltpetre and give him cold baths, and keep him away from that nickering vine . . . I am mightily excited over the coming trip.

Love from all to you all, Allen

TLS

June 27, 1933

Dear Andrew:

Yesterday Chink handed me your letter, and I'm mighty sorry I couldn't write to you before this. I have been in a state of the most harassed indecision. This is no time to describe it, even if I were equal to the task.

Let it be enough for me to say that I am deeply troubled, and I must stay here for a while, for reasons that I cannot explain.

So I cannot come to Cornsilk at present. There is a malignant fate watching over all my wishes to come there and visit you all. And that is where I should prefer to be just now. But I will have to stay here for a considerably longer time. Please tell your father how upset I am by my disappointment—not forgetting George; and say that I'm sorry they had the trouble of meeting those busses.

Nevertheless I'm trying to go on with my book. I expect to finish it this summer if circumstance permits. Last week I went to Gallatin, to the Court House, idly following up some clues about the Arlens—after the chapter concerning them was written. I found that they arrived in Sumner County in 1793, instead of 1798, as I had supposed from family tradition, and that gr-gr-gr-grandfather had a son named Lytle Allen. I don't know what this means. The family dispersed in all directions from Sumner, my gr-grandfather going to north Kentucky, but they did come here from N.C.—Edgecombe Co.

Red is the first of us to get news from Collins[1]—a wire, yesterday, saying that the checks were mailed and the June issue is due in a few days. So I suppose you may still count on him for your article. I believe I would wire for a decision, since he seems to be moved only by telegrams.

I still expect to get down for the 4th. But I'll let you know. Love to you all, and embrace little Sister Polly for me if she's there.

Allen

AL

P.S. Cinina says that the Cabeens are expecting to accept your invitation for the 4th. I thought I'd better name it to you. The Cabeens insist upon staying at the Guntersville Hotel. In strict confidence—the reason for this is that Mrs. C. sleep-walks and has to tie her big toe to the bed, a cruel necessity that humiliates her if other ladies are present.

1. The Agrarians have made special arrangements with Seward Collins of *The American Review* for that journal to be a special outlet for their material.

WESTERN UNION TELEGRAM
Clarksville, Tenn
July 16, 1933

Andrew Lytle [Guntersville, Ala]

CROPS LAID BY AM TAKING BREATHING SPACE WOULD LIKE VISIT YOU AND MR BOB THIS WEEK IF CONVENIENT ALLEN WITH BEN IN CINCINNATI LOVE TO YOU BOTH ANSWER TRENTON KY

Caroline

WESTERN UNION TELEGRAM
Springfield, Tenn
127p July 20 1933

Andrew Lytle [Guntersville Ala]
ALABAMA BOUND ARRIVE SUNDOWN

Allen

Benfolly
Route 6
Clarksville, Tenn.
August 18, 1933

Dear Brer Lytle:

Here we are, after terrific labors, but we are very well satisfied. I hope you are back at Cornsilk, and that the mountain air wasn't too bracing; it might make you discontented with the lowlands all your life. I wish you could have stayed longer, but our arrival at Merry Mont was very timely; the Campbells had just left, and Nancy was alone with the old lady.

Are the Ransoms there? Give them our love. Tell John that I hope he has written a new poem to accompany Red's essay; if he hasn't, to go ahead and write one.[1]

No word from Red since they left for the Indian Territory.[2] I don't see how we can get down there again even if Kirstein comes (as he doubtless will); so please plan to come up. You and John could drive up for a couple of days. We're on the ragged edge of finance; no movements are possible for some time.

By the way, we've had no mail forwarded from Guntersville since we left. Balch's check never arrived. I telegraphed him; he stopped payment on it and sent me another. There's a rather urgent letter there from Stark Young that I'd like to have. I don't think any of this mail came out to the farm. I left a forwarding address at the Post Office, and they probably got mixed up. Won't you investigate it?

Tell your father we haven't gained any weight since we left Cornsilk. I've already told Mr. Wolard, our cropper, about the crimson clover, and convinced him; so we're ordering the seed from Hastings in Atlanta. Our corn at present, though planted three feet apart, is something to brag on; you must see it. If you can possibly get your father to come along with you and John on the Kirstein trip, make him do it. We not only want to see him, we want him to witch us a well, and advise us on the land.

I sent your story[3] to the H&H, but don't expect any word from it right away. I decided on the H&H because I thought it more certain, with possibilities of quicker returns. How's the play? Write us right away.

Love to you all, Allen

TLS

1. The Ransoms visited Lytle at Cornsilk in the summer of 1933 and, afterwards, Lytle and Ransom went to Benfolly to discuss a second symposium. The poem referred to might be "Prelude to an Evening"; an early version of this poem appeared in the *American Review* for May 1934. 2. Warren went to Oklahoma with his wife who was sick. 3. Probably "Mr. MacGregor."

Benfolly
Route 6
Clarksville, Tenn.
August 29, 1933

Dear Generals: [To Lytle and Ransom]

I have letters from you both, but I have been so taken up with the farm and writing that correspondence has been out of the question. I have had two letters from Red in Oklahoma, and although he enjoins the strictest secrecy, I am determined to tell you his news. Cinina has had five hemorrhages, and is in a very critical condition. The poor fellow is beside himself—broke and away from his base. He says that he will know in a day or two whether it will be possible for her to stay on in the Tennessee climate. If he must take Cinina to California, he wants to know if you, John, would care to rent the Burch cottage from him, as his rights to it run through the next year. He is writing to you about that.

Kirstein has not appeared, nor has any word from him; I doubt if he is back from Europe. Stark Young came through Nashville last Friday; we drove over to see him between trains. He is finishing up his new novel, and I think it will be a great piece of work.[1]

John, have you written me that poem? Cornsilk is an excellent place to write an eclogue or a georgic; so put your mind on it.

Since Kirstein has not returned, there is no word from Andrew's story. Red has that other copy of your Backwoods essay, and I am greatly to blame for leaving it there; or rather I should say, it is at the Burch cottage. If Collins isn't sending it to press in the next two weeks, I will be certain to get it. I am delighted that he saw its virtues. I am doing a review for him as soon as I can get round to it in the evenings. I am working now, after book hours, on three essays on poetry for the N.R.[2] It seems that the patrons returned to New York recently, and gave indirect and gentle orders that I was to be solicited oftener; so Cowley's policy is foiled. This is Stark's doings, of course.

I will let you know the moment I hear from Kirstein. If I don't hear, and you all don't hear from me, plan to drive up anyhow early next week. Set your own time. Bring Sister Robb[3] if she's there, or pick her up in Nashville. Sister Carrie jines me in affectionate messages to you all.

Allen

TLS

Tell Mr. Lytle that the recent rain has made our corn look almost as good as his, but not quite.

1. *So Red the Rose* (1934). 2. "Three Types of Poetry," *New Republic,* 78 (March 14, 1934), 126–28; (March 28, 1934), 180–82; (April 11, 1934), 237–40. 3. Robb Reavill, Ransom's wife.

Murfreesboro, Tenn.
Thursday
225 East Main St.
[Jan. 1934?]

Dear General:—

This is a communication, somewhat delayed, as weekly intended for the Headquarters of Army of the Cumberland. The campaign against the Warren county forces has been going, I fear, badly. Treason and spies have given out positions, state of supplies, and mutterings of troops due to lack of pay. Hope to recover original position by several surprise sallies. In this case won't be able to reach Fort Benfolly until after the celebration in honor of the sainted General. If this is convenient to Colonel Radford. If impossible to use your train of transports, wire me at my expense care General Warren, and I'll bring wagon train in by Saturday.

There's possibility I'll make address on Lee's birthday to take Owsley's place (he's been sick) before United daughters in Nashville. They're mighty pore daughters, but I thought it was a chance to get in some doctrine. The invitation hasn't been officially extended yet: so am not sure. In this case, I ought to remain here until that is over; as moving would slow me down on speech and Taylor article.[1] I have, as you see, finished the poem.[2] Is the last stanza any good?

My love to the Chief of Staff and her orderly. Respects to Colonel Radford and lady, Quartermaster-general Meriwether.

A. Lytle, Acting commander, Militia.

TLS

1. "John Taylor and the Political Economy of Agriculture," *The American Review,* 3 (September 1934), 42–47; 3 (October 1934), 630–43; 4 (November 1934), 84–99. 2. This poem has not survived.

July 6, 1934

Dear Brer Lytle:

This ain't much of a letter. Sister Carrie has one for you though. We been in a mighty aggravating swivet. But this weekend ought to get us out. We go to Walling, on Caney Fork, this evening or in the morning, to get Mr. Gordon to read the ms. for technical errors; then it goes off to Scribner's.[1]

I got to work for about two weeks day and night in Nashville from Monday on; then comes Virginia Moore from Virginia and I think you ought to come up and squire her about a day or two, and then all of us come to Cornsilk for a few days. It would do her good to go bar-foot. She's a raving beauty, aet. 30, a grass widder, but she ain't got no grass growin under her feet. She lives in Virginia, but don't take no umbrage at that; she ain't no Virginian except in her sentiments, which is shore flexible enough to stretch in most any direction. But she's a mighty nice proper woman, ain't no modern foolishness about her; belongs to the age of Lily Langtry all except in figger, the which is lissome.

Now don't this here proposition just about meet your wishes as expressed in your last? You said hit would be nice to gather 'em up on the way. Well, you didn't figger in gathering up a prize package to boot.

I done been bothered by these here communists so much about bein in the Ivory Tower that I writ a poem about the same tower, which I enclose.[2]

Write us everything. How's Mr. Bob and Sis Polly? Give 'em our love, we shore want to see em.

Love to all, Allen

TLS

1. *Alec Maury, Sportsman.* 2. "The Meaning of Death."

Clarksville [?]
August 17, 1934

Dear Andrew:

After your letter came about Polly we heard she was better and were tremendously relieved. We thought at first we would come down but not seriously because we knew we would be something else for you all to have on your minds, and we wouldn't be of enough use to you all to justify it. If it had to happen it was too bad that she had to be down in the country. We don't understand how she took bronchial pneumonia this time of year. It is very rare in summer. As soon as Polly is well we want to come down to see her. Meanwhile I know these wonderful women, Miss Molly and Miss May, are giving her better care than she would have in a hospital.

I heard from Little, Brown the other day, and they said they were writing to you.[1] I think it is a fine opportunity, for them no less than for you. Let me know what comes of it.

I have been back here a week now, but expect to return to Nashville Monday or Tuesday. The work goes on, slowly but still it goes on. Miss

Carrie helped me wonderfully. She got her proofs the other day, and they looked fine. [Maxwell] Perkins[2] is trying to bargain with her in very small terms—doesn't want to give her any money, but I think he will. In the meantime we are very broke, more so than usual. There's a chance that the financial crisis will be relieved in an unexpected, though not wholly pleasant way, even if Perkins does fall down; but I'll wait till next week to tell you about it when I know the outcome.

Red came up last week to spend a week with his father, but Miss Emma was so solicitous for him that she followed him in 24 hours, and stayed for the remainder of the visit. Mr. Warren planned a fishing trip for a day with his elder son, but Cinina always did want to try fishing, so she went along, and said she would have to take it up if Red did because "we always want to do things together." They have a new car, a brand-new Terraplane. She is getting very beneficent—is "doing so much for the Radfords"[3] and wishes "there were something she could do for you all." Us, of course, though I'm sure she wouldn't omit the Lytles. To Rose: "I can get Mrs. Burch to give you a tea so you can meet the people who count." Really we have a vast new saga, so great has been the effect of future prosperity. To Manson: "I'm going to do some *real* entertaining at Baton Rouge."[4] And not one of us doubts it for a minute.

Stark will be along next week if he is well enough. He injured his leg and has been in the hospital. You know *So Red the Rose* is a best seller, the first he has had, and I am delighted. As he says, won't his colleagues on the N.R. be pleased?

Let us know how Polly is getting along. And give our love to her and to Miss Molly and Miss May, not omitting Mr. Bob.[5] I know he has been extremely anxious. We are well. Miss Carrie continues around 140. The Radfords send love too.

Allen

TLS

1. Although Little, Brown thought the agreement was for Jefferson, Lytle got a contract from them to do a biography of Calhoun. As it happened, however, the book was never done, and Lytle later returned their advance. 2. A famous editor at Scribner's. 3. Manson and Rose Radford, a young poet and his wife who are close friends of the Tates. 4. The meeting of Southern writers at Baton Rouge. 5. Lytle's grandmother, his great aunt, and his father.

[Memphis]
Nov. 1, 1934

Dear Brer Lytle:

I ain't had no time for writin since I come here,[1] but I shore appreciated your two letters. Miss Carrie seems to have told you all the news. I ain't done nothing but fool with these pupils since I come to Memphis. Writ one review of Freeman's Lee;[2] that's all. They didn't tell me how much work there would be, sort of deceived me without meaning to, I reckon. Twenty hours a week. The result of it is that none of it can be done properly. The others have as much as I do.

I was shore proud to know that Little, Brown got you to do the book.[3] Of course, I don't know about Hollywood. If they would really pay you the money, I don't see how you could turn it down. In the long run the Calhoun would give you more satisfaction, but less money. I didn't do a thing to bring that about but tell Stuart Rose that I couldn't do it, and that you were the man.

Anyhow we'll be seeing you soon. We are coming to Nashville on Nov. 17th—rather on the evening of the 16th, Friday. We will stay overnight in Nashville, see the football game next day, and go up to Benfolly after the game; spend Sat. night there and start back to Memphis about 2 P.M. Sunday. Meet us in Nashville and come down then for the visit. Won't that just about fit into your plan to come in the second half of the month?

Another thing: we're going to spend Christmas in New Orleans. You got to come along. The Warrens and the Radfords are there, and John [Peale] Bishop will be there. The Bishops are wintering in N.O. It won't cost much. We'll sleep on the Radfords, and eat cheap in the French quarter. We plan to stay two weeks. Start planning on it.

Tell Mr. Bob he ain't fer wrong about the preaching. I can feel hit comin on gradually, but I'm fightin hit. Give him our love and Sis. Polly too. We ain't had no news of her for two months. How is she?

Love from us all, Allen

TLS

1. Tate has become a lecturer at Southwestern in Memphis. 2. Douglas Southall Freeman, *R. E. Lee,* vols. 1 and 2, in *New Republic,* 81 (19 December 1934), 171–72. 3. This book was never done.

The University Club
Cincinnati
Saturday
Feb. 9, 1935

Dear Andrew: [Murfreesboro]

Last week I secretly felt that Brother Ben had lost his grip, but Wednesday he telephoned me to come up for a "preliminary conference," and here I am. The main show will be two weeks from, I think, today. So get your eyes in shape, and your *prostrate* in order; don't drink no liquor, etc. You are already being demanded by the people here who are taking Ben's advice to get us for their program. "The Hind Tit"[1] has been read and applauded e'en in the city of the Philistines. What is the world coming to? The situation is this: The Mercantile Library Association is celebrating its 100th year with a dinner. We're to be guests of honor; some of us are to make speeches. It is the background of publicity for the financial drive. Ben suggests [Herbert] Agar[2] as principal speaker from our camp because he isn't definitely identified with the South—he can show that our "message" is for these Yankees here too, and so prepare for the appeal to their money. Brer Ben says that the M.L.A. would back us with about 1000 subscriptions from the start. Tomorrow I'm to lunch with the man who is arranging the program; so it will be definite then. I'll keep you versed in our progress. I'm really quite encouraged. Now take care of yourself, and work up a couple of extra stories. Stay away from them hotels.

Allen

AL

1. Lytle's essay in *I'll Take My Stand.* 2. After reviewing Agar's *The People's Choice* for the *American Review* (December 1933), Tate invited Agar, then the London correspondent for the Louisville *Courier-Journal,* to contribute to the proposed second symposium.

Southwestern
The College of the Mississippi
Valley
Memphis, Tennessee
Feb. 14, 1935

Dear Brer Lytle:

This is the first moment I've had since I got back from the meeting with Brother Ben. You have the worst luck I know of. Take it easy and get on your feet. Luckily the dinner is postponed till March 15th or thereabouts. You, Collins, Agar, and myself are to represent us. I am convinced that we will have the money by June or July. Our real problem is to keep the venture from being swamped by the environment of the trans-Ohio. It will take iron and cunning, and most of it will have to come from you and me simply because Agar is an idealistic reformer and thinks more of Middle Western human nature than it deserves. We will have one man there at least who understands our program, Virginius Hall, an ex-Carolinian, married to one of them rich Taft connections. I reckon some Southern agitation would put him on his feet again. He doesn't need to work, but he has had business experience, and I've told Ben to intimate to him that we would want him as business manager. He'll be flattered to be with us; and remember the Taft money, which Ben says we can tap through him.

Let us know how you are getting along. Better stay in bed a long time, to keep the flu from settling in your eyes. Love to Miss Mary and all the ladies.

Allen

AL

I'm not too comfortable about several phases of the developments, but it is our one real prospect so far, and I suppose it is up to us to try it. It can only fail in the long run.

2374 Forrest Avenue
Memphis
March 7, 1935

Dear Brer Lytle:

I was mighty proud to learn of your improvement and that Uncle John is such a clerkly gentleman. I hope you're still taking care of yourself. The plans for the raid into Ohio seem to be maturing. They've fixed the 29th of this month as the date, and it appears that Agar will be able to adjust that day to his lecture schedule. It will indeed be an interesting experiment. Of course we haven't time to fool with experiments, but since that is all we are likely to get, we'd better take it. The name Lytle is honored among the Cincinnati. It will be pleasant to observe the honor restored to the legitimate line. (I told Brother Ben the tale you told me. He said, "For God's sake, don't mention it here.")

Anyhow we can size up the situation, have a good time, come back and reflect on the prospects. If they aren't good, we will be out our railroad fare.

I thought at first of driving here via Nashville to get you; but on second thought I believe it will be better if we join forces at Bowling Green. I will be pushed for time. The 29th comes on Friday. I will leave here Thursday; that train gets to Bowling Green at about ten at night, connecting with the train from Nashville.

I suppose Red has been writing you about his writers' conference. We're thinking of going, so you'd better jine up for the second Louisiana expedition.

I reckon we better not depend too much on General Ben after (if) we get the money. He's got a little copperhead pison in him, but he ain't going to bite hisself, not effen he can hep it. But he will be mighty good in the preliminary stages, before we give ourselves away.

At the last minute I wrote an article for the *Va. Quarterly.* [Lambert] Davis seemed to like it.[1] Makes me suspicious of the article. But he turned Don's down, on the pretext that it wasn't a literary essay.[2]

I'll keep you up on the news. I'm trying to get some writing done, now that I've broken the ice on the *Va. Quarterly* essay. I think I'll just enclose a copy of it with this, if I can get it back whence it now is. Miss Carrie has been mighty puny with flu, but is better now. I'm feeling right pert—weigh 166. Love from us all to you all,

Allen

TLS

1. "The Profession of Letters in the South," *VQR*, (April 1935), 161–76. 2. This might have been "Regionalism and Nationalism in American Literature," *American Review* 5 (April 1935), 48–61.

March 23, 1935

Dear Andrew:

I enclose the latest from our Ohio entrepreneur, Robert Black. I like the tune of his letters. He naturally wants us to spread the fame of his library. I've told him I would give out an interview the day before I leave. Couldn't you do that in Nashville?

I've written him that we will depend chiefly upon Agar for the speakin', but that you do mighty well yourself. The crowd will be big, but you can wrangle them for a few minutes. I must let him know by Thursday morning whether you will speak. Maybe you'd better drop him a line direct since you now have his address.

I'm forwarding him some biographical notes according to his request for publicity material. I've told him that I would ask you to do the same. He wants it by return mail evidently.

I reckon we'd better go up Sunday night, the 31st, if I can get off. Write me right away, so I will know where you'll be. I may have to write you as late as Friday or Saturday whether I can get off as early as Sunday.

A letter from Red today. He has a $10,000 yearly subsidy from LSU for a quarterly to be called *The Southern Review*. The *Southwest Review* is out of the picture. We'd better get Brer Warren to touch us; his touch is both the king's and Midas'. It's great news.

Love from all, Allen

TLS

2374 Forrest Avenue
Memphis, Tennessee
March 24, 1935

Dear Brer Lytle:

I been thinkin since I dropped you a line yestiddy, how you ought to come to Memphis about the middle of next week, so's we can talk all of it over and know the campaign before we git thar. I'm thinking of takin the editor of the *Press-Scimitar* with us: if I do that he will be with us every minute after we meet in Bowling Green, and we won't have no chance to get our bearings. There's some ticklish pints of strategy we ought to settle in our minds. There won't be time in Cincinnaty. Won't be no chancet to think. It won't cost you much—the fare over here from Nashville by day ain't more'n five dollars.

This here *Press-Scimitar* man is worth capturing. We couldn't get him all the way, but I've convinced him that agrarianism is serious, and he is willing to give us some publicity from time to time. It seems to me necessary that you get here by Wednesday, or Thursday at the latest. Better try to make it by Wednesday night.

We're all feelin good again. Love from all,

Allen

TLS

If you stop a few hours in Nashville and go by the Owsleys, won't you pick up my pretty dressin gown? I left it there and ain't had no pleasure outn it.

Guntersville, Ala.
Cornsilk Farm
May 3, 1935

Dear General:—

I put in a call the other night, over long distance, but your phone failed to answer. I had that day received a wire from Agar, saying he could not locate you; apparently he had tried Louisiana, Nashville, Cincinnati, and Memphis. I got alarmed and thought that something had befallen your menage; then decided better about it. Agar seemed to think that Collins had acted up. He complained that he gave him the prospectus the 7th of the month, afterwards going on a lecture tour. On his return he could not get Collins to answer the phone. He was afraid you were disgusted with some of the editor's behaviour. I wish you'd write me and set me at ease; that all of you are well, and that no untoward event has happened.

I'm going to Tennessee Saturday to fetch Polly home. I'll be in Nashville Sunday, probably Monday: then here Tuesday. You might drop me a line at Murfreesboro. Dad has been trying to get Miss Carrie's ham off, but the rush of spring doings has driven him and the rest of this place until tongues hang dry. He has out twenty thousand tomato plants, an acre of onions; the crops are a planting, and the young turkeys hatching off. Some of us will see to it that it gets off tomorrow or next day. It's only six months old and needs very little soaking; and it won't have the flavor that age gives it: but you might make out with it.

If there is any news relating to the Cincinnati venture, let me know, although I take it things are at a stand still. I'm at work at last, getting shet of an essay[1] before I begin the novel and research.[2] Bobbs-Merrill have been writing me a lot; they are interested about the novel and talk contracts, but I want to see my way a little clearer.

There is nothing here but the long spring days. We begin the mornings at five. I work in the garden and do chores until eight, when I settle down for what work I do. Our garden is doing well, but they worked it a little wet. It is as clean as a colt's neck. Already we have sallet, peas, asparagus, and radishes. In a week there will be potatoes, and the other things are reaching after the sun.

Love to ever one, Andrew

TLS

1. Either Lytle's untitled review of Eleanor Carroll Chilton's *Follow the Furies* which appeared in *The Southern Review,* 1 (Summer 1935), 203–205, or "R. E. Lee," his review of *R. E. Lee* by D. S. Freeman which appeared in the Fall issue, 411–22. 2. Lytle is preparing to write *The Long Night* (1936).

Southwestern
The College of the Mississippi
Valley
Memphis, Tennessee
September 28, 1935

Dear Brer Lytle:

I enclose—confidentially—two letters, one from General Owsley, one from General Davidson.

Their attitude was to be predicted but not in the extreme violence that here manifests itself.

We've got to bring them into line. I gather that John is tired of arguing with them. I expect to go to Nashville next Friday afternoon, October 4th. Couldn't you come up and help me?

Frank's vanity is touched. We didn't consult him! That is bad enough, but to rationalize it with that nonsense about not stepping out of his "field" and sticking to "objective" history (really an insult to Herbert) is about as pusillanimous a stand as I've ever seen taken. Don is simply hurt.

Sometimes I think our group just ain't worth killin'. I hope you can come up. You have influence with Frank. I haven't. I am not equal to the task alone. Don and Frank are absolutely necessary to the book,[1] though they are infatuated enough to believe that we don't think so.

If you come, I wish you'd come prepared to return to Memphis with me. And Polly too. We need a good visit from you all right now. Love to your father.

Yours, Allen [Tate]

AL

P.S. Just got back from college, and find your letter here. You all are having a powerful bad time. Damn the rascals. Since you'll be at Monteagle, can't you easily come down to Nashville Friday?

I've just received a telegram from Herbert [Agar] asking me to advise him which offer to take—Houghton-Mifflin's or Bobbs-Merrill's. So the book is placed. I'm taking a leap in the dark by telling Herbert to sign up immediately. I know its dangerous in view of the sentiment among the babies in Nashville, but we've got to act.

I'll investigate the extra distance to Nashville via Monteagle, and if we can make it, we'll come by for you. Let me know by return mail if you think you can make it. We want to see you all mighty bad.

1. *Who Owns America?: A New Declaration of Independence,* ed. Herbert Agar and Allen Tate, Boston: Houghton Mifflin Co., 1936.

Sept. 28th, 1935
(Later)

Dear Andrew: [Monteagle]

If you and Polly will go to Nashville with us early Saturday morning, we can drive by Monteagle and spend Friday night with you. How about it? The beautiful Mrs. McGehee came by this afternoon and put the notion in mind after I had mailed the previous letter. She looked right peart. She's leaving for Monteagle Tuesday. Your mountain retreat ought to be decidedly improved in charm. I don't know whether Louise[1] is going too.

Love to you both, Allen

TLS

1. Mrs. McGehee's daughter.

1531 Forrest Avenue
Memphis, Tennessee
Oct. 27, 1935

Dear Brer Lytle:

It's about time I was hearing from you. And time you started for Memphis. We're getting along fine—except for cash—and want to see you as soon as you can make it. Polly must come too. She can amuse herself some way.

I've got the essays just about ready to send.[1] I hope to get the ms. in the mail early next week. They seem mighty bad, but I can't make them better now, and I may as well go ahead.

I haven't heard from the Generals since I left, and I'm worried about them. They have probably lapsed into the indifference that we've labored under for several years. I can't go up there again till Thanksgiving.

I wonder if the *Southern Review* is ever coming out. I need the money, needless to say. I heard several people say recently that evidently the magazine wasn't going to continue; they'd asked for it and couldn't get it. That's the way they'll lose their public. But Brer Warren can't be on time. If Miss Emma ever has a young 'un, it'll take her twelve months. I'd be in favor of making that a test of its legitimacy.

Well, I'm powerful ashamed, but we got to pay taxes on Benfolly, and I had to accept the Junior League's offer to serve as "critic" for their Scribblers' Club. A hundred dollars for one afternoon a month for eight months. A hard-faced, bedizened huzzy, with the kept-woman air, wrote a line of verse: "You are as silent as the laugh of snow." I nearly fainted. She must have stolen it.

How's Uncle Dink[2] coming along? Caroline is doing well, but is temporarily interrupted by Mrs. Boyle's De Soto. Love to Sister Polly, and yourself.

Allen

TLS

P.S. Varnell[3] writes me that the gold mine has shown the cloven hoof. Not as good as they expected.

1. *Reactionary Essays on Poetry and Ideas.* 2. *The Long Night* is based on the actual experience of Owsley's Uncle Dink, Pleasant McIvor becomes his fictional counterpart. 3. Tate's older brother.

Route 6
Clarksville
Nov. 20, 1935

Dear Brer Lytle:

I'm powerful glad to hear from you and powerful glad to hear you ain't got no worse'n grippe. It's bad enough. I was in bed two days last week; thought I'd got over it; but my face aches again today. Take keer of yourself and meet us in Nashville *evening of the 29th.* Red and I are still on tenterhooks about the text-book; so I'm afraid to try to come until we get it all settled. If the reply is favorable we will have to partake in an exchange of letters promptly; if unfavorable we'll have to present it to someone else.

Funk & Wagnall's are starting a series of non-fiction, and have asked me write a history of southern literature. I will do it if the other book falls through. I am trying to think of some way to do them both. . . .[1]

So we'll count on meeting you in Nashville. We may get in to Fletcher's lecture Thursday (23rd). Why don't you come on then, and go home with us? You can work on the play here to great advantage. It is practically certain we will be there Thursday. Fletcher will probably come back with us, and I'd like for you to get really acquainted with him. This is the better plan. So let's count on it.

We're mighty anxious to see your gal. You must get her to come see us during your visit. We'll be able to go home with you. It's mighty fine that you've started on the symposium essay.[2] No word from Harper's yet! I'll give 'em this week.

Love to you all, Mr. Bob and Sis. Polly, not omitting Miss Henrietta. Regards to George.

Allen

AL

P.S. You know our fine Alabama Roosters—Cornsilk and Monteagle. Monteagle upped and died the other day. I am trying to decide if it was a sign from heaven. Maybe you can decide. Maybe we should have named him Memphis.

1. Neither project materialized. 2. Lytle's contribution to *Who Owns America?* was "The Small Farm Secures the State."

November 24, 1935

Dear Andrew:

Frank writes me that you are expected in Nashville Thanksgiving day. We will be there by sun on Wednesday. Be sure to come, and bring with you an outline of your article.[1] I've got to get outlines of all the articles to Houghton-Mifflin by next Monday, Dec. 2nd. You don't need to be through—just enough to give them a notion of your subject.

You must be working hard. Bring Sis Polly with you, we want to see her. By the way, Mrs. Waller[2] is in New York; so we can all spread over her domain. Bill has moved.

We both thought your review of Freeman[3] the best review you've ever done. It is a very fine piece of criticism. You do perfect justice to his merits and limitations. The new issue of the S.R. *[Southern Review]* is much better than the first. They ruined my piece, more than it could stand, by bad proofreading—stuck in words and left some out, and changed tenses of verbs.[4] I could have e'en spared Bill Elliott,[5] who got so wound up trying to prove that he knew what everybody else had said, that he could not say anything himself. And I thought Jarrell bad—fresh and pert, though intelligent on the whole;[6] he could have made his points about Miss Ellen [Glasgow] and Stark with less impertinence. There's just something about Jarrell that I don't quite like. He has a very nasty little ego.

We'll be looking for you all. Love to you both,

Allen

TLS

Ain't seen nothin of the McGehees for quite a spell.

1. Tate is beginning to collect material for *Who Owns America?* 2. James Waller's mother. He was a contributor to *Who Owns America?* 3. See above. 4. "The Function of a Critical Quarterly," *Southern Review*, 1 (Winter 1935), 551–559. 5. William Yandell Elliott, "The Modern State: Karl Marx and Mr. Laski," (Fall 1935). 6. "Ten Books," (Fall 1935), 397–410.

Romar Beach
Foley, Ala.
Thursday
[June 1936]

Mes Amis:—

I been lolling around here so any kind of effort is beyond me. The proofs have been coming in, too, in driblets, enough to interfere seriously with the sun and the beach. I reckon the Cup of Fury is drawing to an end, but if the reports are true that it has been 112 in Memphis, I don't see how you can work. This is the finest place you have ever seen. Only six cottages, enough to give it company when you want it, but not enough to give it the organized bustle of a real beach. The gulf is only two minutes from the house, below the dunes, and the water is beautiful to look at, always changing, either from heat or cold. At night, when you walk along the beach, you can feel the heat from the gulf stream whip and lick around your ankles as the waves come in. In the daytime there are a few dog sharks, which keep you from swimming far out. They are very sinister, you never see them, only dark shadows moving rapidly in the water. The boys caught one, and I felt his teeth. They are sharp as needles. But they haven't bothered us, and people here say there is no danger; but it keeps the swimming from being absolutely perfect.

I have been trying to time the end of the book a little better;[1] but the effort, fighting against the inertia of this place, is exhausting. Here is what I have done. When he [Pleasant McIvor] tries to kill Awsumb, his will snaps and fails him. He tries to think of Lovell to make his resolution return, but he can't bring the man's evil features to his mind. He realizes then that vengeance is dead, the rod is broken and beyond mending. He returns to the camp, to lose himself in the war. Ellis's death denies him this. There is nothing left but escape to the hills. I believe this might do it. I just couldn't do much with Lovell at that late date. I may be trying to avoid the issue in two paragraphs, but if I am, I don't believe I can do much more. What do you think of this? I asked Chambers[2] to send the blurbs for the covers of the book to you to see what you think of them. They don't seem bad, but I don't know whether they are any good or not. If you are able, I wish you'd make a few suggestions to him.[3]

Polly said Old Marster flew back from Virginny and admired the clouds. I'd shore like to know what he thought of them. I'll bet they was purty. They's heap better to write about than a pile of rocks. I'd like to know all about the trip and the speaking. Did the little Arsenics call you Uncle? The Davises and Sam [Monk] leave tomorrow for Memphis, then for Princeton. They got the offer of [a] mansion with five bathrooms and private parks. I'm going to be here another week or ten days; then I'll go through Memphis to Murfreesboro. Drop me a note, if there is time and let me know if the end is in sight.

Love to all of you, [Lytle]

TL

1. *The Long Night* (New York: Bobbs-Merrill, 1936). 2. D. Laurance Chambers was then editor and president of Bobbs-Merrill. 3. See Appendix G for the blurb Tate sent.

POST CARD
7/29/36

Dear Brer Lytle: [225 East Main St., Murfreesboro, Tenn.]

We leave here day after tomorrow (exhausted) for N.Y.—393 Blucher St. Fine folks here—real agrarianism, no factories, no rush. Dislike of East, great interest in South and eagerness to learn. Gave them a talk on South & West *vs.* East. Great applause. Will write you next week from N.Y. Love to the ladies.

A.

Monteagle
Sept. 13, 1936

Dear Brer Lytle:

I reckon you're having a big time, and I hate to remind you that plans for the party are developing. We're going to have a big party here the night of the 26th, right after the autographing in Nashville.[1] The Agars write that they may not be able to stay over for it, since Eleanor has got to get back to Louisville and be in West Virginia for a wedding by the 28th. So they are coming down early in the week—how early I don't know yet, but I imagine by Wednesday or Thursday; so if you can get back by then it would be a good thing. They're bringing with them a person named Chauncey [last name?] who is a convert to the Cause and who wants to meet the brethren. We plan to go to Nashville Friday evening (25th) and stay overnight. . . James [Waller][2] has got permission from his aunt to use the house across the road. That gives us six extra double beds.

There's very little news. Nancy is going to school in Chattanooga—much better for her and us. Your father is here now—he reads the reviews assiduously. The reviews are all good except the *N.Y. Times*[3] which was all mixed up.

We've not heard from John, and that probably means that the Warrens arrived for a visit. We haven't heard from them, but the Agars wrote a week or so ago that they had stopped off in Louisville for a day or two. I reckon we won't see them.

I suppose you read Frank's letter. I can't take up the controversy now.[4] I've finished one article and must write another one before the party, after which I must get to my book.[5] I hope Frank is reconciled to the book. He seemed to be in a very good humor.

I hope the engagements at Houston and San Antonio won't keep you from returning a few days early. Maybe you could move up those dates. The Agars seemed upset at the prospect of your not being here; so I told them I would try to hurry you. Everybody sends love.

Allen

TLS

1. There was an autograph party for *Who Owns America* in Nashville on November 26, 1936. 2. James Waller was one of the contributors to *Who Owns America?* 3. Tate is referring to F. T. Marsh's review of *The Long Night, NYTBR*, 6 September, p. 9. 4. The controversy between Lytle and Owsley stemmed from the original plan that the two collaborate on a novel tracing the life of Owsley's uncle. To this end, Owsley provided Lytle, who was doing the writing, with fifty pages of material. As Lytle got into the actual creation, however, the story took on a life of its own and became less and less biographical. Owsley's grievance at this departure explains the open letter addressed to him in the front of *The Long Night;* it represents a public acknowledgement and a kind of apology. 5. *The Fathers*.

Monday
February 2, 1937

Dear Andrew:

In great haste, to borrow some money from you if you've got it. The crisis didn't materialize, but we need some money chiefly because we've got to go to Chattanooga on the 13th, to stay two weeks, with the children while the Campbells are away in Florida. Can you make it fifty? We'll have some money in around the 20th.

I enclose a letter from Eleanor [Agar] that just came. You can see her state of mind—about what we thought it would be. Are you coming up before you go? Try to do it if you possibly can. Love from both,

Allen

TLS

[btw Feb. 2–20, 1937]

Dear Brer Lytle:

Yours just received. We won't leave here until the 13th, so if [D. L.] Chambers sends you the money before you leave just send the loan here. The trouble is that I gave Cath[1] a check for some money we borrowed on the Christmas trip ($25.00), and forgot about it; now it's in.

The news from Stokes and Stockell[2] sounds bad. C. is writing to [Maxwell] Perkins about it. It looks as if they were losing interest before the book is out—the way they did with Alec Maury.[3] Damn publishers anyhow.

Don't do nothin too wicked in Californy. Give our love to Miss Emma [Brescia Warren].

Love, Allen

TLS

1. Katherine Anne Porter. 2. Nashville booksellers. 3. *Aleck Maury* (1934) and *None Shall Look Back* (1937) by Caroline Gordon.

Monteagle
March 24, 1937

Dear Andrew:

Your letter has just come. . . Last night we went over to Tracy to see *The Charge of the Light Brigade,* really a very fine picture directed by one Michael Curtiz. The famous charge was done magnificently, and we both thought how beautifully Curtiz could direct a scenario of *None Shall Look Back,*[1] with your aid on the ground. . . Now your letter suggests much the same thing. I do believe that if Curtiz could read the book he would see in it a fine opportunity—not only cavalry but a big battle like Chickamauga. It is amazing how the technique of putting battles on the screen has improved. If you haven't seen *Charge of the Light Brigade,* be sure to see it; it's the best ever done . . . Why couldn't you do the scenario? It would be a perfect set-up. I can't believe that Curtis Brown, the movie agents, have enough imagination to put anything like this over, and of course they never report what they are doing, if anything. Caroline is always in the dark.

Just on the chance, I'm sending you a copy of the *Turn of the Screw.*[2] You might be able to do something with it. You could do the scenario in movie terms and we'd go half.

Of course these suggestions are most likely very wild and futile in face of the complicated system of things out there. But I just thought there might be a chance for us to pick up something if you could get the ear of one of the directors long enough.

Polly is coming up tomorrow (Thursday) to stay till Saturday, when she goes to houseparty at Beersheba. The Davises and [Samuel] Monks arrive tomorrow too from Memphis. This will be the first society we've had since Christmas.

It comes at the right time for me. I'm just writing today the last few pages of the first section, a total of 42,000 words. It has gone a little slow but very steadily; I have missed only two days since Jan. 7th. I expect to do the second section (about 25,000) much faster; but I can't predict the third. It may be as long as the first. The book will be much longer than I expected.[3] I get a little transition scene going and it turns out to be a big scene. But I can cut later to get it all in focus and proportion.

The Fords are coming in about a month, and K. A. [Porter] almost any time I reckon. As you've seen from her letter, she is leaving Gene [Pressly]. I thought so from her previous letters, and at least so far as we're all concerned it's a good thing. Gene was a little dog in the manger if I ever saw one, and resented all her friends. I imagine K.A. will stay on with us till we go to Benfolly and occupy the cabin on the hillside. The Fords will probably stay on till July; so I fear our trek to Cornsilk must be postponed till later in the summer. I think you'd better come to Benfolly too till your father can get things fixed up and pleasures himself sufficiently with his timber, etc. We can work all this out as soon as you get back. When are you coming?

The sales of *None Shall Look Back* are pretty encouraging. I figure it at about 5,000 so far, since the last we heard, the report of two weeks ago, was 4,000, and it had been selling about 1,000 a week. Twelve cities reported it in *BOOKS* last week, an increase of four over the preceding week. Some indication of the eventual sale will be forecast this next week. If it holds to the twelve or increases, there may be a big sale before it is over. But of course it may lose the ground gained. We can't figure out just what Scribners are doing about it, though they're running big ads five weeks after publication, which looks good. John W. Thomason has done a fine drawing of Forrest that they're using in the ads.

No big news here. John tried to get up a writers' conference,[4] but it seems it hinged on the acceptance of Stark [Young], Bernard De Voto, and Douglas Freeman. They all said they couldn't come; so he has called the affair off. I wrote him that that was a mistake. Such people will never come. Stark's private comment to me was typical. He said he couldn't wear himself out in jabber just for railroad fare. Stark's recent letters have been a little crazy. I don't know what's the matter with him. He wrote Caroline he was "whispering" about the merit of her book into several ears. She wrote back not to do it. He always says these things as if he were doing something extraordinary for you. She told him that among friends such things are spontaneous and more to the effect that people who do them usually forget them the next day. . . I'm surprised at John for wanting to get so much false front for his conference. The best-sellers never come to such things: they're afraid they won't be admired enough. But there's the mystery of John's complicated nature.

Hurry back. Don't fight the battle of Gettysburg with that Yankee woman. You can't win and you'll retire with resources diminished. Love from us both,

Allen

TLS

Dear Andrew: Did I tell you in my letter that I'd got the review from the clipping bureau. Needless to say how pleased I was over it. It seems to me that in addition to appraising the book you've made some important points about the conflict at large. I liked the last paragraph so much. Love and thanks.

C.[aroline]

1. A novel by Caroline Gordon which came out in February. 2. Tate's dramatic version. 3. Tate is writing *The Fathers* (1938). 4. Ransom was trying to organize a Southern Writers' Conference at Vanderbilt.

[California]
Wednesday
[Late Spring 1937]

Dear Allen:—

Just a note. Did [Herman] Shumlin wire you to send him a copy of *The Governess?*[1] I think there is a good chance to sell it to him. Fortunately, he has been wanting somebody to dramatize that for years, but didn't see how it could be done. Shumlin is a Broadway producer, not Hollywood. If he hasn't got into communication with you, write your agent to see him. I explained the difficulties you were having, the business about the other dramatization, but he thought that could be all arranged. If I can find his address, I'll send it to you, because on second thought it might be better for you to send your copy. The James agents might put theirs off on him. Shumlin is the man who proposed the Lee to me, but after discussing it with him, I'm afraid it is impossible for us to get together. Like all Jews he would be hostile to the necessary tragic denouement.

I telephoned the Twentieth-Century Fox again about Caroline's book,[2] but have heard nothing from them. But that means nothing, either way. George [Haight] has been so busy that he hasn't had time to go over the scenario of his brother-in-law, whom he is backing; but I hope to get him to read the book before I leave. You've no idea how complicated this business is, nor how foolish. I'll tell you all about it when I get back. The main difficulty is that from top to bottom every man is ridden with fear. He's afraid to back anything or anybody, because if that person or that script should fail he becomes involved. And the saying is that every man is as good as his last picture. He may have had twelve successes, but if he fails on one, he's out. And when you're out in Hollywood, you are really out. I found out, curiously enough, that Clifton Fadiman recommended my book[3] very highly to [Samuel] Goldwyn. Goldwyn hired him to scout for possible movie material. His recommendations, including mine, showed Goldwyn that he didn't know what Goldwyn wanted; so he was fired. I don't think there is much chance for either of us to sell George's studio a Civil War picture. The studio turned down *Gone With the Wind*—before it swept the country—which means that they refuse to believe in any Civil War picture. Goldwyn is an illiterate Jew who still thinks in terms of the silent pictures. He is a small producer, which means he does only one picture at a time. The others have four or five going at once. And I have no connections [with] them. The directors are mere hirelings. So you see, even if I knew the director of *The Charge of the Light Brigade,* he would not be the proper angle to work. There are three directors who are independent, who get a hundred or hundred and fifty thousand dollars a picture, but they alone are in a position to demand independence of working conditions. Unfortunately I have no way of approaching them. So I'm afraid I haven't been able to do anything for us this time. The only way would be for me to spend time out there, and that I'm unwilling to do this year. In another year, George will either be in a position to demand things, or he will be out. And so I'm afraid we'll have to wait on that. I cannot explain by letter the technique of selling stuff nor how completely mad the whole business is.

I'm delighted that *None* . . . is selling so well. If it keeps up, undoubtedly somebody will buy it out here. Having absolutely no esthetic principles of their own, knowing very little about drama, the movie people all rush to buy anything, with no real understanding of merit or lack of merit, if only what they buy has been approved by others. Then they feel reasonably safe.

I think I'm leaving this week, for I'm very anxious to get to work. I never expected to get into this trip, but I have learned how it is done, and next time I believe I can pick up some money for us.

With love and great haste, Andrew

TLS

I've boughten me the purtiest gazelle coat you ever seen and a medieval skull cap made of the same skin. If I had the money I'd shore bring you and Miss Carrie one, but of course she wouldn't wear it for fear the luxury of it would offend The Muse.

1. A drama based on *The Turn of the Screw* on which Tate collaborated with Anne Goodwin Winslow (1936). 2. *None Shall Look Back.* 3. *The Long Night.*

Benfolly
Wednesday, May 19, 1937

Dear Andrew:

I reckon you been having a trying time. We're hoping Miss May is going to be much better. It looks like she ought to have a little good luck now. The Fords got here Friday, and we've shaken down to a good routine of work. Come this weekend if you can. John is coming Friday to make that speech; so you ought to come with him if you possibly can. I talked to him over the phone the other day, and he seems to be much improved.

We have more sleeping space here than ever before. Even after the Fords—including "Wally,"[1] the secretary, aged 21—are bedded down, there are still two double beds empty. I'm convinced that unless you're actually needed at Monteagle you could do better work here; or rather if you *are* needed, for that would mean encroachments on your time. We separate at breakfast after no conversation and each person retires to his work. Look the situation over when you come.

The Lowell boy[2] turned up twice, and we like him but feel that he is potentially a nuisance. His family decided that anybody who wanted to be a writer was insane; so they tried to have him judged crazy and committed to an asylum. Merrill [Moore] evidently put on his bedside manner and got their consent for him to come to Tennessee, which doubtless in the Lowell mind is not unlike a madhouse. Ford says they are the most dreadful people he's ever seen. (By the way, young Lowell is kin to the Memphis Winslows, his mother being a Winslow and descendant of the Kearsarge man.)

I want you to read the novel[3] as soon as you can. I sort of feel held up until you do. Balch has had a copy of this first section for more than a week, but I've heard nothing from him. I reckon he don't like it. If that's the case, I'll give it to Perkins and feel very pleased.

Love from us all. And be sure to come . . . By the way, Polly ought to come too. I thought C. had written her—she meant to yesterday. Be sure to make her come. There's plenty of room for everybody.

A.

TLS

I hope the widow woman is making your stay in Gadsden pleasant. You might investigate the secretary.

1. Mrs. Jack Tworkov, Janice Ford's sister-in-law. 2. Robert Lowell. 3. *The Fathers.*

Murfreesboro, Tenn.
May 20 [1937]

Dear Allen:—

We got in yesterday from Alabama, after a rather strenuous trip. Polly, as usual, bore the brunt of the nursing and care, while I attended to the driving and public relations. The widow was fat and sassy, and I talked to her some. It war right good conversation. But it looks like she's always studying about eaves-dropping.

We are pleased with Dr. Bass's thorough examination. He says May's condition is due to thyroid trouble. It is the kind which poisons the system but does not produce a goitre. He has put her on a diet and has ordered rest and ease. I think, too, he gives her iodine. There might be encroachments on my time, but I feel I've got to help out with the situation here and at Monteagle until she gets much better. I'll get along pretty well, because they know here that I've got to work. There's nothing I'd like better to do than come down to Benfolly and get in that routine, but I must confess that the temptation is the society, and it's time I did a little self-abnegating. And I feel sure I can work here. After I get under way and things clear up in a family way, maybe we can get together later on.

I had planned to come down this weekend, but Dad took my car back. if I can get James [Waller] or somebody to run me up, we'll come up Sunday or maybe Saturday. And then I'm absolutely not going to move about until I get well under way. I'm mighty anxious to see the novel, but I know you really don't need no advice on it. You can look for me Sunday if I have to come up on the bus. I could get away today, but I in a weak moment agreed to read here in Murfreesboro tonight.

Give the Fords my regards. Polly and I'll run up later when the car is back. I don't know when to look for it, but Dad says he'll bring it back Wednesday. The only trouble about leaving this weekend is that I seem to be doing nothing but moving about. Of course the Gadsden thing had to be done, but I am determined to settle down at once.

With love to you all, Andrew
TLS

[May 1937]

Dear Andrew:

It does indeed look bad[1] . . . John's letter was about as hopeless as could be. He remarked that [O. C.] Carmichael's idea of a literary man at Vanderbilt was somebody to rewrite the catalogue.

We ought to see [Frank] Rand, but I won't come to Nashville tomorrow till I hear from you. Try to make an appointment. We must see that he gets some facts that [Edwin] Mims won't give him. We'd better just tell Rand the whole story of Mims' persecution of Red.

I'm waiting to hear from you because meanwhile I need to work on the review for Red.

A.[llen]
TLS

1. Ransom is contemplating an offer from Kenyon College, which Chancellor Kirkland and Edwin Mims, chairman of the English Department, at Vanderbilt refuse to meet. Tate is suggesting that he and Lytle relate to Mr. Rand, chairman of the Vanderbilt Board of Trust how Mims has "persecuted" Warren and forced him to leave Vanderbilt for LSU. Tate suggests that Mims does not appreciate the critical reputation of the "creative" members of his faculty. Currently serving as Dean, Carmichael is appointed to succeed Kirkland as Chancellor. See Appendix G2.

Murfreesboro, Tenn.
225 E. Main St.
Thursday night
[May 1937]

Dear Allen:—

Of course, as it turned out, Dad did not return yesterday. I should have known with this family's evasions that he wouldn't. He telephoned tonight that he would be up Saturday or Sunday, in which case I'll get up sometime next week. I wanted very much to be there this week so that we could discuss John Ransom's situation. I read your letter in the *Tennessean* again,[1] and it is a masterpiece. Then tonight there was a news story, in which Mims was quoted as saying that he would do everything "in reason" to keep Ransom there. John was quoted as saying that he was embarrassed by the letter, but I can't help but think that he was pleased, and I'm sure that this is the time to bring it out in public, because it would be too late after he has signed up. It has given the administration public warning: they cannot later say that they didn't know anything about it. [James H.] Kirkland was quoted as saying that he had not heard of it except through secondary sources. That puts Mims on the spot. I don't believe you will ever surpass yourself in letters of this nature, although the one you wrote the ladies' club at Clarksville will run it a close second. And I'm sure that the proper people at Vanderbilt will derive infinite pleasure from its publication. The opening sentence is masterful. If it is read widely enough, The Chancellor will be annihilated, for the invective is so pure and the effect so delayed. The bit about the hirelings has long wanted saying. It may remind members of the faculty of the days of their early youth when they went under name of men. Vanderbilt is now to have hanging about it the stable odors of impotence: The old Sultan titillating his eunuched successor and turning over the faculty of geldings for the trustees to spur and beat, but the saddest sight of all will be Don, foaming with fury at the door of the seraglio as Mims plays with the dry paps of the Muse.

I am last working. But I want to see you all.

Love and haste, Andrew

TLS

1. Tate's open letter to Chancellor Kirkland appeared in the Nashville *Tennessean* on May 26, 1937.

Saturday
May 29, 1937

Dear Andrew:

Yours of Thursday just here. We been looking for you for two days, and will look for you early next week.

Your presence will be urgently needed to complete the plans for the dinner to John on June 10th.[1] Red called me yesterday by long distance to offer the *Southern Review* as joint official sponsor of the dinner with the *Va. Quarterly* and the *Sewanee Review*. We now await what news Red gets from Knickerbocker (who will be glad to slap Vanderbilt) and my reply from Lambert Davis.

I've just this minute received a wire from Lyle saying that the result of my attack is likely to be a compensating offer to John from Vanderbilt. Even if John stays, the dinner is still in order—even more so, as a victory dinner to congratulate him on remaining in the South.

The horse metaphor combined with the pap metaphor at the end of your letter is your most masterly. Alas, for once, you're wrong and I was wrong about Don. As soon as Mims got my letter and [a] copy of one to the Chancellor, he went to Don, WHO READ HIM THE RIOT ACT, and told him that he would never recover from the disgrace of John's leaving; he also told Mims that he fully approved of the action that I had taken. When Mims whined that I should have come to him privately, Don replied that Mims ought to be grateful that I had forced the situation before John accepted the Ohio offer. In a letter yesterday Lyle remarked that both Mims and the Chancellor were delighted with the Kenyon offer as a way of easing John out, but that now they were on the spot.

The Chattanooga TIMES played it up for two days, writing both news stories and an editorial with barely concealed hostility to Kirkland.

I have forwarded all copies of correspondence and clippings from the TIMES to *Time* Magazine in New York, requesting them to hold it till Wednesday. I then wrote to Mims, telling him that I had done this, and saying that *Time* would expect Vanderbilt's decision by Wednesday.

Have you seen the Chancellor's weak reply to me? I enclose a copy. He consented to have it published along with mine in the Chat. TIMES, and Julian Harris, at my request, commented: "This letter is printed not only with Chancellor Kirkland's consent, but by the express desire of Mr. Tate." The whole issue is so foreign to the Chancellor's mentality that he could not cope with it, and in his habitual arrogance wrote the first thing that came into his head—which gave his entire case away. (If you can find the TIMES for Wednesday and Thursday, you'll see the whole story. Jimmy Stalhman[2] ignored it, but Jack Nye[3] told Don that my letter had given him one of the greatest pleasures of his life. So we're not without support even in unexpected quarters.)

Please come at the earliest possible moment. John is due back home today. I fear John will not be pleased, and as I wrote him I am ready to face the consequences of his possible displeasure. If this fight had not been made, the cause of literature in the South would have suffered for a generation. Even if John goes to [Gambier,] Ohio, this phase of the fight is won; because hereafter people like John will not be permitted lightly to go to places like Ohio. John had to be sacrificed to that end. But I imagine if he stays at Vanderbilt he will stay under terms so favorable that he will be completely independent.

We need you badly to help with the letters about the dinner and other things connected with it. On the way here I hope you will talk to John and bring me news of his feelings. I naturally have doubts, but I hope in spite of my high-handed methods to retain one of my dearest friends.

Love to you all, Allen

TLS

1. Ransom has accepted the offer from Kenyon and Tate is giving a farewell dinner in his honor. 2. Publisher of the Nashville *Banner*. 3. An important cartoonist, editorial writer, and managing editor of the *Tennessean*.

Monteagle, Tenn.
July 11, 1937

Dear Allen:—

I've had a small piece of bad luck. Trying to pull a bulldog off the Duke, I got a right bad bite to the hand. The doctor keeps me here to dress it; so I'm afraid it won't be well enough for me to leave before you all get off. And I wanted to see you before you took out for the West.[1] There is, by the way, some agitation for a writers' school up here, which, of course, would allow us to dictate the terms. I haven't given into it thoroughly, but will—and if it shows any promise, we might try it out—or at least examine the possibilities.

I'm sorry that you are still troubled by romanticism. I had hoped that the realistic surroundings would temper the degree of the idee fixe: Tell Ford I'll return his book *Trade Routes,*[2] later on in the summer. I read it with a great deal of pleasure. The case is awfully well put, and I cannot help but agree with his thesis. How he has managed to make his central idea so clear by the complicated transitions is a marvel.

When you all return, it is likely to be mighty hot. Why don't you break the trip back to Benfolly by stopping over here. Tell Nancy there are some very handsome and spirited young gallants her age who are waiting to serve her. I heard them playing cop and robbers on the mall last night, and the pool is always open. Polly thought of writing and suggesting that she stay here while you were gone, but Mama is so feeble and May still recovering that we thought they might feel too strong a responsibility and worry needlessly. So we didn't mention it. I went to Cornsilk to see Dad. He has had prostatic trouble. His water was cut off the 4th of July and he couldn't get a doctor. The only one in town was operating, and Dad paced the floor, an old woman got very solicitous she said through her snuff stick—"Tell em they better do something for that man. He's a-hurting bad." I found him with a shirt on and a rubber tube doubled up and hanging and bouncing between his legs as he paced the floor, giving directions about tomatoes.

Well, I wish I could see you all, but I'll have to wait until later. I hope you've got back to work and Caroline doesn't feel impelled to hurry her novel[3] because of the money of hers which Perkins owes. I'm rereading Calhoun for Red's article.[4] His later letters are very fine. The man's insight and power of prediction from generalizations are uncanny, his conception of the social alternative so clear and complete.

Take care of yourselves. Write me your Michigan address.

With love to all of you, Andrew

AL

1. The Tates and the Fords are going to conduct a writers' workshop at Olivet College in Michigan. 2. *Great Trade Routes,* London: Allen and Unwin, 1937. 3. Gordon's second novel to be published in 1937, *The Garden of Adonis,* came out in October. 4. "John C. Calhoun," *The Southern Review,* 3 (Winter 1938), 510–30. This essay is a review of Arthur Styron's *The Cast Iron Man: John C. Calhoun and American Democracy.*

Olivet
July 28, 1937 (Wednesday)

Dear Andrew:

We leave here Saturday for Washington to stay there a week and will get back to Benfolly about a week from Monday. Katherine Anne is making the trip with us! At the last minute there was a vacancy on the staff here, and it happened that K.A. was coming through Chicago; so we plucked her off the train. (She can't go back to N.Y. because Gene refuses to recognize the separation and camps in the apartment like a spider awaiting her return.)

Miss Carrie is getting her last chapter off to Perkins today. How she's done it in this confusion I don't know.[1] Ford remains difficult. . . . We spent the night with the Owsleys at Urbana. . . .

We'll notify you exactly when we will be back. Better meet us in Nashville.

I'm sending along a little change that might come in handy.

We're about exhausted, but ought to recover on the road.

Love to all the ladies from us all.

Love, Allen

AL

1. *The Garden of Adonis.*

Benfolly
Friday
[Sept. 10, 1937]

Dear Andrew:

Your letter was waiting for us when we got back from Memphis yesterday. We didn't go till Sunday, and stayed longer than we expected. I reckon your father is better now, or we would have heard from you again. The glucose injection sounded a little alarming, but I suppose it wasn't since it came so long after the operation. We were very much surprised by your account of your father's attitude. No one would have thought that he expected to die. Maybe as soon as he is out of the hospital he will recover his buoyancy.

Please let us know how things develop. Nancy has started to school or I would drive in today. Come up when you can. K.A. is getting restive and will probably leave us soon. She expects to go back to Houston for her nephew's wedding and then go to New Orleans, perhaps for the winter.

I'm getting back to work, and with New Orleans as a spur I'm going to finish up as quickly as I can. Just yesterday I had a new idea which will simplify the whole thing from now on—a very simple idea, and one that I could probably see immediately in somebody else, but it has taken six months for me to see it for myself.

Love to you all. Tell your father we expect to see him soon running up and down between the rows.

Allen
TLS

Murfreesboro, Tenn.
225 East Main St.
Oct. 14, 1937

Dear Allen:—

You got my telegram yesterday. That's the state we've been in here with a sick man and a wedding. Polly decided while we were in the hospital that she had better go on and marry early, so that she and Jimmy [Darwin] could get back and get their house started before the winter rains set in. In the midst of this Chambers came down for Stokes and Stockell birthday, and I had to take him to Chattanooga. He gave me a pep talk on getting started to work.[1] I didn't need it, but I've made arrangements to get down to it just as soon as the wedding is over. The arrangement is not quite what I had expected it to be, but with my limited means to consider I did I think pretty well. I decided to stay in Nashville for three good reasons, the library, swimming, and another of a private nature. It looks like I have to cut off myself pretty completely to work, as well as turn on the economic pressure. As long as I'm spending money, and a limited amount at that, the pressure will be sufficiently strong to get me started. The only pleasure I've promised myself is to run up to Benfolly on the weekends. I'm keeping the fact of my being in Nashville a secret.

Dad is coming along fine now. I take him to the farm the day after the wedding. His wound hasn't healed completely, but he gains strength daily; and I think as soon as he gets to the country and occupies his mind with crops, he will mend more rapidly. The wedding is eleven-thirty

Tuesday morning. Come Monday night if you can. If that don't suit, prepare to stay over Tuesday night if you can. Whichever suits working conditions. You might drop me a note.

With love from all of us, Andrew

1. Lytle is beginning work on *At the Moon's Inn*.

Nashville
October 25, 1937

Dear Andrew:

I have just returned from my father's funeral, and I decided not to let you all know until it was all over. He died last Saturday, the 21st, at Covington, Ky., after being struck by a taxicab two months before. He was apparently getting better, but his age prevented the absorption of blood-clots which attacked his heart and caused sudden death. He suffered none at all, and we are the more reconciled to his death because there was no hope of his ever walking again. He was seventy-one. After a brief service in Covington, Varnell escorted the body to Washington, where burial took place yesterday.

I am in Nashville for a day or two on business. We hope to get down to see you all early in November. Please plan to come back with us for a good visit. Is it convenient for you all to have us? Miss Carrie joins me in love to you and Mr. Bob.

Allen

AL

The Woman's College of
The University of North Carolina
Greensboro, N.C.
House Address: 112 Arden Place
February 9, 1938

Dear Andrew:

Well, here are the full professors, nicely settled in a large, comfortable, furnished house in a pleasant subdivision. We emerge every other day to give one hour of our time to the college. Prof. Carrie's class is at eleven; mine at two, which means that I have every morning to myself. The college is big enough to lose yourself in, making it hard for people to find you; and since the faculty is better paid than the one we belonged to in Memphis, the spirit is better. Old Dr. Smith, our boss, informed me that he didn't intend to boss, that he expected to see us socially only. There may be a few malcontents, but so far they haven't been troublesome.

Altogether, in view of the money, it seems to be a gift from heaven. The defects in the gift will appear later, of course.

Every afternoon I go to the well-equipped Health Club of the YMCA, and I already have a good violet-ray tan over muscles that are hardening after fifteen years of disuse. The Club has all the gadgets, and when you come over you can step right in.

We are leaving Saturday for New York, whence I will go on to Boston; we return the next Saturday. As soon after that as you can you ought to come over here. We can give you a room; more than that you can have the large, light, and warm attic to work in, should you not want to work in your bedroom. It is a two-story house with plenty of moving space in it.

I've worked every morning since we got into the house. This is going to be a good place to work. Ain't no bad company around here for you to mess with. Better come on.

We haven't got mixed up yet with any of the North Car'liny literati, but that will come, I fear. Paul Green[1] has "welcomed us to the State," and I reckon we've got to be welcomed soon or later; but on the whole we expect to be mysterious and snooty.

Give our love to all our friends. And write what you are doing. . . . I don't want to sound sententious, but just before we left I had a conversation that convinced me it might be good for you to be far away from Nashville for a while; what was said to me scared me a little.

Love from us all, Allen

TLS

1. The playwright.

March 19, 1938

Dear Andrew:

I've been working every day since the Eastern trip; hence the silence, except for some letters to Don about his book,[1] which is indeed fine. I work slowly but daily, and I expect to be done by June at the latest. The trouble is that the last part of the book will be very different from the first, as a result of the interval.[2]

We're going to New York again on April 1st to stay until the 9th or 10th. We've just decided that you need a change, not a jollification but diversion. You ought to take a bus to Greensboro towards the end of the month, and go on to N.Y. with us. We are too many to stay with the Radfords, but they can easily put you up. The whole trip would cost little. The expense account for C. and myself last time, including my trip to Boston, with ten days altogether, came to less than \$70.00; that included transportation. I am sure you could do yourself well on $40.00 at most. The only transportation cost would be a round-trip bus ticket Nashville-Greensboro, which is about $12.00. Say $50.00 for the whole thing. You could take in the Smithsonian in Washington. Dissipation would be bad for you, but a quiet trip, good. Last time we did no drinking, and we expect to do none this time.

You will have heard from Eleanor [Agar] by this time, but for us a trip to Louisville at present is out of the question. We had urged them to come over here and join us at Wrightsville Beach; when they couldn't do that we planned the N.Y. vacation.

I ought to say that, being such plutocrats now, we can easily lend you the price of the trip.

How are things going? We miss you all the time. Better come. You're on discipline now, but sometimes the results can be got by contagion. I need some of that too. Love from us all,

Allen

AL

1. *The Attack on Leviathan* (Chapel Hill: University of North Carolina Press, 1938). 2. *The Fathers.*

The Woman's College of
The University of North Carolina
Greensboro, N.C.
March 19, 1938

Dear Andrew:

There's some news from Baton Rouge that I don't know if you've heard. I forgot it this morning. It's staggering enough to justify an extry letter.

Katherine Anne and Albert Erskine[1] have announced their intention of getting married in April.

Let it sink in.

They already have the Little House in the country, and are setting out I think it is forty trees. A year from this summer we can go down and see forty dead trees around a deserted house. Albert will say nothing. K.A. will say that she couldn't possibly foresee that Albert would develop such sinister qualities. . . . I am convinced that even this isn't the last attempt. There will be others. And they get younger all the time.

We're going to count on you for the N.Y. trip.

Love from all, Allen

1. A twenty-seven year old English teacher at Louisiana State University who was also, at the time, managing editor of *The Southern Review*. Porter was forty-eight.

Nashville, Tenn.
2304 West End Ave.
Thursday
[Spring, 1938]

Dear Allen:—

I'm tempted all to pieces. I found your two letters here on my return from going over parts of De Soto's route. My eyes went bad from too steady reading and not enough sleep. On an hour's notice I left for Arkansas, Texas, and Louisiana. I met a man, an old gentleman who has studied De Soto for twenty-five years,[1] in close communion with Swanton of the Smithsonian; and he is going to let me pick his brains. He has a complete report of long years of study, done by the Smithsonian and himself, and I must go back within the week and spend the time with him in Little Rock copying and going over many things with him. He has old maps, original editions, and special translations of authorities, and he has stuff dug out of the India house in Spain. He tells me that Swanton managed also to get the list of names of people in the expedition before the revolution broke out. So you see, unless something comes up, I just won't be able to take an Easter vacation. There are only two copies of this report in existence, and he won't let it out of his possession, but he is willing to give full cooperation. As he says, he has no literary ambition, but he is willing to lend his time to see that the historical basis of the novel will be right.[2] I'm so afraid that something will happen to prevent this meeting, that I can't let anything stand in its way. And yet I shore would like to take a week off and pleasure myself with you all. I miss you considerable, and I've got to get up there and see you all before spring is out; but I'll have to time it just right. Spend a week in Greensboro and a week in Washington. Tell Caroline that I've found some Smithsonian reports that she must look into. I don't have them immediately at hand, but I'll check up and send or bring them along. It's bad that things can't be timed any better, that we can take off at the same time; but I have reached that stage where research and ideas are butting each other. This means that in a month or so I will have no personal life whatever until the book is done, or I am done. It's strange how we fight off the terrible exigency, plunge in and out of its cold pool then pull for very life.

I usually start the day reading [François] Villon, [W. B.] Yeats, or from the *Selected Poems.*[3] I never noticed before how very close the relationship exists between all of your poems. Of course I knew it, but I've noticed with fresh surprise how often the fundamental imagery recurs. There seem to be almost certain key words that draw each poem to its fellows. Of course, you've always said that you are writing only one poem; but it's wonderful the subtle variety that you get out of the same adjectives. Aside from the fundamental view and judgment of the meaning of experience which is common to each poem it is this use, it seems to me, of the same image and symbol which successfully makes each a part of the whole. It is a curious thing how contemporary Villon is, after once you get over difficulty of an older French, which I solved by rereading it aloud; and with Yeats the only time I feel that I am reading poetry of a fixed period is when he labors too much the particular symbols of his metaphysics, if you can so call it. There is a pleasant sound, but where the quality is lyrical, the lyricism fails because you slowly begin to feel a kind of religious undertone which, being private, cloys the sound that you first liked. I wonder if a poet's metaphysics, to make the poem have the right kind of ring, ought to be a metaphysics closely related to formal religion. This presupposes, of course, that the reader will have sufficient formal religious instruction himself to follow the poet's intention.

One more thing and then I'm done. Before I close and get to work, let us speak of Paris and Helen. I confess that I foresaw all when they sat up all night together at Benfolly. But must Troy fall again? Will the forty fruit trees be uprooted to make another horse? I wonder. It is fascinating to conjecture. I will hazard this theory which opposes yours. Here is a Paris without direction, but one who has the genius to admire both his Helen's charm and talents. To serve her and admire her will give him what he needs and her what she wants. And perhaps now Menelaus is wearied, being old indeed at the first rape. How many times, surely we know time's progress, how many times can the sound of war be bruited about the embattlements surrounding her ladyship's power? Not forever surely. But I grow sententious. And with this I leave it.

I miss you all right smart, Andrew

TLS

1. Colonel Fordye. 2. *At the Moon's Inn* (1941). 3. Tate's *Selected Poems* (1937).

Murfreesboro, Tenn.
225 E. Main Street
June 14, 1938

Dear Allen & Caroline:—

By the time this reaches you I'll be on my way to be married. I didn't expect to do this until I finished the book, but I decided a week ago that I didn't want to wait any longer. This is right hard for me to tell you all, because it will be the first time in our long friendship that we haven't seen things alike. It will grieve me not to have your sympathetic support, but there are three things a man has to do alone; and this is one of them.

Outside the family I haven't any closer attachment, of course as you know; and I can hear what you are thinking and will be saying together, but I love you anyway.

I'm going to Memphis and just marry, with the families there; drop out of the world for three months and start to writing. I'm going West for a while—then to Monteagle for the fall. My address will be here until I know the other.

I suppose Sam had to send on that vulgar gossip column. I suppose a man who has been subject to so much enforced charity all his life hasn't much left. Edna [Barker] had already written me about it and predicted his comment.

Love, Andrew

AL

WESTERN UNION

Athens Ala 20 555 P

Mr. and Mrs. Allen Tate
[Womans College University of North Carolina
Greensboro NCAR]

MARRIED AND ON OUR WAY WILL WRITE SOON OUR LOVE

Andrew and Edna[1]

1. Lytle married Edna Barker of Memphis on June 20, 1938.

10511 Almayo Avenue
July 1, 1938

Dear Allen:—

May brought your letters to Memphis, just before we stepped up to the altar rail. They were powerfully comforting, as I knew they would be. I suppose now on looking back, that the introduction at Southwestern was a fateful moment. I must confess that I felt not the slightest inkling of what it meant. I suppose the important events in life begin quietly, gathering strength so unobtrusively as they progress that the denouncement doesn't seem inevitable until it is spent. As a matter of fact, we had no thought of marrying any time soon. I never really thought I'd marry at all, nor did Edna. Then that spark as Dad would call it, set us on fire. I decided there was no sense in carrying on a distant courtship and a book at the same time. I thought we might as well begin with a greater risk than we would ever have again. After you know your mind, there's no point in hedging. A man should leap into the marriage bed, not go sniffing at the sheets. I first satisfied myself that Edna knew what she was getting into. She is eager to serve the Muse. My difficulty will be to prevent her from making her life too completely mine. I have never been so sure of myself, and the common burdens already seem lighter. After we had made up our minds; we delayed barely a week; and it was done.

If I had known positively that you all were coming through Tennessee, we would have waited; but I didn't expect you to leave N.C. until the book was done[1] and I know too well the uncertainty of closing chapters. Besides getting down to grappling with adelantado, there were other reasons for no delay. We wanted to take the vows before it was noised too much abroad. The newspapers had already been calling up to verify a rumor that we had been married at Monteagle. Marriage is certainly a time when it's nobody's business but your own and your immediate intimates. Not long before Memphis had outdone itself in vulgarity over the nuptials of some baron and a local product. There was every kind of spread and numberless pictures—even of undergarments. The poor man and his affianced were taken in every possible position but one, and imagination had been irresistibly drawn to supply that lack. An author wasn't much meat but I meant for it to be no meat at all. Edna managed the business well, even to leaving the poor photographer cooling his heels at the church door while we went out through the priest's entrance.

And here we are in California. George Haight played Brother Ben, staking me to the wedding and a house out here with all expenses paid. He had been trying to get me out to stand god-father to a little girl, and so that explains the distant West. We are going to Monteagle in the fall, but at this season of the year there are too many people to keep you from writing. Here there is no one. I've taken your advice about not going to work immediately, but it's a good thing to get out of the world for a while. You want to be alone and find each other out. I had to take the house for three months, and that's probably just as well, for it will allow me to get in a good spell of work. I wish we could have come to Connecticut, but since we can't, I thought it would be a good idea to drive to N. C. in the fall. We'll be back about the time school opens. Your book will be off your mind and Ireland[2] in it and Caroline won't as yet be deep into the Indian country with her traps and long rifle.[3] What is she going to do with Fossegrius von Isarthal[?]? When I last saw him, he didn't look much like turning into a bar dog. And she's not the woman to leave him at the swearing rock.

Be sure to have galleys sent out here. I wish I could read it before it goes off, but that, I suppose, is now impossible. Write as soon as you get good settled in Connecticut. Edna is writing as soon as she gets the kitchen and house in better order. With love to you both.

Andrew

AL

Do you have Red's Eyetalian address?

1. Tate finished *The Fathers* in West Cornwall, Connecticut, on July 21. 2. Tate's family originated from County Antrim, Ireland. 3. Caroline is preparing to do research on her next novel *Green Centuries* (1941).

Allen Tate's
Long-Awaited
Great American Novel
THE FATHERS
coming on September 23rd—$2.50

West Cornwall, Connecticut
July 10, 1938

Dear Brer Lytle: [Los Angeles, Cal.]

We got your letter yestiddy, and mighty glad we were to get it too. I reckon you did the right thing to go out to Hollywood, especially if Cousin Edna is devoted to the Muse, as I'm sure she is. Didn't her old professor teach her that the Muse was a good thing to be devoted to?

We got here Thursday night, and I started to work next day (this is Sunday). I've promised Balch the whole ms. by this coming Friday, and he shall have it even if a few details aren't what they ought to be. So it will soon be over. Balch is driving up here to see us this evening—he's only forty miles away at his country place. For the first time in five years I can see him with conscience.

Miss Carrie says the book is good, and Balch is enthusiastic. They're putting on the steam, advertising. I'm adorning this letter with a sample of it. I took it off a letter I got from Balch yestiddy. . . . By the way, I hope you all will be back in Tennessee by the 23rd Sept. Stokes and Stockell want to give a party for the book on that date (publication); if we were at Benfolly, I'd say no, but being in North Carolina we will have a pretext to come to Tennessee. Then you and Cousin Edna can come over to Greensboro with us for a visit.

This is a mighty good place for a vacation. A fine lake, tennis courts, and fishing. I ain't sure yet I'm going abroad. Bro. Ben says it depends on whether he can close the deal for a loan of $600,000 between now and

August 1st. Just a little change. If Nancy had stayed a day longer at Sister Louise's[1] house she would have been ruined for life. She shore takes to luxury. I felt like Miss Carrie's Cousin John Meriwether when he visited his Brother Hunter in Kansas City."That marble palace was so damn fine, it kept me awake all night." I couldn't sleep to do no good.

Red's Eyetalian address is care American Express Company, Genoa, Italia. Harriet Owsley[2] said Miss Emma's way was being paid by LSU for study abroad.

We got here exhausted, and Miss Carrie is plumb wore out. So am I but it don't make no difference; I could finish the book standing on my head, I've got going so. As a mater of fact I'm finishing it in an abolitionist house. The owner is a niece of Henry Ward Beecher. At my back is a bookshelf containing Olmstead and Miss Kemble's journal. At any other time it would give me a feelin' of snakes, but I don't have no feeling at all.

Our best love to you both.

Allen

TLS

1. Ben's wife. 2. Frank's wife.

West Los Angeles, Cal.
10511 Almayo Ave.
Tuesday
[Summer 1938]

Dear Bre'r Tate:—

I'm shore glad you done got done stumbling about your kinfolks' burying grounds. I feels lak hit a load off'n my mind, too, exceptin any load, however heavy, don't seem more'n a fly bite to these here Injuns and Spanids, the way they a-tromping me down. I named it to the child bride that looks lak she a widdy-woman fore she's been married good. I reckin that's what I git for digging around in foreign folks graves, folks that's hard to git the smell of. Your own kin you can take liberties with, bring sort of up to date, lak what Mr. Eliot means when he tell a body about tradition, but these here Spanids a-stinking of blood and them Injuns a-scalping and yit doing no good.

It's mighty pore timing that we can't get our work done at the same time; so we can really celebrate and pleasure ourselves together. Come what may, me and the child bride will be in Nashville the 23rd of September, God willing, and I hope to have enough done to frolic just a little with you and Miss Carrie. She, in spite of her conscience, will feel real good at it, becaue I think she'd about give you out. I got a lot of pints

I want to take up with her that churn and foam in my head. I been able to go off and hide before, but them hiding days is over now, and I'm glad of it. It's a good solid feeling to be eating your own bread and heading your own house.

I hope Brother Ben makes his loan and you can have a pleasurable trip. Tell him to take you anyhow, because you don't need money. It somehow always turns up when you need it, and when the time of repayment comes up, if we ain't got it, they can't jail nobody no more. Tell Miss Nancy that that ar yeasty luxury will swell a body up. Hit's Babylon and Ninnyvah. She'll have much more fun in a good stout hewn-log house. Ever now and then when I gits tared, I think about Cold Water and the mill pond I'm going to have there and the dog-run with its streams of water running in the little park beneath it. But that's a temptation now, until I pile my rocks on them twenty-five thousand you seen.

I expect we'll have to clean up some things in Tennessee before we go to North Carolina. We'll have to follow you all up there, if Dad hasn't ruined my car by the time we get back. He will have had it for three whole months and there's no telling how many fields of cotton it will have bounced over and how many bolts shaken out and carburetors clogged with clay.

Our love to you all. Write along and let me know what you are doing. You got time now more than I have.

Andrew

TLS

West Cornwall, Connetycut
August 2, 1938

Dear Brer Lytle:

We was shore proud to git yourn of Chuesday. Hit don't make no difference which Chuesday hit was. I knowed you was up agin hit with them prehistoric Injuns and Spanids, but hit ain't no more'n none of us is used to, as Macijy's[1] mammy allowed when pappy give her the Chrismas gif. Just so hit don't keep the child bride from gittin' her arnin' done hit won't make no difference.

I ain't goin' to the ole country I reckon. Brer Ben ain't gittin' his eight hunnerd thousand dollars soon enough. I told him I didn't need all that fer the trip, but when I named it to him he says he didn't want to be chinchy. He wants us to go to Canady for a coupla weeks at the end of the month, and I ain't a'carin ef I do. I reckon we'll ketch us some feesh. Miss Carrie may go too, effen ole Miss Carrie at Merry Mont don't git no worse. She was took a week ago with a raht bad spell.

Old Marse Phelps[2] was here for a few days. He ain't so good. He ain't gittin' no work done, and he ain't young enough to be a playboy no longer. Now I'm a-tellin' you, Miss Una shore is a card. She's his old woman in case you forgot. She named it to Miss Carrie as how she hoped one of Marse's literary character friends would write him a Ode, or something, so'd she could jest sing sing hit to herself when she's a-warshin' the deeshes. Ain't no man can do nothin' effen his woman acts thataway. She tells him he's the greatest genius for a hunnerd yares, so's they ain't nothin' he can do. Eeffn he writes a piece of rhyme, hit's writin' down. Fellers like us got to be writin' up way above ourselfs all the time cause that the only way to git hit done. We got to prove we're somebody. Effen we done proved hit to ourselfs that we're somebody without doin' no work, ain't no use doin' the work. Tell Child Bride I'm gittin' ready to write a Ode to Brer Lytle so's she kin sing hit when *she's* warshin' the deeshes.

This was a good place to finish the book but now I ain't doin' nothin'. The presence of all these Yankees is bearin' down on me, and I ain't pleasurin' myself like I ought to. We'll be seein' you all in September. I ain't sendin' you galleys because bound copies ought to be ready next week. Hit was too late to git your ad-vice. Love from us all to you and Child Bride. I declar, she's a raht peart gal.

Yourn, Allen

TLS

1. A reference to Micajah Searcy, a character in Lytle's "Old Scratch." 2. Phelps Putnam.

The Woman's College
Greensboro
September 14, 1938

Dear Andrew: [Los Angeles, California]

We're just here and settled out on the edge of town. I'm thinking of going to Nashville next week, to be there by Friday morning, the 23rd, but I ain't sure I'm going unless you and Child Bride will be there.

Please let me know right away. I will have to leave here next Thursday at noon to make it.

I assumed that you would have received *The Fathers* two weeks ago, when I inscribed copies in the Putnam office; but now I learn that the personal copies are being withheld till three days before publication. Your copy is being sent to Murfreesboro. The book is full of errors owing to the rush of getting it through. There's one very bad misstatement of dates on page 117.

Love to you both,

In haste, Allen

TLS

Andrew, did Polly ever get her andirons? Please get yours & Edna's from Puryear[1] when you're in Nashville.

C.[aroline]

A P.S.

1. Edwin Mims' son. His wife was also Clara Puryear Mims, Puryear being her maiden name.

West Los Angeles, Cal.
10511 Almayo Ave
Saturday the 17th of September
[1938]

Dear Allen:—

I was just about to write you at Stokes and Stockell, because I haven't known where to find you for the past three weeks, thinking you were somewhere in Canada. I've been so busy with a recalcitrant Muse that I delayed too long in writing you. We planned especially to be back for the party, and will get in Nashville that Friday morning at seven thirty-five from St. Louis. You know a man working and with a fresh woman on his hands don't have much time for correspondence. But I tell you, true love turns water into wine. I'm like a new man, maybe not new but sort of like a ship that's been going along on a few flopping pieces of canvas and then feels topsails and mizzen go out.

Be sure and get there. Isn't Caroline coming? Or is the school open and you both can't get off? of course, I'm anxious to see the book but more anxious to see you. I somehow feel now that you've got it off your chest that you'll have a fresh welling up of poetry. Neither one of us has done the work we ought to have done in the last few years. There's no need to tell me about this misery of fitting words together. Marriage nor nothing else will ever free me from it. I'm so slow and my mind works so bad that it shakes my confidence in myself. I feel now and have felt for several years that I've got another periodic burst of creative energy, but when I get down to it, what I do doesn't seem to justify the expectations I had of myself. The world ain't nothing but Caroline's morning favor,[1] but it looks like it's hard to leave it alone. We are going to Monteagle and will spend the fall and probably the winter there, and I'm hoping to stay right there until I finish De Soto, except for one take out to come to North Carolina and see you all. But before we do that I want to have something substantial done.

I've got to stop and do a lot of things about getting off. This trip back is longer than coming out. I made the mistake of taking the northern route. It's about a day longer and one or two changes. The andirons were delivered, I think, to Murfreesboro. We are mighty proud to have them and they'll set in the cabin at Coldwater where we can always look at them when you aren't there. Jimmy has had a bad return to his amoeba. He is medicine fast but is now better. That's probably why you haven't heard from Polly.[2] He's taking a lot of cream etc. Don't say anything about it, because he's sensitive on the subject.

With love to you all from us, and it'll be a fine homecoming to see you both.

Andrew

TLS

1. Lytle is making an oblique reference to Gordon's short story, "A Morning Favor," *The Southern Review,* 1 (Autumn 1935), 271–80. 2. Lytle's younger sister and her husband, James Darwin.

Monteagle, Tenn.
The Log Cabin
Oct. 7, 1938

Dear Allen:—

We are settling down here, and the accumulated dust and cobwebs are gradually clearing away. I suppose it was an inherited optimism, but I had no idea we would be so long getting to the mountain. The cabin[1] was dirty and disordered and I seem to have fathered many assignations during the idle season. Edna [was] taken down with the red throat the day after you all left, and then she had to go to Memphis and get her stuff together. I borrowed a truck and brought her and it up here two days ago, and here I mean to stay, barring one or two sallies into the world, until the Adelantado is buried beneath the waters of the Mississippi.

I finished *The Fathers* a week ago. I was so moved I wanted to write you at once, but it was late at night and [I] postponed the letter, for which I'm sorry because the things I wanted to say have lost their first edge. The book is really magnificent. "The Abyss"[2] is almost overpowering and part of its power comes from surprise. The slow pace of the first two sections, especially "The Crisis," in no way prepares you for the terrific shock, rather than the series of shocks, of "The Abyss." When I was reading "The Crisis," I thought you had missed your timing. The pace was that of a longer book. I didn't see how it was possible, without undue haste, to bring your story to the catastrophe I knew was necessary, although I didn't know its exact nature. "The Crisis" worried me as I went along. It seemed to add building detail but really nothing that you didn't put into the Pleasant Hill part. I took all this back after I had finished. In fact, without "The Crisis" the book would be unbearable. The greatest display of skill comes after the scene on the river. That is really the end of the family's story. Of course I knew why you had to go on, but I don't see yet how you managed to raise again the suspense. Pity follows terror, and it proves to be stronger. I always thought before that either pity or terror produced the katharsis. Now it seems obvious which is the true order. The Jason-Medea part comes off, I think. There is a roughness when the boy calls up his ancestor. The transition is too brief. Something is needed to focus the reader's attention here. I had to go back and pick up the verb. I believe it's because you don't realize that Lacy is in a condition to see visions. You know the strain, but the Lacy telling the story forgets in the logic of his narrative to make the reader aware of the boy's physical condition. I was not satisfied until he dropped in the yard and lay unconscious six weeks. But the few pages in there are some of the most beautiful prose I've ever read. The book has to perfection the double level meaning and ought to sell well. There's a good story but every moment the feeling of fatality which never fails is with you, and you sense that there is a meaning of terrible importance which we may never know nor dare to know. I think even the casual reader will find this undertone enhancing the story of character and circumstance. May and Mama have almost finished it. They sit up nights reading, and we got a note from Mrs. Jervey praising it in her way. I think this makes the point. I wanted to say more, but the sun's drappin' and I've got to bring things in for the night. The Nashville visit was mighty harried, and I'm getting so I can't git no pleasure out of roving around so much. Now that our agrarian society is broken up and there's no real society no more it's hard for a body to think of how to live. We are going to Coldwater[3] as soon as it's possible and there retire from the world by limiting it greatly, working and studying and doing a little farming. Beyond seeing you all and a few other people I don't keer much whether I see any other face.

This here marrying don't answer no problems, but hit's shore fine. I got a woman is a cracker-jack. I'm sorry she wasn't born sooner or me later.

Love from us both and write when you kin, Andrew

TLS

The Hessians keep guard in the front hall, and the fire comes through their armpits, and I think of you whenever we look in the fire. I don't believe nobody could send or receive a better and more fitten present.

1. Lytle's father bought this cabin on the grounds of the Monteagle Sunday School Assembly in 1907. 2. Tate's novel is divided into three parts: "Pleasant Hill," "The Crisis," and "The Abyss." 3. A family lot with a spring so cold that, according to Lytle, it would crack an egg dropped in it. Lytle sold the place during the depression.

The Woman's College
Greensboro, N.C.
October 10, 1938

Dear Andrew:

I'm mighty proud to get your letter and appreciate it the more for the difficult circumstances of its writing. It's hard to move into a place like the Log Cabin after it has been uninhabited. But once you're settled I believe you all will really enjoy it.

I've been meaning to write to you but kept putting it off till my arm got better; it's a little better the past two days. As soon as we got back from Nashville, I developed five vicious abscesses in the pit of my left arm, and I've been simply knocked out. The fifth was lanced yesterday. There's a new little one, but the doctor says it may be absorbed. If I hadn't been in pretty good shape, I reckon I'd have been pretty sick.

I'm delighted that you like the novel. I felt too that the transition to the vision of the Grandfather was a little abrupt, and if I had had more time I might have smoothed it out. But I felt too that it had to be sudden or not at all. There was the dilemma. Our lives are a constant regret that we can't do things better. I wonder we don't all go crazy. I felt that the scene of the killings—Yellow Jim and Semmes—was too brief, in actual reading time; but then it had to be all action, and I decided that anything else added would be padding. I learned a good deal in writing the book, and though it is pleasant I am not beguiled by Stark's remark that it reads like the tenth instead of the first novel. I am sure that I can do better, and I think maybe I will.

We were just saying that you ought to send us some of De Soto to read as soon as you can. I have a feeling that seldom misguides me that you are going to do a magnificent job, and do it in a way that will surprise us all. Aren't there any parts ready to be looked at?

My arm is aching; so I must stop with compliments to Edna. She can't know how fond of her we are already, and how much we both admired her natural behavior and good sense. You've got a fine girl, and I believe it's going to be one of the best marriages ever made. Our love to you both,

Allen

TLS

The Woman's College
Greensboro, North Carolina
November 3, 1938

Dear Andrew:

Caroline has to go over to the Watauga country, so we're going next week, and being so near Nashville, we shall run over there for Saturday to get BiBi back from Dr. Sanborn[1] and to see the football game. I ain't trying to tempt you away from your work, but I just wanted to let you all know that we'd be there in case you were going to be off the mountain anyhow. We'll be in Nashville just over Saturday, starting back Sunday morning. We're going to stay with James Waller. As you know, Caroline don't like football; so I'll have an extra ticket for either you or Edna. I just say this in case you all might possibly be there.

I hope you got the Injuns and Spanids roped and hogtied. I ain't doing no good at all; seems like I can't get my mind on nothin. Of course, I'm just now getting well of my infections, the last of eight abscesses being just about gone. But that ain't any real excuse. I hadn't done a real piece of long work in a good many years, and I'd forgotten the empty feelings afterwards. Miss Carrie has a real start on hers, and seems to be going ahead rapidly the last few days.[2]

Balch wrote me the other day that *The Fathers* has sold 11,000; so I reckon I'll have a little cash in the spring for the first time. I'm trying not to think of ways to spend it.

We send our love to you both, and we do hope you've just finished a chapter.

ALLEN

TLS

1. Herbert Sanborn, Chairman of the philosophy department at Vanderbilt. He loved dogs and had bred one of the Tates'. 2. *Green Centuries.*

The Woman's College
Greensboro, N. C.
November 26, 1938

Dear Andrew:

We were mighty glad to get Edna's letter, and of course *we* want to be there for a Christmas party. James [Waller] writes that his Aunt Louise will let us have the house. But before we go ahead with the arrangements we want to be absolutely certain that the party won't interfere with your work. There's no party in the world that will justify breaking into a good stretch of writing, and you are the only judge of this. If we don't have the party, we thought we might come by for a day or two, then go up to Merimont, and perhaps down to Memphis to see Mrs. Winslow.[1] Just our visit would take your mind off the work somewhat, and the party more so. But you decide. If you could send us a wire about it, that would help. Miss Louise wants to know what to expect.

Love from us both, Allen

TLS

P.S. The price Miss Louise asks for the summer is $150.00. That seemed reasonable to us. Is it?

Don't wire; write by return mail.

1. With whom Tate had collaborated on a dramatization of *The Turn of the Screw*.

The Woman's College
Greensboro
December 9, 1938

Dear Andrew:

We've been talking over the Christmas plans again and we've decided that maybe the houseparty is too complicated, unless you all have gone ahead and committed yourselves to it. How about this as a plan? We will come on to Monteagle around the 19th or 20th, and then if you all want we will all go to Memphis, we to visit Mrs. Winslow and Edna her family (again if she wants to) for a couple of days. Then since the Agars want us all to come up there, we can proceed to Louisville, and thence to Brother Ben's. Or we can change the order of these visits. We should have to go to Louisville a few days before the 28th because on that day the Agars leave for New York. I am writing them now to find out if they can still have us.

Miss Carrie says that the thing about this plan that recommends itself highly is the fact that she and Edna would be sitting around while the colored folks do the work.

Let us know what you all think. I don't mean that we should have to make all those visits. We could pick and choose, or not go anywhere if the spirit didn't move us.

Love to you both, Allen

TLS

Monteagle, Tenn.
March 21, 1939

Dear Allen:—

Caroline writes that you have staved off what might have been the flu by going to bed. I take it this is the last desperate effort to put off work. If it is any comfort to you all, my pain has settled down to a steady ache, like some deep abscess which it would be fatal to uncorrupt. I've just learned that I've got to do over this month's work to give it tension. The sense of loss would be more acute but for the feeling that I'm moving all the time in one of those caves whose mouth opens into an underground sea with tides and whirlpools separate from the known cards of navigation. In Peter Martyr I came across an account of such a cave by a mariner who followed Columbus. I'm sure there is nothing like this off the coast of South America, but the description of it managed to give me the feeling of the sinister peril of the new found lands, producing genuine horror because of the felt necessity that the Christian sensibility must shed its old skin before the terror of a new horror which the old was incapable of feeling. Maybe in Savannah or after it[1] we can get some relief from the common pain and put the slow winter behind. I move along in spurts, hope for steady stretches, but my reading is such that I can't take it all at once. While I digest one segment, the other churns. Nor can I find the books I really need. In between I get what writing I do done. I'm finding it hard to limit the Peruvian venture. It is introduction, but it struggles for a main share of the story.[2] I'm trying now to find a balance between something too discursive and something too brief.

Axley[3] writes about holding a round table discussion on the writing of biography, another on the article or essay. I might have something to say about biography, but I haven't written enough articles to be competent. Anyway, it seems to me articles are written for bread and meat, and I don't see how you can generalize anyway. I don't believe I'd have accepted the invitation at this time if I had known all it would entail. I can't take out time to prepare anything and only hope that leading a discussion means getting it started. What did you all do at Greensboro? Well, we may be able to pleasure ourselves anyway. I'd like to go up those waterways a piece and see if Lee's works are still in existence. Perhaps they are too far back to find.

The manager has been away and so we've just got the keys. Edna will go over today and find out what the cottage needs. James [Waller] says his aunt doesn't want to spend any money on the cottage; he'll have it attended to. It won't be long now, and we ought to pleasure ourselves together and establish a good working routine. By then maybe you'll be at it and we can all stand together against the summer distractions. The winter's gone by right fast. We've only left twice to go to Murfreesboro and Alabama. There's no news from Nashville, except that Don's textbook promises to sell exceptionally well.[4] Beatty says already he has a new spurt of energy and good feeling. The old melancholy is [dispersed?]. This seems to bear out your analysis of his hunger for power. The Beattys,[5] Lon [Cheney], and James [Waller] came up this last weekend, Floy says she proposed to Richmond that they give up dieting and spread out into middle years. She asked me with faint envy if I could eat all I wanted, and I said, "Yes. Nothing put it on or took it off." And I with four dollars and fifty-two cents in the bank returned more than faint envy at their talk of a lot of money coming in this year and ways of avoiding income tax. Lon let one of Houghton Mifflin's agents have his mss. Maybe this will put him in line for that scholarship.

The readings at the Jerveys[6] barely keep going. Abbott [Martin][7] still comes over, the last time with three well-bred ones, and I was much the worse for their whisky next day. Edna had to get up and make the fires and prepare for the Nashville contingent. We've got a cook that Dad brought up, Lizie's sister. So far she seems contented. Through Abbo as social agent we tried to launch her in Sewanee. There was some success, but I don't think Willy Mack, Abbo's pick of the Sewanee bucks was quite virile enough for Jesse. She probably remembered her place in George's [Timmons] harem. You know the one. He used to cook at Cornsilk. She makes fine bread, though, and that is worth many sacrifices for summer and society will be here soon.

Chambers seems a little bitter that I didn't give him Lon's name, but I thought Caroline might want Scribners first to see it; and it is just as well, for if H. M. doesn't take the book, he will now be more anxious to read it sympathetically. I don't know really what he thinks of my start, in spite of his glowing words. One of his readers thought of the New England poet [E. A.] Robinson. I surmise that such produced doubts in their minds of its saleable qualities.

The way Miss Carrie of Merrymont is making her end is heartening. And awe-inspiring, when you think of that will which has made a compromise neither with man or God. It's a sorry thing to consider that the world we know lacks any mold for making such as she now. I don't believe people are going to toughen with age any more. There's going to be a rapid crystallization which will crack and break into such curious pieces that the junk-heap of social security will seem the right keeper of the old and prematurely weary. And if the old can't have either the dignity of good or evil, what's going to happen to the rest of us?

John Wade reports you will stop over there the fourth. We were going by and will try to make it then, too; but unfortunately, before I knew how much time it was going to take, I accepted Dyer's[8] invitation to spend two or three days with him before the conference. We may have to do this, because I've written inept letters which show too little enthusiasm. If we can't change the dates, we'll see you Wednesday afternoon.

Well, take keer of yourselves until then.

With love from us both, Andrew

TLS

By the way, if you have Flaubert's biography, will you bring it along for me to borrow?

1. Lytle is referring to a Writers' Conference held at Savannah in April. 2. This section does not appear in *At the Moon's Inn* but was published independently as the novella "Alchemy" in *The Kenyon Review,* 4 (Autumn 1942), 273–327. 3. Not further identified. 4. *American Composition and Rhetoric (1938).* It went through several printings and at least three revisions. 5. Richmond C. Beatty and his wife Floy; Brainard and Frances Neel Cheney, a writer from Smyrna and his wife. 6. General Jervey taught mathematics at the University of the South. The E.Q.B. club met in the homes of the various members. 7. Also taught at Sewanee. 8. Gus Dyer, a teacher at Vanderbilt.

Greensboro
March 22, 1939

Dear Brer Lytle:

I'm proud to have a word with you, and prouder to get a word from you. I know what you're suffering, at least I can imagine it. I suppose I didn't suffer quite as much with *The Fathers;* if I had, it would be a better book. The Georgia excursion won't hurt you. The danger lies in the early stages. I plan to get down to it as soon as we arrive in Monteagle. That will be the charm. I did that way before. We went off on a trip, and the first day we were back on the mountain I wrote the first sentence of *The Fathers,* and went on from there. I've decided that I'd better write the next one in exactly the same way in all respects: that is, get a tone and point of view in the first sentence, have a final objective, and then let the point of view discover what lies between beginning and end.

Maybe I oughtn't to tell you, and I know you will keep it entirely to yourselves. If it got talked about it might not happen. Dean [Christian] Gauss of Princeton came by here Saturday, and virtually made me a proposition. The Carnegie Foundation has given him a lot of money for an experiment in the Creative Arts—music, painting, sculpture, and literature. All but the last are installed, each with its head. I gathered from his tone and things he said that I am his leading candidate for the literature, though his committee has two or three other names, and the result of their deliberations will not be known until after April 10th. Two things make it desirable, very desirable: the money, which though not named would be much more than here, Gauss let me understand; and the fact that Caroline wouldn't have to teach. Teaching is getting her down. It doesn't really bother me in small quantities. Other things favor it—a good school for Nancy, who will be no worse off with Yankee students since she already has here all Yankee teachers; the Yankee teachers at Princeton would be better Yankee teachers, not their cast-offs. Against going there is my great dislike of crossing the Line; but in Greensboro the satisfaction of being below the Line is largely symbolic, since to all intents it is a Yankee town. My colleagues here are getting on my nerves more than the Southwesterners did. So I don't know what we ought to do. Of course, I don't know whether the final proposition will be made. Miss Carrie, who is never too optimistic, got the impression from the interview that it is really all sewed up, and that Gauss is merely awaiting official authority. I don't know.

Another thing about it is that I've persuaded John Ransom to come here in the fall of 1940.[1] I say persuaded, but of course we are not that attractive; he will get the largest salary ever paid by this college, and because he needs big money he is coming. Yet if we go to Princeton I will feel that I am deserting him in the wilderness. Of course, John is never bothered by environments, and I don't feel as obligated as I should with somebody else. This news too is most secret. It will not be announced here until next fall, but it is all fixed.

If you all must visit Dyer, why not do it after the conference, and meet us in Atlanta on the morning of the fourth, or rather since you'll be driving, on the evening of the 3rd. We could drive down to John Wade's the next afternoon. In Atlanta I have to make a talk that Balch arranged at a book shop, but we can get away after lunch. On the fifth at noon we appear in Macon, thirty miles from John Wade's, and that afternoon drive on to Savannah. At Macon we are to speak at a breakfast given at the Macon Writers Club. (John Wade got us into it.) But we can be visiting and talking all the time. By meeting us you prolong our visit, without depriving Dyer of his. Tell Edna she must be for this plan.

Love to you both, Allen

TLS

P.S. If I were you I wouldn't worry one moment about sticking to Axley's assignment. The subjects we [were given] don't mean a thing. I expect to talk about the first thing that comes into my head, just as I did at the Seminar here.

1. Ransom did not go; he accepted a Carnegie Professorship of Poetry at Kenyon and remained there.

The Woman's College
Greensboro, N. C.
March 28, 1939

Dear Andrew:

Our plans are getting very definite now. We expect to get into Atlanta on Monday, the 3rd, at about seven o'clock, and go to the Atlanta-Biltmore hotel (Mr. Axley is paying the cost; he is paying yours likewise; ain't no use economizing, since expenses are about all we're likely to get.). Now you and Edna can plan to get there at the same time. John Wade says that he has urged you all to come; we can go to Marshallville the next afternoon.

A telegraph yesterday announced the death of old Miss Carrie. We can hardly believe it, and I doubt if she can either. Caroline isn't going to the funeral; she's just sending a check for the amount of her railroad fare, which will do them more good than her presence. Now the heirs will begin the war over the division of the place.

Love to you both, Allen

TLS

Monteagle, Tenn.
Saturday
[Spring 1939]

Dear Bre'r Tate:—

I've been meaning to write you ever since we got back. We collapsed for a week. I think it was the return to fires that got me; and then we had to go to Murfreesboro for the day as they expected us to come by on the way back—and so it has went. I was afraid when we didn't hear that the Princeton thing didn't come through, and I had pulled myself together to write when Caroline's letter arrived.[1] Well, five thousand ain't so bad, and two years may be the most perfect amount of time to spend there. You may find that so much school work will take energy which ought to be reserved for your own business. I think you ought to watch this. You know what you want to do and how long it takes for germination, but I'd like to see you get on that long poem sometime.[2] You probably will be able to save and take time out before the Carolina proposition takes form.

I've been demoralized and am having a terrible time getting back to work. I need books that are hard to get, and the Peruvian sections are going slowly. I know what I want to do, but somehow I can't find just the way to put it. I discovered at Sewanee some material that may help, but it's going to take a couple of weeks going over it. In the meantime there are the bird dogs. They are beautiful pups, and I've got them routined now so that I don't have to think about them so much. I'll be glad when you all get here. The hum of work will be supporting for all. Problems which take a long time to work out alone may be solved more quickly by discussion. It would be fine if we could work out the routine we had at Cornsilk, and this time we won't have such a sharp break between the workers and the players, so the players won't have such a hard time.

There's not much to write from here. I just wanted to pass the time of day before I bow down to the grind. I'll send you that five dollars and I owe you for a breakfast when the Savannah people mail what other moneys they intend to divide. Tell Caroline we'll plant their seed just as soon as it dries up a little. I have to haul the dirt, because it's so poor about the cabin.

Well, we had a good time together, even if they did push us hard. Take care of yourselves and drop notes now and then.

With love to both'm of you, Andrew

TLS

1. Tate became Writer in Residence in Princeton's Creative Arts Program. 2. "Seasons of the Soul."

Monteagle, Tenn.
Wednesday, May 31
[1939]

Dear Brother:

I've been writing you for two weeks, but I'd always postpone it until after the day's work and then I'd be dry. And there ain't nothing to write about anyway, except that we've had too much company. The [Lemist and Jane] Eslers (author of the *Grey Fox*)[1] came by and took six bottles of Bromo-Seltzer and us to the Derby. I picked up a bacillus and was in bed for a week after they left. Now I'm getting up at five and the work seems to go better.

Miss Louise is doing about the cottage considerably—so I imagine she'll have it in shape for you. Mrs. Waller, I hear, has been sick all spring with high blood pressure and that James has been a model son. Somehow that's a world going for an old war horse like that to be turned out to graze. I got a letter from Lon [Cheney], saying his book[2] had been taken by H. M. [Houghton-Mifflin] and that Red was going to be around Nashville for a month or six weeks this summer; that's about all the news from Nashville. Frank [Owsley] hated to see you all go above the line, but he doesn't realize that your presence in an Eastern school will have nothing to do with your set of ideas one way or the other. And it will bring pain to the right set of scalawags. I suppose Mims has disintegrated so that you can't enjoy a little malice in considering his reaction to the news. And I'm afraid I've noticed a little envy and the wrong kind of respect in quarters where you shouldn't expect it. I'm no longer shocked but it is discouraging that there are conceptions of characters which may still be shaken.

The Bovary book is swell. It was demoralizing for a week—if Bovary took five years the Enemy of Man seemed to say—and then Chambers writes he wants to come by and give me a pep talk or have me go there. I haven't the money to leave, but would prefer to see him in Indianapolis because I'm going to ask him for more money. I've just gotten hold of the proper bibliography and a book I'm now reading is going to make me do considerable rewriting in the Peruvian section. I made the mistake of trying to hurry with writing before I'd read enough. When I get through this book, I'm going to write one with the closest kind of a plot. I need the discipline back.

You all make haste and come on. We'll be looking for you the sixth. It's just as well you didn't try to come over before commencement. It has been raining all spring; the mornings are cold and clothes damp. It's only fair working weather.

Tell Miss Carrie I'll be glad when she sheds all them mss.

With love, Andrew

AL

1. A play about Machiavelli and the Sforzas. In a twelve-week run on Broadway in 1929, Lytle played the part of a clerk. 2. *Lightwood* (1939).

Monteagle, Tenn.
October 10, 1939

Dear Allen:

Elizabeth Buntin came up here about a week ago, on a Friday, saying that St. Blaize was going to be sold Monday. (She says that I got the name confused. That another place is called St. Blaize.) Well, I knew that you couldn't act that quick, and after a whole day's discussion, I got fifteen hundred dollars from George [Haight] to make the down payment and take over the insurance mortgage of five thousand. In the midst of the dealing I got down with a severe case of flu and Edna had to close the business part of it. Mrs. Buntin nearly ran her crazy in the process.

The movie people have all been cut thirty percent on account of the war, and George wasn't as flush with money as he might have been; and I didn't want to risk buying the Buntin place unless I paid Elizabeth the entire amount cash. This is the turn our plans have taken. It looked to me as if it was this or nothing. We really preferred the brick house, but as I began to think of the difficulty of paying for it, I realized that it might prove a trap and undo what it was supposed to do. The other place will pay for itself.

But lying between what was to have been your place and the brick house is a hundred and fifty acres with an old log house, weatherboarded. It sits on a rise with trees around it and has a cave with a good spring flowing out of it. This can be bought, and I think for about twenty-five hundred dollars. I haven't seen it, but this is the report from one of the Buntin boys who went up to look at it. There is also a fifty acre plot belonging to a Jew in Indianapolis. I understand he will take five hundred dollars for it. Now if this house suits you all and we can buy it, it will make our places join and ought to work out better than the other plan. If you want more land, I'm sure that more can be got reasonably; and if you sell Benfolly for a good price, you will have money to fix it up to suit you; fence it and put cattle on to bring it up, for I'm told the spring is strong enough and has a good flow for such a business. The road from this farm runs straight to ours, and it's the kind of road we can visit on horseback. In fact all the roads about there are good horseback roads. If this doesn't suit, and you don't want to do much farming, there is always the brick house. You can never tell exactly what Elizabeth will do, but I think she will be glad to part with the brick house, if you all prefer that.

I don't know how set you all are in the place we bought, but it seemed to me that I had to act, or it would all go by the board. But I know we can work out something. We plan to move around the first of the year, as soon as we can fix the house up a little and get water and lights. The T.V.A. will give us all lights for one down payment, at the most demand that we use five dollars a month worth of current for the first year.

When we get up there, we will scout around and we will take pictures of the adjoining place to give you some idea of what it looks like and describe the interior. It may not have any possibilities, but if necessary you could add on to the logs and take off the weatherboarding.

The sound of the house in Princeton and the surroundings, with easy country walks nearby and a garden and fruit, sounds fine. We may possibly dash up before we go to the country, see you all and talk, for by that time we ought to have more information about the country. I have already traded with tenants and ordered fourteen acres put in wheat for bread, but I am not going to do much farming this year, certainly not until the book is done. May has made an appeal to come to Murfreesboro and help out with Mama,[1] who is failing; and so we will go there for a month or two. I don't want to leave here so soon, but what we save can go into fixing up the house. Chambers came through with a hundred dollars without my asking for it. I wrote while in bed with the flu. Some way it must have touched a sentimental spot. He says the book business is better than it has been in a long time. I don't know whether this is special with him or general.

De Soto with flu and farm has suffered, but after this letter I get back to work and, God willing, no more interruptions. Edna is going to try to make the house livable without my assistance. George volunteered twenty-five dollars a week until the book is done. And another thousand later on to fix up the house and buy tools. Dad has given me a pair of mules. Well, well. There's something strange about all this. Here am I a penniless man writing a book who by June will owe $16,000 and have a deed to a farm.

We miss you all every day. This is the bird dogs' birthday, and they are to get a pound of meat apiece. Write us soon, but don't interfere with no work.

Andrew

TLS

1. Lytle's grandmother, Molly Nelson.

16 Linden Lane
Princeton, New Jersey
October 16, 1939

Dear Brother:

I've been getting round to a letter for a couple of weeks; so yours was just what I needed. I think you did just right in getting the so-called St. Blaize place before it was too late. After all, we had lived there only a few days. And I am sure that you can find us another one that will suit us just as well. The adjoining place of 150 acres, with the log house, sounds mighty good; with the Jew's 50 acres added, and it would be quite large enough for us.

As a matter of surprising fact, we have already had a nibble at Benfolly. The prospect is looking it over now. I've named it to him at $10,000; it didn't seem to frighten him; and he has replied that he will make me an offer in a few days. I might come down to $8,000. That ought to leave us enough to fix a good place up, after the purchase price was paid.

We are in the midst of a visit from Bro. Ben and Sis. Louise—which is quite strenuous. I've discussed selling Benfolly with Ben, and he's perfectly agreeable; I made the point that while Benfolly is mighty pretty, Nancy could never make a living there; and making a living is one of his favorite programs.

As to the work here, I have it all concentrated into two days; so I think there will be ample time for work. I just got it organized this week, and expect to get down to hard labor Monday, as the visitors leave.

In other respects, it is a fine place to work. We see nobody—everybody lets us alone. I am not bothered with any academic conferences or routine; I'm responsible only to Dean Gauss, who doesn't care what I do. The boys are all very smart and well-prepared, in that slick Eastern way that doesn't mean anything; my best boy is from West Virginia. I can see already that as far as the teaching goes it is going to be easy; the boys require no stimulation; they came here all primed for work.

What you and Edna ought to do is to come up before Christmas, and stay until it is time to go to the farm. Come as soon as you can. Caroline has already described the house; we have lots of room and good working places.

Don't worry about the $10,000 debt. The Lord will provide. He always has and there ain't no reason to think he'll quit if we help him a little. Have you filled out the Guggenheim blanks? I saw [Henry Allen] Moe,[1] and he seemed concerned that you hadn't got the blanks; he said he would send them immediately. . . . George's twenty-five a week is really better than a Guggenheim. Why not have both? It wouldn't be any too much. Love to you both,

Allen

TLS

1. An official of the Guggenheim Memorial Fund from 1925–1967.

Monteagle, Tenn.
October 31, 1939

Dear Brother:

Polly has a little boy. He came in but not a-bouncing last Friday after about twenty-four hours labor. Seven and three-quarters pounds, which seems a lot for such a little woman to carry. Named for the father. Polly took her pain with a good deal of courage. Staid on her feet for a long time, but when they got bad she took to bed and sent kin and husband out of the room, as she didn't want them to witness her humiliation. Dad was on hand early, several days early, with a new home-spun suit, hair cut and shave. He dropped all matters, business ones included, including two slow payments on a car which I was urged by the company to pay. Even borrowed money don't do you no good. This morning he wrote a card saying the milk let down all right, and that the baby, which was a lazy one from the dope given at the last, took two or three pulls at it. Polly had a radiant look about her next morning, and I think the arrival has given Jimmy a desire to do something about himself. He is better and looks better. I hope appearances are not deceptive. Edna stayed with Mama while I drove May down, hot water bags, pans, bedding, food for months. She only had one bad eye spell which the bags and hot water conquered. Kate [Savage] Zerfoss[1] told her it would be best not to go down. She bought two pair of new glasses and went in training for the event, but all went by the board.

I filled out the Guggenheim blanks and hope for the best. George may not be with his company in March, as the war has caused upheavals in California, cutting the industry's income by a third. I suppose he'll come out on top, because he's good at it, but I don't want to be such a drain. Not doing much on the farm. Planted fourteen acres of wheat with a tenant, which will give grazing for chickens and bread later on. We've decided not to do anything about fixing it over until we go down, and at this stage I put it as much as I can behind me. Never did I think I would be a dark-fired tobacco grower.

Have you had a satisfactory offer for Benfolly? If Jimmy does well, he and Polly will try to sell their place and get one near. We can get a real community if they do. The cold weather has set in here. It's brisk and fine, and we hate to leave. I think now we'll go about the first of December. Lon had a successful book party at Zibart's[2] and goes to Atlanta for another, where his friend [Ralph] McGill is talking the book up.

The set-up at Princeton sounds fine, house and working hours. We are going to come if we can. It all depends on the money. We may have to save to paint the house. Chambers is coming down here in ten days to see what I have done and speed me up. I'm doing pretty well. Putting the first section in final shape, cutting and rearranging. It reads much better and the banquet scene will be tighter. I'm leaving the Peruvian part until I can use it in the last half.

When you can, write. Every time you pass Brooks' store, look the other way.

Love to all of you from us, Andrew

TLS

1. A long-time member of the Monteagle community, married to Dr. Thomas Zerfoss, Sr. Dr. Zerfoss practiced in Nashville for many years. 2. A bookstore in Nashville.

16 Linden Lane
Princeton, N. J.
November 13, 1939

Dear Brother:

On the whole your news sounded fine—Polly safely through, Jimmy better, the book moving, and Edna (I judge) keeping a stiff upper lip. Miss May's collapse seems to be the only complication. We're just the same. I was doing well in getting my two essays organized, with some writing done on them, when this past week end dealt us a body blow. The Agars came, and at the same time my ex-sister-in-law, Bess, to see her boy. We were all scrambled up together, and nobody got a chance to take a bath but Eleanor [Agar], who bathed all the time. We were glad to see them, but observed after the first greeting that there wasn't much to talk about; as a result we talked all the time to drown out the silence. Bess has a neurotic impediment in her speech; so she comforted us by just listening. She's very pathetic; she thought up to five years ago she could buy everything; she still has the money, and is bewildered because it won't buy what she wants. Herbert [Agar] can't eat; he manages to get a little food down by priming his stomach with liquor—drank eleven Martinis before dinner, and consumed a shaker afterwards like wine. Old Mr. Robertson dropped dead day before yesterday; so Herbert now officially moves up to the head editorship of the [Louisville] *Courier-Journal.* He looks like a ghost, and is setting off on a strenuous lecture tour. His two children hung around him all through the visit; occasionally he would answer them from a great distance. The daughter, Agnes, is the most beautiful creature I have ever seen—tall and ethereal; the boy is a phonograph record which plays Herbert over and over again. They both worship him. We've met their mother, a hard and intelligent lady of the early fifties who looks sixty; a critical and drastic mind that would not be sympathetic to the Agrarian oratory.

Now about you all coming up here. All in the world it would cost you is the gas and oil, round trip, and that's very little. You could save on food on the trip by making a Warren journey—practically non-stop except at bathrooms. This is really a village, and there's nothing to tempt you out of your money. When you went into New York you would be the guests of the Agars, as we expect to be. What you will spend on gas and oil through December going back and forth between Murfreesboro and Huntsville would easily pay transportation up here. We could just put the car away. We use ours about twice a week. Besides you could get some work done—which you can't do looking out of the window at Niobe. Now you all come on. And the sooner the better. If you must be with the ladies for Christmas, come now, and go back by that time.

The other day I got a card from Red (still with the Eyetalians) saying he intended to stay on "because it is so interesting." Then a letter came describing the prodigious amount of work he is doing on a prodigious number of projects. He casually remarked that if he got a renewal of his Guggenheim, and LSU refused to extend his leave, he might resign and trust to luck for the future. What has come over him? Did Miss Emma see that remark? I doubt it. I think it would be very foolish of Red to start freelancing at this time. It is much rougher going than when I started in 1925. I have no idea he will really try it.

We had a nibble at Benfolly, as I wrote you. Mr. Posey wrote me, and I heard later that he had been out there several times to look it over; but he hasn't said anything further to me. I priced it at ten thousand. I could take less if the new place we get is cheap, and I could have enough money left over to do some fixing up. I named it to Brother Ben when he was here last time, and he's perfectly agreeable. I believe the best thing would be for us to wait till you all get settled, and get the feel of the neighborhood, and then you can pick us out a desirable place. We can get to work on the thing early next summer. Meanwhile I will be looking for a buyer for Benfolly.

Ain't no Brooks' store here, but there's some just as bad. I ain't bought nothing but a raincoat and a necktie.

We're mighty anxious to read the revised Part One. I have more time here for some reason than I had at Monteagle doing nothing. We're hoping that you all will come. I believe you will enjoy the visit, which we need worse than you all do. I feel like I was living in a motel, or on an ocean liner; nothing beyond physical vision has any existence. Love to you both,

Allen

TLS

Monteagle, Tenn.
Dec. 3, 1939

Dear Brother:

Them letters were so good I been trying to wait until I had something fitten to write. But the days here have been mighty worrisome, with a series of interruptions beginning with Chambers' visit. I finally made the statement aloud and to myself—the mistake was in speaking aloud—that I wouldn't stop any more except for death, contemplating my own. I had no more than got the words out of my mouth when a car ran over Dad's brother in Texas,[1] knocked him fifteen feet into the air, killing him instantly. My Nemesis chose the longest possible distance, a week's time. Dad was here on the Robertson business, for which I had to take somemore time out, but which I think was well spent as it winds the business up and gives us back certain properties—and so, after the first shock, he got into action. I was to fly to Texas, as his clothes were in Alabama, and he was afraid of getting among the clouds. I said, "He's your brother, and you've got to go." It ended up by telephoning to Guntersville and having the clothes meet us at Fayetteville, while we drove to Memphis to catch the night train. Fortunately, the dogs were in Alabama, running wild after birds.

Last night we got back to a cold house, and this morning I'm beginning with letters—the old routine. On the way we stopped over at the Cheneys, took in the lousy Alabama game and a pleasant party afterwards. Everybody asked after you all and several said they had had letters. Beatty spoke of the old guard hunting up their firelocks and saltpetre to try another Bull Run on New Jersey soil. I feel like telling them to hang up their rusty pieces before they blow up on them. Floy Beatty has built a new house and it's a nice little house. Edna went out and spent a morning with her. In language a city gal hadn't heard Floy bemoaned Dr. Sanborn's negligence, or rather indifference, as to the organic pleasure of her dogs and seemed a little envious of Bibi's constant popularity. Lon [Cheney] didn't sympathize, as one of them has bitten him twice. He says his book has sold twenty-five hundred copies, and he has plenty of ideas for others. He looks like a new man to me. Frank [Owsley] is fixing over his farm house, and I think they expect to spend a good deal of time out there. Harriet [Owsley] looks brighter and better. She's had some kind of crisis, which probably was eye-strain and overwork, for when she came by here, she looked gloomy and bad. That's all there is to report on Nashville. We didn't stop long.

I got a letter from Red, too. Everybody seems to have heard from him. I didn't write because I thought every day he was on the high seas home. You all wrote Cinina had been seen on the New York Quais. I wonder if he is home sick, if so many Eyetalians everywhere about set him to thinking of his own people. It might be a good thing for him to break from academic life, even though freelancing is more hazardous for his years and the times. He works fast. It might be his salvation, or he might spend the time once spent on proofreading and teaching in Bohemia or Eyetalia, I don't suppose any of us ever escape, lacking brutality or the bloodspurting energy of the Sixteenth-century, the draughts from your defeated caves. I remember Caroline saying once that you can't afford to waste a moment: all conspire to snatch away what time you reserve for your work. I was more ignorant then and didn't believe it. I suppose a man must act and live always companion to sudden death. But that takes a hero's discipline.

Well, well. Think of Nancy a slim young lady. She must be very beautiful. She writes to Dear Uncle Andrew and Cousin Edna which shows something of what the quality of her wit will be, for, says she, "in spite of how hard Daddy worked on her lessons this summer, she is not doing very well in Algebra." And she thought the pony rides were a little previous for birthday gifts. And I sympathize. Tell her, if we had known the pitiful thing she received was to have been the only gift and that she had also turned young lady, we would have done somewhat better. I know what a trouble it must have been for her to take time out from all her whirling to write. It wasn't necessary.

That was a fine description of the evening with the Agars. I can see Caroline getting more and more restless as Herbert lies stilled among his children. That must have been an evening. Her face must have had that peculiar look of desperation she has for a mangy dog by the side of the road. If he's shooting dope in his throat to lecture to women's clubs, he's done for. For an ambitious man he is pathetically misguided. He can't talk, at that slow rate, himself into the Presidency. It's a curious thing, but I wonder if he ever asks himself why he went to Louisville. The only reason for going there was to make himself strong locally. There are no candidates at large. Like all deck A, expensive Hotel-living cosmopolitans his daring, and I think it was daring for him, return to a local place had no more imagination than supporting the immediate policy of a newspaper. He should have remembered that Judge Bingham used what power he has to assist the tobacco farmers. I think this explains his stupid behavior with *Free America.*[2] I feel right sorry for him.

Well, I've about run out. Tell Caroline I'm going to take her advice about tobacco farming and tell her I'm proud and envious the way she works.

With love from us both, Andrew

TLS

1. Robert's younger brother, Foster Lytle. 2. Agar's short-lived magazine for which Tate served as an editor in 1939.

II

1940–1949

The letters of the forties deal with a different set of problems. Reflecting the uncertainty of the times, much of the exchange is given over to either Tate or Lytle indirectly taking up the question of where he should live and what he should do. And it is no surprise that the only year for which no correspondence has been found, 1946, falls in this sequence.

Although this section includes, among other things, an allusion to Tate's first, brief divorce from Caroline and his analysis of *A Name for Evil* (1947), its central concern is with first, Lytle's, and then, Tate's editorship of *The Sewanee Review.*

In a letter dated October 23, 1941, Lytle tells Tate that the imminent dismissal of William S. Knickerbocker is going to leave open the editorship of the *Review.* This and subsequent correspondence shows both Tate and Lytle agreeing that because of the suspension of *The Southern Review,* the time was right to transform *The Sewanee Review* into a quarterly of distinction; that such an aim required funds to pay contributors; and that Tate was the one man with influence enough to carry it off.

After about a six-months' break, Tate, concerned about the state of their friendship, reopens the correspondence. Although there are no letters on the point, it seems that Tate was passed over as editor when it became clear that he would demand funding, and Lytle was drafted for the job because, as one who was already on the faculty, he could hardly refuse. Only a few letters appear during Lytle's term as editor, and these deal mostly with material being published. Attention is next drawn to the *Review* when Tate reports to Lytle his plan to get funding from the Rockefeller Foundation. Successful in this attempt, he soon assumes editorship of the *Review* not only with money for contributors but also with a paid staff. It is during this period that Tate gives Lytle suggestions about "The Guide," a short story of Lytle's he publishes. But Tate's role as editor is cut short because of his and Caroline's marital problems. In October 1945, he resigns. Although neither man was editor of the quarterly for long, both made a decisive difference—Lytle began the practice of including fiction and Tate got it on its feet financially.

After leaving Henry Holt, Tate took on a series of positions including one at New York University and another at Chicago, but in this sequence of letters, the next return address is Princeton where Tate returns to the lecture circuit. Lytle, in the meantime, has written from the University of Iowa and the University of Florida where, when the section ends, he is teaching and preparing to build a house.

Murfreesboro, Tenn.
225 East Main St.
Saturday
[January 1940]

Dear Brother:

Well, you see where we are. Trapped this time by the weather. With water off and the near-zero weather it would be useless to go back just yet. I feel caught, like a fly in the mouth of a dog. Edna is enjoying the freedom from cooking and cleaning, but her pleasure don't do her no good. Fortunately, I am back at a spell of reading for the next section; so I don't consider it so bad, that is, so bad as it might be, being here.

Them purty, sinful gamblin' tools was sent down at last from the mountain. No more broke matches for rats to gnaw on. We shore are proud to git em. I know living up there with all them rich folks you ain't got no money to go spending on such handsome presents. I reckon you just got so accustomed to running with rich folks that you find money looks to you just like hit do to them.

I haven't made my transition from Spain yet, and it is worrying me to death. When I think of all those chapters Miss Carrie turns out, in spite of guests, young lady daughter, and dogs, I am filled with shame. But shame don't help me much. De Soto has turned into an old man of the sea, but maybe I'll git stout and lusty enough to shake him off. By the way, is it true that Herbert [Agar] has had a nervous break-down? I heard it from somewhere. From your reports it was inevitable. I hear that John Wade still talks of the letter Caroline wrote him after leaving Georgia. He said it [had] more typographical errors but was the best and wittiest letter he had ever come across.

Polly and Jimmy came up with the baby for several days, but refusing invitations to go out was so difficult that they left in a few days. They have asked for your address several times, and I have always forgotten to give it to them. I think maybe they want to send a picture of it. It is a cute little baby and looks very much like Dad, although it has Jimmy's stern Indian-nature. Never laughs but stares you down. We wired for Dad to come up Christmas and received his vaguest diplomatic message. "Weather bad. See you next week." We haven't discovered yet what the real reason was, for we haven't seen him.

We hope to get back to the mountain in a day or two. Write when you can. I'll do better when we get back to base.

Love from both, A-

TLS

16 Linden Lane
Princeton, New Jersey
January 28, 1940

Dear Brother:

It's so cold here in this house that the first thing I thought of this morning was this letter. It's just like the temperature at the Log Cabin. This house just won't get warm. This is Sunday; I've been back from the hospital since Thursday noon; feeling pretty good but sagging a little in the belly. The operation warn't nothing; if it hadn't been for the gas on my belly afterwards it wouldn't have been a bothersome as a bad cold. Though I'm still weak, I imagine at any rate that I feel generally better than I've felt in years. You can carry pizen around in you and accept it as normal until you get it out; then you know it warn't normal. The doctor said the appendix was mighty bad looking, like some he had taken out in the middle of the night. Brother Ben was there presiding over the ceremonies, symbolizing the junction of Science and Big Business. The worst part of it was at first, the gas they give you to knock you out before they apply the ether. They slipped up behind me and fastened a mask over my face before I knew it. Even after I was unconscious I kicked and busted a strap they had over me to hold me down. But I didn't talk any, and I didn't have no ether dream. I'm glad it's all over. Brother Ben's Christmas present cost him a little under three hundred dollars.

We kept thinking that you all should have come here instead of Murfreesboro. This is about the quietest place we've ever lived. You could have gone right on working. And Edna could have gone on being a lady, like she said. Are you all going to be at Monteagle next summer, or is Chambers going to let his share-cropper live on the farm? We're mighty anxious to know, so we can make our plans. It seems we can't have this house over the summer; the landlady wants it. (We can have it next winter again.) So since we've got to move somewhere we thought we might come down to Tennessee. Or if you all go to the farm, could we get a place to stay nearby?

It might be the last summer for some time we can come back. I've got to make a hard decision in the next ten days. I've been asked back here for next year with a nice raise from five to six thousand; but there's no commitment beyond next year, though it is quite likely I might be reappointed from year to year for some time. But I can't run the risk since I've been offered a job by [Archibald] MacLeish[1] at the Library of Congress, that would be as permanent as any job could be. I don't like the idea, but I can't help it. I don't like a library; I don't like the atmosphere of Washington; and I don't greatly like the idea of working for MacLeish, who is at least one-fourth fake. I wish to God I could get a suitable job in the South. We were just saying yesterday that if a place even like Sewanee would make me an offer, what a relief it would be. But I daresay I've more chance of being asked to come to Oxford or Cambridge than to Sewanee, or even to Austin Peay Normal at Clarksville. It's bad morally to be working at something with which you have no connection, so that your feeling for it is on the cash nexus basis. I don't mean that it isn't pleasant here. As a matter of fact, there is absolutely no trace of the employer-employee relation. If what writers are looking for is to be treated with consideration and honor, Princeton is the place: but some of us are not looking for that; at least we want something else first. This place has its defects—largely the same ones that Sewanee has, complacency and inertia—but on the whole it is far too good for the Yankees who have inherited it. They must have had something good a hundred and fifty years ago.

I've just been informed that when I leave I will be consulted as to my successor. If you want the place for a year or two I think it could be managed. The opening would come right after the publication of De

Soto,[2] the psychological moment. They realize it is hard to get just the man they want. The qualifications are as follows: a gentleman; poverty, so that he will be interested in the money; a sufficient literary reputation; young enough to communicate with the boys; an un-academic point of view; and negatively, the lack of a regular job. You have all the qualifications. Very few have. At present, they can think of only three men who meet the requirements, from all the United States: [Edmund] Wilson, [John Peale] Bishop, and [Richard P.] Blackmur. Wilson is the weakest candidate because his approach is historical and academic. Bishop's personality is too fancy. Blackmur is a little eccentric. There's something against all these men; so if you want the job, it will be evident to them that you have no disabilities. We must keep this quiet, so that I can spring it as a surprise.

This reminds me that Ole Brer Bishop is coming here tonight for a lecture and a visit. Then next week Brer John Ransom comes for a day or two en route to Yale where he is lecturing. Recently I had a letter from Red enclosing the final scenes of his poetic drama.[3] I just don't want to write him about it. He's evidently expecting great things of it. But it isn't good. There are fine passages in it, but it doesn't come off. Tinkum Brooks[4] writes us that she had a formal letter from Miss Emma, bearing the news that she had strained a ligament in her back. We couldn't at first see how she did it; she don't ever lift nothing. Then we saw it; they ain't but one way she could have done it.

Maybe I'll be able to get down to work now the pizen is out of my system. I hope DeSoto is going well. Edna's long letter was greatly appreciated; likewise Polly's Christmas card. But naturally Polly didn't say how Jimmy was. How is he?—I've got to get in bed, it's so cold. Our love to you both,

Allen

TLS

1. As Librarian of Congress, MacLeish wanted to establish a "Consultant in Poetry" position and have Tate fill it. When Tate chose not to fill the newly created post, it was left vacant until he eventually accepted it in September, 1943. 2. *At the Moon's Inn* (New York: Bobbs-Merrill, 1941). 3. *Proud Flesh,* later rewritten as the novel *All the King's Men.* 4. Cleanth Brooks' wife.

WESTERN UNION TELEGRAPH
Princeton, NJ
11:53 AM March 30, 1940

Andrew Lytle [Monteagle, Tennessee]

MR. MOE[1] IS SENDING YOU 2500 DOLLARS

Allen (name spelled "Allan" on telegram)

1. Of the Guggenheim Foundation.

16 Linden Lane
Princeton
May 9, 1940

Dear Brother:

Miss Carrie has just written you all, but before the print is dry I am offering an entirely new suggestion. As soon as we talked it over, it was obvious that it was the only simple and sensible thing to do.

You all come to Princeton, and we'll spend the summer here, with forays to the beach at Asbury and into New England for visits. This is the best plan possible for *work,* and that is what we must do. The Florida plan would guarantee us pleasure, without making the work certain. The northern clime would keep us invigorated, and we could have all the summer pleasures. You have no idea how pleasant Princeton is now the leaves are out. It is like Sewanee, with modern conveniences. And we were just saying that this house is the best we have ever seen for several people to work in at the same time. Three are working in it now. You would take Bill Brown's[1] place. We have an establishment already operating. Beatrice doesn't want to leave Princeton. Edna could pleasure herself, with no cares or labors. If we went to Florida we would have to pioneer a new household economy, get set in it, and the moment we were set the summer would be over. Here you all would just slide into the going concern.

Now don't let the beach dazzle your mind: we can get to a beach here in forty minutes. We can get to New York in one hour. We can get to Connecticut for small vacations in 2½ hours. This is the place to spend the summer. Princeton is virtually deserted through the summer, and the people we see will be people we want to see, not transients who drop in and waste time.

If you all come, it will make it possible for us to stay—which is what we really want to do, have wanted to do all along, but gave up the idea when it seemed you all had to go to the farm. Tell Cousin Edna not to let no Lytle romanticism take her off to Floridy where she would cook all summer; follow the Tate realism and let Beatrice do the cooking.

At this point I believe I have Edna won over already. We just have a letter from Mrs. Jervey saying Edna has been taking anti-tetanus shots.

This is the place to relax after that. And since we're going to be here, you all might as well come as soon as you can. No use waiting for June.

Love to you both, Allen

TLS

1. William Slater Brown was a novelist married to Sue Jenkins.

May 24, 1940

Dear Brother:

Well, it's settled at least. You all's coming here is the very best thing for us all, and besides we will have a fine time. If you rent the Log Cabin pretty soon, why wait till the end of June to come? Come any time after June 11th. That's Commencement, and in the weeks preceding it Bro. Ben & cohorts will be here; but after that nobody. The sooner we get into the summer routine the better.

I forgot to tell you about the lake here—three miles long—with canoes and sailboats available. That will improve the prospect for you. Sister Edna can paddle in the water all day long, while we work.

It looks like General Jervey is right, but I'm not yet sure. I think he's dead wrong about the Germans ever attacking this continent. I think Lindbergh is right. My feelings are divided between hatred of the British and love of the French, and on the other side I dislike the Germans. So I don't stand anywhere.

I am trying to start the novel,[1] but as usual I can't get the right tone; and I have so many interruptions. But quiet will reign in a couple of weeks.

Love to you both, Allen

AL

1. Tate attempted to write two other novels but finished neither of them. This one is possibly his projected sequel to *The Fathers*.

May 27, 1940

Dear Brother:

We may get off by the middle of the month. Edna is in correspondence now about the house. There is one thing that may possibly delay us until the end of June. George [Summerford] has cataracts and I took him to Kate Zerfoss to keep him out of the hands of a Birmingham quack who was going to take his money and endanger his sight. I don't think there is any real reason for me returning with him for the operation if I can make all the hospital arrangements beforehand. It will be a good idea to get settled in the summer routine as soon as possible. I'm afraid I've gone stale. The trip to Princeton will give me a break, and there I can get into the long pull. Right now I feel like a spent horse coming up to the rope.

This month has gone by with mighty little done. I can't keep away from the radio, and that gives me a late start in the morning. My feelings are mixed too. I long to see the English punished for their sins and stupidity, but did you notice that the Nazis forbade the Dutch from drinking beer. If the Germans hold London and the industrial region of the midlands in ransom for the English fleet, I believe the British would give it up. Where would that put us, even if in the intoxication of victory Hitler does not try to establish a military hegemony of the world. It's going to be like Rome, with all the loot of the world passing into Berlin, and you will find the loot will come very quickly and thoroughly. The English king, that poor stuttering symbol, will be brought out in some feast of victory to talk for the amusement of his captors. This may not be so far afield, except that I can't believe the French army won't meet the emergency, unless their thirst has undone them. Spending all that money on the Maginot line and then not extending it far enough.

I would take Lindbergh more seriously if I didn't think he wanted the Republican nomination. And there is an ugly and evil fatality hanging about the boy hero. I want none of him. The gravest thing about a German victory, as I see it, would be the political effects here in this country. Playing on the fears of the dispossessed, Brother Ben's buddies will virtually establish a political as well as financial tyranny at Washington. And there will be enough truth in the situation to maintain it. If it turns out that finance-capitalism has betrayed itself through its English peers, then some other group will do the same thing, for it may very well be that the power of this country will have to play an Alexandria to the German Rome. It always worried me how an agrarian society could be maintained in the face of the necessity for a mechanized army and navy. You can have a Republic when the smooth bore rifle is an effective weapon. But when you've got to have tanks and antiaircraft and machine guns, you will bring about the kind of organization to maintain such an army. Nationalism has played Judas to Christendom. It may hang itself but its credits won't buy any potter's field. And the imitation to hang to the Swastika will be an old and pot-bellied Christ, too weary to come again.

I'm going to stop thinking about this thing until events become more urgent. After all the damage was done in the 16th century, and I'd better try to return to that.

That lake sounds fine. It's better in many ways than the ocean. You can't really swim in the ocean.

Love to you all, Andrew

TLS

[Note added by Edna:]
Andrew is very worried and discouraged—the first time it's really been bad. It's just been so darn long—& slow; he can't write at that pace any more & he can't write to suit him if he does it faster.[1] It's like sitting down to the same dish at table for the hundredth time—he just has to learn. Why not write him if you think it's a good idea, you're anxious to see what he's done, how he's managed to dramatize something [so] broad so inclusive & so unending in exploitation possibilities, or whatever's appropriate. He's feeling, you see, it's too enormous for him.

P.S. He doesn't know I've added this—I'm going to write soon, Caroline.

Love to you both, Edna

1. Lytle does not publish another book-length narrative until *A Name for Evil* (1947), and Edna says he is worried here that he can't conclude *At the Moon's Inn,* which has been practically finished for several years.

May 30, 1940

Dear Brother:

Your letter doesn't sound any too cheerful, but as I see your situation (from a distance, of course), you are, first, stale, and second, teased away from your center by the war. What you need is this trip up here; and I think you need to have the ms. read by fresh eyes. You have stared at it so much that you can't see it; and Edna has probably told you that it is good, so often that you don't believe her. All this is to be expected. Turn off the radio if you're still working; but sink into it, if you're not; make it definite one way or the other. And come up as soon as you possibly can.

It all depends on the condition of the main French army, and on whether Italy stays out. This debacle, if it becomes general, is probably the way capitalism must collapse in terms of war.

The buying of the farm is still the best thing you ever did.

I go down to Washington to broadcast over CBS with Winkie[1] Barr on Sunday, at 3:30 E.S.T. The subject is Plutarch's Lives—sufficiently remote from the present world.

Stop worrying. You've been at Monteagle too long. Love to you both.

Allen

AL

1. Stringfellow. Along with Huntington Cairns who served as moderator, Mark Van Doren, and guests, Tate appeared as a panelist on the weekly CBS radio show "Invitation to Learning" from 1940 to August 1941, when he was dropped from the program.

Monteagle, Tenn.
October 2, 1940

Dear Brother:

We are at last about settled down to the mountain routine. We had to go to Murfreesboro and Nashville to see the ladies and arrange for disposal of eight mongrel pups. The pups had enough style from their mother so that we got rid of all of them in two days. We got down to business more quickly than I had expected. I've been writing well for three or four days and feel that I am reaching some kind of a stride. I saw [Alexander] Guerry[1] accidentally and had a short talk with him. We were interrupted and I am going over again later. Knickerbocker[2] happened to be passing at a distance, Guerry pointed him out and that allowed me to bring up his attack in the *Sewanee Review*. Guerry asked what issue and said he would read it. Afterwards I doubted whether he would understand the allusion.

It's been rather fine here, no interruptions except occasional whirlwind visits from Dad. He went up to the farm for me. Apparently I have a good tobacco crop; it has been well handled. If only nothing goes wrong now. The corn was better than expected and is about seventy cents a bushel. I mention this, as you ought to get something out of yours this year. My mind is much relieved since apparently the crops will make the mortgage payment and even taxes.

We shorely do miss you. Coming here is leaving the best society for none. If we could only always swing between two such good extremes. I may be over-sanguine about being let alone to finish this book, but I have a feeling that we won't be disturbed much. The only temptation is the fine fall weather. We have fires to break the morning chill, and we let them die out by noon. Try to take walks in the afternoon, but so far we have only napped. That's a good working sign, as I need not point out. I suppose people like us ought to be grateful for any place that will support us while we work, and certainly artists have had to take their bread where they found it, but now there doesn't seem to be much sympathy or understanding behind the provender. You can be almost as isolated in this country as you all are at Princeton. This hostility and indifference to the arts will finally dry them up and leave only propaganda, a thing the state can use. I think it's this condition that makes it so hard to work now.

This is just a note. I'll write later when I get a break in my stride. Take keer of yourselves and let us hear when you feel like it.

With love from us both, Andrew

TLS

1. Vice-Chancellor of University of the South. 2. W. S. Knickerbocker, editor of *The Sewanee Review*.

November 5, 1940

Dear Brother:

I been aimin' to write you these past ten days, but I've had a streptococcus infection in my writing hand. I took gas yesterday and had it lanced; so it's better today. The air's been mighty thick here, and I ain't got nothin' done but the radio, and that none too well. The broadcasts are to make a book which Random House thinks will make a killing.[1] I'll need it because the latest news here is that I'm not to be asked back next year. I begin to hope it's so. Maybe I'll get something done.

It was fine news that you were on a good stretch of work. Let us know what you all are doing. I send cheque for $75.00—more in two weeks. Doesn't this leave a balance of $51.00 still owing to you?

Miss Carrie will finish this.

AL

Dearest Edna:

You'd never think from our slowness in writing, how we've missed you all. It was positively painful at first. Your picture in the big hat was on top of that bunch of pictures, lying around on the table. I had to turn it face down, made me so homesick to see you. I send some pictures by the way. Henry [Church][2] keeps at it.

Allen's hand is much better this morning which is a great relief. He is having eighty allergy tests Monday—if this present infection is gone by that time.

We were in New York Sunday. Saw K. A. who is at the Murray Hill hotel having teeth taken out and put in. Also Eleanor Agar who had just come from the first rehearsal of her play. K. A. and E.[3] didn't get on any too well.

Have just been out to vote and MUST get to work. Will write when things quiet down a bit. Love for you both,

Caroline

TLS

1. Tate has been doing some broadcasts, which are to be published as *Invitation to Learning* (Random House, 1941). 2. Heir to the Arm and Hammer soda fortune. 3. Albert Erskine, Porter's current husband. They are soon to separate.

Monteagle, Tenn.
November 18, 1940

Dear Brother—

Your letter came while I was in a good stretch. So I haven't been able to answer before this. That's fine news about the radio book. It beats the Guggenheim for the sale is bound to be tremendous. You'll probably have trouble pulling it together from the records, for I should imagine it ought not to be too episodic. We haven't heard a full program. It's almost impossible to keep up with time. Sunday I got it just as you were reading the close of Rousseau. It's very strange to hear you and not be able to talk back. The experience is not altogether pleasant, particularly when the program is incomplete—sort of like the Ouija board.

Are you absolutely sure they aren't going to ask you back? The experiment has been such a success I can't understand what grounds the committee will have to discontinue it.[1] They must be able to get the money. It might be a good thing for your work, if the radio book will help you. I went over to see Guerry again, but his child was being operated on so I didn't get to talk with him. I should have gone before. I suppose I've felt a kind of reluctance, and yet Sewanee should be as good a compromise as anybody could hope for.

We are so icegrown here there's nothing much to report. I have had the minimum of interruptions and two long working periods which have advanced the book. Only three days of winter, but those severe enough. We are still planning to establish ourselves in New Orleans for at least three months. Perhaps we'll go in several weeks. I am paying for the removal by talking informally at U. of Chattanooga. I'd rather not break up here until the first of the year—but it's harder to get lodgings after the festivities begin. And then, too, I've bought a lot of wood and I can't bear to go off and leave it.

An old song started me to thinking about my dead the other day, and since then I've been dreaming about them. The dreams were fuller than such dreams usually are. I've almost had connected experiences, and though they were brief they were long enough to restore the feeling of life, and in the daytime that brevity filled me with pity & fear.

I read all the educational articles. They made a powerful indictment, and it was a pleasure to read yours again.[2] What you did to it improved it. I remember in the other ending the use of intelligence seemed a little too general, asking maybe for definition. Brother John's[3] was in his most political vein. It does not defend the old order of scholarship but I see little chance for his article to offend it. He speaks of revolution, yet leaves the impression that the old guard will purge itself. The old job was well done—now move into green fields—I longed to read the direct, unequivocal statement.

This is about all. Much oblige for the check. You don't owe me fifty-one—only forty-five dollars. Take your time. I'm in no hurry.

Both of us send love, Andrew

AL

1. The question is whether Princeton is going to renew Tate's appointment as Poet in Residence. Tate retained the post from 1939 to 1942. 2. "Miss Emily and the Bibliographers," *American Scholar,* 9 (Autumn 1940), 449–60. 3. "Strategy for English Studies," *Southern Review,* 6 (Autumn 1940), 226–35.

Nov. 28, 1940

Dear Brother:

I'm sending you all another cheque—for $40.00—it was $121.00, as I recalled after your last letter. If later in the winter you all need some money, up to a couple of hundred, just tell me; by May I could make it twice that: Now remember this.

I still don't know definitely my situation here. I suppose I should have assumed that I shouldn't be asked back. Doubtless I've embarrassed the Committee by offering myself for renewal. But this isn't a social situation: it's business. I'm doing a kind of work I like and do well, and I saw no reason not to tell them I wanted to continue it. I may get an offer from Columbia University next week—not so good as this—less money, about $4,500.00—but only eight hours a week. My negotiations with St. John's are broken off permanently, on account of a bad mess over the radio program. [Stringfellow] Barr was fired: they didn't like the way he did it, and besides he wanted $10,000.00 a year. He is now very sore at us; has accused us of stealing *his* programs; and is (behind our backs) trying to get CBS to discontinue the program, on the ground that our "debased performance" is injuring St. John's prestige, since the public identifies the program with St. John's. I thought Winkie [Barr] had improved, but he's the same old Winkie. As a matter of fact he stole the program from [Robert M.] Hutchins of Chicago:[1] took it for less money. He pretended to us that *he* persuaded CBS to put it on. In the process of his being fired he said nothing to us; his vanity was so great that he was still pretending that our jobs depended on him; we could have stood by him but when we learned that his "vacation" was permanent, we had committed ourselves to the winter program. CBS will not discontinue the program.

John was here two weeks ago; made a great hit with the good students; was hated by the English professors. [R. K.] Root wouldn't go up and meet him after the lecture. John is a queer bird: we felt he wasn't really here. His leaving Tennessee has been a disaster, and I am partly to blame for it. I pushed him into Ohio.

I wish we were at Monteagle with you all. I feel something which is very nearly fear the longer I live in this section. There's no communication with these people, who respond to nothing, not even to each other. Ceaseless activity but no life.

We were mighty pleased that you had done a good stretch. Miss Carrie has been doing right well too. I am trying to get together a book of essays for spring publication—either New Directions or Putnams.[2]

When do you expect to go to New Orleans? I reckon Edna will go out the first day and get her that easy job. We think of you all constantly and miss you sorely.

Our love to you both, Allen

AL

1. President of the University of Chicago. 2. *Reason in Madness: Critical Essays* (New York: G. P. Putnam's Sons, 1941).

New Orleans, La.
627 Dumaine St.
Dec. 17, 1940

Dear Brother:—

I meant to write you before we left—but your letter came in the midst of preparations and last minute business. The weather was still bearable at Monteagle and I had the finest pile of wood I have ever seen, but Edna was anxious to get here and try to locate a job in the Christmas rush. But I think she thought Tennessee was going to have a mild winter. We stopped over in Chattanooga for two days where I talked at the University for $50.00 and that got us well settled in our house.

For it is a house. It's the quickest transition we will ever make. We took a long time on the road, stopping over in Montgomery to see the godfather who gave her the $100.00 this summer. We got in Saturday night, had found the place Sunday, and this is Tuesday and we are practically settled. Places are scarce and high; so I take it as a good omen that we struck down so quick. It is a slave quarters done over. One large two-story room, white walls, plenty of light, and a fireplace. Nice looking cast iron stairs lead to the bedroom and bath. The bedroom has a balcony and underneath is the dining room and behind that a pretty good kitchen. The courtyard is small, with a fountain, tall cave and banana trees. We have complete privacy. No night clubs or street bars enough to be disturbing. The French market only a few blocks away and Jackson square just two. With the square we hope to pacify George who has shown a strong case of nostalgia. He bucks at the leash and the only way to make him follow is to drag him along, which is rather embarrassing. He has already advertised us on the street as dog beaters.

Wood Carper[1] wrote Abbo [Martin] that the students considered it an honor to get in your classes. It seems to me this gives you a great advantage strategically. Carper merely reports the general opinion, and I believe the authorities will listen to this, as they seem more concerned with success than with examining its nature, except, of course, in your case the popularity condemns their futility. Let me know how it goes. Perhaps it's just as well that the St. John's offer fell through. That would bind you to teaching longer hours. If you have to stay in the East, Columbia might gave you greater freedom and the city would probably be cheaper than Princeton. In the old days 4500.00 would have served mighty fine.

In my own case Guerry seems very anxious to get me at Sewanee, but so far he hasn't been able to locate the money. The Foundation turned him down. I asked if he wanted me to see what I could get you to do, but he said wait until he went East this Xmas, when he proposes to try there again. I got indirectly that Knickerbocker showed no sympathy with the idea, and Guerry was disgusted. But he couldn't go over his head to put me in the English Department which I wouldn't have agreed to anyway. It is his plan to put me on my own if he can raise the money. He told me it was a shame that he had to pay certain people who did routine work and couldn't divert that money to having somebody like me there. So it hangs fire. I'm going to try to get the Guggenheim extended for a few months and then possibly go to the farm. That may work out well. I've got good negro tenants who are brushing a mighty clean broom.

It is some better in this country than in the East, but it's only in degree. The dry rot spreads. I suppose I prefer a familiar corruption to the dehumanized surroundings that you all confront. What is so hard is downing the spectre of insensibility for which you work. It is bound to pervert and destroy in time all effort in the arts. I feel more & more like me reaching out for a solid thing to hold to, and grasping snow candy. I've had a feeling for some time that John was damaged by the change, that perhaps he holds a certain resentment. If loss in standing on principle does such damage, where lies the evil? I don't know. Perhaps it's the old trouble. Perhaps the kind of principle maintained there cannot flourish by making a clear-cut fight. The code duello was very careful of the quality of the antagonists.

Is Miss Carrie going to see her father this Christmas? If it's not too far maybe she can come by here & try the couch in the sitting room. Hope she works away, and I feel I'm going to, because I know there ain't any chance to see you all any time soon, as much as we want to. We shore miss you and study about you a heap. Maybe sometime everybody will be done [with] a piece of work at the same time, but traveling visiting ain't the same as riding over and sitting a spell in the cool of the evening.

Love from us both, A-

AL

1. A graduate of the University of the South, now at Princeton.

Dec. 22, 1940

Dear Brother:

It's mighty fine to picture you all beneath the banana trees and the sugar cane. I wish we were there. Today there's a weak sun above the Jersey murk, a sort of "leaden-eyed despair"; the scene requires bad poetry to do it justice. We've done nothing for Christmas. I must broadcast Christmas and New Year's eves. The good thing about the season is that it will stretch to Feb. 5th, so that I can finish up two essays for a book (12 in all) that Balch is publishing in March. Title: *Reason in Madness,*[1] from *Lear.* Since my quarrel with Putnam's two years ago they have been eager to publish anything I give them. The radio may have something to do with it.

Well, I'm hired for one more year; or maybe it would be more accurate to say that I told them I wanted to stay, and they have let me. But I am telling them that I am making other arrangements for 1942–43. That will indicate that I will not wait for their favor again till the last minute, and it will put squarely before them the possibility of a permanent appointment or nothing. I believe the real reason they are keeping me is that they couldn't think of anybody else.

You remember I wanted to get money for an annual series of lectures on literary criticism. Sister Louise was about to give it; then Roosevelt was reelected. I told it as a joke to Barbara Church, and she almost wrote the cheque on the spot. (As a matter of fact, Henry is writing it tomorrow.) $600.00 a year for four lectures on *The Language of Poetry,* for five years, under the auspices of the Creative Arts Program. Henry insisted on poetry against my proposal of literary criticism. I thought he ought to have some say about it.[2] The Confederates have been very much at 58 Cleveland

Lane. There's a big party for next week—the Aubergonois and Miss St. John, their English old-maid, 2nd cousin of the Duke of Norfolk. She looks more like the Duke's horse.

There's a sad tale about Bill [Brown]. He steadily went to pieces after you all left: he departed Friday, not to return. He was stealing liquor and not working. Then he took another form of escape in falling in love with Richard Blackmur's wife[3]—a born fool of the New England variety. She was giving him liquor "because you were so cruel to him." When we told Bill he had to go, she thought that we ought to keep him so that they could have their affair without inconvenience. There is general human weakness here, but I seem to detect a specific New England quality in it. They were to be allowed to indulge their personal feelings at the expense of an established social situation among the persons concerned. It never occurred to Bill that since I had brought Blackmur here I could not harbor a man who was openly seducing his wife. Red was right: it is the snake pit. In three months there has been a hideous transformation of Bill's character from weakness into corruption.

As to Sewanee: I hope you will get in touch with Guerry early in January, and then let me know what luck he had in N.Y. Getting this money from Henry Church (small though it is) puts me into a favorable light with the Carnegie people: Gauss said as much the other day. At the same time I can't very well speak to the Carnegie people unless I know what Guerry has in mind; it would be better if he wrote me a note describing in general terms his plans. Without that anything I do is presumptuous. And I think something can be done.

I am sending you a new poem[4]—the first in 18 months. But I have some others in mind. Let us know what progress you are making. It will probably take a while for you to get used to the bananas. And did Edna get her job? And have you seen the Baton Rouge people? The Ransoms are spending the holidays with the Warrens.

Love from us all, Allen

AL

P.S. Harcourt Brace refused Katherine Ann $500.00. She got other offers, big ones; now H-B has given her $7,780.00. She has bought herself a scarlet evening cape. Doubtless she will get her a nice pipe organ. Albert [Erskine] is now as if he had never been.

1. *Reason in Madness: Critical Essays* (New York: G. P. Putnam, 1941). 2. Henry Church, heir to the Arm and Hammer Soda fortune and patron of the arts, edited and published *Mesures*. Under Tate's editorship, the four lectures in this series were published by Princeton under the same title in 1942. 3. Helen Dickson Blackmur. 4. "False Nightmare," *New Republic* 104 (24 March 1941), 399.

New Orleans, La.
627 Dumaine St.
Feb. 2, 1941

Dear Brother:

I've been too busy to write. The weeks have swished by, and every week I've been too tired to compose a decent letter. Towards the end of December I copied a short part of the Florida section and sent it in to [Henry Allen] Moe, asking for a three months' renewal.[1] In January I did about forty pages, which is a lot for me. I feel a little better about the book now that I am in the wilderness proper, but I still have grave doubts as to whether it is a novel or not. And today, I'm going to try to divide what remains into four parts, covering the four months more we will be here. That will give me two weeks rest and six weeks to revise and pull it finally together.

After a month's red tape Miss Edna got her job, working for the social service branch of the Louisiana state government. At ninety a month and five cents per mile for car service. This is a big help, because it's been hard not to live up the Guggenheim. Money seems to fly away and we don't live particularly high. It's the incidentals like cleaning and eating out and picture shows that get us. Already I can't understand her conversation: it is entirely alphabetical. She says you can see the entire confusion of a totalitarian state in her office—reams and reams of sociological and wordy reports, dictaphones which terrify her, detective work, a sort of governmental peeping Tom. She has figured it costs about a hundred dollars to do the office work on one case. But it leaves my days altogether free, and I have the best working conditions I've ever had. The days are long, the weather occasionally bad and, if I can just hold out, I see an end to De Soto.

We went to Baton Rouge while Cleanth [Brooks] was in the east and discovered the Ransoms visiting the Warrens. The stage was set for an uninterrupted discussion of the movies, golf, the villainies of Moo-saliny, not to be confused with the Italian people who are brave and the oldest and most cultured people of Europe, when suddenly upon this undisturbed scene, this holy day setting of joy and feasting upon the lotus flowers (enumerated above and prepared from the oil of the finest olives: Re Umberto) when suddenly the great betrayer, accompanied by his consort, whom I took for a walk and entertained at dinner, though she didn't understand the Italian I spoke to my friends and didn't even (five months later) come by to thank me and say goodbye, appears like the insect he is, darkly upon the horizon. The messenger of ill will, the once soundly tromped Tinkum,[2] the Louisiana Fixer.

We meet at a cocktail party at the [Robert] Lowells. Enter the man with the iron mask and his entire entourage. The villain summons what arts of diplomacy he has and asks, in his most agreeable manner, about the vacation on the continent and all the things that have passed while there. But really he was at his worst, quizzing, quizzing, quizzing. Did I make a hundred? The villain is a confused villain. On the other side of the room, his consort learns from the pioneer how the hope of the country lies in the middle west, the country which is just beginning and where all young men should go. When the consort asks why the west should just begin a hundred years after its settlement, the trail blazer pauses and smiles blandly. The party continues at the messenger's lodge, who grows a little bitter and complains that her food was ruined by the help of the volunteer in the kitchen, who thinks that she is the only one who can cook. Just as the conversation begins to grow, the man with the iron mask steps forth and calls quickly for charades. By this time Lowell hears in detail of the villainy. The consort says she would like to use her little dog George in the games. "We'll play dog in the manger, and I'm sure you can have a dog if you want to; you can have anything you want—even a dog." I lack a dictaphone to transmit the placing of emphasis.

For two days and nights we play charades. In the last five minutes of the last game, the man with the iron mask lets it down and discloses his old and charming manner. Later they come to New Orleans and Cinina says to a perfect stranger, "I have no relatives or friends in the world." At a farewell party they go to Ioway, forcing the Lowells to leave an agreeable apartment and move into theirs, inheriting Mamie who is the only one I will let do my linens and dishes and a cat, with one can of food. The cat's life grows daily more precarious.

These are some of the highlights of our visit to Baton Rouge. I've been very depressed on many counts, not so much with the old wound but the new one and regret the small part I had in the Nashville trial of principle. By the way, that was a very annoying circular from Don. I wrote him a stiff letter and said I wanted my share of the royalties.

I've wrote out. We been hearing you for the last month over the air, and it's still mighty natchel to hear your voice but a mighty pore way to visit. Edmund Wilson sounded like old Ford. Write when you can. I ain't going to be able to do much corresponding. Give everybody my love and tell Miss Carrie I hope she's doing well and pushing the book along.[3] I wish I thought mine was in any way as good as hern.

Love from us both, Andrew

TLS

1. Lytle is seeking an extension of his Guggenheim. 2. Brooks' wife. 3. *Green Centuries.*

New Orleans, La.
627 Dumaine St.
Feb. 17, 1941

Dear Brother:

I been waiting to find the "False Nightmare" to write you, but the weeks have slipped by like days, and here comes Miss Carrie's fine long good letter, and I feel guilty it's so long and fine. I feel like I ought to send a check.

I like the poem very much. It's one of the best you have done. Without trying to make any relative comparisons, I put it with "The Mediterranean," "Aenaes at Washington," and "Message from Abroad," and the "Message" I like better and better.

The success comes particularly from the almost terrifying thing to be said tightened to the point where it don't seem tight. Intended or not, the simple rhyme and short line opposed to what it delivers takes you by surprise, so easy and direct does it make the poem seem. The shifts are sudden, too, perhaps too sudden between the italicized stanzas and "In bulled Europa's morn." The corn, torn doesn't tie it together as well as the change in the rhyme plus the feminine ending of gloating and floating. If the whole poem was the nightmare, instead of the introductory part, this would be justified; but as I feel now, it's a little jarring. But I'd like to wait and see and I ain't no poetic critic noway. And anyway it's a fine poem.

I told Cleanth when he was here how bad I thought some of the recent fiction was they had printed, the Albrizio[1] for example, and I was just about to ask why they hadn't taken "Port London," which I think is one of Caroline's best stretches of writing, when we were interrupted and the conversation shifted. Cleanth's position was that maybe he didn't know, but then it's his place to know. It was probably a good thing at the time that I didn't say anything, for it was just after he got back from the east. But I am going to pin him down for my own satisfaction. Of course, I may be wrong, in the sense that it's a part of a novel, but I thought it had its own unity, and the Albrizio piece had no unity nor anything as far as I could see. So they haven't any grounds there. I can't make out whether it's because Red has been away and is still away, or whether it's because Cleanth is politicking so much, because I believe he does know what's good. I did read the critical resume of novels and was shocked.[2] Lon [Cheney] was here at the time and I showed it to him. I think he was shocked but of course pleased. By the way his present novel shows great improvement.[3] He has handled some very difficult stuff with great skill. The boy as a white nigger, for example. It's entirely convincing and sympathetic.

I can't find Caroline's letter; so this may find you gone to Cincinnati. When you write her, tell her to be sure to stop by here if she can make it. There's nothing to offer but oysters and a little drinking, but they might refresh her on her way and the sight of her would freshen us up like nothing else but the sight of both of you. I'd send this to Cincinnati but I've forgotten the name of the Towers Ben works in and I can't bring myself to write him in care of Mrs. Fleishman. Of course, that's because I've been so pore so long I feel like a man, no matter how stout he is, nor how loud he said "I got the power," would in the end be whupped by a nine hundred thousand dollar house which he didn't build.

Our love to you both, Andrew

TLS

1. Gene Albrizio's "The Bereft," *The Southern Review,* 6 (Summer 1941), 454–88. 2. Don Standford reviews thirty novels in an essay entitled "The Beloved Returns and Other Recent Fiction," *The Southern Review,* 6 (Summer 1941), 610–28. 3. *River Rogue* (1942).

March 2, 1941

Dear Brother:

Yrs. of the 17th rec'd. Miss Carrie's done gone to Floridy and come back. She went from the wedding in Cincinnati to Guthrie, and on from there. She wanted to come over to N. Orleans, but had to come back to work. She hopes now to finish in July. Do you reckon De Soto will be done by then? If he is, couldn't we go to a beach somewhere? I believe Cousin Edna would like this.

No news here, except that I've read the galleys on my book of essays,[1] which ought to be [out] on April 4th. Yes, and Winkie Barr has been frustrated in his attempts to fire us from C.B.S.

There's a terrific mess at Vanderbilt. I enclose a letter from Dr. Sanborn which explains it. Evidently Pomfret[2] is out for blood. I see no use in a publicity campaign. Don suggests the formation of an alumni committee to represent the more educat[ed] minority against the illiterate Board of Trust and the Administration. If Don will do the organizing, I will join him; but I have little confidence in his powers to act.

Cleanth & I wrote letters to the *Alumnus* on the Vanderbilt "literary tradition," in reply to some false and complacent remarks in the November issue.

Tell us how the work progresses, and how Edna likes her job after so much labor.

Don't bother to answer this. You need the time. Love to you both.

Allen

AL

1. *Reason in Madness.* 2. A dean at Vanderbilt; a committee is liberalizing the curriculum, much to the distress of the more conservative members of the faculty.

New Orleans, La.
627 Dumaine
March 15, 1941

Dear Brother:

I've been a little late in sending the Vanderbilt stuff back, but here it is. I wrote Don a note and the doctor a short one. What can you do with stupidity, arrogance, and proletarian methods. Edna doesn't like her job, but she likes the money. The sociologists now are making them account for every five minutes of their time. How they expect the girls to get anything done and stop every few minutes and account for themselves is beyond me. I've just received word from Moe of a three months' extension: $500.00. What a lift that will give me. I am in the middle now. Hope to get done by July, but can't tell yet. Maybe we can get together at a sea shore. We'll probably go to Monteagle for the last stages, but may stay here.

Two of Edna's co-workers listen regularly to "Invitation to Learning": Think you are the best—don't like [Mark] Van Doren. Wonder what [Huntington] Cairns is doing on the program.

Our love, A

AL

P.S. That pore visitor last week didn't get a bewildered word in.

New Orleans, La.
627 Dumaine St.
April 28, 1941

Well, Brother, we are mighty proud. The book came yesterday. We turned the pages and seen our names. I feel sort of exposed setting out in front of so much distinguished prose. As for Edna she's been feeling exposed anyway of late and will be able to carry the honor better than me. It's a good looking book and well set up and we're mighty glad to have it ever which way you look at it.

With all the things going on around here I'm in a press. Did a good month's work but it hasn't taken me far enough along. I'm trying to get out this fall, but it will be late fall. I don't see how I can do it, but some way it's got to be done. I could see my way clear if I didn't have to recast that first section. I'll declare you all have had enough trouble and sickness: Caroline's letter had the tone of an old campaigner who had seen many wars, and I can see she's writing at her best and that the book will be her best. I've been looking into *Flowering Judas*[1] recently. As fine as it is, it is not as tough as Caroline's work. There is a certain female impurity which Caroline lacks, and I believe this is the thing a woman writer will naturally find the greatest hazard. With a man it is easier to obliterate himself. His difficulty is to subdue the idea. At least I find it so. The love scenes between Outlaw and the girl in no way disclose either the sex or a writer. They are fully rendered. A man and a woman behave like a particular man and a particular woman under given conditions, so that the pages of the book disappear, the people come live in their world.

I am beginning to feel that I take hold of a book the wrong way. I find straight narrative difficult and feel the need of some cross pull which in its bad phase turns into the envelope. Perhaps some day I'll work it out, but I'm certainly having a time now. Certain sections come off. If I can only pull the thing securely together.

Well, I've got to go to work. We go to Monteagle about the first of June or last of May—love from us both.

Andrew

AL

1. By Katherine Anne Porter.

Sept. 14, 1941

Dear Brother:

This ain't a letter. It's just to urge you to let me have as soon as possible a copy of Peru for the anthology.[1] At the first mention of it John Bishop was all for it. There may not be much money for rights of translation, but if Dodd, Mead publishes the anthology here, in English, there will be a second fee; and meanwhile you might get magazine publication.

We got here Wednesday (10th) in good shape. I've already seen Dr. Wolf, and he says I am in fine condition. Miss Carrie is already sewing. Nancy is in new disgrace: the school is reluctantly taking her back, informing us that the faculty voted last spring to expel her. Truancy, lying, and insolence were the charges against her, in addition to low grades. I don't know what to make of it. She seems subdued now, but it won't last, I fear.

We're hoping that Edna is now getting a little rest. We were too much for her.[2]

Around November 1st I will have $300.00 idle; so keep it in mind. It might make the difference between ease and anxiety when you take Edna from the hospital to Murfreesboro on the farm.

Will write more later.

Love to you both—or rather all three,

Allen

AL

1. *American Harvest: Twenty Years of Creative Writing in the United States*. Edited with an introduction by Allen Tate and John Peale Bishop. New York: L. B. Fisher, 1942; Garden City, N.Y.: Garden City Publishing Company, 1943. 2. The Lytles are expecting their first child.

Monteagle, Tenn.
Friday
[September 1941]

Dear Brother—

We miss you very, very much, but are glad you arrived without mishap. Edna has rested up and together we finished doing over the baby bed. Now the proofs are coming in and they are asking them back on 24 hr. service. As soon as I get them all in, I'll recopy the Peru and send it to you. If you think it needs revision, and there is time, I'll rework it. I want to smooth it out as much as I can before sending it to you.

I hope Nancy has discovered that the world is more complicated than she thought and will come through the school with flying colors. Much oblige for the offer of the $300. If we need it, we'll let you know. Guerry finally came through with the house.[1] We are delighted, as I had begun to worry about moving Edna and a baby in winter weather, and while she would be so weak. We are moving as soon as they do some painting. Will write later.

With love from us both, Andrew

AL

P.S. I am sending Caroline's box.

1. Alexander Guerry, Vice-Chancellor at Sewanee, offered Lytle a house in exchange for several free public lectures.

Oct. 23, 1941
Sewanee, Tenn.

Dear Brother:

I've been in bed with a fearful cold, Edna has now taken it, and we have as well had further troubles with the Kirby-Smiths over [the] hospital. Edna is so accustomed to taking things into her hands that I let her go out to reserve a room before I checked with Alex [Guerry], who had promised to arrange the matter satisfactorily. He had forgotten; the Kirby-Smiths stood fast; so that the situation has become more complicated. Either the Vice-Chancellor has to humiliate them publicly or we have to go to Tullahoma, unless the Kirby-Smiths listen to advice and on their own revise their decision. It has upset Edna, as the arrival is not so far off, her doctor is still vacationing but returns this week, and the cold gives little cheer. Enough of our difficulties.

Of course, the moment I heard Knickerbocker was out I thought of you. I didn't realize the Princeton business was over this year or I would have taken it up with you. My position must be reticent until Alex brings it up. Whereas it has been the talk of Sewanee, Alex has never mentioned it to me. The only indirect statement from him to me was made when we first moved over. He said he hoped we could work out a more permanent arrangement. Now I don't really want to stay here and get involved in teaching, particularly since the farm seems to promise well. But if the book flops,[1] I may have to consider some kind of an offer. In which case I will bring up the proposition of dividing the chores between us. This he will understand as he himself has told me, the time I first mentioned you, that the *[Sewanee] Review* was a job to itself.

Of course, there will be opposition. Abbott [Martin][2] has kept himself rather remote since we arrived. I have several un-friends here. This will not extend to you, and your reputation, although it may not be understood, is known and will have sufficient weight. Alex wants to make this the literary and cultural center of the South. I think the idea would appeal to him. It might resolve itself down to a question of money. I think he genuinely likes me and would consider what I had to say. I think it better not to discuss this with anybody, even the General,[3] now. I believe a premature leakage would ruin it. It would give a weapon to the considerable body of sympathy for Mrs. Knickerbocker.[4] There is danger that the dismissal will rebound on the Vice-Chancellor. There is some feeling that I have been brought here to take his place. Under no circumstances must the charge of conspiracy be made. Guerry himself being a new man has to move carefully about upsetting the status quo, although he is stubborn and willing to take what risks are necessary to achieve the end he believes in.

I don't know what good I would be on a magazine, but I could assist you. I don't really know whether I would be a good teacher. I would have a real interest in making this the cultural center of the South, although even that may be too late. I certainly will do all I can to get you all back here. It goes without saying that it would be fine to be on the mountain together. Even if we move to the farm, you would be in striking distance.

For the time being the strategy is silence, at least until rumor becomes factual. If you have any other suggestions that have occurred to you since you wrote, send them on.

I must stop now. When does Miss Carrie's book come out?[5] What news on the advance sale? South America is too far away, but still you might establish a base, even temporary, and for us an objective.[6] I think the chance here is good, particularly if you can supplement with some money.

With love to all. My wits are so addled from cold this may not be over clear, but I'll write later.

Andrew

TLS

1. *At the Moon's Inn.* 2. A professor of English at University of the South. 3. Jervey. 4. Knickerbocker was dismissed because of his unpopularity with the administration. 5. *Green Centuries* (1941). 6. Tate had considered arranging a lecture series backed by the Pan American Union to be delivered in South America, but the plan failed to materialize.

October 24, 1941

Dear Brother:

I hope I haven't got you in hot water. After I wrote you the other day, I let my imagination get the better of me, and a letter to General Jervey followed yours.

It never occurred to me as a remote possibility that he would show the letter to Guerry.[1] But that is exactly what he did. I suppose I just didn't consider the amazing innocence of the General.

However, I didn't give the General the source of my information that Knickerbocker was leaving. So if Guerry confronts you with it, you can truthfully say that other people besides you know it. I have heard it from two sources since you wrote me: Bob Daniel, and a man at Columbia to whom evidently Knickerbocker had written.

Guerry denied to the General that K. was going to leave, and therefore, said he, I am not looking for another man. I don't know what to make of this. It may mean that he wouldn't have me, or it may mean that he has already found somebody and is keeping him hidden.

Maybe the General will show you my letter. I hope he does, so you can see just what I said. I made the point that I was not interested if you were.

How is [The] Foundation coming along? Give Edna our love.

Allen

TLS

1. Vice-Chancellor at the University of the South.

Sewanee, Tenn.
Oct. 29, 1941

Dear Brother:

That was a right bad blunder for such an old campaigner, but don't let it worry you. I can't tell yet how far it will tie my hands. Nothing has been said to me about it. It's too bad I didn't write my letter to you sooner, giving you a report on the general situation. Now that you have it you see why the General's move was so ill-timed. The only disagreeable part is the waiting, which had to be done anyway and which is bound to be unsatisfactory to you. I can't see how the situation has been fundamentally changed, though, unless Alex feels his hand has been forced. Even so, I don't think that would keep him from seeing what a good thing it would be to have the *Sewanee Review* in good hands. I haven't seen the General. When I get a chance, I'll maybe talk with him in case he feels any embarrassment.

We have been worried with Edna's cough. She lies in bed, coughing and reading *Green Centuries*. I'm in the midst of writing a speech, and so get it only at off times. We like the way the book looks and the illustration gets very well the feel of the cave-like gloom of the wilderness. We are mighty proud to have it and will write very soon. Edna has started a letter, but she feels too bad for writing and is somewhat alarmed, for her time draws nigh and this cold is draining her resistance and, unless she gets rid of it, will make it hard to take ether if she has to.

Caroline, there's no doubt this is your best and a great book. I've only got as far as the love scene. There's no halt anywhere; it moves and accumulates as it moves. The description of the Dawson spring is perfect. It does the trick and brings the family alive. I won't write any more now but will wait until we finish reading. Of course I think maybe you've lost something by changing the opening scene. At least I missed it. I got the feeling of the thing that would draw him on. But there's certainly nothing wrong with the way it does open.

With love from us both, Andrew

TLS

I'll mail the Peru tomorrow.

Sewanee, Tenn.
Dec. 22, 1941

Dear Tates:

Just a note to say how much we enjoyed your last letters. We have never caught up with our routine yet. The little Dona Pamela[1] keeps all three of us busy, day and night. A loud voice and a little piece of flesh, so busy doing nothing, as Edna says, when she is awake, has certainly taken hold of this household. She has begun to gain, prefers to sleep by day and yell by night. Edna is coming along, but she is suffering now from a discomfort which often goes with carrying so much weight. We had thought to go, not to Murfreesboro this Christmas, but join Polly and Jimmy in Huntsville. This was only on the grounds that May was kept uninformed. But Dad, in the shape of Mercury made the land leap up before him and disarranged all plans, so that now we go nowhere, which we decided to do anyway, as Edna ought not to travel and I doubt if the baby ought either.

If you can stand the long jaunt, we hope that you will be able to make the trip south. We are mightily anxious for you to see the little girl and for us to see you. If the weather stays mild, you can put up at Monteagle. Here there is one bedroom. Dad will be around with Franklin[2] to keep fires going. He stays there when he comes up. Now that the baby is safely arrived, he has been attending to his cotton and we haven't seen him and the food for which he has exchanged tomatoes. It had cut our bills tremendously. It looks like it will be a long time before the book repays the advances, if ever now that war has come. Chambers says the book market was doing well until Pearl Harbor. Now he doesn't know what to think. I wrote him that you would probably be looking around for another publisher; so you will hear from him. He is probably as good as they come. I don't know how they work, but I believe they have got to work differently to sell books in great quantities, or even in moderately good quantities, granted that the book is any good. I know he will do the best he can and feels that the book and his money will allow him.

Your interview with [Maxwell] Perkins was superb. When business men are grieved and shocked over the discussion of money, there is occasion for alarm. Gilbert Govan[3] says he had trouble finding anything about GC *[Green Centuries]* from Scribner's before publication. He says he wrote them and, I believe, got no reply or a slow reply. I'll check up on this when I see him next.

Could Gauss be lying? Or disturbed over the success of the experiment? The academic world is a strange place. I incline more and more to the farm. George Haight suggested that he put up some money to do over the house, as a refuge from the West Coast. But now I don't know whether I can get the supplies to fix it up, but it was certainly generous of him. He gave Pamela three hundred dollars to be set aside in case she got sick and needed doctors and nurses. I don't know how we would get along without the Brother Bens and the George Haights.

I am returning that letter about tobacco chewing. It certainly is one of the most remarkable I have ever read. That lad certainly shows all the making of a writer.

With lots of love from us. Edna wanted to add a note, but I haven't time to wait for it. Drop a card and let us know when you will make it this way. We might meet on neutral ground, in Murfreesboro, or even Nashville, if it is towards the end of the month. Mamma is so lightheaded these days that it's a problem for anybody to stay at home. She set the house on fire while May was up here. It was only God's mercy she didn't burn herself up. John[4] happened to be awake and heard her.

Andrew

TLS

1. Their oldest daughter was born November 16, 1941, the day before *At the Moon's Inn* appeared nationally. 2. A black boy who was Robert Lytle's driver. 3. Librarian at University of Chattanooga. 4. Probably John Nelson, Lytle's cousin.

January 26, 1942

Dear Brother:

I've been getting to this since before Christmas, although in the meantime I can't see that I've accomplished anything else. I've been running from one place to another on a treadmill. The South American anthology has taken most of the time. That is now finished, so far as I am concerned.

At the last minute our Bolivian advisor said we couldn't use your Peru because the Latin-Americans, in spite of their Spanish blood, think of the conquest as we do of Sherman's march; and they don't like to be reminded of it. So we took the "Washing of Brother Macon" from *The Long Night,* and asked Chambers for his consent, which he gave. Is this all right with you?

As to Peru, why not get it out as a small book? Chambers said something about this when I saw him in Indianapolis; and it gave me a still better idea. There's a little press in San Francisco called the Colt Press which does beautiful books and pays the author for them. They're doing one for Edmund Wilson and they asked me for one. I could easily send the ms. out there. Tell me what to do.

Doubtless Miss Carrie has written you of her difficulties. It seems that she has had bad luck all round. She wants to change publishers, and this is the worst possible time. They are all shaking in their boots. We had counted on *Green Centuries* selling enough to justify an advance which would see us through a year and Nancy through her last year of prep school. Now that is out of the question. I could probably get $500 from Balch, and Caroline not more than $1000. But we can't do much with that. We could alone, but Nancy is the expensive item.

The job here, as I wrote you, is over, although the Committee is quarreling over my successor, one of them, [Willard]Thorp, [is] still holding out for me. It seems that the candidate to succeed me is Julian Green,[1] whose value is enhanced by the fact that he is a refugee. He's a good novelist but critically naive, as my boys said last year when he lectured here.

In this dilemma, I am considering an army or navy job, and I urge you to do the same, unless you've got some money on tap that I can't see from this distance. There are all kinds of jobs in both branches—Intelligence, and Public Relations mainly, which pay according to rank. If we went into the service we should get commissions—captaincies at our age I should think, in the army, and senior lieutenancies in the navy. I am perfectly serious about this. There will be nothing for writers elsewhere in the next few years, perhaps longer. The suspension of the *Southern Review* is typical. If you are interested, I will tell you where to write and whom to see.

Part of my time, a large part, since I got back from Indianapolis has been spent working up publicity about the *Southern Review*. So far we've got editorials and articles in *The Nation,* the *New Republic,* and *Time*. And at Indianapolis I got a petition up with 231 names to the President of LSU. (By the way, I saw it passed to Knickerbocker, and he refused to sign it.) We were seriously hampered at first by the preposterous statement of the editors announcing the suspension. We've had to tell everybody that the editors didn't really mean that they agreed with the university policy. That announcement is a perfect example of Cleanth's humorless political intrigues.

The hysteria around here is appalling. if I could get my army commission by February 9th, when the second term begins, I would resign from the university. As an example of what the hysteria will do to intelligent men, Gauss the other day stopped me on the campus, and it soon became apparent that he expected the Creative Writing group to disintegrate under the impact of the accelerated program. I told him it wouldn't happen, but I could see that he would not be convinced. The only change in enrollment for the second term is a net gain of three. Willard Thorp had to take the figures to him to convince him.

I suppose the war will postpone any change at Sewanee. I was very much amused by Knickerbocker's demeanor at Indianapolis. He came up to speak to me in his usual fawning way, and spoke of you and Edna as if he were your most intimate friend on the mountain, and of Pamela[2] as if he were her uncle.

If nothing else works out, we plan to spend the summer and next winter at Monteagle. The summer would be fairly expensive, but for the winter we could get a small compact cottage, easily heated, for very little, I imagine; and if Brother Ben would not send Nancy off to school, we could keep her there and tutor her. Nancy herself likes the idea of this. I think it might be good for her. She has matured wonderfully in the past four months. Her poems knocked me over. Parental fatuity is capable of any exaggeration; yet I am convinced that the poems have remarkable things in them. Our problem is to make her responsible, without making a fool of her. So far I've said very little to her—merely that they contain good lines. What amazed me was the objective use of imagery—not how she felt.

Our present feeling is that if we can get enough money together to live on for a year from this June, it might be better if I don't succeed in getting a job or a commission in the service. I would get a novel written (it's pretty firmly in my head already) and Caroline could do her next book.

I've been wanting to read over again both *At the Moon's Inn* and *Green Centuries;* and I'll get to it next week. How are the sales now? We saw an ad in the Sunday *Times* for *At the Moon's Inn,* which must mean that the sales have picked up at least a little.

I'll let you know how things turn out. Meanwhile let me know whether the army interests you. We might be shifted around the country a little, but probably that wouldn't hurt us.

We've assumed that Edna's trouble just before Christmas was cleared up, not having heard more about it. And how is Pamela? Our love to all three of you.

Allen

TLS

1. Green was born in Paris of American parents. He returned to the United States to attend the University of Virginia and to serve in both World Wars. After WWII, he returned to Paris. 2. The Lytles' daughter.

Sewanee, Tenn.
Jan. 30, 1942

Dear Tates:

I have done little else than read [Marcel] Proust since I got the present, or I would have written sooner. The war, our precarious situation, even to a dwindling of moneys, has not been able to arouse me from it. The last chapter of the first volume, "The Red Shoes of the Duchesse de Guermantes," is one of the most overwhelming things in literature. I'd never read further than *Swann's Way.* I suppose I never would have gotten around to the whole thing without the books at hand. Very much obliged.

We enjoyed the last letters and the shock of surprise over Nancy's poems was tremendous. I suppose all her headstrong energy should have prepared me for it, but I had forgotten the great difference between a child's viewpoint when she reported that her father was a banker and adolesence [sic]. There's no doubt that she's got something and that that something is going to be very good. It's all the more amazing when you consider what you might expect from somebody her age. There is another remarkable thing about it. Most children turn away from everything their parents represent.

I suppose going in the army or the navy would be a good thing, and perhaps we could be of some use if we were put to the things we could do. But I would hate to lose valuable years doing something somebody else, somebody younger and with quicker reflexes, could do better. Naturally if the situation gets desperate enough, men our age will be called. I should think, offhand, that there will be enough men coming of age each year to fill up the fighting forces: and somehow the Intelligence or propaganda doesn't appeal to me very much as a way of making a living. I certainly think you would make a mistake, unless you absolutely had to do it. Of course, you were speaking of it primarily as a stop gap, but it might prove to be a right long gap, and expensive as to time. It is perfectly true that this is a bad time for literature, but commercially speaking there is no good time for poetry and higher criticism. The war has hurt fiction, may hurt it more; but after the country settles down to fighting and if the war isn't brought too close home to us, that is, if we don't actually have to meet an invasion of the continent, there may be some place for fiction. I feel that, at least for myself, it will give me a breathing spell for study and writing which will be an attempt to overcome my flaws. The flaws which Caroline has pointed out are grave, her judgment of them acute, and I am going to try to do something about them.

Of course, one never knows absolutely which course is the right one to take. As diverse as we are as writers, we certainly have this in common. We do not have to travel all over the world looking for the stimulus as people like Hemingway do. I learned this, among a great many other things, from you. And yet even as I say this, I think of Ford. I often wonder if he would have continued to write but for the last war which his talent used to extricate him [from] the bog of his social exile. Of course, you can never be sure of these things, but the violence of war to my mind neutralized the equally violent confusion he got himself in with his various women and so turned him again to writing. He, naturally, is a special case; but then all men may need the experience of war, which is usually deprived us in the regimentation so common everywhere. The new weapons may restore an experience a seventeenth or eighteenth century man took along with all other experience.

The situation at Sewanee is this: it can give no technical training. There is fear that it will be hurt, that students will go where they can get a degree and find a place waiting for them in the army after graduation. The faculty is debating a summer session, giving diplomas in three years' time. From getting money, from all sides it looks bad for a liberal arts college. If Guerry had ever intended to offer me a place here, the war has postponed that indefinitely: but to show that he had it in his mind he did offer me an Academy job for a year or two which I took to mean that he wanted to keep me on call. There will be two or three of these jobs, full-time teaching jobs, paying two thousand in cash, some allowances for a house, and free food at the Academy. I thought seriously of taking it, although it would mean no writing, until I decided to move to the farm. I have refrained from giving Guerry my decision until I wrote you. I would go fully into his expressed wish to establish the liberal arts here: tell him that now is the time for the *Sewanee Review* to take the place of the *Southern Review,* and that you might take the Academy job until Knickerbocker's contract expired, when you would be made editor of that and do more or less what you have been doing at Princeton.

I don't know how this appeals to you. I hesitate to propose it, because I think you've been teaching long enough. If we go to our farm, why don't you all go to Benfolly? With you there, you could get your brother Ben to farm the land, and certainly fifteen hundred dollars ought to carry you well there. Would Ben stake Nancy and even you all to such a venture? You might even sell Benfolly and find a place near us.

If you did buy a farm near ours, with your reputation and Caroline's why couldn't we start a school of writers all our own, perhaps not, certainly not to be reasonable, in the immediate future but not too distant future. Those snob schools in the east which make lads pay high to wash dishes we could turn into farming and writing schools. That is, for supposed exercise, make the lads improve our farms. We might even bring in one or two other teachers. This should be done only if necessary. I should prefer to do a little farming and write.

It has been hard for me to make up my mind to go to the country. It has been very pleasant here, but I believe it is the only sensible thing to do: and then I have debts. George Haight never tires of being fairy godmother. When he was here he gave me three hundred dollars, which he had won at poker, to lay away in case Pamela got sick and we had to call in an expensive doctor. Then he opened the question of the farm and said that unless we fixed up the house before we moved up there, we would never fix it up. He is giving the money as an outright gift, with no strings, attached so that I will be able to write. If the war is brought to the West coast, I will offer it as a place of refuge for his children and Justine. His understanding equals his affectionate generosity, so that I feel like making the venture. To think that you all could be nearby would relieve me of my remaining uncertainty about the change.

That's a good idea about sending the Peru section to the West Coast. Will you do that? If they don't take it, maybe Chambers will put it out later. Do you suppose I ought to offer it to him first? At any rate before I accept the other people's offer, if offer there is, I can take it up with Chambers. I don't think the *Moon's Inn* is going very well, but Bobbs has promised to try to do something more about it. I noticed in the Book of the Month bulletin it was in a list of best sellers for January. That may mean very little, that a few stores so reported it. Certainly Caroline has been badly treated, and I'm not sure that Bobbs has done all they should have done by me; or that they had the wit to know what to do. Of course, turning in the mss. so late was a drawback. The war makes it hard to complain. My own doubts as to the popular appeal further tie my hands.

Knickerbocker is impossible, of course. He led me to believe he had only seen you at a distance. He has never seen Pamela. He is plainly unbalanced and not responsible for his speech and acts. He talks incessantly at the sandwich shop, coherently for five minutes and then he is off. I was so annoyed at the editors' notice in the *Southern Review*[1] that I didn't write a letter of protest. Politics is all right up to the moment of decision. To continue it afterwards is not an act of manhood.

Caroline: I meant to write a letter all by itself in answer to yours, but I've taken it to heart instead. Both ways it gave the kind of encouragement I need, although you have way yonder overestimated my talents. Many times I think that the accident which started me writing was not a happy one. I haven't a thing in my head just now to do. I have enjoyed this winter, taking it easy and reading, staying up late at night without the guilty feeling of bad work on the morrow.

Let us hear soon; especially if you want me to mention your name to Guerry.

With love from all of us, A.

TLS

1. In the Winter issue, 1941, there is an announcement that the magazine faced suspension with the Spring issue.

16 Linden Lane
Princeton, N. J.
February 6, 1942

Dear Brother:

I've been pondering your letter for two days, until I should know a little more clearly what I wanted to say. You have made me review my whole situation very critically. Since I wrote you last we have been in Washington, where I saw some Congressmen and a couple of army officers. The results were vague but may lead to something, yet not too quickly to keep me from exhausting every other possibility.

I think you are right in believing that the service would not be [a] stop gap, but a long gap; that both attracts and repels me. I fear it, and yet because I am convinced that the state of war is going to be our permanent state—that is, for at least a generation—I reason that I might as well be in it, because out of it I will face something like liquidation. It is true that poetry and criticism have never paid, but indirectly they have led to jobs which virtually amounted to pay. I think that is all over for us; if it is ever restored it will be for the next generation.

I know this reasoning is too pat. It will very likely be possible for us to dig in somewhere and scrape up a living; but then there is the problem of Nancy. It has been nearly two years since Ben remarked that he would send her to college; he made the offer when we were first at Princeton, and he was impressed with me for the first time. Although he knows that my leaving here this June will not be due to any fault of mine, the business mentality cannot escape its pattern; and he is bound to think there is something wrong with me or I could have kept the job indefinitely. (He would think I could keep it because he wanted me to keep it.) No, Brother Ben will not stake us to a new venture at Benfolly. He is still the same Brother Ben—munificent when we don't need it, but canny when we do. Nevertheless we will probably go either to Benfolly or, as I wrote you, get a small cottage on the mountain.

As to the Academy jobs, I'd like to hear more about them and especially whether Guerry would commit himself to your plan so far in advance. You are already settled on the mountain and could just slide into the job. It would be harder for me. But I would certainly consider it very seriously if it might lead to the *Review* in a couple of years. So let me know the results of your next talk with him.

If Guerry has any gumption at all, he ought to see that the collapse of the SR *[Southern Review]*—which, John writes me, will probably be followed this summer by the flop of the KR *[Kenyon Review]*—gives him the whole field for the *Sewanee Review.* A subsidy of about $3,000 to pay contributors would be all that is needed. I believe that could be raised. In fact, Wood Carper, who is very much interested in this plan, says that he can get it from the alumni.

I am sending "Peru" to the Colt Press today. If they make you an offer you can put it up to Chambers.

There was an interesting and depressing end to my negotiations with Gauss. Last year, when I was reappointed for the third year, two members of the Committee remarked that the "policy of rotation," which required a change of the incumbent every two years at least, seemed to have lapsed. This gave me the idea that I might possibly expect to be here another year, or two more, making the entire five years of the Carnegie grant. I had no reason to expect it, yet it seemed possible. In a talk with Gauss the other day, he said that the Committee had decided *last year,* when I was reappointed, that the policy of rotation *must* go into effect at the end of my third year. So Gauss told me [a] very pointed lie; and I am wondering why he did it. It was wholly unnecessary; he could easily have said that the Committee had just decided it, or that *he* had decided it—since he is the Committee, the others being his yes-men. I am very depressed by this. Doubtless administrators have to lie on occasion, but I can't see this as such an occasion; and I can't see Gauss as the kind of man who would tell a gratuitous lie. Moreover, he ought to have known that the grapevine might have given me the facts which would expose the lie. I am perplexed.

You have already received Nancy's letter. The prospect of being a godmother has given her a tremendous thrill. She immediately telephoned all her friends, and boasted about it. I am relieved that you too see something in Nancy's poems. She has evidently written a good many, but these two are the only ones she will show us. I suppose there is nothing we can do about her or for her, so far as poetry is concerned. It would be a great mistake to press her about it; and we must face the probability that she may not continue it. She will be living in a difficult world. There has been a vast change in her this year. She still has and doubtless will always have this violence of nature, but I suspect that she will never be wholly committed to it; even now I can detect in her a constant observation of herself.

We plan to come to Tennessee unless I get a job of some kind and will probably come down anyhow for a while. The mountain will not be as attractive without you all; so we are thinking about Edna's suggestion that we come to Headlong Hall.[1] I would see it as immediately possible if the schoolhouse were practicable. Neither of us remembers it distinctly enough to judge. But we can go into these problems later.

I am more and more convinced that George Haight is a very remarkable friend. It is one of the incomprehensible things; it must be accepted as something unpredictable and final.

I suppose it is just as well that we are not to be here next year. My dislike of this part of the world is rapidly mounting to hatred, and I must get away from it.

Our love to you all. Kiss Pamela for me.

Allen

TLS

P.S. Nancy said your letter to her was the most wonderful she had ever received. You said things to her that we couldn't have said; they were just the things that will be good for her coming from you.

1. The first name of the Lytles' farm in Portland.

February 17, 1942

Dear Brother:

I enclose a note from William Roth, the man who runs the Colt Press.[1] His first reaction is very good; I believe he will do the book. Even if Chambers wants to do it, I would urge you to let the Colt press go ahead. In the long run a limited edition (recall K. A. P.)[2] will do more for you.

What's the news on your front? There's been a startling development on ours. The development has far to go yet, but it is at least something. Last Tuesday I had a long distance call from Philip Davidson of Agnes Scott College, and yesterday a letter, offering me the editorship of a new magazine to take the place of the SR *[Southern Review]*. Davidson said that the money was in sight, but not yet in hand, and he must wait until it is before he makes me a legal proposition. The thing ought to come to a showdown within two weeks. I would do part-time teaching in the Univ. of Georgia, Agnes Scott, and Emory, in rotation, in addition to the editing. All three colleges are backing the project.

What do you think of it? And how would you all like to move to Decatur, where the headquarters would probably be? We could have a good time running this magazine. I don't know how much money there will be, and of course they may try to give me one of their men to help me; but I imagine I will be able to write my own ticket.

We simply can't believe that this thing is real. And I am going ahead and making my formal application to the Navy tomorrow. Wood Carper was here yesterday, and I showed him Davidson's letter. He says it gives him an opening to bring the Sewanee situation up when he sees Guerry in N.Y. on Thursday at an alumni dinner.

If the thing in Georgia really comes off I'll wire you. Meanwhile please keep it entirely to yourselves. Our enemies are not above sabotage.

I've been so depressed by the Pacific situation that I haven't been able to sleep. We're in for rough times.

Love to you all.

Allen

TLS

P.S. Each of us thought that the other had written you about the picture. It's a fine one, and now you and Bro. Ben face each other across the length of the downstairs rooms.

1. See Appendix H. 2. After being published in *Hound and Horn* in 1930, "Flowering Judas" was republished that same year as the title story of Porter's first short story collection. The six stories were printed in a limited edition of 600 copies.

Princeton
March 2, 1942

Dear Brother:

It's mighty good news about the job at the Academy. A thousand dollars is a lot of money, particularly in that part of the world. We are both struck with the very cheerful tone of your letter, the only hopeful word we've had from anybody. If I don't get out of this region soon I'll have to be put in a padded cell.

The situation in Georgia is still hanging fire. It's the money, of course, in spite of the fact that they have told me that it is "in sight." Meanwhile if you want to talk to Guerry, go ahead. Wood had a very frank talk with him—frank on both sides. Guerry said that if he could possibly help it he would not recommend K[nickerbocker] to the board for another year, that he had already told him he'd have to go because he had done more harm to the University than anybody else ever connected with it, etc. But when Wood mentioned me, Guerry became a little cagey, asking: "Do you think he would be a good man for the job?"—as if he might be thinking the opposite. No doubt it is the work of [Edwin] Mims: I would bet anything he has already consulted Mims on this question. But Wood went on to explain that he was personally very enthusiastic and that other alumni were, and that perhaps some money could be raised to pay contributors if I were chosen. Maybe this influenced him, but Wood wasn't sure.

I would much rather be at Sewanee than in Georgia. The Georgian society would be more varied but it would also be more harassing. That is, I'd prefer Sewanee if Guerry saw the point about the *Review*. There would be no point in taking it over as it is—a graveyard for second-rate professors.

The Georgia situation is complicted by the fact that before it came up John had proposed a merger of the KR *[Kenyon Review]* and the SR *[Southern Review]*. Red and Cleanth feel that the merger might be the only way in which the KR could survive, while the Georgia magazine could get started without the SR name and subscription list. I contest this view because John proposes a budget of $8,500 for the merged magazine, $2500 of which he would have to raise. But since he has *some* money already, why can't he go on alone? The amusing feature of the situation is that Red and Cleanth see John's offer as a gesture of perfect nobility which would perpetuate the name of the SR. I see it as partly that, and also as a way of boosting the subscription list of the KR by about 1000 and as also a talking point to raise money. All of which is perfectly legitimate, but there's no reason not to see it realistically. So I've put it up to Red and Cleanth to decide whether they would rather survive nominally with the KR, or have a full-sized Southern magazine carry on the name. I suspect that John will win the decision because he is being noble, while I out of an interested motive would want the name and subscription list of the SR for the new magazine.

I hope the five classes a day don't wear you to the bone.[1] It sounds tough, but you can stand it for three months. How long are the classes? Forty minutes, I suppose. And what are they?

As to Guerry, I should think that you might talk to him pretty soon. The Georgia matter may come to a head any day; when it does, I will not be able to hold them off very long.

You say that Edna accused you of giving Pamela pneumonia; but I gather she didn't really have it. Which reminds me that Laura Auberjonois came down with it last Wednesday, but after four days of sulfanilamide she is ready to go home from the hospital. She had fever of a 105.

Love to your two ladies.

Allen

TLS

1. Lytle has taken a temporary position at the Sewanee Academy.

April 19, 1942

Dear Brother:

Edna's letter came the other day, and we gather that you all have been pretty busy and hectic. The five classes a day are enough to get a body down. We'll be leaving here in a little more than six weeks, but what direction to take we don't yet know. So many things are hanging fire. The Navy is the only prospect so far completely eliminated; the others aren't actually prospects but some of them [may] become so.

What we were thinking of for the summer was the possibility of renting Mrs. [Elizabeth] Buntin's brick house, the one you all were interested in at first; and then if we liked it we thought we might sell Benfolly and move into your neighborhood. Miss Carrie shudders every time she thinks of Benfolly, and I recoil at the expense of living there. We need a small farm but a real one. At any rate Mrs. Buntin's house would be a good place to spend the summer, and we could scout around from there. I had an offer of $6,500 for Benfolly last year. I believe I could get $8,000 now.

But the main purpose of this letter is to urge you to take the job in history at Sewanee. You could do some farming from there, and spend three months at the farm every year. Of course, we are right at the center of the hysterical excitement about the war, but it is not hysteria, it is rather a long view that I had before 1939, that the next war would liquidate people like us; and God knows when we will get another chance to function. I think a job is very important. For God's sake take it!

I gather from Edna's letter that, at the time of writing, we probably knew more about the Knickerbocker situation than you all did. Guerry wrote to Wood Carper asking for a statement about Knickerbocker, but Wood couldn't write it; it was an inconsiderate request. It was perfectly all right for Wood to tell Guerry orally what he thought of K., but that's very different from writing it. Wood believes that Guerry, like most executives, wanted to pass the buck by getting other people to support his decision to fire K. Besides Wood was definitely on the spot, since he had urged my case; so he wrote Guerry that he couldn't plead for a friend unless the job was already open, i.e., unless Knickerbocker was already fired. Guerry wrote back a very curt letter. And that's where it stands now, except that Guerry wrote to Diehl at Southwestern about me, but for some reason hasn't written to Princeton.

We simply don't know what to do. Houghton Mifflin are angling for Miss Carrie,[1] and if they come through the advance plus what I can get from Putnam's will easily see us through a year. Sarah Lawrence College has practically offered Miss Carrie a part-time job at $2000, and I may get one there too filling in for Horace Gregory. Cleanth [Brooks] writes me that Red has accepted a full professorship at Minnesota,[2] and that there's a move in the department there to get me to fill his place. I don't want to go there. I have been interviewed by members of the Donovan committee—Coordinator of Information—and I saw the inner workings of the office. I doubt if I could last two weeks. The propaganda is on a cynically low level, and nobody I talked to there believed in what he was doing.

How do you stand in relation to the draft? I supposed you registered in February, as I did. My order number is 14,578 in the national lottery; but since the local board has only 1500 numbers, mine becomes 967, about two-thirds up. For a while dependents will mean exemption, but not for long.

Caroline has written a long first chapter of her new novel, and it is very fine.[3] I spend practically all my time running around interviewing people. I spent a lot of money getting up this South American anthology for John Bishop, but now John has been fired, and I may not be paid for the work. I'd be willing to contribute the work towards the war, but I can't afford the $250.00 I've spent doing it.

Since you all will not be at Monteagle we are not sure that we want to be there all summer. We simply won't descend upon you all at the farm. Could you let me have any information about Mrs. Buntin's house, or would it be better for me to write her direct? And what is her address?

We're mighty anxious to see you all, not least Pamela. We're coming down for a while anyhow, either to the mountain or to Benfolly, whatever we decide to do. Love from us all to you all.

Allen

TLS

When Edna[4] says her sister [Jane] is going to use the cottage the first two weeks in June I can't make out whether she means the cottage on the farm or the Log Cabin at Monteagle. Would you consider renting the Log Cabin this summer? We could stall around somewhere till Sister was through with it. If the ladies wanted to come up any time during the summer we would be delighted, of course, and I would turn the housekeeping over to Miss May while they were there. Also Mr. Bob could use us for a halfway station on his way to Headlong. But please don't consider renting it to us unless it really suits you. You know there are dozens of cabins we could rent there.

C.

TLS

1. H. M. has indicated an interest in publishing Caroline Gordon's fiction. 2. Warren left L.S.U. after *The Southern Review* was suspended and took a position at the University of Minnesota as professor of English and director of the Creative Writing program. 3. *The Women on the Porch* (NY: Charles Scribner's Sons, 1944). 4. Lytle's wife.

Sewanee, Tenn.
April 23, 1942

Dear Brother:

We have just come back from Nashville and the farm. I wrote you a letter to send by air, but it got lost in the movement. The logistics of moving this family is now very complicated. As a result Edna is sick with a bad throat and several degrees of fever, but we think the baby has escaped. It is rather difficult as I am at the Academy from seven until two, and tomorrow I am there all day up to midnight on guard. You would not like it. It is a twenty-four hour a day job and requires a certain kind of mind and a certain kind of talent. I can think of nothing more wearing. Day labor would be far preferable.

At last I got a line up on the situation here. It took me some time because my hours and Guerry's did not meet. And he was away a great deal of the time. He still refuses to commit himself on Knickerbocker. Your recent letter explains much, but the real fly in the ointment, I believe, is a recent Southern college meeting at Nashville. He enquired around and got the idea that you would be difficult. But since he is accustomed to intrigue, he minimized the reports; but you must understand the sympathy existing between college executives. I made a full and complete argument about the magazine and the necessity for the University to have distinguished men on the campus and just what prestige you and the magazine would give it. How much he discounts what I say as a friend and how much he discounted it otherwise I have no way of knowing. At any rate he has not yet made up his mind about Knickerbocker, and nothing would happen until he does. But I believe he will keep on working around until he does see the light.

Now here is the situation otherwise. Mrs. Buntin has deeded the little farm to Sinclair, he thinks so that she can cut him off in her will. At the moment he has put an old carpenter in the house who is running it for him. The carpenter is doing some building and fixing up the barn and improving the place generally. So renting that is out. He will sell, I believe, for five thousand dollars. Whereas you could not do at the start much real farming, you could have your garden and make enough wheat and hay and corn to feed several cows and even run a few sheep. Sinclair is doing it. It has that wonderful spring on it and a creek. The government payment ought to pay your taxes.

The little schoolhouse has had corn in it and broke through the floor. It would take a while to get it in shape, besides moving corn. The thing to do is go to Monteagle and stay until July. By that time we will have the house in some kind of shape. We are putting in two bathrooms, making an upstairs and a downstairs apartment. You all could occupy the upstairs one. Then you could look around and see what you wanted to do, whether to settle in that country or not, and we could talk everything over. The time you spend at Monteagle would make it possible to see Guerry. I've noticed that he works better that way. For example, if I hadn't called him over to Monteagle that time, I don't believe he ever would have had the idea of getting me on the campus, even though I was only six miles away. You wouldn't mind if your occupancy of the cabin overlapped a few days with Edna's sister: nor would she mind. The ladies will never move out of M'boro again.

I myself am torn about teaching here next year. I don't think I am going to do it. I may weaken at the last moment. So far no definite offer has been made me. I dislike teaching heartily. It is merely a question of money, and unless we can save enough out of the salary to justify us, we won't stay. I will know more about it after I get to the farm. Another thing. I don't know whether George [Haight] would be putting up this money to fix up the farm, if he thought I would not settle down to writing. But more of this later. In wartimes, of course, there would be certain advantages to being here. But I can think of disadvantages. And what if I am called? Wouldn't Edna be better off at the farm?

I will write again soon. I am so rushed I can scarcely think.

Our love to all of you. Pamela is very, very cunning. She is going to be a big girl.

Andrew

TLS

April 28, 1942

Dear Brother:

We still don't know whether you all want to rent us the Log Cabin. That's the basis on which we could occupy it, since you would easily rent it to somebody else. If it were not rentable at all, it might be different; but I gather that cottages will be in demand there this summer. Also, is there much furniture left? That is, enough for us to get by on? We need a double bed for us and a single bed for Nancy. Under the circumstances we can't consider company. We'd like to know about this as soon as possible. We're in a swivet of uncertainty—but I take it no more than you all are.

It isn't clear to me whether the offer you've had from Sewanee is from the University or the Academy; if the latter, it might kill you even though you all could eat; if the former, I still urge you to take it. You could do some farming from that distance, and the farm would remain as a base underlying the cash income from the job. It isn't as if the job meant giving up the farm altogether. Of course, if you have a new subject for a novel and can get right to it, the farm is undoubtedly the place to go. But nobody could expect you or anybody else just to sit down and "write" in times like these. George is too intelligent to require that or even have any feeling about it.

Yesterday after your letter came I saw Gauss on the campus and told him your report of Guerry's feeling that I might be "difficult." He laughed and said that his letter to Guerry adequately covered that point. I doubt that Guerry had received it at the time you talked with him. Gauss couldn't have written it before Wednesday of last week. But as you say it all depends upon whether Guerry can get rid of Knickerbocker. He is evidently writing all over the country trying to get a job. I suspect that Guerry would rather have it appear that Knickerbocker is leaving of his own choice. We'll just have to wait.

Meanwhile Miss Carrie may get a part-time job at Sarah Lawrence which along with our publishers' advances might see us through next year; but of course we'd have to live in New York. And I want to leave the East.

I'm inclined to think that Sinclair Buntin has a buyer for his place if he will take $5,000. We could easily sell Benfolly for $6,500. I would any day rather have the Buntin place. It is a nice house, and the land is good farming land. From this point of view Benfolly has always been hopeless. Now that Merrimont is broken up there's no reason for Caroline to be in that neighborhood.

Caroline has read this, and says that since we can't leave here until the 7th of June we couldn't get to Monteagle until around the 12th or 13th since we are stopping in Washington for a few days. By that time Edna's sister might be gone. It might be as late as the 15th, if we visited in Nashville for a day or two.

Let us know your plans as soon as possible. We'll let you know ours. Love to your ladies.

Allen

TLS

Sunday
[May 1942]

Dear Brother:

You all must think we are mighty slow arranging affairs at this end, but things here have not been straightening themselves out quickly. I literally do not have the energy to compose a letter at the end of the day, now that the Academy has put off on me the commencement play. Pamela has been sick with bowel trouble; at the same time Edna was down with a strep throat and fever, so that she had to take sulfathiazole. It doesn't take much imagination to see our state. They are all well known. Edna still lacks strength and is run down . . . but there [have] been no pleasant doings around here.

I haven't written you, even, about the record.[1] There is no doubt that your poems gain by your voice. As often as I have heard you read them, and not so often at that, the record gives them a distance almost in time, a mysterious, prophetic quality. I had the strange feeling I was hearing this familiar but strange voice coming out of an ancient time, released perhaps from a buried Ilium. There was a stern, admonitory quality to the tones, given maybe by the drive of the whirling disc, but it was very effective.

I would like to write a long letter. I have a great deal to say, much about Knickerbocker, and other things. But to come quickly to things you want to know. First of all, Knickerbocker is doomed. He said so in my company and everybody but Guerry says so, and as he does not deny it, I'm rather certain he is definitely out. Your information supports this. I would almost bet that you are in the V.C.'s mind as his successor. I have heard no other name mentioned. I've made myself clear that I don't want it, although Guerry seems to want me to stay on the mountain. He has made me a proposition, one temporary and the other permanent, neither one of which has to do with the English department or the *Review*. This is encouraging, and I wish that you would hold back on the L.S.U. offer as long as you could. It would be worth it to have the prospect of our being together here in the winters and on nearby farms in the summers. That would decide me in accepting my offer. It is not to teach at the Academy but at the University, temporarily taking history and perhaps one class in creative writing. The permanent offer is too contingent now to have allowed to mention, but it might work out well as a buttress to writing. Sewanee has its drawbacks but they would not be so oppressive as L.S.U. I should think. Tell Caroline I have spoken to all the head men at the Academy about Manson [Radford]. I can't do anything until I am certain he doesn't go into the army. Could he make a trip down here to be seen. The only drawback there, I think, is the need for bachelors to live on the floors with the boys. At present there will be only one apartment vacancy for a married couple in the building. This might not suit Rose and Manson. Enquire.

Now about the cabin. We have written Edna's sister that she must expect to let you all have it the middle of June. This is all right as we told her you all would probably want it. But there is another hitch. Mercury has offered it to Ladies. Mama was enthusiastic, but since she doesn't know me now or has little mind left this enthusiasm lacks authority, but not to Mercury. May would not commit herself. So that is the situation there. I don't think there is much chance in their going, but there is a chance. Why don't you take it the last two weeks in June, planning to stay on if they don't come, or looking around for another house if they do. If you insist, you can pay this year's taxes, which are around seventy dollars.

With the gas rationing, now that things move so fast, this is not going to let us see you all much. Therefore the first moment we get in shape at the farm, we want you to come up there.

It would have been so simple if Dad had not had the romantic idea that Monteagle would be fine for Miss Molly, when it will probably mean her end if she goes. She's nearly ninety and terribly confused. But Dad is full of plans, now since he sold twenty-two bales of cotton for over three thousand dollars. He has weaned us almost completely, forgotten he gave me the cabin; has taken it back and plans to begin all over again.

The moment I get my breath I will write again. I like, Caroline, the sound of your change to Houghton. The fanfare they will give you may be that very thing needed to do which the complacency of Scribner's failed to do. I have stirring vaguely a glimmer of an idea. Our love to all of you. Tell Nancy we have taken the first pictures of Pamela. If they turn out well, we'll send them on.

Andrew

TLS

Of course another thing—the war situation is changing so rapidly, we might be in a training camp before another six months. This thought keeps any permanent plans tenuous. Another thing—I'm afraid of getting caught in a university.

1. Tate has recorded a selection of his poems for The Library of Congress.

Monteagle, Tennessee
December 9, 1942

Dear Brother:

There is something wrong, and I think you ought to tell me what it is. If I have done anything to offend you or if you disapprove of me in some general way, you ought to tell me. Or if you don't quite know what it is, I think you ought to face it and make up your mind about it, and then tell me. In any case, you have a definite obligation to tell me.

I may be wrong, but I think I see further than this personal aspect. You seem to me to be going through a severe crisis, and your attitude towards me may be only a phase of this crisis. About this I have only one thing to say: You ought to meet this crisis with clear and energetic ideas and not, as you seem to be doing, in a daze in which you are not completely alive. You ought to do this at any cost.

If there's one truth of human relations above all others, it is that we *are* our brothers' keepers. I refuse to sit by and see you gradually dissolve.

However, I feel that I must reassure you on one point. If I am wrong about your crisis, if your attitude is personal and directed towards me, I will accept your grievance as final; and I assure you that I will withdraw altogether, without a struggle. I only insist that you ought to tell me what the grievance is, because I am at least due a hearing.

People simply cannot fade away from each other after fifteen years of our sort of friendship. If they part they must do it with understanding and complete clarity.

I have forborne to write this letter for nearly two months because I couldn't stand to add to your anxieties. I write now only because I think that it would be dangerous to withhold it longer.

Allen

AL

Monteagle, Tennesee
January 11, 1943

Dear Brother:

Since Nancy will be catching a ride I will not be coming to Sewanee much; so I am writing you about that article I left with you. I had just finished it, but looking it over again I can't see that it is good enough to stand as a magazine article, though possibly it may do for its purpose in this Dictionary. I want you to use your own good judgment, of course, but I would feel more comfortable if it were supressed. I wrote it in one day, and it shows it. I gave it to you precipitately because I was eager to give you something, but this has mis-fired.

I have been blind, but now my eyes are wide, if reluctantly, open to the fact that I shouldn't have taken it upon myself to help you so extensively in getting your editorship under way. You haven't liked it, and I haven't been writing to acknowledge it. It is, as you know, an extremely complex matter which extends far beyond the *Review* into other causes. I don't think any amount of discussion will remove those causes; so I am opposed to discussing them, as I assume that you too are opposed. Time will either cure or aggravate this loss of confidence between us, and I think that all that can be done now is to acknowledge the loss—an acknowledgment which honor demands. Silence on this sad matter, on your part, will sufficiently acknowledge it to me.

There will probably be one more manuscript from a poet solicited by me—Weldon Kees, who is extremely good.

Aff. Allen

TLS

Sewanee
Jan. 14, 1943

Dear Brother:—

Some times there are simple answers to questions. I say this because I believe that if my car had not broken down over the weekend and the press delayed, you would not have written that letter. Of course, I wanted you to help on the *Review* or I wouldn't have let you. The only thing that has troubled me is this: your usual generosity and affection for your friends has in this instance led you to do almost everything for the magazine of an institution which has less than a claim on you. This has worried me a little, especially since I have felt some chagrin at editing it at all, when you have the perfect qualifications. My own are limited, my interest more so and my position temporary. Perhaps I should have made my feeling in this matter more directly clear, but I thought you understood my reticence. As far as I am concerned, there has been no loss of confidence in you. My affection and my admiration for you professionally is as great as ever. I do not, as I once did, believe everything you do in the realm of action fine and sound. There is merely the maturity of judgment, either right or wrong, and has really nothing to do with a long time friendship. Nobody remains static nor is any relationship even towards yourself, constant. I tried to explain something of this before Christmas.

I have had a set of galleys made to bring over, and I will Saturday if you want to fool with reading them. The galleys won't be complete until tomorrow or Sat. morning. But I would like for you to see what is in the issue and to pass judgment on it.

Affectionately, Andrew

AL

Monteagle, Tennessee
January 15, 1943

Dear Brother:

I'll be looking for you tomorrow with the proofs. I have never felt that I was trying to help an institution, but you and the cause of letters which must be served whoever is sponsoring it.

I don't want to seem relentless; but I do think we are back to my first letter on this subject. There is something I have *done* that you don't like, and it shows conspicuously in your bearing toward me. I have done many things for a living that I didn't want to do, but I have never felt that I have acted so far out of character that I have been compromised. I think, then, that you owe me, however painful it may be for us both, an explanation of your view of my failure of action, for it seems that action is the plane upon which you place it. I agree with you that relationships change, but the normal change need never break the old relationship if it was soundly based. Ours was; so there is something specific, not mere alteration of time, which explains your attitude.

You can well understand how much I need your explanation for my own continued well-being, particularly if this is a matter in which I have failed you, or in which I have reduced my scale in your eyes.

I'll be here all day tomorrow; so come at any time. There is a slight grievance on my part, wholly impersonal, which I feel that I ought to explain to you.

Yrs., Allen

AL

Monteagle, Tennessee
May 16, 1943

Dear Brother:

I am sending you my Mesures lecture[1] which I haven't had time to revise very much; and I won't have time, since I am trying to finish my book[2] by the end of July; but if you want it as it is, you are more than welcome to it. I don't know whether you would have room for it in your summer issue; but if you are going to use it I should like if possible to have it appear then.

Yrs., Allen

TLS

P.S. Your spring issue is even better than its predecessor, even though it lacks anything as brilliant as the [Wallace] Stevens poems.[3]

TLS

1. The general topic for the Princeton Mesures Lecture in 1943 was "Poetry and the Actual World." On April 8, Tate read "Dostoevsky's Hovering Fly: A Causerie on the Imagination and the Actual World" which appeared as the lead article in the summer issue of *The Sewanee Review,* pp. 353–69. 2. *The Vigil of Venus: Pervigilium Veneris,* Tate's translation of and introduction to the Latin text, was published by the Cummington Press in Cummington, Massachusetts, 1943. 3. "Dutch Graves in Bucks County," *The Sewanee Review,* 51 (Winter 1943), 14–15.

Sewanee, Tennessee
May 19, 1943

Dear Brother:

I am glad to get the Mesures lecture. We needed a lead article for the summer issue. Of course, it is very fine and will distinguish the number. [Delmore] Schwartz said something about sending in a piece on Dostoevsky and the man who did the piece on Faulkner[1] promises another on the same subject. So it happens that, with luck, there will be a kind of symposium, with special treatments to support your treatment of a general critical problem.

Tell Caroline I wrote [William] Meredith[2] today.

Yours, Andrew

TLS

1. Harry M. Campbell, "Experiment and Achievement: *As I Lay Dying* and *The Sound and the Fury*," *The Sewanee Review,* 51 (1943), 305–320. 2. A young poet who had graduated from Princeton and served as a reporter for *The New York Times*. Two of his poems appeared in the 1943 Winter issue of *The Sewanee Review,* 20–21, "Navy Field" and "Airman's Venture." He also contributed to Tate's *Princeton Verse Between Two Wars: An Anthology* (1942).

Monteagle, Tennessee
May 24, 1943

Dear Brother:

I am glad you like the lecture. I was just thinking that if you haven't already sent it over to the press I might go over it once more, since I'm taking a couple days' breathing spell, and save proof corrections. I have to go to Nashville tomorrow but I'll be back Wednesday night or Thursday morning. If it is already in type it won't make much difference, and of course I'll keep corrections down to the minimum. It has just occurred to me that Willard Thorp might do you some reviews. He has been doing them free for the *Va. Quarterly;* so why not for you? Willard does a very competent job of reviewing, particularly in American literary history.

Yrs., Allen

TLS

Portland, Tenn.
Rt. #1
Oct. 18, 1943

Dear Brother:

I am still hard run. I have been in Alabama a great deal, under difficult travelling conditions, with the added embarrassment and trouble of picking up my family and setting them down on people while I go about business I have to attend to but don't want to. Jimmy [Darwin][1] is not well and cannot do much. I hope now that we will be selling out there, but how long it will take I don't know. I've already made two recent trips to try to sell some farms. Each trip has boosted the price of Cornsilk, as there are several who want it, but it delays us here, getting ready for winter. Tell Lon[2] the lights have finally been approved, but the Northington man now tells me I have to get my neighbors' houses wired before he will run the line. If he had told me that earlier, we probably would be fixed. I don't know what we would have done without Lon in this matter, as it will not be possible to live here with pleasure without waterworks.

I've had no chance to finish the story.[3] If we can get our own apartment ready to live in and let the rest of the house go for the time being, I will be able to get down to work again. It is tiring to be thwarted in these material matters, like one of those dreams of running in molasses with a monster after you.

I lost your note, but I would certainly like anything you can drum up for the *Review*. [Walter] Watkins[4] had got hold of certain things. I was glad in a way to carry on for another issue, as I need the money. I got a call from Washington in regard to working in the war department, writing biographies of generals, etc. I am going to decline it, a kind [of] journalism, I imagine. Forty-four hundred, which would mean a repetition of Sewanee. Hard as this winter promises to be, I think we will stick it out here and give this place a thorough trial, although I have had so much trouble with it, at times I've grown to dislike it.

Watkins said something about you reviewing Red's poems.[5] Has he put out another book? Did you get a copy of the last *Review*? It has several weak articles, but it was the best we could do. If you want to write up these poems still, I would like to have them.

No more now. I've got to catch up on back correspondence.

Yrs., Andrew

TLS

1. Polly's husband. 2. Brainard Cheney. 3. Probably "The Guide." 4. Watkins was supposed to take over editorship, but because of a breakdown he went home on indefinite leave. Lytle remained editor for an additional issue to allow the administration time to make other arrangements. 5. Horace Gregory reviewed Warren's *Selected Poems, 1923–43,* in *The Sewanee Review,* 52 (Autumn 1944), 575–78, 587.

The Library of Congress
Washington
Reference Department
December 15, 1943

Dear Brother:

I am about to leave for N.Y., but I must get this off to tell you that Red's poems have evidently been postponed. So that review is out, at least temporarily. Bill Meredith's long poem hasn't reached me yet, and it is likely that *Poetry* is taking it. I am sending an article of my own which you are welcome to for this issue or which could be held over for spring or summer, as you think best.[1] Several times I have written Alex [Guerry] that if Long would tell me his needs for spring and summer, I would try to get what I can. For obvious reasons I have hesitated to write to Long direct.

My correspondence with Alex since mid-October has been frequent; every letter I get from him increases his stature in my eyes. The approach to the Rockefeller Foundation was a ticklish affair; but Alex gave his consent; and I am to present the case for the *Review* day after tomorrow in New York. The chances for success are very favorable. It would mean about $4,000 a year for three years. If we could ever get as many as 3000 subscribers (not wholly improbable) the *Review* would not need outside help. I am convinced that Alex will cooperate to the fullest extent. I am making a point of consulting him on all business matters, and he seems to appreciate it—after his experience with Knickerbocker.

It is mighty fine that Corn Silk brought such a good price. That and the Huntsville lots ought to ease your situation enormously. I want all the news of you that you have time to send me. How is the writing? Mine is at a standstill, but I expect (with Fannie [Cheney's][2] expert help) to go ahead again on *office time* right after Jan. 1st. I have worked out a technique of dictating the first draft which is wholly changing any style I had, but it is certainly no worse. We want you to give Edna our love and tell her that we think of her most affectionately.

Yrs., Allen

AL

P.S. Bad news about Jimmie. Has Polly had another baby?

1. Tate's "The Techniques of Fiction" appeared in *Sewanee Review,* 52 (Spring 1944), 210–225. 2. Frances Cheney was Tate's assistant while he was a consultant in poetry at the Library of Congress.

Portland, Tenn.
Jan. 18, 1944

Dear Brother:

Your piece[1] came here, and I didn't get here until after Christmas. I have been commuting between Alabama and Sewanee. I had to put the family in Memphis and then go get them. Since our return here we have been mud and ice bound. I finally got the county to build me a new road, change it so that it would take in some fine trees in front of the house and move the road farther away. It is a beautiful road, but we can't use it. They promise to rock it as soon as they can get in. I am now trying to get ready for turkey raising, which I promised the government to do for the light line. It is going to be hard to get the material for houses, etc. I wish I didn't have to do it.

I sent your piece on to [Tudor] Long[2] for spring publication. As I wrote you, I mentioned to him your proffer to help in any way and he said he wished he had time to run up and see you in Washington. Since you have written Guerry about this and I have mentioned it to Long, I gather that Long doesn't want any help but wants to be an editor on his own during that time. I suggest you let the matter drop unless you hear from them. Did you have luck in New York about getting your money. It certainly will make it possible to do the thing in the proper way and give the magazine a start whereby it could carry itself. I don't feel so bad now about telling people that if they would contribute gratis to keep the magazine going, it would work into a paying thing.

We got your announcement of Nancy's marriage.[3] They will make a go of it, and they certainly were in love. I hear reports that they are staying in Miss Daisey's [Bagley] house at Monteagle. Monteagle is certainly a backlog and has proved a refuge for me many times.

Winding up the estate[4] has taken far more time than I could afford, and Jimmy hasn't been well enough to push it along. He is better this time of year, and they won't go West until later. They had a little girl in June. Named Mary Nelson.

I have been working some on my short story.[5] I would like to get it finished before the turkeys arrive. No other news with us. Our love to the Cheneys.[6]

Yours, Andrew

TLS

1. "The Techniques of Fiction." 2. The head of the English department. At that time, this position made Long titular editor of the *Review*. 3. Nancy Tate married Percy Wood, a Vanderbilt student in psychiatry, January 3, 1944. 4. Lytle's father, Robert Lytle, had died early in 1943. 5. "The Guide." 6. The Cheneys were also living in Washington at the time.

The Library of Congress
Washington
Reference Department
April 26, 1944

Dear Brother:

I very much need for *my first issue* the story you are working on. Can you finish it by early July? Please try to.

It seems that Red may succeed me here for one year.[1] Why he wants to come I don't know, but he seems to be excited by the prospect.

We leave for Tennessee in exactly two months.

Yrs., Allen

AL

1. Warren is appointed to the Chair of Poetry, Library of Congress, in 1944.

Sewanee Review
Portland, Tennessee
May 13, 1944

Dear Brother:

I have been waiting to see what time I would have. Your note came when I was in the first press of the turkeys. My preparations were not of the best and the weather was fearful, cold and constant rain, and I was trying the feather boards which I did not understand. Then in the midst of everything—more than Edna and I could do—Jesse up and leaves. Slips in the night and takes her clothes, and without seeing us, slips away again. Always there is the Alabama business which won't be wound up. But we have a girl new who is cooking and the promise of one to help me with the turkeys after strawberry picking . . . so I may be able to get the story to you by July. If you are willing not to count on it.

It is a hard thing to do, and I don't yet see all my way clear. I could make a story of it, but I want to satisfy myself that I have solved the problem. The beginning is right, the ending I vaguely see, see its direction, but the rest has not had time to come.

I am making a heroic effort to get this place in a material way pretty well established this year; so that I can cut loose from it. Edna can do more now that she has had an operation. So we are eased on that score. I've done a good deal, but there is much to do yet. Lon got us the lights, I got a new road cut, et cetera, but none of these matters are completed entirely. For example, there is some bad wiring which I have been trying to get mended for six months.

At times I do not see my way clear, but if I am right, this place will beat for me universities, hack work, as a [way] to live while I work. The times are difficult anyway, but I have hardened myself to the responsibility of my present condition, so fairly recent, and it does not wear me so. It's a gamble, but I am too deeply in to pull out, even if I knew of another gamble that might seem more propitious.

I have learned much that will be of use. For example that regeneration is far more difficult than [restoration?]. The Reconstruction and the after years are much plainer to me now. The war has made me able to compare the process of restoration, with an old house, an old farm, and the scarcity of materials and men . . . .

I ran into Miss Daisy Bagley the other day in town. She told me of Brother Gordon's death. I am very sorry. I am going to write to Caroline the moment I have a breath.

No more now. I wish I could promise the story. Make your plans not to count on it, but I will try.

Yours, Andrew

TLS

Portland, Tenn.
Route 1
Oct. 16, 1944

Dear Brother:

The copy of the *Review* came today.[1] It looks very fine, and it certainly is loaded against big and little guns. Even the local snipers will not waste their mouldy powder but will creep from the laurel, where they have been lurking. I've read some of it, and it gave me the feeling you have only when you are seeing the thing completely turned off. Your notes at the end were just right. With no sociology to mar it, the *Review* will not be embarrassed as was the *Southern* by Pipkin.[2] It will not only carry on but will in many ways be much better. I don't think Sewanee can fail to understand now what it is to have you there. The obvious fact, at least, that you have the widest literary connection in the country all are bound to see. I'd like to hear what reactions you get when there is time for the full impact to be felt.

I am drawing nigh the time I can begin to work again. This has been a hard and frustrating year. Recently we have been threatened with losing our crops. Until a week ago I had three acres of dark, two of one sucker, and two of burley[3] in the fields, with a frost predicted, wet weather, with no sun to make it drop. We cut anyway and of course damaged our crops. Fortunately, nearly half of it was in the barns, but I have had to run around and find barn room and beg and steal more sticks. And my tenants are leaving. It is unpleasant to live in an unfinished house, where everything is inconvenient and the marks of thirty years of tenants confront you, but after I get it underpinned and my turkeys sold, I mean to drop everything else until after the war and get to work.

I have owed you this letter for some time, but each week has been like the last.

I hope you can hold out up there, for it is important that the *Review* hold our profession together in these uncertain years. There will be nothing like it anywhere else in the country. It has already made me hurry through the maze.

I am enclosing Patty's [Patton] letter, which is for you all as well as me.

As ever, Andrew

TLS

P.S. Here's a check for a subscription.

1. Tate has become editor of *The Sewanee Review*. 2. Charles W. Pipkin helped Cleanth Brooks and Robert Penn Warren found *The Southern Review* at L.S.U. in 1935. 3. Kinds of tobacco.

The Sewanee Review
Edited by Allen Tate
October 20, 1944

Dear Brother:

I am mighty glad you like the new *Review*. Everybody here seems to but Henry Gass[1] (even [Howard] Baker likes it) and I only surmise he doesn't from his silence. But the 10 paid advertisements ($650.00) are alone enough to quell opposition, and when you add to that the $1,400 of gift money, the picture is complete. We printed 1200 and the issue is exhausted. We are actually recalling copies from bookstores to fill subscriptions. We may have to put the type on the press again. Whether they really like it here or not is irrelevant, at least for the present; money talks, even at Sewanee.

Alex is like a little boy with a large all-day sucker.

The whole thing comes down to a very simple matter. For the first time they have somebody really interested in doing the job, and they are backing him with money and a full-time assistant.[2] That's the whole story.

We like Sewanee very much. The social life is harmless, and we always have our fingers crossed because we have other resources outside Sewanee.

I am writing Cousin Jinx about Dr. Patton's death. He was quite a hero in his own way.

I hope the turkeys and the tobacco shake down soon, and you get back to writing. I am advertising you in the hope that it will put pressure on you—in addition to the pressures of the farm.

Yrs., Allen

AL

1. Major Henry M. Gass, one-time Headmaster of Sewanee Military and instructor of classical language. 2. Mildred Haun.

Portland, Tenn.
Route 1
March 27, 1945

Dear Brother:

I got your note, and I will have the story ready by May the first. I have been working on two stories, trying something from two different angles. At the moment I have set aside the first story, as it promised to be rather long and I have been too interrupted to work it out. The other story, called, "The Guide," has a duck hunt for scene. I've done about three thousand words. It will run two or three thousand more. This I will send you and then get to the other. Whichever you think best I will submit to the contest.[1] I am getting up at three and four in the morning to get my writing done without interruption from the farm, which is a very hard thing to operate in these times. Ordinarily I would like it better, for I believe for me it is the simplest way to make a living and get any writing done. A university does not serve for me. But now the difficulties are supreme. If I find they require heroism, I will sell the farm. I am no hero.

The *Review* certainly keeps its standard. It is mighty fine that it rises in circulation, which is a mighty comforting judgment. I am mighty glad you are drawing together [John Peale] Bishop's stuff[2] and making a stir about it. Otherwise I am afraid his value to the profession would never have been focused, and so it would have largely got lost.

No more now. It is a little after day, and I have just been interrupted about a corn planter and a man with the cow pox.

Andrew

TLS

1. In collaboration with Prentice-Hall, *The Sewanee Review* sponsored a Southern literary contest in memory of John Peale Bishop who had died April 4, 1944. 2. After Bishop's death, Tate worked with his manuscripts in order to bring out a definitive collection of his poetry. The volume, *The Collected Poems of John Peale Bishop, 1892–1944,* was published by Scribner's in 1948.

The Sewanee Review
Edited by Allen Tate
May 7, 1945

Dear Andrew: [Portland, Tennessee]

I think the story is magnificent[1] and we are going to use it in our July issue. I am not sure that the story shouldn't have a different title, like "The Mahogany Frame," or something like that. On the very last page (27) the phrase "descending night" seems to me to lack edge. Perhaps you don't want it too sharp but I suggest something like "falling night." I am not sure that the very last sentence is clear; it is after a moment's reflection but I think it ought to hit you immediately, or is it clear at all? There remains a little doubt in my mind whose eyes are the eyes in the mahogany frame. If they are the boy's isn't the shift in point of view in the very last sentence of the story pretty violent?

These are the only questions that I would raise about the story at all. Please be thinking about them. In a few days we shall send you proof and you can consider the problem when it arrives.

I am just wondering whether you would be willing to sacrifice the squatting lady from Chicago? Not altogether—just the part about her where she squats.

I think perhaps we ought to enter this story in the Contest.[2]

It is a bird in the hand. As we print material entered in the contest we must run a note indicating that it is entered; so if the story is printed without such a note it can't qualify in January for the prize. Please let me know about this as soon as possible.

I am leaving this afternoon for two weeks in Washington and New York and haven't time to point out all the fine things in the story but they are there. Please address your reply about the Contest to Mildred [Haun].

Ever yours, Allen (m.h.)

TLS

1. "The Guide," *The Sewanee Review* 53 (July 1945), 362–87; later published in *A Novel, A Novella and Four Stories* as "The Mahogany Frame." Appeared in *O. Henry Award Prize Stories of 1946*. 2. The John Peale Bishop Memorial Literary Contest.

The Sewanee Review
May 24, 1945

Dear Brother:

I am sending you this duplicate set of galleys without corrections in order to save time. We will transfer your corrections to the original.

I hope you will consider the ending in the terms I wrote you about. I'm afraid it isn't very clear as it stands. The more I think of the lady from Chicago the more I believe she ought to be toned down (certainly the squatting passage), for the violent shock to the boy, or what would naturally be the violent shock of the story, is not visibly registered in any reaction of his. The passage as I see it is the climax of his lesson in evil and in how he should behave towards it. I believe this will be driven home if you can point up the identification with the grandfather at the end.

It is certainly a fine story. It has a sobriety and restraint and a kind of savage objectivity which are new in you. And the story I am convinced opens up a new vein which will yield a great deal in the future.

Yrs., Allen

TLS

The Sewanee Review
June 15, 1945

Dear Brother: [Route 1, Portland, Tennessee]

We thought all your revisions and additions were excellent. I could wish that you had made a little more of the end but it is certainly effective and perfectly clear now. In reading the page proof two words smote me between the eyes and I took the liberty to change them without your consent. I tried to telephone you but was told that you had no telephone on the Portland or Franklin or Springfield exchanges. In dictating this letter I hesitate to use the words but you will know what they are. I felt that omitting the words did not materially decrease the shock of the total obscenity of the scene on the boy's sensibility. To fight for these two words and to win would have been a victory on a front of no strategic importance. I hope that you will bear with me in this because I hate like the devil to change anything without the author's consent. You know how I would object to it.

Yours, Allen

TLS

P.S. How is the other story coming along?

Portland, Tenn.
Rt. #1
June 20, 1945

Dear Brother:

I got your note. The two words will be all right. I wanted the brutal and complete kind of obscenity which first shocks and then neutralizes itself, as a kind of exhaust to the professional tension of the hunt. It is always a question of how far to go. I am sure now that the obscene abandon of the lady from Chicago was too much (I overheard the report of this incident), as the circumstance of life is often too much for art, insofar as it would jolt the reader out of the story to reflection on the author's taste; and yet even this for a limited audience was right.

I am not satisfied with the ending. I hoped to find the time to work on it more. You lose something when you try to be explicitly clear. Perhaps I should have done something to show the boy's reaction to the end of his introduction to evil, just before the last flight of the birds but such would have weakened the end. You can't have two climaxes. I thought the moment of action would serve as the means to solidify and focus his experience, from feeling to apprehension and thereby make sudden the change from boy to man.

After all this was the subject. The boy's inheritance, his romantic image of the ancestor, the uncle who was being destroyed by a society which failed to serve and fulfill his character: all such had meaning but the meaning was subordinate to the subject and the material out of which the subject was built up. At one time I would have been more interested in the more restricted use of the material.

The story I originally started has spent itself in this one. I will use the material probably in a book. I've got a short novel in mind[1] and I will probably get on it this summer. More later. This issue of the review which came after I started this note, which has had many interruptions, is mighty good. It is certainly holding up. Randall [Jarrell] is showing a weakness every now and then, almost sentimentality, certainly half truths. "The State"[2] is not a good poem. The cat business instead of doing what it proposes to do makes the poem miscarry ludicrously.

More later, Andrew

TLS

1. Lytle is making plans to write *A Name for Evil* (1947). 2. *The Sewanee Review,* 53 (Summer 1945), 427.

The Cheneys
Tuesday, October 3, 1945

Dear Brother:

Lon tells me he has mentioned to you the ordeal I am going through at present.[1] I am glad he did; I wanted you to know it before the gossip reached you. Ever since this matter has been in the critical stage, and especially since the decisive stage, I have had a strong wish to be with you; and I hope that will be possible soon. I had hoped you and Edna might still be here when I arrived; for I wanted to see Edna too. I must go back to Sewanee on Thursday, in the afternoon, and I will be at Benfolly all day Wednesday, but shall return here by six o'clock. I explain this schedule just in case you might be coming in the next couple of days.

Yrs., Allen

TLS

1. Tate and Caroline Gordon are having difficulties. They were divorced in February 1946 and remarried in April.

The Sewanee Review
December 11, 1945

Dear Brother:

You have won the short story prize.[1] Prentice-Hall will send you a cheque very soon—$200.00.

In haste, Allen

AL

1. For "The Mahogany Frame."

Iowa City, Iowa
244 Quonset Park
March 5, 1947

Dear Brother:

[Paul] Engle has told you about the sudden move here.[1] I felt the need to go away to finish my book;[2] I also needed the extra money for a new car, which I was lucky to get by walking into a strange place and saying, I'm going to Ioway, with a wife and two children.[3] I have to have a car by Tuesday. I got it by Wednesday.

Of course, we got here in the dead of winter, with thermometer dropping twenty-seven degrees in five hours, and the Quonset hut was rather depressing. It's a washwoman's country, and Edna was a little bitter about leaving a good cook and a commodious house, to be shut up in narrow quarters with two children and do nothing but wash and iron. But things are easing up a little, although we've been through a siege of sickness and are not quite out of it.

Engle says he had a pleasant meeting with you in New York and further said that you were coming out in March, which is fine. I got a note from Red, who is riding the circuit again, and he mentioned the piece for John Ransom's birthday. I, of course, would like to do it. It will be very difficult, but I hope to get my novel over sometime around the first of April. I have postponed it twice. Maybe it will end itself by then. I will have it nearly done, when you come. I am anxious to get you to read it, and I wish I could get it to Caroline's eyes.

No more now. I've got to get to work.

As Ever, Andrew

TLS

1. Lytle has accepted a position as lecturer in the University of Iowa School of Writing. 2. *A Name for Evil.* 3. The Lytles now have a second daughter, Katherine Anne.

March 18, 1947

Dear Brother: [University of Iowa]

I am mighty glad to get your note and to know that a part of your manuscript will be coming soon. Meanwhile, could you lend me copies of THE LONG NIGHT and AT THE MOON'S INN? My copies, because of cramped living quarters, are stored away in trunks. I will see that they are returned to you. I want to get them read here in the office[1] before your manuscript arrives. I will see you in about five weeks.

Yours, Allen Tate

TLS

1. Tate served as the Editor of Belles Letters for the Henry Holt Publishing House in New York from 1946 through the spring of 1948.

Department of English
University of Iowa
Iowa City, Iowa
March 24, 1947

Dear Brother:

I have already drawn several hundred dollars from Chambers on this book. As you know, I have never been absolutely satisfied with Bobbs-Merrill. He certainly rushed *At The Moon's Inn* onto the market without proper preparation. It sold much better in England, and although the material might have been too remote for present sympathy, still I don't see why it should have sold so much better there than here. However, Chambers had the option on the next book, and I thought I would give him another try before taking the matter up with him.[1]

I wanted you to see this one, for your criticism, but I was already bound when I talked to you. Of course, I'd feel better with a firm where you were, but that will have to wait, I'm afraid.

I've got no copies of *The Long Night* and *At The Moon's Inn* here. We came only for the four months, to end in June. Engle has asked me if I would consider an offer to come back next fall. I told him I would, but I'm not sure that I will accept or just what the offer will be. We are living in a Quonset. We will have to get better quarters.

May has had a stroke and is slowly dying. Polly thinks that she has had two, and that the second one affected her sight and mind. It is very sad. When she went to Memphis to have the cataract operation, I felt that the end was near. There was no more she could do about her eyes.

My best to Caroline. We will see you next month.

Yours, Andrew

TLS

1. *A Name for Evil* (1947).

Cornsilk
Portland, Tenn.
July 2, 1947

Dear Brother:

I wrote Chambers to send you a book as soon as he printed any, and as he has sent me mine, although it doesn't come out until August the 8th,[1] I suppose your copy is on the way. I am anxious to hear from you and Caroline about it. It seems rather short in print, but treating it from the first person and with a frenzied kind of tension it could not be any longer.

I tried to write it on several levels of interest, with many cross references of implication. When I sat down and read it right through, these references seemed vestigal and the story overwhelming all. I've lost perspective or recovered a fresher critical insight.

I experimented with this: how far can you take the form of a certain book *(The Turn of the Screw),* deliberately take it and make something else; do this so that the ancestors will be clear, make it even a comment on the ancestor, without having it said it is derivative, "it is just another . . ."

It seems to me that when the chief meaning of a book lies in the symbol, that symbol must have two qualities: one, it must be common to society, that is, it must not be too private; two, it must not intrude upon the story as symbol (that approaches the danger of allegory). Therefore your actors, especially the protagonist, will through the action of the piece describe and qualify the symbol.

The legend of *A Name For Evil* is the attempt to regenerate, and the failure to do this in our time. My myth is the Thammuz or Adonis myth, modified as it would be in a Protestant or Late world: that is, where all is will, there is sterility and the sacrifice cannot generate spring.

Perhaps the piece is too short to deal with this, but it seemed to me, that I did at the time. I would like to get your comment on this, when you are able to write.

Duncan Kenner Brent has sent me a philosophical piece which I am still reading. It is called "The Image." I am going to send it to you with a view for considering it for publication. I don't know whether it is a thing publishers would care to put out, It might be important. You would know more than I about this.[2] If you can't use it, you might know of some place it could be sent.

Affectionately, Andrew

TLS

1. It was published on August 11, 1947. 2. Tate is working for Henry Holt. The essay was on Plato.

Cornsilk
Portland, Tenn.
July 20, 1947

Dear Brother:

I am sending that manuscript called "The Image," I wrote you about. The first part might need reorganization and perhaps condensation, but it seems to me on a first reading to be pretty good. Let me know what you think of it as soon as you get time.

Hope you are all well.

As Ever, Andrew
TLS

Henry Holt and Company, Inc.
Publishers New York
257 Fourth Avenue
July 29, 1947

Dear Brother:

Your letter reached me in Utah[1] and *A Name for Evil* was here in the office when I returned. I had so much work piled up that I had to wait till this past weekend to read it. I think perhaps I ought to wait another week before I write you to let the story work a little in my mind. I *am* a little too conscious of the close parallel to *The Turn of the Screw*—even down to the last word, "alone," in the book. The story has very considerable power, and the tone is maintained throughout. First, however, let me tell you the things that trouble me. It seems to me that Major Brent should have a simpler reason for coming back to haunt the place; I find him more credible in life than in death. His desire in life to destroy his posterity is not necessary to motivate the delusions of the narrator and to get into motion the narrator's compulsion to kill his wife. Major Brent's mania in life is a serious metaphysical burden for the story to carry, and I feel in it a melodramatic diversion—a distraction not an extension of the symbolism. I am a little worried too by Moss: what does he do? If you merely wish to show that there too Major Brent is having his way in killing off the narrator's heir, I feel that you go to greater lengths to get this said than are necessary. But the slippery problem of moving the lateral and the delusive levels of the story you have managed beautifully. There are some very fine scenes—in these I think you have surpassed anything you've written before; for in the past you have depended upon mere action to a large extent; here you've got the rounded scene, one after another.

I wish you had been able to hold the book back for a month or two to get sufficient perspective to take out the immediate stylistic influences of James. There are echoes of James' rhythms, some of his mannerisms, and even his phrases. In *The Turn of the Screw* James never lets the Governess reflect philosophically; all her observations bear upon her defense and support her "version"; I think you somewhat overdo this phase of your story. There is too much abstract meditation on good and evil, and its style is a little high-falutin, with occasional reversions to the colloquial phrase. And isn't the mist in the last scene unnecessary? It stands there as a piece of machinery—the old machinery in the story—and it casts a sort of Gothic romance air over the whole story: for the first time I feel there is no credible, literal equivalent of the delusive level.

I am writing this between telephone rings; but I didn't want to wait any longer. *A Name for Evil* is a powerful story, and it is "morally" convincing. It is nothing less than a triumph to have written it under the circumstances. What next?

Yrs., Allen

TLS

1. This trip probably marks Tate's attendance at the annual Utah Writers' Conference. Tate and Lytle frequently attend.

The State University of Iowa
May 6, 1948

Dear Brother:

I have meant to write for some time: I have received various messages from you from time to time; but with Engle away[1] I've been snowed under here with thirty students. In spite of good assistants, if you are going to do a good job with these people it takes a great deal of time, so much so that I don't much think I'll come back. Your boy [Paul] Griffith[2] seems to be back at his novel; he had a courtship with a girl here and somehow that broke off and upset him. I think that is the reason for the delay on his novel to you. He's a bright, but sensitive person and has done good work with his students here.

I was wondering when you want what I'll do for the *Sewanee Review* on John Ransom.[3] I tried to find out the time when Red was through Nashville, but I couldn't get any explicit knowledge from him. I see by the *Times* that the summer issue is the one. I think I may have something to say, but if you don't like it you won't hurt my feelings if you don't print it.

I've another matter I want to broach in this note. I've been thinking for some time that a serious criticism ought to be done on Caroline's work. I have thought Red was the person to do it. I've been turning it over in my mind for a year or so, if she has no objections I would like to try my hand at it.[4] I don't feel equal to it, since I've limited what critical faculty I have to criticism of what I do when I work, and this is another sort of criticism but closely related. You might take the matter up with her, and I thought I would take it up with John then. A good time might be when her next book comes out, if that is not too far away.

This is just a note to get off before the railroad strike and the airways will be crowded. Let me hear from you. In the meanwhile I'll be working on the Ransom piece.

What is this rumor of Popery I hear?[5]

Affectionately, Andrew

TLS

1. While Engle was on sabbatical leave, Lytle served as Acting Head of the University of Iowa School of Writing. 2. Assistant to Lytle at Iowa; Tate is bringing out his novel as soon as it is finished. 3. Lytle's contribution became "Note on a Traditional Sensibility," *The Sewanee Review,* 56 (Summer 1949), 370–73. 4. "Caroline Gordon and the Historic Image," *The Sewanee Review,* 57 (Autumn 1949), 560–86. 5. Caroline Gordon joined the Catholic Church in 1947 and Tate two and half years later.

The State University of Iowa
May 25, 1948

Dear Brother:

Thanks for the note. I had supposed John Palmer[1] knew I was to do something, as the last time I saw him I asked when the issue was to come out. Red had told me to send the mss. in to you, and I supposed naturally that he had made some mention of this to you. At the last minute John [Palmer], after I had written a kind of short eulogy, said he didn't want such, that you had done that, and so I did the best I could. But no more of that. I wouldn't have bothered, but thought I ought to say something, even in my halting critical way.

It will be good to see you all. I hope our times do meet there.[2] I'm sorry now that I agreed to go as I thought it would begin when I end here. We have to give up the house and there is a lapse of ten days, which means we will go to the farm and then back to Mo. Edna may not be able to face it, by the time she has cleaned two houses in rapid succession.

I didn't get your book but have seen it.[3] I didn't realize what really a large body of work you've done. I'm sure my copy is at Portland, and I'll be mighty anxious to see it at more leisure. This is just a note. We are exhausted in cleaning and closing the house and winding up the mss.

Aff., Andrew

TLS

1. Palmer took over editorship of *The Sewanee Review* with the Fall issue in 1946. 2. At the University of Missouri. 3. *Poems: 1922–1947* (1948).

"Brinkwood"
Sewanee
May 29, 1948

Dear Brother:

Here we are, the Woods (all 4)[1] and the Tates, having descended like locusts three days ago upon Phin. [?] Percy, a saintly young man. But the occasion of this note is your fine piece about J. C. R.[2] John Palmer brought me the galleys yesterday. You put your finger on something that nobody else has seen, and it gets to the center of J. C. R. And it is beautifully done. But for the chance of your writing me, we should have missed this.

We stay here till the 15th or 16th of June, and expect to reach Columbia, Mo., on the 17th. I fear we shall miss you there.

Yrs., Allen

AL

1. Nancy, her husband and two children. 2. "Note on a Traditional Sensibility," *The Sewanee Review,* 56 (Summer 1948), 370–73.

Confederate Hall
Columbia, Mo.
June 7, 1948

Dear Brother:

I found your note here, forwarded from Iowa City.[1] We left there the last week in May, since we had to get out of the house and I had to get to the farm on pressing matters before coming here. It looks as if, still we travel the maximum miles. I never would have agreed to come here if I had not thought I could stop by on the way home. But it is good to see Ward [Dorrance] and he has an awfully pleasant establishment and Edna will maybe get some rest from closing of one house and opening another (with waterworks out of order for the first four days).

I am glad you liked the J. C. R. piece. I wanted it to be a little sharper, but the time element was against me. It pleases me that you feel the point was made and not too badly done. I never feel any too sure of myself in such writing. I hope we will get to see you. We will try to stop over one day if possible. It's so dry at home and I have so much stock. I'm afraid to leave decisions that might arise to my tenant, although he is a good man. When I arrived home, I found a north wind had been blowing for two weeks, and no rain to speak of since the middle of April.

Tell Caroline I have written Miss [Gottlieb?]. The appointments had not been made by the time I left Iowa, but I recommended G. highly and her chances are good. I also wrote Maxwell, asking him to reassure the lady.

I hope we see you here if not, maybe at Monteagle before the summer wastes.

As ever, Andrew

AL

1. Lytle is attending a ten-day workshop at the University of Missouri. He is in charge of the novel segment.

466 Nassau Street
Princeton, New Jersey
October 22, 1949

Dear Brother:

Caroline has already written you about your essay on her.[1] She could be scarcely more pleased with it than I am. There is no better study of a living writer; it may even be the best. What I admire most I suppose is the perfect coherence and resourcefulness of your approach, and the case with which you have found the terms to set it forth. I know that this ease is never really ease; it is always the result of labor. After a third reading I am at a loss to find any fault in it. There is a rightness not only about the overall view, but also in the particular discriminations. What you say about Lucy and Rives on the battlefield, and the ending of *The Women on the Porch,* is exact and profound. And what an astonishing job your reading of "The Brilliant Leaves" adds up to!

Twenty years ago some of the boys seemed fleeter of foot; but now you have passed us all. I wish I were capable of such an essay.

We have doubled back to Princeton[2] which we like now because there is no official connection—dinners swapped, official calls, etc. We spend one night a week in NY. What kind of life this is only time will tell. I am in a working way again, and no longer have a phobia about typewriters. No poetry; but two essays done and two more in the making, besides the book on Poe.[3] I did a little trial flight with Poe recently, as a lecture in Baltimore: I came out with things I never knew I thought about him. I'll send it to you shortly.

I'd like to know what you are into now. I will not try to give you our news of the past year: we've been in so many places I can't remember them all; but chiefly Chicago,[4] where the money was good.

Aff., Allen

1. "Caroline Gordon and The Historic Image," *The Sewanee Review,* 57 (Autumn 1949), 560–86. 2. The Tates have bought Benbrackets on Nassau Street across from Willard Thorp. 3. This projected book finally becomes *The Forlorn Demon: Didactic and Critical Essays* (1953) with only two essays devoted strictly to Poe. 4. During the first part of 1949 Tate served as Visiting Professor of Humanities at the University of Chicago.

Gainesville, Fla.
University of Florida
Bldg. "G"
Oct. 27, 1949

Dear Brother:

Of course, I'm pleased that you all like the piece in *The Sewanee Review*. Your letter was my first knowledge that it had come out. I had just written John Palmer to ask him if he got the mss. I was fearful as I hadn't a copy of it. When I got done, I was too tired to make one. Your praise of it, and Caroline's which just came in today, was worth the work on it. And really, you know you read and like things, but you don't really read them until you do something like this. I wouldn't take anything for the experience, although it was troubling because I don't do this sort of thing much. In the end all I did was try to understand why I liked Caroline's work, and in the process it developed a vague feeling I had had about historical writing. I noticed in a place or two that the magazine left out sentences, which confused [Leo] Tolstoy and [Sigrid] Undset. It may have been my fault, but I don't think so. To show you how solid was my fare, after my juices began to flow, I felt I had barely touched the work as a whole and could have gone on and on. This is really the final test, I think.

Of course, I didn't mean to make so much of the "White Goddess,"[1] the terms don't really matter, or they do of course, but what I was concerned with is the one-sided masculinity, which is the unbalance of nature and the assumption of the god-head, which no society at equilibrium could assume. It's just a pleasure really to know how good it is. I was tempted to use "The Ice House" but I thought "The Brilliant Leaves" more nearly fitted into the general position. I never got before the full effect of the bone-buyer of his obesity so resembling the decay of death and the full ramifications of his sinistral obscenity. If you all are pleased, I am pleased, and I was certainly pleased with the reading. Of course, you know, I ain't no Christian. I jest does the best I kin. And you say I ain't been baptized.

Brother, I signed that paper and sent it on.[2] I didn't know much about the controversy. I heard of it second-hand and spoke to I believe it was [Karl] Shapiro, the poet from Baltimore, that I met at the writers' conference in Indiana this last summer. I only felt that the committee made a mistake referring to his [Pound's] political predicament. It would have been better strategy to give the prize for the poetry; at least it seems better strategy. The ugly part of which you refer to I didn't follow. One thing, this is the frontier down here, in a sense, and I've been trying to get under way on my next book, which at least I have, but I'm not quite sure yet what it is, I've got so many elements I want to absorb into it, and my point of view is worrying me. You mentioned that you came out with things on

Poe you never knew you thought about. Don't you think the writing of a thing is to discover what it is. Otherwise you wouldn't write. And to make too close an outline is to make a thing, or tend to make it stillborn. Be sure to send me the Poe piece.[3] I will be anxious to see it.

I've been meaning to write you, was about to when your letter came, as I sold Monteagle to the Woman's Association. I explicitly took the ladies over and showed them your grandfather's desk and a chair which was yours and was not to be included in the sale. I don't know what you want to do with them. I didn't see any reason writing before the sale went through. It might not have. The manager had made me right mad, telling people it wasn't for rent, or that he didn't know where "the man" who owned the house was, and when I heard he surmised I was dead, I thought, feelings and all, I'd better pull out of Monteagle before I hurt him, or somebody got hurt. You might write Huey Wooten to take care of it. You may remember him. I got him to take out the few things I reserved. He hauled them to Murfreesboro for me. I wouldn't waste too much time. When those ladies move in there and get to doing the place over . . . although Miss Irene [Weaver Williams], I'm sure, won't let anything happen to them.

We like it down here.[4] The manners are good, as they were thirty years ago, but you also have the remnants of the Puritan breakdown. But the people are generally mighty nice and I had to get out and educate these little girls and was getting a little tired of worrying over money. Edna couldn't take Ioway any longer, although I expect it is a better university, at least up to a point. You can see on the student body's face here the stamp of all the runaways in American history. It's very curious. That's not all of them, but it makes it hard to reach through to people that are just hearing about higher education, after the Educationists have taken over. The head of the Liberal Arts here is making a fight, but I'm afraid it is a rear-guard action.

We finally had to set in to build a house, the accommodations were so bad. Edna didn't want to do it. The idea has made her flighty and nervious [sic]. She said it would interfere with my writing, and it will; but it may be I have to undertake such things to get writing done. I'm getting up earlier in the mornings and working regularly for the first time in a year.

Let me hear from you. Tell Caroline I'll write her soon.

Aff., Andrew

TLS

1. A term made famous by Robert Graves' book *The White Goddess: A Historical Grammar of Poetic Myth* which appeared in 1948. 2. The paper involved the awarding The Bollingen Prize for poetry to Ezra Pound. 3. "Our Cousin Mr. Poe," *Partisan Review,* 16 (December 1949), 1207–19. 4. In the fall of 1948, Lytle accepted the position of Lecturer in Creative Writing at the University of Florida in Gainesville.

III

1950–1959

Despite some of the real difficulties the letters of this period reveal, in many ways they show it to be a comparatively settled time for both men. Although for a couple of years Lytle still returns to his Portland farm in the summer and Tate continues to lecture in such places as Italy, India, and Oxford, both men establish for themselves a kind of base. When the section opens Lytle is situated in Florida preparing to move into a new house, and Tate soon accepts a tenured position at Minnesota.

As for literary concerns, the letters here offer some of the richest material of any section. The file contains Lytle's letters discussing Gordon and Tate's *House of Fiction* (1950), Tate's poems "The Buried Lake" and "The Swimmers" (1952), and many of Tate's individual essays in *The Forlorn Demon* (1953). It also includes Tate's enthusiastic response to Lytle's essay "The Working Novelist and the Mythmaking Process" (1959). "You have defined," he says, "the orbit of fiction for the future." But by far the most extraordinary exchange is a discussion extending over a series of five letters dating from December 4, 1954, through February 9, 1955. These letters are almost wholly devoted to Tate's reading of and Lytle's commentary on the novel still two years from completion, *The Velvet Horn* (1957).

The sequence is interspersed with references to such occasions as The Fugitives' Reunion at Vanderbilt in 1956, Tate's renewing ties with the Lytles when he delivers the Phi Beta Kappa Address in

Gainesville in 1957, and Tate's pleasure on receiving an advanced copy of the *Sewanee Review* celebrating his sixtieth birthday. But the correspondence refers to less happy circumstances as well. Not only does it cover the period of Tate's prolonged separation from Caroline, it also records other personal matters occurring in 1959. In May of that year Edna writes Tate that Lytle is ill and in a few days is going to have to undergo a serious operation; and in August Tate talks about the depression he feels now that the divorce from Caroline is upon him. Perhaps the strength of their friendship is best determined at this time not by the genuine concern that comes through on almost every page of the letters, but by the practical support they provide for each other. After the operation, Tate begins work to establish a Professorship for Lytle at Vanderbilt, a Chair of Southern Literature. And before Tate's marriage to Isabella, Lytle visits the couple and makes clear his complete acceptance of Tate's private decisions. The sequence concludes with a number of letters taken up with plans for the Christmas vacation the Tates and Lytles are going to spend together.

Gainesville, Fla.
University of Fla.
Bldg. "G"
March 22, 1950

Dear Brother:

I've been meaning to write you, particularly after reading the piece on Poe in the *Partisan Review* and the "Three Commentaries."[1] I had seen Eliot's piece,[2] and I thought it was rather weak, lacking any clear definition or technical exposure. You can't just say a thing is bad but has had good influence, without going into it. It seems to me you have a fresh and coherent handling of Poe. Are you working further on it, or will you let it stand as it is? By the way when is the *House of Fiction*[3] coming out? The parts I have ready by Caroline are splendid and very helpful.

I have not done as much work this winter as I had hoped to do. I have not had or forced myself into steady enough stretches of work, but I think what I am doing is alive.[4] It reads to me well, but my subject is still unclear to me; but when I get further along I expect to know which threads are subordinate and which central. [Note in margin:] Did you ever do anything about your grandfather's desk?

I haven't got a copy of *The Long Night*. Somebody either stole or borrowed it, but I wrote Chambers to send one to the address you gave. If he can't locate one, I'll write Nashville and see what can be found there. I will certainly be proud to have it considered for such a prize.

You all must come up to the farm when you get to the Cheneys in July. We ought to be there then. My trade here was to have the summers off, but it's a state institution and their sales tax didn't raise the money they expected, and I was told I might have to teach the term this summer, as we are on twelve months salary and, like clerks, are supposed to put in twelve months work. But I thought when I knew my way around a little better then maybe you would like to get away from the winter for a lecture down here. It's a strange country, the wilderness once you get off the highways and the educationists are gaining strength everywhere else. But I'm left alone and have plenty of time to work. I must be slowing down. The other day I felt for three days the kind of oppression you must feel when you are dying, and I dreamt continuously of the dead.

Aff. to you both, Andrew

TLS

1. "Our Cousin, Mr. Poe," *Partisan Review,* 16 (December 1949), 1207–19; "Three Commentaries: Poe, James, and Joyce," *Sewanee Review,* 58 (Winter 1950), 1–15. 2. "From Poe to Valery." 3. *The House of Fiction: An Anthology of the Short Story.* Edited by Caroline Gordon and Allen Tate, New York: Charles Scribner's Sons, 1951, 1956. 4. Lytle has already begun work on *The Velvet Horn,* a novel he will not complete until 1957.

465 Nassau Street
Princeton, New Jersey
March 27, 1950

Dear Brother:

I am sorry I bothered you about *The Long Night,* except that it got a letter out of you. We found our copy yesterday. This house is so small we can't unpack everything; enlargement waits upon the money which we will probably never make.

I remember you asked me before about the desk. I don't remember it being at Monteagle. Are you sure it's mine? What does it look like?

"I must be slowing down," you say. Well, I'm glad you're just now feeling it. I've been in the doldrums for a month, the end of winter apathy which I've felt for about five years: I can't work, and don't even want to. The Poe is the last finished piece of work. I peg away at odds and ends, chiefly getting things together for my book on Poe. The essay you read is a bird's eye view. But I'm constantly distracted by greed—lectures here and there, to make more money in order to have none. By the end of April I will have given eight since October, and I haven't a cent. I would be proud to come to Floridy some time.

The Tennessee trip is uncertain again, but we still hope to make it. We had a touch of Sewanee today. Margaret Myers, with Hobart (now a loutish but nice adolescent), stopped here for lunch on the way to New York. If I had her energy I'd go a long way. She informed us that she takes Cousin George's breakfast to him in bed. "It's better for him that way," she says. No doubt it is.

We hope you all are well.

Aff., Allen

TLS

P.S. Saw Red about a month ago. The mask is completely petrified.

Gainesville, Fla.
University of Florida
Bldg. "G"
April 14, 1950

Dear Brother:

I was glad to hear from you and have been meaning to write sooner: but I have so many interruptions and have to use what will I have to keep at work, haltingly I'm afraid. I wrote Chambers and he sent a copy of *The Long Night* to the secretary, but said that he had to have it back. I had written him that it was only to be borrowed for six weeks.

The desk, I don't know how I got it into my head it is yours; but it must be. I think it is mahogany or walnut—it was in a dark corner at Monteagle and I didn't look at it too close. I think it's got a roll top on it, and part of it is locked. There is also a mahogany rocking chair. Maybe you will run up to Sewanee when you come down this summer and see. It is understood that it didn't go with the sale of the cottage, but I don't know how long ladies' avarice will dull their memories.

Money doesn't go anywhere now. Every now and then I take out the Confederate money Aunt Tean [Tene] left me and wonder if it won't come in good stead. At the rate we are going we'll be as bad off as Europe. I usually can show a legitimate loss on the farm, but this year it shows three hundred dollars profit. But I don't know where it went. The Cheneys brought Red by the farm, their lunch and all, one day last summer; but he didn't stay long and I looked for the mask to crack every time he took a bite of food. John Palmer says he and Cinina will be at Sewanee for a month. They may be there now. He was looking for a farm to buy, but I don't really think he means to do it. He will never meet the specifications he wants, and I doubt if there is anything very cheap in land any more in

Tennessee. You've almost got to farm it to afford it. His movie version of his last novel came to town,[1] but I can't see books done into movies any more, nor movies for that matter. I went to see *Bovary*[2] and left before it was over. I don't know whether the movies are getting worse or me better. It takes a heroic kind of energy to be an artist, and I've about concluded that, everything else being equal, the difference between a minor and a major poet, is energy. These forties and fifties have a powerful shadow. You ought to be at your best, but you have to rely too much on the will, I believe. But I never saw such energy as our little girls have.

Bryant Cooper[3] came back from Nashville and reports that Doctor Mims says he is making more money than he ever did. Some University here in Florida gave him twenty-five hundred dollars for five lectures. Their hearing must be bad to listen to him repeat himself so often. He is also working on a book: tracing the number of times The Virgin Mary appears in literature.

I will close on this, as I know it can give you infinite speculation on the mystery of God's ways to man.

Let me know if you get to Tennessee. I've got to go up for a week soon on farm business.

Affectionately, Andrew

TLS

1. *All the King's Men* (1949). Produced, directed, and screenplay by Robert Rossen. 2. Directed by Vincente Minnelli (1949). 3. A Vanderbilt graduate who taught philosophy at Florida with Lytle.

Gainesville, Fla.
1927 W. Church St.
May 19, 1950

Dear Allen and Caroline:

This is to tell you how much I like *The House of Fiction*. I have ordered it for next fall's class for my advanced students. Unfortunately they rarely run over eight or ten. I am thinking about using it for the lower division, but the classes there run only an hour and I am not sure that they can in any way be ready for it. I've been using Brooks and Warren.[1] Their comments are generally pretty good but never used, since the instructor such as I makes his own comments; and their choice of stories is on the whole not too good. I can see where the book would serve other instructors, but not the way I try to talk.

That's the reason I find your comments exceptionally good. They stand on their own and are properly restricted to the point of view in which the book is composed. I have long wanted someone to deal with [Somerset] Maugham and place [Ernest] Hemingway. I think in both instances the treatment is neat, brilliant, and just. Particularly is it needed for Maugham, since he is thought among the faculties to represent the best in fiction now going. I don't know how long writers will continue to be invited to read with students. I am appalled at the professional teacher's fright and frozen stare when he is called upon to teach something without prestige of past acceptance to support him. It makes me wonder how sound any of his judgment is. I've noticed that any modern fiction the art courses give, certainly here, is always second rate and always read for some residual reason. And I can't believe their defense which is, that the students are not ready for the best. It means they don't know it, or are afraid of it. I don't know why I should be surprised, except that fresh evidence of the corruption of learning seems always a shock. I hope you make a lot of money out of the book. You will without doubt in the proper quarters receive the praise it deserves. It's a wonderful title.

Now that we are about to move into this house I have been building[2] I can no longer fail to confront my book. I used to read to avoid getting down to it, and do other things. I am a little terrified that I have to set in to building to escape the confrontation with my problems. I tell myself that this will be the last postponement.

Are you coming to Tennessee, or will you go to Indiana[3] direct? I hope we will get to see you before the summer wanes.

I'll write you later when I've gone more thoroughly over the *House* . . . I am now pressed with the end of the year and my conscience.

Affectionately Andrew

TLS

1. *Understanding Fiction* (1943). 2. 1822 North West 8th Avenue. 3. Tate is to teach in the School of Letters at Bloomington.

1822 North West 8th Avenue
Gainesville, Florida
June 5, 1951

Dear Brother:

We are packing up for the trek to Tennessee. These opening and closing of houses are wearisome to Edna; and I find that movement is less pleasing to me with each year; but there are many reasons why I want to hold on to that farm. I hear that I have been considered as a permanent member of the staff here; but there is no formal announcement to that effect, although the head of the department told me when I came here that he would like to consider me as a fixture; but, to allow me to go away for the summers, which the rest of the staff can't do, I am appointed lecturer, which ranks above the full professor (that means nothing, of course) and allows for arbitrary pay and hours of work. The working conditions are good, all my mornings to myself and few classes. As long as these little girls have to be educated I don't want to move them too often; so I would like to stay here. It is pleasant.

I'm glad you're taking Red's place out there,[1] but I don't know why you should bother with tenure: you move every Tuesday, as they used to say of my father.

Tell Caroline, on several readings, "The Waterfall" is mighty good.[2] Why are they making so much of [Scott] Fitzgerald? Arthur Mizener's book was good. I haven't read everything, but I can't see him as the figure they make him out.[3] I think I have at last the point of view for my present book. What I have done was write the first section, but found it only introduced itself.

This is a note to say why don't you come by the farm and stay while you are around Nashville. It's not far from Indiana. I was there one summer. You come to Franklin, Ky., and about ten miles south of it, you reach a red brick house on the right, up a rise after you have crossed a bridge. They have cedar stumps in the yard. Turn right; go to where the road makes a T, turn left and in about a mile you will run into my mail box.

Aff., Andrew

TLS

1. Tate accepted a tenured position at the University of Minnesota. 2. "The Waterfall" first appeared in *The Sewanee Review,* 58 (Fall 1945), 532–43. 3. Mizener's *The Far Side of Paradise,* which came to be the standard biography, was one of two important books to appear on Fitzgerald in 1951. The other one was Alfred Kazin's *F. Scott Fitzgerald: The Man and His Work,* a collection of the best critical essays to date.

456 Nassau Street
Princeton
June 9, 1951

Dear Brother:

I'm mighty glad to get your letter of the 5th. Yes, we move every Tuesday, but it will be a new feeling to know that I won't have to move unless I want to. I get less mobile as I get older. We had become so attached to this little place in the past year that we wanted to stay here indefinitely.[1] But we have to make the money to pay for the renovations, and we couldn't have done that with the salaries we were making. Nancy and Percy [Wood] and the little boys will occupy the house for at least a year. Percy has just started his psychiatric residency at the New Jersey State Hospital nine miles away. Under the circumstances it is a fine arrangement for us.

Lon [Cheney] is with us, and will probably go on to Bloomington with us, where he will begin his next book.[2] He hopes to get the ms. of the present book ready for his agent by the time we leave, two weeks from now.

At Bloomington, Tennessee will be a new temptation, but I doubt that we can make it this time. I've got myself in a jam: before I signed up to teach this summer I had agreed to go to Harvard and give a paper at a symposium; and I'll have to fly there from Bloomington, and get back in three days. We all used to take thousand mile trips at the drop of a hat, but age has made them seem formidable.

Caroline's novel is now in galleys.[3] "The Waterfall" is the first chapter, but since it appeared it has been entirely rewritten. I'm glad your own book is coming along. When a sizable part of it is done I hope you'll let me read it. I'm into a long poem,[4] but it has bogged down, and I can't seem to do anything else effectively until it is out of the way. When that will be I don't know.

Affly, Allen

P.S. Last winter Don and Theresa [Davidson] stopped here for a day. Don surprised me by taking a stiff drink of whisky and becoming very gay!

1. Benbrackets. 2. *This Is Adam: A Novel* (1958). 3. *The Strange Children* (1951). 4. "Seasons of the Soul."

POST CARD
Tour del Banaco
logo di Gardo
9-17-52

Dear Lytles: [University of Florida]

I had a wonderful visit in Rome (a week) with those fine folks the Foxes;[1] then some *toresismo* in central Italy. I am now on Catullus Lake,[2] a few miles from Sirmione with Cal and Elizabeth [Hardwick] Lowell[3] the [Stephen] Spenders, the [Cecil] Day-Lewises, and other oddments of the British. From my hotel room I look across a lagoon to the ruined castle built in the 13th century by Santi's[4] patron, [?], Grande della Scal-[?].[5]

Affly, Allen.

1. George and Bea Fox. 2. Tate is at Lake Garda, the home of Catullus. 3. Robert Lowell and his second wife whom he had married in 1949 after divorcing Jean Stafford the preceding year. 4. Raffaello Santi (Raphael). 5. The castle is probably Scaliger Caster.

University of Minnesota
November 4, 1952

Dear Brother:

I am sending you a new poem—or rather Part VI[1] of a long one I've been working at about two years. But each part is complete in itself, and I will probably end up with a number of related poems that do not form a whole. You will see that it is in *terza rima,* a stanza that has never been used in English with perfect success. I suppose I undertook it just to increase the difficulty. Yet it does offer unique opportunities for the brief scene or "vision"; and that is really why I use it.

I had a nice letter from Bee Fox the other day telling me she had sent you and Edna an article about me from an Italian paper. I've never seen it: I went off on a tour the day before it appeared; and afterwards, in the confusion of Venice, could not find a copy. If you still have it, won't you please send it to me?

How is your novel coming along? I've heard fine reports of the opening chapters. I have just received Red's long poem,[2] and hope to read it this week—a sort of historical novel in verse.

We have almost completely withdrawn from the world: I get up at four and begin work; and to go to bed at nine. Caroline works steadily at her novel.[3] I suppose we've begun to feel how little time is left—*much* less than has gone before.

Affectionately, Allen

AL

1. "The Buried Lake." 2. *Brother to Dragons* (1953). 3. *The Malefactors* (1956).

Nov. 16 [1952]

Dear Allen,

I wanted to write a note to say how much I enjoyed reading "The Buried Lake" and how much I admire it. I take it this is the name of Part VI? What is the name of the poem?[1]

I have not seen it before today, but I think now that I like it best of your poetry. Not that I would not agree that several others are equally as fine—but here the poet and the poetry act upon the poem with your most perfect unity, I think. And the result is a gentleness underneath the fire of it as striking as the day-night, light-dark . . . . images themselves. The stanza is fine for stress of these; it is interesting, it is refreshing.

Please accept the tribute of my delight and my praise, such as it is. I'll not write more. It reads so beautifully I wish you'd make a record of it.

Edna

Happy Birthday soon[2]

1. The poem was never completed, only "The Maimed Man," "The Swimmers," and "The Buried Lake." Tate proposed to do six or nine parts, to make it a complete book. 2. Tate's birthday is November 19.

Gainesville, Fla.
1822 NW 8th Ave.
Sunday
Nov. 17, 1952

Dear Brother:

I've been waiting to answer, hoping B [Fox] would send on the article from the Italian paper. You have to watch that Old Christian (born between the two ararats) she sometimes gives the word for the deed. Maybe we can write her and have her relay it between here and Minnesota.

But I was mighty glad to hear from you and get the card from abroad. I didn't know how long you were going to stay over there—you are getting more and more a public figure, but so long as you go to bed at my old hours and beat me at rising, I reckon you are pretty safe. And stay withdrawn. Now I falter at those hours which were so easy for me when I was younger. The frayed will still works a little but it is hard now for me to arise at five-thirty, which I have to do if I'm ever going to finish this book, as my students this year are excellent and you know how that takes it out of you. There is a nostalgia for that ability to withdraw as you all are doing, which I know will be denied me—you can't marry at thirty-five, beget a family, and expect any such peace and close quiet in late middle years. Pamela already has at least eleven suitors of a sort. They bring snakes now and stand in the yard; they will bring themselves later and jet planes and I don't see how I'm going to stand it, a father and grandfather fused into one, for I will not be allowed the irresponsibility of the one and perhaps [am] unequal to the responsibility of the other. It's wonderful how a metaphor can turn into the living evil. I don't know whether it was one of Pamela's friends but Edna found a snake squirming over the kitchen floor the other day, and when she got a neighbor to help her deal with it, it crawled into a small hole in the wall, which they stopped up with paper and I later boarded up. It looked like the deadly coral snake (northwest Gainesville has more of them than any place in the world) but it might be the kind that looks like it which is harmless, but who can tell evil's colors when it is squirming and the head has already withdrawn into the foundations of the house? Good Christians that you [are] now may be you can tell, but I'm afraid I'm a pagan.

Lytle (1986)

Andrew Lytle (about 1945)

Lytle's wife Edna (about 1938)

Lytle on honeymoon in California (1938)

Andrew Lytle at Harper's Ferry with Tates on trip to Civil War battlegrounds (1928)

Edna Lytle and daughter Pamela (1943)

Photograph of a painting of Allen Tate, Caroline Gordon Tate, and their daughter Nancy (1928)

Allen Tate with John and Ben, two of his and Helen's sons (1969)

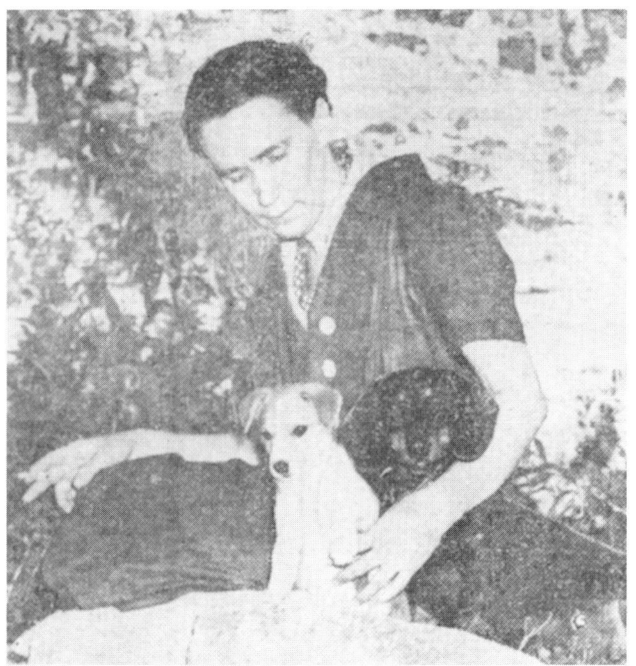

Caroline Gordon Tate (1937)

Caroline Gordon Tate (about 1970)

Caroline Gordon, Allen Tate, and Sally Wood (Paris 1932)

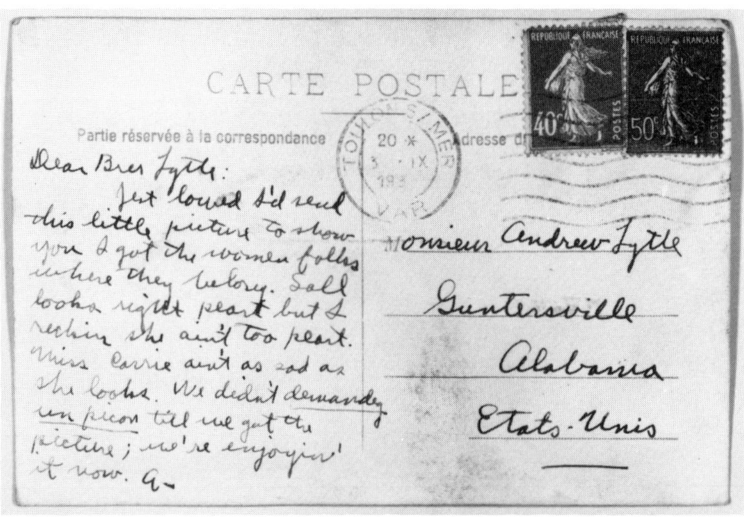

CARTE POSTALE

Partie réservée à la correspondance

Adresse

Dear Brer Lytle:
Just lowed I'd send this little picture to show you I got the women folks where they belong. Sall looks right peart but I reckin she ain't too peart. Miss Carrie ain't as sad as she looks. We didn't demand un picon till we got the picture; we're enjoyin' it now. A—

Monsieur Andrew Lytle
Guntersville
Alabama
Etats-Unis

Postcard Tate sent to Lytle with the photograph

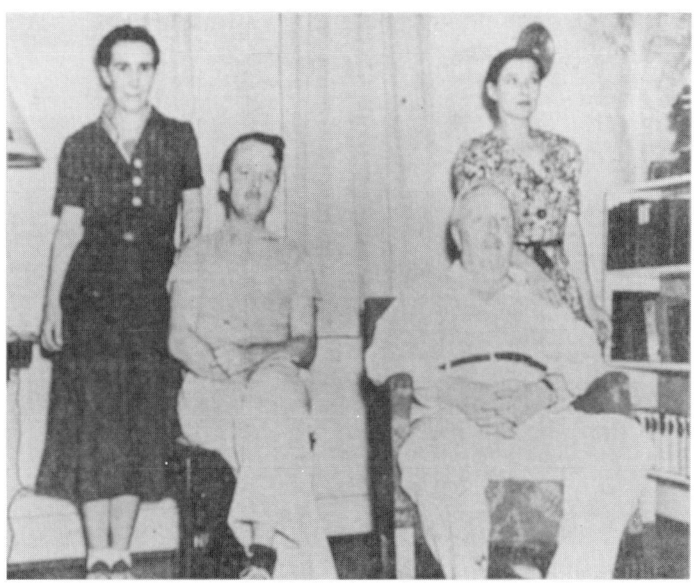

Left to right: Caroline Gordon Tate, Allen Tate, Mrs. Ford Madox Ford, Ford Madox Ford (1937)

Photograph taken at Bill Bandy's wedding breakfast, Paris, 1929.

Seated, left to right: Caroline Tate, Titus's clerk (invited because Ford refused to sit at a table of 13), Mrs. Horatio Krans, Leonie Adams, Virginia Hersh, Alice Bandy, Zonola Snodgrass. Standing, left to right: Horatio Krans, Lee Hersh, Ford Madox Ford, Paul Snodgrass, Bill Bandy, E. W. Titus, Allen Tate.

A luncheon at the Tates' house for the celebration of Allen Tate's seventy-fifth birthday on November 19, 1974.
Clockwise, from bottom: Louis D. Rubin, Jr. (seated on floor), Eudora Welty, Harry Duncan, Cleanth Brooks, Lewis P. Simpson, Francis Fergusson, Morton Weisman, Allen Tate, William Jay Smith, Joseph Frank, and Howard Nemerov. Also present on this occasion but not shown in the photograph were Denis Donoghue and Radcliffe Squires.

All Andrew Lytle photographs courtesy of Mr. Lytle
All Allen Tate photographs courtesy of The Photographic Archives of Vanderbilt University
Photograph of Bill Bandy's wedding breakfast courtesy of Professor William Bandy

I believe you are going to do like Yeats and make the last span the best. That's a tremendously fine poem.[1] I haven't worked it all out yet but it shows a resurgence of power and your gifts, and I know the time left will be the best time. But first I want to say how moved I was by the oration its clarity, felicity of style, holding the essence so clearly, so brightly-hard that those who listen are fixed in truth and cannot wander. I see that when I have been using communication (as I talk a good deal about its breakdown) I have assumed the communion beneath, which of course is now lacking, except in individual cases and even then you must communicate through something outside yourself. I have thought of it as love, but I see the dangers there, lacking divine love. I hope you gave this oration in Europe, for the guardians there were the first sinners. And you will forgive me, I know, but I would have given a Bishop's ransom to have witnessed behind an arras, with a hole in it, your visit with the Pope.[2]

I just think the poem is the best you've done, well almost; the entire poem will be. Edna who is critically so much smarter than I reads it more lucidly, but then our readings come out to the same thing. It has done what it set out to do, and a paraphrase would be murder. I wish I could talk with you about it, where the half-spoken communication relies upon a deeper and fuller communion, because finally I think or have come to think what a clumsy vehicle words are. To say anything close to meaning depends upon art: I suppose that is why it is so hard a thing to do, because of words, their stiffness. We who use them have to make them the real thing, whereas in life they are nothing but counters; and even in intercourse they release far more than they exchange. If I were there instead of here, I would like to tell you not only how fine the light-dark images are but also the sound-silence ones, in all their varying degrees of life-in-death and death-in-life, and that you used the dream to contain the mortal progress, you dream at night and night is this mortality, and light is divine love into which you awake. But when you put it down like this, you deny all the other suggestions and relationships. Were you punning on Homburg? I could only think of pinched hotel as being pinched in the grave, which leads you to images which put him in hell, which maybe only suggest it in night which is life here. Is the aging child not only the child's innocence the man must have to enter Heaven but is it also the condition of man in the modern world? It seems to me the particular power of this poem, I will put it very badly, comes from the reverberations of suggestion. The inheritance of western man is as faint as a suggestion but technically works with the same persistence as the Lady of Light, invisible, immanent; you lead us to think of Orpheus and Eurydice; that is, shades that they are you evoke them in the very quality of shadiness and, incidentally qualify what you are doing with the dream. You make the reader specify as the Master said to do.[3] (I know he is not your master.) You suggest yourself, the Mediterranean, the ladder . . . well, I won't go on and destroy the effect of the poem. But it's good, I tell you. When are you going to finish it and we can see it all?

I'm working away a little faster now and see my way more clearly. After three years I begin to see the final structure. I had thought to be doing maybe three novels, but I now see how I can do it in one. I'm thinking about calling it *The Water Witch.*[4] In different ways we seem to be involved in a fairly central subject. I leased the farm for three years and that ought to give me the time by leaving me more energy and lessening the draw of care. I think the man I leased it to will do right by the farm and himself and me, or else the care will be increased. We'll stay on down here and won't have to undertake our migrations twice a year. So maybe I'll get the book done.

By the way, how do you think we can help [Monroe] Spears[5] on the *Review*. The trouble with the Rockefellers is they can't get away from promotion. They want to give the money right but can't get away from the moneyness of it. If they could be made to see that a Review just doesn't need a start to keep it going but has to have a permanent subsidy. If that fails do you have any other approach to the moneybags? Spears is a fine choice for an editor and Ned McCrady[6] a brilliant choice for the Vice-Chancellor. If they are just given a chance there.

Well, I better bring this to a close. Let me hear from [you] on this matter, our best to you both.

Affectionately, Andrew

TLS

1. "The Buried Lake." 2. Jacques Martain helped Tate obtain an audience with Pope Pius XII. 3. Henry James. 4. He will work on it five years longer and call it *The Velvet Horn* (1957)—his magnum opus. 5. Spears became editor of *The Sewanee Review* with the Fall issue of 1952. 6. Edward McCrady was appointed Vice-Chancellor of the University of the South.

November 19, 1952

Dear Andrew & Edna:

This is only a note to thank you for your very nice, appreciative letters. You see very clearly what I tried to do in the poem, and so far nobody else has. I haven't got a title yet for the whole thing; it may not work out as a "unified" poem, but a series of symbols of water and light. Another unpublished part (III) you haven't seen; so I send it along.[1] It's based on a lynching I saw outside Mt. Sterling, Ky., when I was eleven. I'm sure at some time or other I've told you both about it. This is the only copy I have, and I'm sick of typing it; so please mail it back at your convenience. It lacks the scope of "The Buried Lake," but it's sharper and more active.

I'm glad, Andrew, your book moves. What we do is often by chance. I have never expected to write any more verse; then all these images began to rise. We just have to wait and be patient. We'd like to see some of the new book when you're ready to show it.

Affly, Allen

AL

P.S. You're exactly right about the "aging child." I'm changing "Homburg" ("weak specification") to "top hat," even sharper and more grotesque.

1. "The Swimmers," (1953).

Gainesville, Fla.
1822 NW 8th Ave.
Nov. 24, 1952

Dear Brother:

I've copied right away the poem, fearing the responsibility of the single copy, which I am returning. Haven't had time yet to read it carefully. There's a clarity almost sensuous about the images in their immediate impact on the boy which gives the dramatic situation the reverberations beyond the occasion. It effaces the naturalistic violence by means of the innocent view, the tension thus set up enriching the action as it leads the reader towards the center of a mystery.

I believe I like Homburg better, the play on man's town and maybe I follow the suggestion too far but I see all those stacks of bones, tangled like giant Jack Straws in the prison camps, the dead, half-dead, and quality of death there—but the most fearsome of all—the kind of crazy geometry of the sight, the utter inhuman sight of the inner truth the reduction by man of mankind to this abstraction.

Affectionately, Andrew

AL

University of Minnesota
Feb. 10, 1953

Dear Brother:

The enclosed letter from Douglas Jerrold is self-explanatory. I couldn't help him much—I'm so far from historical materials.

Caroline leaves in 4 weeks for Univ. of Washington to teach the spring quarter: I go East for 2 weeks to pick up money lecturing. There's no fun any more.

Affly, Allen
AL

By the way the Hopkins symposium is pretty good, but too much of the social science mentally has infiltrated it. I hope you get your essay in.[1]

1. "How Many Miles to Babylon?" *The Hopkins Review,* 6 (Spring-Summer 1953), 101–104.

Gainesville, Fla.
Monday

Dear Brother:

I have been meaning to write you, but as I was involved and had been for six weeks in getting my central intelligence into the realm of the dead, in this instance history preceding the present action, and getting him there without the reader's awareness until he had already become involved, by witnessing its resurrection and so freed of the static dicta of history, you know how hard it is to write letters, which always tend to divert you and which are as easily tempting as reading in such instances. But I think I have happened on something which might become a technical device able to obviate the clumsiness of backward-looking, the flashback etc., which even when skillfully done tend to make you aware of the mechanics of writing and so lose [for] you the sense of witnessing or partaking in the action. But even so I have been reading, or rereading your essays to tone me up,[1] and found that what I had done was nothing new at all, but maybe a renewal. I suppose it's always so. Your point in "The Symbolic Imagination"[2] which seems to deal as much with your sense of the angelic as the angelic clarified my experiment, insofar as it showed the only way to approach the supernatural is through the natural. This emphasis seemed to me the particular value of the discourse on Dante, as "The Angelic Imagination"[3] showed me the simplest term to show up the flaws in writers like [Carson] McCullers, [Truman] Capote and [Tennessee] Williams, not that these don't have other flaws which make them pretty second-rate, although the last book McCullers showed more sincerity and truth, except that she didn't know it and so did not end her book, ending it where she started, ignoring the growth of the center of action.[4] I suppose I wouldn't read these people if students didn't ask questions about them. I'm so slow a writer and have so fumbling a mind that if I get anything done, over and above the demands of family and job, I have to restrict myself sharply. But these people are angelic even if in a poor way by trying to deal with essences, such as ghosts and qualities of evil, so that there is no distinction between nature and supernature. You have affirmed my comprehension of that risk of the leap into the supersensual through the senses. These are certainly fine essays, the one on Longinus and the new criticism[5] particularly I liked. I've been meaning to ask you why, in "The Hovering Fly,"[6] you didn't mention the abrupt marriage of the young girl to the adventurer, which seems to me to be the underpart or counterpart to the death and fly. It's the final comment and focus of the worldly family, the illusion of innocence, as well as another exposure of the irony inherent in the situation. I haven't thought it out, but it seems to justify the long and full treatment of the family in the center of the book.

Are we to meet at Sewanee on these Fellowships? I hope so, although it's going to be pretty hard for me to get away. I wrote Spears about it. I thought this issue of the *Review* was good and liked very much the story by [Danforth] Ross. He seems to be teaching at Minn. Who is he? "The Buried Lake"[7] is as good as I thought it was. It's certainly good to see you getting better, for the fifties not only ain't much fun but they are turbulent with the waste fumes of the thirties and forties. But then I've never been gifted with much energy. That's a terrible deprivation. I can't take off, like you to foreign parts, with a growing family like I have.

Aff., Andrew

TLS

1. Lytle is reading *The Forlorn Demon: Didactic and Critical Essays* (Chicago: Regnery, 1953), a volume of articles Tate had previously published elsewhere. 2. First published as "The Symbolic Imagination: A Meditation on Dante's Three Mirrors" in the *Kenyon Review,* 14 (Spring 1952), 256–77. 3. First published as "The Angelic Imagination: Poe and the Power of Words," in the *Kenyon Review,* 14 (Summer 1952), 455–75. 4. Probably *The Ballad of the Sad Cafe.* 5. First published as "Longinus," in the *Hudson Review,* 1 (Autumn 1948), 344–61; but afterwards reprinted as "Longinus and the 'New Criticism'" in *The Hovering Fly, The Forlorn Demon,* etc. 6. First published as "Dostoevsky's Hovering Fly: A Causerie on the Imagination and the Actual World," *The Sewanee Review,* 51 (Summer 1943), 353–69. Later reprinted as "The Hovering Fly." 7. The poem had just been published in *The Sewanee Review,* 61 (Spring 1953), 177–80.

University of Minnesota
May 12, 1953

Dear Brother,

I very much enjoyed your good letter. Of course you needn't suppose—as you don't—that I don't know how tough those technical problems are; that's one reason why I've never written another novel. At any rate the difficulties of poetry, whether greater or smaller, are more congenial.

Whenever you have a good portion of your ms. ready to be looked at I wish you'd send it to me.

I am in the doldrums again—sheer physical exhaustion I suppose, after three lecture-reading trips since the middle of February. It wasn't exactly avarice. We had to accumulate money to leave here, since I can't send any back from my salary in Italy. We expect to go over around the middle of July, though my duties don't begin in Rome till November 1. What the duties are I don't yet know. I suppose they couldn't be heavy. I have been asked to go to Oxford for six weeks on the way,[1] but I think I'm declining because of the bad company, which will be a lot of social scientists topped off by a young man named Peter Viereck,[2] whom I can't stand.

I doubt that Monroe has the money to bring us to Sewanee, though I wish he had and wish too there were time. I am not greatly impressed by the applications so far. Donald Justice seems good, and so does Danforth Ross. (Ross by the way is from Clarksville, and a cousin of Caroline's.) Flannery O'Connor is very good, but she has already, I understand, got a Kenyon fellowship; so I don't understand her appearance on our list. I suppose we may leave that to Monroe.

Well, we ain't as young as we were. As for me, as I get older and physically weaker, my mental powers seem to increase; and the irony doesn't please me, because I'm getting short-winded. But we can't have everything. As you know I have always resented having to make a living; as the Freudians say, my ego-satisfactions are not only not connected with the struggle for a living, but frustrated by it. But there is no relief in sight! I am in Sewanee a couple of days in March, and decided again that I'd like to settle there in my old age on a small unearned increment, if I could get it.

Love to Edna.

Affectionately, Allen

TLS

1. As part of a Fulbright program, Tate spent the summer lecturing in the American Studies Program in Oxford and the fall and winter as a professor at the University of Rome. 2. Professor of history at Mount Holyoke College. His volume of poetry, *Terror and Decorum* won the Pulitzer prize for poetry in 1948.

54 Hodge Road
Princeton, New Jersey
August 6, 1954

Dear Brother, [Harvard, Mass.]

It looks like we can't make it up to New England, even to Chatham to see Ben. I just can't face any more driving than is necessary. We've decided to see Ben in Cincinnati on the way to Minnesota. I'm mighty sorry about this because Minnesota is pretty far from Florida, and our lines intersect very seldom. If you possibly can please stop here on the way South, if only for a day. We'll be here right along until about Sept. 15.

For one thing I would like to see what you've done on your book. I've done very little work in the past year, but now I'm ready to go, as soon as I arrive in the Twin Cities. I've worked better there than anywhere else in many years, mainly because the city is so uninteresting that it is easy to withdraw and look inward.

Nancy is all right again. The trouble was largely the small house. It was all right for a middle-aged couple without children, but for the Woods and their three children it was hopeless. Caroline came back in April, sold the small house and bought this large old Ruskin Gothic mansion at the other end of town. I don't need to describe it to you. It's not unlike the Nelson house in Murfreesboro. When the children yell in one part of the house they can't be heard in another.

I couldn't quite get it clear from Bee Fox what you are doing at Harvard. She said some sort of "international" course.[1] It has been so long since I taught any kind of course that I shudder at the prospect of my first class.

After a year in Europe I scarcely know where I am. Caroline throve in Italy. My digestion got worse and worse. I will never again agree to stay in Europe more than two months at a time.

Love to Edna and the children. I'd love to see them before they are grown and married, as they will surely be in two winks of the eye.

Affly, Allen

TLS

1. Lytle was teaching at the International Seminar of the Harvard Summer School.

Belmont, Mass.
330 Waverly St.
Tuesday

Dear Brother:

I'm sorry you don't feel up to coming by here, but we'll stop on the way home. It won't be so long now, as this seminar is over in two weeks. Driving in this part of the country is awful. I have caught on to it, I guess, and they seem to know what they are doing, but the blending of traffic terrifies me. I don't believe I could ever live here again. Pamela and I drove up from Florida, Edna [and] the other children flew.[1] I was late getting here, having just come in from the conference at Salt Lake City,[2] and the last day we pulled out of N.C. at four in the morning. I had hoped to spend the night in New Jersey, but I got on that turnpike and couldn't get off; the traffic shunted me over the Washington bridge just at the time of the evening traffic, I took a wrong turn and found myself down by the ships and docks. It was raining and I had a hard time turning around, and by grace I got on the Merritt turnpike, exhausted, in torture, and that was like driving through a spaceless, unlocated abstraction. There were no motels, no place to stop and the traffic not giving you time to look or turn. I blindly turned off in desperation and found myself in the [quiet] country of the rich. All was quiet and peaceful, a man was walking a little dog, but it was a maze, no motels there, no hotels. Some lost soul advised me to go to the Boston post road, and there, it was dark by now, I fell in with the trucks, three and four abreast, charging like beasts, I was so exhausted that by this time all sense of reality was gone, and I found myself charging between them, turning in the dark, the lights glazed from the rain like a reflection from some inferno. There were no motels here either. Finally we stopped out of the last faint streak of will and found a woman who would take us in. I'm still not recovered.

I shouldn't have come, and I shouldn't have brought the family, but I didn't feel like letting Edna run the children for the summer alone. Incidentally I am [in] what is called, grandiloquently, the International Seminar of the Harvard Summer School. It is divided into three parts, economics, politics, and the humanities, I'm in charge of the humanities. It is made up of young men and women from Asia and Europe who have made some impression in their own countries, they are philosophers, painters, poets, etc. None of them studied for my thesis, which is yours, the matter of communion between east and west and in societies as opposed to communication. So I've had to improvise. I guess we've done very well. I got along fine with the colored folks, but the Europeans know it all, or think they do, particularly a German, who talks too much and is often rude. I should have been working on my novel, as it was going well when I left off; but the University likes for me to go a few places every now and then, to sustain my position in Florida. Harvard is a big name with them. I figured it's another indirect way to sustain the family, but the cost has been high. You don't do any good at these things. I refused at first, but they thought it was money, and I couldn't make it clear and I don't talk well over the telephone.

I'm very anxious for you and Caroline to read what I've done on the book. If it comes off, I intend to dedicate it to you both, but it's a risky book. I've let a few students read it, and one or two other parts of it. It goes slowly because I am discovering it as I go along. I have a central intelligence who speaks all languages (in a sense) and who is based vaguely on Uncle Jack Lytle. It's, for one thing, an effort to transfuse the essence of certain myths which recur through time within the conventions of a given society. All such ideas merely begin a work, the work takes over. But my feeling about symbol is that it should suffuse, not be too apparent, the action and not be an emblem which is outside the action and can only be a kind of guide and maybe not the best kind.

We'll be looking forward to seeing all of you shortly after the twenty-fifth of this month. I'll send a card or wire that day.

With love from us,

Andrew

TLS

1. The Lytles now have their third daughter, Lillie Langdon. 2. The annual Utah Writers' Conference under the direction of Brewster Ghiselin.

1409 E. River Road
Minneapolis, Minn.
November 15, 1954

Dear Brother:

I get worse all the time about letters, evn when there are no distractions. The trip out here was difficult, and until last week we were living with friends, until this house should be available. We are nicely settled now, and look ahead to the snow, which ought to confine us and encourage work.

I hope you will send that section of your novel. We can both read it now without our eyes being pulled in six other directions at the same time.

Every spare minute since we've been here I have spent on the poetry anthology[1] I told you about. It's just about done, and I hope by the first of the month to get down to real work.

We still talk about the Lytles' visit in Princeton—a memorable week. Practically everybody we know is deteriorating, or at least holding their own. It seems to me that you all are better than you ever were.

Red has written some new *short* poems which I hope to get this week.[2]

We send our love to you all. Please give those fine girls a kiss for me.

Affectionately, Allen

AL

1. *Modern Verse in English: 1900–1950,* ed. David Cecil and Allen Tate (New York: Macmillan Co., 1958; London: Eyre and Spottiswoode, Ltd., 1958). 2. These eventually make up part of the collection entitled *Promises: Poems 1954–1956* (New York: Random House, 1957).

1409 East River Road
Minneapolis 14, Minn.
December 4, 1954

Dear Brother:

I read your ms. about a week ago, then put it aside to let it simmer in my mind. In its present structure I had difficulty following the action and the relations of the characters, and I wanted to see whether it would become clearer after a few days, or the opposite.[1] You have two wonderful episodes—the water-witching and the hunt-seduction-knifing episodes.

But the continuity is tough, there's no doubt about it. I can't see that you would lose anything by making all the complicated family relationships perfectly plain at the outset; and I don't think this would involve a radical change of method. What you are doing here is, it seems to me, an extension of Faulkner's method in *As I Lay Dying*. But there are certain respects in which your attempt to extend it makes you liable to its disadvantages. You will remember that the scene in AILD is very narrow: all the action is concentrated around the body of the mother and the necessity to bury it in her chosen ground. The soliloquies are short, and the range of consciousness in all the characters is very narrow. But your "soliloquies" are so long that they cease to be that: they have so much in them that one has to remember at times that *all this* is being said or thought by so-and-so. For the action has reached such magnitude that it is severed from the actual interior monologue, and remains merely within the point of view of, say Lucius. Since this is true—if it *is* true—it would seem to mean that in extending Faulkner's method so far as all that, you have virtually abandoned it; and it might be better to make certain alterations that would give you all the advantages of *your* method, without the disadvantages of *his*. This would mean, of course, that you would have to give up the opening narrative by Sol Leatherbury—in fact all the quick entrances into the minds of the merely flat characters, who don't really illuminate the main action.

I suppose soliloquy isn't the precise word for what you set out to do; but whatever that word is, it seems to me that it has set a trap for you in another way—that is, the extreme rural Southern idiom. For example, the opening gambit by Sol Leatherbury is so extreme in this respect that it erects an almost insuperable barrier between the reader and the exposition of Cree's death. The death is so important to what follows—it is the critical event—that surely it ought to reach the reader in the round, so to speak, and not cluttered up with an almost phonetic transcription of the idiom of a poor white, whose involvement in the situation is remote and whose point of view is not sufficiently informed to give the incident its symbolic weight.

On this general question of Southern idiom, it seems to me that you and Red have gone rather wild—so wild, in fact, that it is no longer in the interests of a naturalistic verisimilitude, but a kind of virtuosity that runs away with you both. There are two writers of the older generation who do this thing better than either you or Red—Elizabeth [Maddox] Roberts and Caroline; and there is a very young one, Flannery O'Connor, who is a master of it. Just read her "The Circle of Fire," in the *Kenyon.*[2] She has instinctively hit upon what seems to me the essentials of the matter. The local idiom is recreated cheifly through word order and rhythm, with an occasional local idiom, and all done with the *minimum* of distorted, or phonetic, spelling. Caroline, as matter of fact, learned this from Ford, who would let a character say (in our spelling) "It warn't," only he spelt it just "want," because the apostrophe halted the attention of the reader at an irrelevant effect. Hardy too was a master: his Wessex peasants spoke a much more extreme dialect than our poor whites, but if he had rendered it literally it would have been unreadable. Then there's the problem of the colloquial idiom of the gentry—of Jack Cropleigh, for example. Some of his flights of idiom, in the midst of "educated" language, are highly effective; there's a kind of Elizabethan invention and abandon, and it's good. But when you are in the mind of a character, however, or rather in whatever idiom he may conduct his interior monologue, I am sure that it should be represented on the page as straight prose, with only an occasional exception which one's sense of fitness alone can justify.

I haven't at all communicated to you my admiration of one telling effect after another. It ought to be your best novel. Again, as to the method, I should think that the more you simplify it the better. Shouldn't your concern be to make the central action as obvious as possible, rather than, as you intimate, to keep it back? Since the book seems to be Lucius' "education," couldn't you get it pretty quickly established in his point of view? If you do that first, then you can depart from it as necessary. As the method now stands, I confess that I don't yet know just *what* the central situation is, because I don't know just what kin all these people are to one another. Is there any advantage in not getting that laid out before the reader as soon and as lucidly as possible?

We are settled in for the winter. I am trying to get the last loose ends of this anthology gathered up, so that I can get down to real work. I say real work, but it is not the work I want to do. I have written only five poems in eight years, and if I don't get back to verse soon I may never. Like John Ransom.

Are the Foxes down there? If they are give them our love. News from Princeton is good. Nancy is on her feet again, and will doubtless be all right until they get into another muddle of debt and psychotherapy. Give our love to Edna and the girls. They are gals after my own heart.

Affectionately, Allen

TLS

P.S. I'm sending you a book in a few days that I've learned more from than from anything I've read in years—*God and the Unconscious,* by Victor White.

1. A first draft of *The Velvet Horn.* 2. "Circle of Fire" was first published in the spring issue of *Kenyon Review,* 1954.

Gainesville, Fla.
1822 NW 8th Ave.
Dec. 11, 1954

Dear Brother:

Your astute reading of the mss. so far is going to be a big help. I suppose finding the proper structure for this novel has caused me more trouble than anything else I've ever done. I deliberately didn't tell you what I am now finding I am doing, because naturally I wanted to see how it struck you. I hadn't realized how confusing the family relationship is; Edna has said the same thing. I think one reason for it is that I had so much trouble recreating the physical world, and even learning about the people, that I had to plunge in where I could in an exploratory way, to involve them, to see what they were. I started out with an incestuous theme, which I feel is pretty strong in our society, maybe in any country society; but what is incest? I also wanted to locate the action between 1880 and 1910, which I take to be the last moment of equilibrium in the western world, that is, the pause, the hiatus. And then too a certain vice of mind, which seemed to be growing, the vice of indirection has been a terrible struggle. Of course, incest itself lends to hidden veiled allusion, but at one point I found that I had a monologue within a monologue within a monologue. It took me a year to break that down. I think I've [got] this somewhat well in hand. But the truth is I've never been able to approach a subject chronologically. It's flat and dull, at least to me, when I do it. But how to control this surrounding of a subject, not so much on the surface, as within levels of consciousness, whose virtues are real but whose risks are plenty?

You saw the effort, a later effort, as I originally opened with the Water Witch section in Lucius' p.[oint] of view, to extend the method of AILD. You are quite right about that, and about what has happened. I see now that the falling of the tree is merely the occasion of the release of the various forces which will make the action. In fact I had already been seeing it, but needed your explicit criticism.

Here's another thing. I started out with Lucius as the central figure, but found I was getting more and more interested in Jack. I still have got to decide this before I can go on. I suppose it would be better to place it initially with Lucius and identify Jack with him, which I did in the buggy ride scene but also allow him to understand the larger implications of the action and enveloping action. For he is the water witch, in the limited and symbolic sense and he is consciously so.

Let me think aloud here in a kind of paraphrase of what the action now seen ought to be. When the Cropleigh parents are blown up in the steam boat, the oldest son, Beverly, withdraws into the wilderness and takes his brothers and sister with him, all except Jack who is only partially involved. What Beverly is doing is resisting, refusing the common plight, the human involvement in the dualism of good and evil after the expulsion from the garden of innocence. What happens is that Jack refuses to go along with this and so does the Doctor brother, but the brother Duncan and Julia, the younger ones, find in a kind of play which the wilderness offers that which strengthens the love between them. This is particularly so on Duncan's part. So that society in the form of a half indifferent Aunt, and Joe Cree, her son and Julia's cousin, take her to make a lady of her at the time of adolescence. When Duncan sees her again, through Jack's revery-dream, not only as taken away but as engaged to Joe, he is awakened to the full meaning of his love, through its deprivation and out of this, in the night on the hunt commits the act. This fact will be withheld until the end. Joe Cree thinks he is the father of Lucius. Until Julia tells him otherwise, and she, trying to keep him at home and Lucius at home, in anger lets it out. He commits suicide by letting the tree fall on him. That is, out of his egoism, keeping the world established no longer has any meaning. This order he has tried to keep is so involved with the old vanity that he can't take it. But Pete Legrand, the outlander, the stranger, thinks he is the father of Lucius. He is the man of power, the exploiter, the raper, the man denied the sensuous innocent delight in the world's business. At heart he is a sentimentalist. His capability for love has been destroyed by the scar and the deprivation of it earlier. Now, being able to hold the mortgage on the property which is Julia's and Lucius's, he thinks he wants to unite himself with his deprived wife and son. But he doesn't want to wait, the conventions of mourning he wants to violate, he oversimplifies the situation and tries to force it before it is ready (ignoring the life between Julia and her husband Joe Cree). So his brutal routine of power is brought into play, which is his real self, and she tells him (maybe, I'm not sure) that Duncan is the father, at least she indicates the doubt of Lucius's parentage. You see I haven't gotten the incidents this far worked out, but anyway Lucius must overhear or learn, and this will take him back to the Peaks of Laurel, to the daughter of the hag there; but in the meantime his cousin and friend has married her sister and wants to make the family respectable, and when Lucius wants to use the sister for the plunging of himself into degradation, violence results. It will be Jack's part to try to save Lucius; it may be at the sacrifice of his life to do it, to save Lucius. Now that I have set this down, it sort of seems to be that Jack is the protagonist.

The subject then is what happens when you refuse to accept man's state, after he has been cast out of the innocent state. Jack as water witch is Beverly's spiritual counterpart. He doesn't go like his brother back into the garden, which he knows can't be done; but he is rebellious against the god-head. Only Jack fully knows and understands the past. That's my trouble about making it clear, the relationships.

The society itself is the kind of enveloping action. It is the world, and I want varying degrees of love's imperfection and miscarriages as an enlargement of the scene and for emphasis to the incest, which I take it is as far as love can go in refusing to accept the condition of the wandering of the outcast state, the seasonal turn of nature and life which never allows the permanent fixity of a state of innocence. That's why I used the flat figures, really as voices first. In the Wake scene they will take on more substance. You know how a thing can happen in the country and it will reach home before you do. I didn't want Sol to really embody the symbol. That's why I chose such a character. He merely reports the fact. I had thought that how little he saw in it would have its effect. I know that the idiom needs much more attention. And I will watch the mechanical diversions of it. I was aware that in the haste of writing some [of] it I hadn't worked it out. But this, I do think. It is not poor white necessarily, but that the idiom was basic to all speech, just as I feel that the gentry were more homespun except in certain families than I at least had previously considered it. I know this is my big problem. I'm glad that you think that it is effective in Jack's use of it, at least sometimes. He speaks all tongues, often with irony as well as his identification with all men.

It's hard to work it out, ain't it? The thing is your technical knowledge doesn't help too much when you're doing it. It's hard to get the real critical distance when you come to revise. I don't want an actual naturalistic verisimilitude. What you told me is what I tell my students, and I'll have to look at it, but I want the idiom to match the imagery and tone which is more complex. Suffuse it even.

I don't know how far I can let the imperfections of love intrude upon Lucius's story, his initiation. Maybe I'd better do it, or try to do it, and cut it if it doesn't work.

How does this seem to you?

I'll write you later. We are doing pretty well. I'm glad you approve of the girls. If I can just live long enough to get them started some way.

Affectionately, Andrew

TLS

I don't want to bother you with this now. It's helped me to put it down here. But does anything occur after this paraphrase?

1409 East River Road
Minneapolis 14
December 23, 1954

Dear Brother,

I'm glad you didn't find my comment entirely useless. It is always dangerous to say anything about a manuscript at that stage because it might mislead the author. But I suppose we've got to take the risk—the author as well as the commentator.

It seems to me that at present the progress of the book is being held up by the absence of a plot structure; and as our old friend Aristotle said, a plot is an action, not a quality. You seem to me to have a group of "confessions," each character exhibiting his inner quality, but this quality is not being moved toward a resolution. I confess I am a little surprised at your statement that you are not yet sure whither the whole entanglement is heading. Hasn't it all got to be centered on *one* character, or at least the relation of not more than two, with the others acting in the end rather as "messengers" or as catalytic agents? Of course, there are many fine novels which lack anything like so rigid a structure as that, but it seems to me that, given your tendency to invention and extension, which can easily run away with you, the tighter structure might well be borne in mind as a kind check.

Isn't a part of the trouble also in your intention—a secondary intention, at any rate—to depict a whole society? Well, [Honoré de] Balzac came to grief on that rock; and I am inclined to the extreme view that "society" is not a subject for fiction, except insofar as rendered detail of scene, etc., must be there to create The Direct Impression of Life. The society comes into fictional being only as a quality of character and action, not as an end in itself. I can deliver myself of this wisdom because I have been and still am to a great extent a victim of its lack. It has occurred to me in recent years, in retrospect upon our early days, that we made the South, and especially the Old South, an object of idolatry, in the strict sense of the word: we were worshiping a "perishable god." I have come to the view that no society is worth "saving" *as such:* what we must save is the truth of God and Man, and the right society follows. We thought that the South was an historical problem; it was actually a theological problem. We were like Oedipus at the end of his life: he sought peace at a certain "place," Colonus, but what he found was a grove sacred to the Eumenides, and the "peace of place" was his being swallowed up by Mother Earth. Place in itself is nothing, and I find myself emphasizing this point as a result of your remarks last summer; for it seems to me that "place" does not sustain us; we sustain place, and through it nature will give back to us only what we have put into it.

But all that has nothing to do with your practical problem. Now this matter of the "envelope," the narrative within a narrative, even to three stages beyond the first narrator. As we all know, technical problems are never merely technical. They are partly, and perhaps even initially, problems of the way we *see*. Knowing you now nigh on to thirty years, I would say that a certain modesty, a certain *pudeur,* leads you into the snare of the first-person narrator, or a series of them. You let these various Masks speak for themselves because you feel that you ought not to take charge of them. I can't help thinking that if you could get your own consent to do it, your technical problem would ease up considerably if you just began thus: "Cree went over and stood under the great white oak, and seemed to be fixed on the spot as it began to fall." You see what I mean.

You've got some wonderful material in that ms. and you *must* do something to realize it with the greatest possible force.

We certainly enjoyed getting the picture of Edna and the gals—a fine Christmas greeting. We're having Dan Ross and his nice Minnesota wife for Christmas dinner, and that will make it a little like home. Our love to you all.

Affly, Allen
TLS

Gainesville, Fla.
1322 NW 8th Ave.
Jan. 5, 1955

Dear Brother:

The only trouble with our old friend Aristotle is that he was talking about plays, and furthermore plays whose fable the audience and the authors already knew; so that the plot in a sense was already given, and the author reshifted emphases and interpretation. The novelist can't count on this today. What the novel has added to the scene, as you know is the panoramic effect. When you begin with feelings about and vague ideas, as I am doing for the first time, a plot would stultify the creative act, because you don't know enough when you begin. The people have to come alive through the author's enforced exploration of his people in situations. I started off with Lucius but Jack began to take over: that's why I said I was unsure. Of course, I have an idea and a clearer sense of where the novel is moving than I've indicated, but I'm sure that any plot in a novel so conceived, that is, without a fable's outlines, must grow out of the complication. The skill and the risk is to control it as it comes up from the unconscious. The trouble with this is that when you write it, it gets somewhat set and is therefore difficult to rebegin and find the moment to see out of the fragments the true form.

I had thought to begin on the periphery and move towards the center increasing the tension until it narrowed towards the climax. Surely you didn't get the feeling they were envelopes. Each segment is separate, whether it is an action or not. Perhaps this is wrong, but it seems to me you are thinking in terms of a play. Each segment, though, has to do, with varying degree, with the central situation. Maybe this can't be done. Maybe it's absolutely necessary to deal with one or two persons. I have always bucked against this limitation. And, of course, you are right: I feel the author should be anonymous except in the work. I can't work any other way. Whatever that feeling is, I suppose it's why I'm a writer instead of a politician.

This business of place and location exposes perhaps a temperamental difference between us. You know you've always been a wanderer, and yet you've never wandered in your mind because you live there. You've never felt much for the natural world, whereas with me, in the aspect of growing things, which locates you, it's been my great struggle to give it up, so that my interest would not be so divided. I don't see how you can save the truth of God and man except in terms of the conventions of some society. You might have a private salvation, but we were born at such a time and were formed by conventions whose fragmentations had not reached such a stage of dissolution as they have now. They had meaning. Indeed there would have been no Oedipus without an ordered state, and certainly no Antigone without Creon. Naturally religious belief is the spiritual core, but theology isn't the only discipline. And what were we to do, or how move or speak, when the theology of the South was so inadequate and the older Catholic institution, which once was all pervasive, absent. The South's crucial situation was that the trading religion you mentioned once did not express, indeed contradicted, the experience of a people involved in the turn of seasons and the mystery of growing [. . . page missing[1]] boudoir is a vulgarity so extreme that the spiritual poverty and corruption is there finally as the adversary Emma [Bovary] has all along confronted. She went to the priest for salvation, and he was of the enemy too. And this is made clear by the natural objects of bread and wine, which the priest and the atheist discover is the means of their fellowship at her wake. Now without the presence of this bread and wine, seen and tasted in Emma's house, the comparison to the sacramental counterpart could never so well be made. I remember now after years the old gentleman sitting with his toddies and the little nigger boy fetching them in *Penhally*. As great as James is it is hard to visualize his actors. But I don't want to get off on this. That's a mighty fine piece of yours in the recent issue of the *Sewanee*.[2] I do think we have to reckon with this lack in James and then read him for what he does, in spite of it. You're right, to wish him a mistress is aside the point; and yet this wound, if wound it was, will be found in his work. The imagination does not require much experience, but it does require the risk of the loss of self in the abyss. James, I believe, hovered above. I wonder if on the crucial occasion, he ever plunged. I haven't read him all, and I reserve judgment, and what I say is tentative nevertheless finds in my reading his limitation.

To me the writing of a book is an exploration and a self-discovery. I began this one out of a need, not the only need, to discover what is ever recurring in the human consciousness as myth or myths. Whether I had read Jung before or after this, I don't now remember; but this equates with his archetypal theory. Of one thing I was certain, the turn of the seasons and the meaning implicit in this turning. This is a beginning, I know, but for a people who live by the land, it is the body of the world; and this contradictory but all necessary body is the point of departure for the search of meaning. Theology is the science of sciences, as you say; but it can err, since it's made by man. Life everlasting is a theological concept, but it is viewed in terms of time. Eternity is timeless. When I did my section on Jack's dream-revery, he discovered in a certain area of the unconscious a sense of eternity, that there is no past, no future, only the present instant, which never dies. But only man can experience this in dream or revery, which is also timeless. There is another thing about Christian theology, and this is expression of a deeper thing, which has always puzzled me is its attitude toward woman and man's basic union with her. Was it St. Paul, "Better marry than burn"? Why this negative attitude? Does it come from Christ's attitude to his mother? Which I hadn't thought of until you mentioned [John] Layard, was it? Alan Watts says that the chivalric concept of woman was Manichean, not Christian. I don't know enough to check on this, but the predominant father-son relationship is a thing I've got to certainly unravel, and I feel it is connected with the Christian concept of sex, which concept has clouded the sense of sin, which actually is a "missing of the mark."

Well, wish me luck in this book. I may not be equal to it. It may miscarry in a big way, and if it does, it will show most plainly in the structure, I suppose. I feel that the novel is so young that we have got to experiment with it, learn from those who have gone before but not let the past grow rigid and kill. A lot of my action is in an area of the consciousness and the border line between the conscious and the unconscious. Maybe this can't be done, but it's not Balzac. I would like to take up your bet, but I don't have much energy, as you know. I have read the missal, I had Father Flye's for the De Soto book, but I can't promise to read it every day. Whatever salvation is for me will have to lie in my work. I don't know whether I've got the energy to be saved. With growing responsibilities and work which becomes all the time more difficult, although I'm stronger in many ways, the demands on me deplete me more. If you can find those books, I'd like to see them. Maybe I can order them somewhere if you don't.

Did you know Miss Daisy Bagley died of cancer in December?

Write me another good letter, and tell Brother he's been a help too. I respect his judgment so considerably that I have trouble finding where it misses the mark with me, and where it doesn't.

Love to you. I hope it won't be so long before we see each other again. And I'm mighty glad to get the good news of Nancy and Percy. I guess he'll see in the end that the world is not one big sick bed, at least not a Freudian bed.

Andrew

TLS

1. Unfortunately, it seems a page of this letter is missing. The topic shifts from discussing the instinctive religious sensibility of the Southern people because of their closeness to nature on the bottom of one page to an analysis of Flaubert's Emma Bovary, on the top of the next. It also seems that Lytle now directs his remarks more specifically to Caroline. 2. Lytle probably means Gordon's "Emmanuele! Emmanuele!" which appeared in the 1954 Spring issue, pp. 181–222.

1409 East River Road
Minneapolis 14, Minnesota
February 9, 1955

Dear Brother,

The high and fast dialectic shooting back and forth between you and Caroline has left me far in the rear. So this is just a note about odds and ends.

But I go back to your letter of January 5, and pick up the point about "place and location." Because of the peculiar temperament of my mother I never *lived* in a place, but was bounced around from one to another; so there is this difference between us that you speak of. I agree that you need place and the natural world; but I think that, when you generalize and say that the truth of God can be saved only through the conventions of some society I believe you are wrong from almost every point of view. In the first place, if you are right, Christianity could never have risen; it bucked the conventions of the Roman world. (Look at *Marius the Epicurean*[1] again: [Walter] Pater's whole problem is to find out whether the New Religion had any relevance to the ancient society represented by Marius; and mind you it was a beautiful agrarian society, rooted for centuries in the land.) On the other hand, it seems to me beyond dispute that every writer has got to use what is given him. Since you see the problem as you do, you must approach it that way. But again I do not believe it is the physical, natural place *as such* that even you need; you evidently need it as a matrix through which you can make concrete and sensuous a transcendental unity. The corporate entity of the people making up a society makes the place, not the place the corporate entity. There was nothing inherent in the natural landscape of Tuscany that issued in the Sienese culture:[2] even Sienese *nature* was created by the Sienese. I come more and more to the view that much of our agrarian thinking twenty years ago was much more modern than we realized: we were setting up the means as the end. The means is of crucial importance. But having agreed that the agrarian is superior to the industrial society as a means, we tended to rest the case there, and thought of the agrarian as the end. I would almost reverse your statement: "There would have been no Oedipus without an ordered state," to read: There would have been no ordered state without Oedipus; for the reason why the ordered state of Thebes was in trouble was that the divine order represented by the priest-king got off center. I can't help thinking that the modern conception of "society" is a version of the well-known heresy of "historicism"—the idea that the state is first and the religion second, as the mere expression of the state. Another version of it is Erastianism.[3]

Well this agrument could go on forever, and I suppose its value lies in its sharpening our tools, when they tend to rust from disuse. More later.

Affly, Allen

TLS

You see I don't agree that John Ransom has a good theological mind. He makes up his theology as he goes along—mixture of odds and ends from old Dr. Ransom plus a little eccentric Aristotelianism. So far as I know he has never read *any* theology—Calvin or Luther or St. Thomas, etc.

1. Pater's historical novel (1885). 2. The culture of Siena, a city in West Central Italy which was finally annexed to Tuscany in 1557. 3. The doctrine of Thomas Erastian which declared that the state had supreme authority in church matters.

WESTERN UNION TELEGRAM
Gainesville, Fla.
[Nov. 19, 1955]

Allen Tate [2848 Irving Ave. So., Apt. 4]

THEN SUDDENLY THE NOON TURNS AFTERNOON STOP TIME, FALL NO MORE WITH LOVE.

Andrew and Edna[1]

1. The Lytles sent this telegram to Tate on his fifty-sixth birthday.

University of Minnesota
November 21, 1955

Dearest Lytles,

When the operator read the telegram to me at 2 A.M.—after an all-day birthday party—I had a bad moment of paranoia, until I heard the signatures, when sanity returned. It has definitely turned afternoon, but time is still falling. I feel like a fatigued grasshopper.

I wish to God I could see you all soon.

I am going to Sewanee for three days—Dec. 1, 2, and 3—and then to Tuscaloosa to give the Phi Beta Kappa speech on the 5th. Back here by air on the 6th. Will you all stay put over Christmas? I will probably go to Princeton if I'm not broke. Caroline is spending a lot of money in Rome, but not extravagantly, and I may just hibernate over Christmas. She has decided to stay on till January to be with Fannie and Lon, who fly to Rome on Nov. 30.

What a life we live in our old age.

Love to you all, Allen
AL

P.S. Percy & Nancy are flourishing. A little professional success was all that Percy needed, and this is reflected in Nancy. Those *particular* troubles are over, though no doubt others, incident to our fallen condition, are necessarily latent.

Gainesville, Fla.
1822 NW 8th Ave.
Dec. 27, 1955

Dear Brother:

I've been trying to write you, but we had a spell of sickness, thought to go away for Christmas; then found the old empty purse kept us here. I tried at the last minute after getting your note to see if there was an opening that would get you here to speak; found again that they set it up a year in advance, due to the kind of machinery which runs this place. Anyway the Phi Beta Kappa is set here for January; so I've set the machinery in motion, if it would suit you, to get you here next year for that. To get a man to speak here, you've got to have a group or something or the other to sponsor it. It's such a poor way to manage a speaking program, with the best money going to the journalists and such-like, and with the pseudo-democratic assumption that all the colleges have to be represented, which actually works out that the topical names of the moment and the speech and so forth mostly get their people in. However, there are a lot of the younger instructors and so forth who want very much to see you and hear you, and others too, of course, and it is under way—but how can anybody know what he wants to do a year hence. But I thought that if you and Caroline could get away for several days, we could get somebody to stay with the children and at that time run far down the coast for a little sun and water. And I will be free of mind to enjoy you all before the next plunge under, if there is any more. You always feel that nothing more will come, and of course that day will show itself, too.

I'm sorry the telegram woke you up. It was supposed to have gotten there in the morning, but I guess you were away from home all day. Lon called last night and told us about his nephew's death and the flight back from Rome; so I guess after all you were all in Princeton with Nancy and Percy and the young. We tried to do with cheer and tinsel and baubels with a few presents for the young, for I was set on not borrowing any money for presents. You know I had a tornado, as if to make me freshly aware, begin at the farm and knock down a tobacco barn, then skip five miles away through my woods carrying seventy-five chickens and tearing up a town. It showed me how narrow a margin we operate on, as it took practically a year's rent to replace the barn. I don't carry much insurance, but pusillanimously took out more after this disaster. We rent it to a good man for money rent. It is so far away I could not operate it otherwise. He has done much for it, but the time is coming when I will have to sell it, I'm afraid. As you know, I've never been able to make the choice between writing and having to do with the land; but at last, when it is almost too late, I guess I will have to. Anyway, with the book off my mind,[1] I can view it with care and composure. We are outgrowing this little house here, the baby sleeps in our room which means we have no room or privacy, which didn't seem to matter before she came and since we always went to the farm for summer. The tenantry has deteriorated, the mechanism of farm is worse (they even feed cows in large lots here in Florida by push buttons.) I have heard of two houses at Beersheba for sale, around four thousand each, with dining room and kitchen off to themselves. That's twenty-five miles from Sewanee, but it's in the woods, with no assembly grounds, and the houses at Sewanee I imagine are right high. You might keep that in mind; we might even go up there in October when we go back to Vanderbilt[2] and look around. I see it, it's the only way to get a real house with the kind of money we have; and I had thought, for ourselves at least, that it might be fine to go there for the summers; and then when the time comes, Edna and I could live there for eight or nine months of the year; then spend the hard winter months in Florida, maybe by then with me just lecturing enough here to carry us along or maybe getting a shack near the warm waters. For the first time I think of old age, and of how fast we move towards it; and it would be wonderful if Beersheba could appeal to you. But you could make your sallies into the world. Dr. Mims does; he says he is making more money than he ever did, but maybe I told you this. Maybe you, or we, ought not to think so far ahead, when you take the risks of an art, I guess you live up to the hilt in those risks. And always will.

I'm still trying to get away from Bobbs-Merrill. Chambers, I hear, is out. I will try again with the new man in January. I can't sign a contract with anybody else or get an advance, until this is arranged. It's hard for me to do business when I am working. I'm in the last quarter of the book, see it all for the first time, and with luck ought to finish by March, then revise the rest of spring. I will take your advice to the extent of making the structural changes in the beginning to make relationships clear; but a part of my trouble with the reader must remain, as the matrix of the structure deals with two kinds of present tenses. In a certain area of the unconscious there is no time, only the images of the present, even though they have happened in past time. These images operate on a conscious present. The rhythm of the book alternates between these two present tenses. I am trying for something which is not naturalism. I happened to reread Frank's piece on spacial form in literature,[3] and I guess I am closest to that, without being conscious that I was doing it. It may fail, but that's the risk I am taking. Unless you are going to experiment with fiction and try to force from it what may be implicit in it, there's no real involvement of interest. You may remember the garden of Eden section, the roving point of view is placed in Jack's mind at the border of consciousness and unconscious revery. It rises and dips there, as a man going under and out of water, which is the way all reveries, hallucinations, and visions operate, I think. Anyway, when you all read the whole, you will see it, I hope.

Love to you, and let us hear how things are, and something of the last Roman pilgrimage,

Andrew

TLS

1. *The Velvet Horn*. 2. The original date set for the Fugitives' Reunion at Vanderbilt was October 18–20. 3. Joseph Frank, "Spatial Form in Modern Literature," *The Sewanee Review,* 53 (1945), 221–40; 433–56; 643–53.

University of Minnesota
March 28, 1956

Dear Brother,

Your good long letter of more weeks ago than I like to remember has been on my desk every morning; and now I have the letter of March 19. I look ahead [to] the reunion with the usual mixed feelings. If we can only get away from the public exploitation enough to talk a little among ourselves, it will be fine; but it does mean that Randall [Stewart] and the Chancellor are trying to account for every minute, public and private.[1] We will be staying at Cold Chimneys, and Fannie writes that she has room for all of us, since she now has the house of late lamented Sister for the overflow. We are bringing with us from Kansas City a nice young couple, the Howard Adamses, dyed in the wool Confederates, as only Missourians can be, and perhaps also some Princeton friends now in K.C., who "want to see the South for the first time" under the auspices of "people who are the real thing." All very pleasant, but complicated. I think the Lytles and the Tates ought to have a private agreement to disappear for a good part of one day—after our program is done—just for a private jollification. I would have preferred October too.

I haven't the slightest idea what I am going to say on our program. I wish I knew what Red will do. I will try to write out something, perhaps three or four pages, a basis, and then after I get the feel of the audience just talk off the cuff. But I will send you a carbon the moment I have the written part finished.

As you know, Caroline is Visiting Professor at the Univ. of Kansas (Lawrence) for the spring semester, and I have been virtually like a Princeton-N.Y. commuter. I've flown down three times since Feb. 1st. She comes here Friday for her spring vacation. We were so broke after the Italian binges that she felt she had to take the job. It's a grim place, and she has had a hard time, but it goes better now. I wish I could take off the entire week of the reunion, getting to Nashville a couple of days ahead of the program, and I wish you all could too. We could have some fun before fatigue sets in. Could you? We might.

I am mighty glad to hear that the novel nears the end. I do wish you could get away from Bobbs-Merrill. You've suffered from their limitations more than 25 years.

Love to you all,

Affly, Allen

TLS

1. The Fugitive reunion at Vanderbilt was held on May 3–5, 1956. The proceedings of the conference are in Rob Roy Purdy, editor, *Fugitives' Reunion*. Nashville: Vanderbilt University Press, 1959. Stewart was chairman of the English department. Harvie Branscomb was Chancellor.

Gainesville, Fla.
1822 NW 8th Ave.
May 28, 1956

Dear Brother:

Just a note to ask you if you left a topcoat in John's car. I found one and brought it back here, thinking it must be yours. General exhaustion has kept me from writing before, but now that school is out, or about to be, you'd better write me where you want it sent. I'll get a box and post it.

Well, no time for conversation. Got a letter from a man named [Lawrence] Bowling,[1] which you must have got too. I can't see the point of it much. Such things are premature burials.

In haste, A

TLS

1. Bowling was a student of Davidson. Taught at the University of Alabama, among other places, wrote "An Analysis of Davidson's 'Lee in the Mountains,'" *Georgia Review,* 6 (Spring 1952), 66–88.

Ambassador Hotel
Cambridge, Mass.
Sept. 27, 1956

Dear Brother,

I am about to take off on a jaunt to India, with stopovers in Italy and France on the way back. Hence I write this brief message lest I disappear somewhere forever in the mysterious East. I have been almost daily aware that I did not answer your note written right after the reunion. For me the most satisfactory part of it was *our* reunion.

I leave on October 7th, and expect to return about December 19th. The

State Dept. is sending me on the Specialists Program. It came out of a clear sky early in August. I have got leave from Minnesota for the fall quarter, with—thank heaven—67% of my salary. Caroline will stay in Princeton in a new house that we bought this summer—rather a very old house, but in almost perfect condition, and set in an acre of ground.

When I get back I don't know what our situation will be. I think Caroline will live in Princeton permanently, and I will live alone in Minneapolis. There is nothing about all this that you don't know.[1] Now that the separation (without divorce) is a fact, I have an entirely new set of anxieties. I know you all will not mention this at present. I think it is Caroline's privilege to speak of it if and when she wants to speak.

I hope you got your book finished this summer. In the midst of my anxieties I couldn't write letters. About all I could manage was the seminar here. It came off very well.

I am staying here until October 4th, when I go back to NY for final preparation for the flight. I can't stay in Princeton, and I can't bear NY any more. I am sorry not to be in Princeton when Nancy's baby is born—now almost any day. The crisis of her parents has been a little hard on her in her condition, but she seems to bear it with equanimity; and Percy has been very fine.

My love to you and Edna and the girls.

Allen

TLS

P.S. That old coat of mine. Just use it when you work around the yard in cool weather, or give it to some deserving colored boy, if such can be found under desegregation. I'm sorry I burdened you with it.

1. Caroline and Allen separated for the second time in 1955.

POST CARD
Bombay
10/20/56

To: Mr. & Mrs. Andrew Lytle [University of Florida]

Arrived last night, exhausted. Haven't had time to look around but feel little curiosity: it's like a great Mediterranean city. Five days in Delhi; now a week here giving a seminar. Your friends the Kirklands at airport to meet me. Rome, Nov. 3–17; Paris, Nov. 18–Dec. 1; London, Dec. 1–8; then N.Y. Love to you all,

A-

Gainesville, Fla.
1822 NW 8th Ave.
Feb. 7, 1957

Dear Brother:

I was sorry to be away when you called, but Edna said you had a good visit over the phone. I was late in returning and you were gone, or I would have phoned again. My trip to New York was I feel highly successful. Edna told you that after eight months of a quiet battle I got away from Bobbs-Merrill, and without acrimony or hard words passing between us. That was, I guess, why it took so long. I hated after so long an association to leave without good will there. It was so unnecessary.

After I finished the book, I had a long wait to hear which I did not understand. Several publishers wanted to see it, after having read the part in *The Sewanee Review,*[1] particularly Little, Brown and Knopf. I had sent it privately to David McDowell, one of the senior editors at Random House, since at the time I was not free from Bobbs. The news is that he has pulled out from Random House and has formed a publishing concern with a lad named Obolensky, the son of Alice Astor and the chief heir of Vincent. He also has written a novel which is a pretty good first book. The house is well-formed, and with plenty of credit and money will get a good start. McDowell was the man who quadrupled the sales of New Directions when he ran it for [James] Laughlin. He did it by pounding the sidewalks and just plain selling the books. Laughlin fired him because he was making him money and afterwards he went to Random. He left there because he was finding it more and more difficult to get backing for his books. He says the sales manager is only interested in merchandise and juveniles now and that the taste of the house is leaving with one of the owners who retires and that [Bennett] Cerf turned down two of his books without even reading them. He feels it is getting too big. He has fine connections, and so does his sales manager. They are going to bring out only four books this fall and concentrate on selling them. I thought it a good risk, knowing this lad and knowing he feels he can sell literate books. He gave me a three thousand dollar advance, a fine contract, and in it the agreement to spend five thousand dollars on an initial advertising, in the first three months. He also promises me to go to every major city in the country and see the book stores and the major reviewers, and write letters to the others. I just feel that, with all this and being so closely bound in with their debut, and after examining the care of the house's foundation I couldn't go wrong. Young Obolensky is serious and means to back this up, leaving everything in David's hands. Anyway this is it, and of course there will be some risk, but there is also the risk of having to divide between others the moneys and promotion of a big house, with the danger of getting lost there.

We've been trying to pick a date for you [to] speak here. When does your vacation begin and end. There are certain conflicts in the two weeks in March, and we want to pick a time when we can get a good reception. A Monday is the best time. The vacation here is around Easter, I'm told. It looks now as if the end of March would be better, or what about the end of February? I know you don't want to write letters now, but pull yourself together and think about this. Also, can I call that number instead of person to person which is more expensive. That is, will only you answer it?

Well, brother, so long. I wish you would remember that in your troubles now an artist can use them very well, in that curious way which such a devotion is able to take its distance upon the object, itself. Everybody does not have such a way of withdrawal into the proper work.

With love, Andrew

TLS

1. "What Quarter of the Night," *The Sewanee Review,* 64 (Summer 1956), 349–397.

Oak Grove Hotel
230 Oak Grove Street
Minneapolis, Minn.
February 12, 1957

Dear Brother,

I am pleased and relieved to get your letter. My nice talk with Edna left me at a loss because I was very high and afterwards couldn't remember it all.

At last you are free from B-M, and I am delighted. I think you've done just the right thing. David McDowell has become the best editor-publisher in the country, and he may change the whole direction of commercial publishing. That, at any rate, is what I hear and what many people hope from him. You've got at last the perfect arrangement and the new novel will get around as none of its predecessors did.

Now about coming to Gainesville. My vacation is March 18–April 2, and that seems to be a bad time for you. I've agreed to go to Iowa City, April 27–29, but I could come to you before that. I'm looking at your letter again, and I see that the end of March might do; it would do for me, after the 18th.

That wild trip to India and Eurpoe almost did me in, but I'm recovering. Yet, in another sense, it is worse than ever, because I know I can't deal with my situation through a succession of flights, and I must now sit back and take it.

Write me soon and meanwhile love to you and Edna and the girls.

Affectionately, Allen

AL

P.S. Remember me to the Foxes and the Kirklands, please.

Oak Grove Hotel
230 Oak Grove Street
Minneapolis, Minn.
February 23, 1957

Dear Brother,

I'm mighty glad to get your letter. If March 25th will do for the lecture-reading, I'd like to settle for it definitely. I must be in Chicago, on a jury to award a prize, on March 29th–30th; so April 1st would not be too good, as my visit with you would be only two nights. I could come down on the 22nd and leave on the 26th or 27th.

I'm fond of the Foxes but I don't want to come all the way to Florida to stay with them when you all are there. I am sure they will understand. Your study will do for me nicely. As to a bathroom, I need one very seldom.

What I'd like to do at the "lecture" is to begin with some remarks on modern poetry (about 10 minutes) and proceed to the reading of three or four poems by other people, and ending up with my own.

I'm glad you're putting the final touches on the ms. I have a hunch it's going to be your biggest book. I hope you'll let me read the galleys.

There's trouble in Princeton[1] and I'm feeling a little down; so I won't even try to make this a real letter.

Love to you all,

Allen

AL

1. That is, with Caroline.

University of Minnesota
February 27, 1957

Dear Brother:

I'm sorry I had to ask you to change the date. The situation became complicated, first, by Chicago (29th) and then, after I had written you, by the necessity of [a] trip to Princeton. I can get this in only between

Gainesville and Chicago; hence, the earlier date with you. I hope this isn't too difficult. At your leisure write me what you'd like me to do at the "lecture."

In haste, Affly, Allen

AL

Gainesville, Fla.
1822 NW 8th Ave.
March 3, 1957

Dear Brother:

It doesn't matter so much about the date. We merely wanted a propitious one. Mondays always draw the best crowds. Thursday is not too good, as there are progress tests in the University college at that time. But then few of these students would be likely to come anyway. I hope the news from Princeton is not too worrisome. The suggestion you made in your other note for the talk is fine. Anything you want to do. When will you get here? And how long can you stay? Try to stick around a few days anyhow, get here as soon as you can and stay as long as your other arrangements will allow. Archie Robertson, the head of the department, thought you might like to go fishing on the Crystal river for a day, and there will be a few people who will want to meet you. More than a few, but we want to limit it and not let the public take your time and energy.

B. Fox called for your address, insisting that you stay over there, "to save Edna." She didn't realize that they would be seeing you and we wouldn't. B.'s help is like Pierre Bezuhov in his Masonry phase,[1] but she is a good woman. If she really wanted to help, she could have invited Pamela to spend the night there while you were here. But we've got a comfortable bed and you will be all right here.

No more now. Sit down and write a note when we can meet you. The Eastern airlines comes to Gainesville.

In haste, affectionately, A—

TLS

1. A character in *War and Peace* who, as a Mason, tries to improve the lives of his peasants but ends up making their situation worse.

Thursday—11th

Dear Uncle Allen,

This "epistula" is late as mine always are. *The Greek Myths* are wonderful books. As of yet I've read sixteen pages into the first and find it absolutely fascinating. But I find my time so short these days and the afternoons so pleasant that reading, especially pleasure, is mostly neglected.

This afternoon has been a rainy one. Mother, Katherine Ann and Langdon went to the P.T.A. supper about five-thirty and left me all by my lonesome. With nothing better to do I wandered around in the downpour picking flowers. I also managed to mess around in the kitchen and came up with a horrible batch of cookies. They look as if they'd been sat upon but are still eatable.

Surely you must remember lines from Shakespeare's *Macbeth,* "Methought I heard a voice, 'Sleep no more! Macbeth doth murder sleep.'—the innocent sleep" and so on. For some reason those words are my favorite.

Speaking of sleep, my eyelids droop and my bed looks very comfortable. As the hour is late, I must draw this to a close but do with much love. I think of you everyday and look forward to seeing you next year.

Your daughter by love, Pamela[1]

AL

1. Lytle's first daughter.

April 11, 1957

Dear Uncle Allen,

Thank you very much for the book *The Secret Garden.* It is so good!

We are fine. Daddy's going to give me horseback-riding lessons either early next year or late this year. My birthday is on May 12th and that's almost here, so I can hardly wait. Every time near my birthday, things get exciting! Packages come from different people, and Mama won't let me go near the linen closet. She won't tell me why but I think I know. Thanks again for the book. I love it and you.

Hugs and kisses, Katherine Ann [Lytle][1]

AL

P.S. You're my sweetheart.

1. Lytle's second daughter.

Gainesville, Fla.
April 1957

Dear Brother:—

I have been meaning to write you every day, to say how fine your visit was, how it renewed old ties and showed again the lack of memory, which as we grow older we must increasingly live by. All separations are fragmentary deaths, which here and now we continually rehearse. I am sorry things didn't go better at Princeton. It seems to me late now for such an impasse. I could hope for a renewal of your domicile. The inherited wandering of the blood is reaching an acute degree with you, and I just wonder if you shouldn't restrain it. You know, you have of certain acts regarded them as if they were autonomously determined—beyond the will, which they are not. This attitude of yours is so long established, though, it will be hard for you to do anything about it, I guess.

The artist is a harried creature, and this long poem you are doing is so much better than anything else it seems as if you have come to that moment, and that form, which releases the fullness of your gifts.[1] The enveloping action of the earlier poetry has been history saturated with the Greco-Roman inheritance, and the action the conscious knowledge of self before it. Of course, this is a paraphrase—but now there is something very new and passionate more of a personal involvement—and all restrained, but the restraint merely shows the feeling fleshed and bleeding. Perhaps this is overstated. But it is so good that you will compound your sorrows if you don't spend all your time finishing it. Your temptation is to assume in your person the paradigm of the fallen state, that is, this wandering of exile which we all know, the one common reminder in all the degrees of our impairment. If as you believe, I think, that the knowledge of God is through your neighbor how can you pause long enough to know? Certainly the artist can in his art, but is that enough? Maybe. I don't propose to know, and I'm not really advising for who can. I am merely thinking out loud in your presence which is the habit of friendship and love—

Edna wrote you the publishers want me to come to New York the middle of August to help sell the book. I've never done this before, but am willing to now—in hopes of maybe getting more than the advance, as the girls make greater demands. And since I am involved with their debut, I felt I should do what they wanted me to. It's harder now I guess, to sell books. I've just been reading the galleys, and it seems my best although the author is not to be trusted in this. John Ransom is officially retiring, as you know, this year.[2] He is a friend of David's[3] and gave me the money to complete the book. To my knowledge none of his former students has inscribed anything to him, and since time is narrow with him now, I thought the moment had come to do this. All along I had meant to do this for myself to you and Caroline, as I felt this book would be worthy. But if it is as I feel, that I too am coming to my best work, we are younger and I will be able to wait for a better book. This is hope, I hope not false hope. But it can sustain that last flare, where if it is to be done, it is plainly shown that there can be no meandering of the will. It is a risk I wouldn't take if I didn't have hopes of going on; and if where there is such closeness, there would not be easy understanding and sympathy.

I am going this week to Tennessee to see about selling the farm, making that choice between two trades I love which should have been made years ago, but I was not man enough. I am depressed in a way and wonder about risking my dependence upon this University. It will be a small stroke against my oscillations which is my form of wandering.

Well, Brother, we love you, all of us—and Pamela is reading in the myths.

Affectionately, Brother—

1. Only "The Maimed Man," "The Swimmers," and "The Buried Lake" of a proposed six- or nine-part poem were ever completed. 2. From Kenyon College, Gambier, Ohio. 3. McDowell had, in fact, spent his freshman year at Vanderbilt, but when Ransom left Nashville, followed him as a sophomore to Kenyon. So, their friendship was of long-standing.

University of Minnesota
Minneapolis
April 24, 1957

Dear Brother,

I, too, had meant to write, to you, about my wonderful visit; and now I have your moving, even disturbing letter. What you say is all true. In 1952 ("The Buried Lake") I struck my real vein and part of the panic since has been fear of losing it—a fear aggravated by my personal troubles and my flights from them. My hereditary pattern of flight is a given thing, the course of which the will may alter but, it seems to me, not the movement itself or its velocity. As you so well observe, I fused it with the Trojan-Roman cycle, but that no longer contains what I have to say. Apart from these personal nuances, I have reached a point at which nothing less than the fullest exploration of my resources will suffice, and I recoil from it; it is another facet of my fear. But if I can *sit it out* a little longer, the sleight may return—which is only to say that I may be subdued to that patience which is the will of God.

You are wrong about *one* thing! My *Reactionary Essays* is dedicated to J. C. R. But I think what you are doing is more than proper; it is necessary. I should have felt just a little uneasy otherwise.

I will be through at Cambridge on August 20, but I see no reason why I couldn't fly down to N.Y. for the debut. You don't give the date, and I can't put my hand on Edna's letter, but I believe she said the 15th. So let's count on it. Where will you stay? We might get a suite of rooms close together at some hotel like the Algonquin or the Gladstone.

Just this moment the departmental secretary has brought to me the galley of *The Velvet Horn*. I'll get down to it this weekend, and read it, uninterrupted.

By this time you will probably have sold the farm, and I know your feelings. Yet it seems to me that the decision *in substance* was made ten years ago and is only now being enacted. You will not regret it, though you will be haunted by it for a few years.

Tell the girls I enjoyed their letters, and ask them to write to Uncle Allen. I know that Langdon[1] would write if she could. Kiss all four of your ladies for me.

Affectionately, Brother

AL

1. Lytle's youngest daughter.

Oak Grove Hotel
230 Oak Grove Street
Minneapolis, Minn.
May 28, 1957

Dear Brother,

Here's a copy of the statement I've sent to David McDowell. It says only 1/10 of what I think about *The Velvet Horn,* about which I will write you at length this week end. I'm just back in my classes after three weeks with doctors and tests. So you must forgive the delay. I've got the ulcer but not acutely, and there's something a little wrong with the heart which will require a radical change in my way of living. I am undertaking this now.

So, more later. Love to Edna and the girls.

Affly, Allen

AL

Gainesville, Fla.
1822 NW 8th Ave.
June 5, 1957

Dear Brother:

I've been worried about you, feeling you were either sick or in the slump of self-laceration; I'm glad to get real news and of course glad you liked the book. David will be glad to get the little statement. I think they have been slow to come in. Edna has not been well, in a very nervous state from pain in leg and neck. I sent her to Memphis two weeks ago for a thorough examination under her brother-in-law's[1] guidance. None of the fearful things showed; what had scared us was a half inch difference between her thighs, and the doctor thought the nerve might be dying and didn't think she should wait until all of us went up this month. But the news is good: she has a thinning disc in her neck and calcium deposit in her hip and the possibility of a too active thyroid. These matters are not light but they are concrete and maybe there is something to do for them. Anyway our fears are banished, and she has been relieved of a household, taking only the baby with her. I'll follow with the children the end of this week or the first of next, and on June 17th go to Salt Lake City.[2]

I take it your own heart murmur is subject to the cure of less tension in the heart and more regular ways. You know the trouble I find in the middle of the wood is that you have to act, even to yourself, to recover the source. There seems nothing new to know in the world, no people you want to charm or discover; even those you love seem at times remote in your lifeless view. This means that you have only to sink a little deeper to bring it up, freshen life and art; that way maybe you can banish the world thickening about you. The ways are obvious and simple. To me, although sometimes it fails, it is the early morning light which quickens me afresh, even though the leap is slower and the light somewhat diminished.

There's an old friend of ours really in the mire of the world. He has great energy, but what will happen when that lessens. David McDowell sent him the galleys of *The Velvet Horn* two months ago, wanting him to give a blurb or review it, which he refused to do. He hasn't even read it yet.[3] Isn't that curious? There is a curious letter to David I will show you sometimes, which is strange indeed.

I'm glad you feel the way I used the interior monologue was successful. You know that was my hard technical problem, how to keep the two kinds of time from confusing each part of the action. What I wanted was the sense of the eternal presence of all action through moving time. So that is a comfort. I of course want to hear more what you think, but I don't want you to fatigue yourself now feeling bad, no doubt as you do. Finding words gets wearisome when vitality gets low.

The Memphis address is: 175 West Chickasaw Parkway, Memphis, 11.

Affectionately, Brother

TLS

1. James Hogan. 2. Lytle attended the annual Utah Writers' Conference. 3. Donald Davidson.

12-A Farwell Place
Cambridge 38, Mass.
June 25, 1957

Dear Edna,

I'm mighty glad to get your letter. I'd heard about your illness from Brother and still later news *via* Caroline in Princeton last week. Yes, it may not be fatal, but it *does* hurt! Yet I'm a little sorry, in my own case, that my disturbance moved, about ten years ago, from my head (migraine) to my chest and stomach—the region, after all, of the vital organs. I've had bursitis in the shoulder, and the pain was so dreadful that I wished somebody would shoot me. I know how you feel.

You see, from my address, that I'm trying to carry out my plans, and that a visit to Monteagle seems impossible. I get through here August 29th, but by that time you all will be back in Florida, and Brother will have made his trip to N.Y. I still hope, indeed expect, to fly there for the occasion, even though I may be able to stay only a day. I'm terribly sorry not to see you this summer and also to miss seeing Polly—to whom you will, of course, give my love of thirty years? I would dearly love to see her. Give my love to Amelita,[1] and to old friends roundabout when you see them either in Memphis or on the mountain. Take care of yourself. You work too hard. The Lord will look after the girls and the domestic routine while you are getting well.

With love of old, Allen

AL

1. Nancy Tate's mother-in-law.

Monteagle, Tenn.
July 31, 1957

Dear Caroline:

I've been meaning to write you any day, especially to tell you how fine it made me feel that statement you made for David [McDowell].[1] You are my closest and best reader, and have sustained me over certain low morasses of the spirit. It's not that you want to be widely and popularly read; you want to be understood by your peers and betters and also have something that will carry it a way. Edna is in no shape to come to New York, I think; especially since ten days ago her mother had a stroke and Edna had to go down there and help nurse, [which] I thought unnecessary, since there were nurses available. But anyway she is back now and looks some better and the pain comes and goes; and we are off tomorrow for Florida. The packing is in hand at last. Polly got off with her children today. She looks well and as Marjorie Cooney[2] said she must have suffered so along with Jimmy that now he is released, she is too. She speaks of him as if he were in the West.[3]

We wished you and Allen could have been here. Mr. Fults seemed to think it a kind of lapse on your parts (the postmaster, you remember) and asked about you. I want to come down and spend a night with you, if they will let me. Anyway I want to come down. I'll find out what the score is when I get there. I think these are the boys for me, and you too. They try to sell books. There's a party. You must try to make it. I don't know quite when it is, but I think it is the fifteenth.

No more now. We are exhausted and out of whiskey.

Affectionately, Andrew

TLS

1. See Appendix I. 2. The Lytles' next door neighbor in Huntsville. She and Uncle Dave Macon were the stars in WSM's beginnings. 3. Polly's husband, Jimmy Darwin, died three days before Christmas, 1956.

12-A Farwell Place
Cambridge 38, Mass.
August 3, 1957

Dear Brother:

I was just about to write you to get the date fixed when your letter from the mountain came. The 15th is much better for me than the 18th would have been. My seminar is out at 11:00 and I'll try to get the first plane to N.Y. If there's no room for me at the apartment, I'll stay at the Princeton Club; but send me the apartment address and, if possible, telephone number.

Too bad about Edna's mother. We're all reaching the age of casualty, one after another.

I noticed you said, "It's the 15th, *I think*." Let me know definitely as soon as you can.

And has Caroline been asked to the party? I ought to know this.

Love to all four girls.

Affly, Allen

AL

P.S. Mr. Fults behind his barred window *is* a real ghost. How much easier life would have been had we been born covites named Fults!

Oak Grove Hotel
230 Oak Grove Street
Minneapolis, Minn.
September 24, 1957

Dear Brother,

I'm mighty glad to get the inscribed copy of the *Horn*. I had just started rereading my other copy day before yesterday. I see all sorts of things I had missed, and I will report on them shortly. I hope it is still selling. It got off to a good start, and had the right kind of reviews for the purpose. I'm curious to see what the quarterlies will do with it. There's nothing like it in Southern writing, or anywhere else.

When I got to the Princeton Club three days late to pick up my mail, there was a message to call you. My car was parked in front and I couldn't; so I sent the telegram. I don't even know whether it would have been convenient for me to come. At any rate, I couldn't. I had to get back here to attend to my part in a textbook collaboration,[1] as my collaborator was leaving a week later. I wish I could have come; it would have done me great good to be with you and Edna.

I came out of the summer in pretty good shape, and things went better in Princeton than in several years. I was there two weeks, and had a good time. I think that the house there, the garden, and the job at Columbia are working wonders.

I may go to Nashville Christmas. Couldn't you all come up for an old-time jollification?

Love to Edna and the two remaining girls.[2]

Affly, Allen

TLS

I marvel how you got through that long spell of parties and drinking.

1. *Modern Verse in English, 1900–1950,* edited with David Cecil (New York: Macmillan, 1958). 2. Pamela, the oldest girl, has left home to attend St. Mary's at Sewanee.

October 3, 1957

Dearest Allen,

I have been meaning to write you several weeks and tell you how disappointed we were you didn't get to Fla. I hope you can manage a visit here before long.

Getting Pamela off to school was quite an ordeal. She needed everything and nothing she had was suitable for that climate. Certainly will help if *The Velvet Horn* does a lot more selling. This was far from the only angle, as you may know, and I reached the place the week she left when I ceased to sleep. She got off on a Friday, we collapsed Sat.—& tried all Sunday to call you.

Pamela's letters are very enthusiastic so we are feeling real good about her. She is finding her studies difficult which does not surprise me. When she writes me of spending an evening with two of my nephews, I feel like I'm dead looking in on the next generation of "us" sitting around on that mountain. My brother's youngest, Edward Barker, is the senior class honor student at S.M.A. and my sister's youngest, Holt Hogan, is teaching forestry at U. of the S. I wish I could have seen you all in N.Y. but there was so much to attend to here—and after Monteagle (which was pretty strenuous & rowdy) I was in no shape for any effort, what's more extra effort. I'm better now, have gained nine pounds, and I hope you are, too. We found Polly and her children perfectly wonderful and a real experience to be with. We are trying to work out something together with them on the coast here Christmas, but she's a poor letter writer and we haven't heard how the idea strikes her. How does it strike you? Too.

Did you know Miss Irene [Weaver Williams] died in August?

My mother had a stroke this summer. She is making a remarkable recovery. She is past eighty. Write when you can. We love you here and want you here. And write Andrew about *The Horn*—the lack is felt here of the first flood of letters—but of course.

Always, Edna

AL

12-A Farwell Place
Cambridge 38, Mass
August 14, 1958

Dear Brother,

I can't be with you, and I'm distressed by it. Tomorrow is my last class, and I must read term papers over the weekend. I am dead tired. This past week has been very rough. I wish I could talk it over with you. Last weekend, as the result of drinking, C.[aroline] did something absolutely appalling—real paranoid delusions which led to her insulting an innocent woman who is little more than a stranger to us both. I don't know what to do next: More—but not of this—later.

Affectionately, Allen

AL

25 Aug. 1958
Morning

Dear Andrew—

I thought you might be interested in seeing the enclosed.[1] Haven't my copy yet, but I hope to get to the bookstore today.

My writing is coming along at a better rate; I believe I'm more acclimated. I have a short story that is clearer in my head than in my pen. The two main characters have haunted me like the Eumenides, although one of them is such a weak character that it embarrasses me every time I think of him. (Probably he's really me and one of us must go.)

This is being written at work and I must close. Please write what you are doing and when I am going to see you again.

I had almost forgotten: a young Mr. Fagan applied for a job here and gave your name as a reference. Seems he only wanted a short-time job and they didn't hire him.

Affectionately, Allen

TLS

1. Enclosure is missing; reference unidentifiable.

All Souls College
Oxford
March 14, 1959

Dear Brother, [Gainesville, Florida, USA]

I have owed you a letter for months on more than one count. For one thing I have never acknowledged in writing your moving dedication;[1] for another, there are certain matters that I should have made you privy to as long ago as early December.

I am sure you've heard about these matters by grapevine, but I should have preferred to tell you first. Last fall I asked Caroline to let me get a divorce. She is opposing it, as I expected she would—as I virtually counted on her doing. Something drastic had to be done to clear the air. As I told you in Cambridge, I had planned, had indeed prepared myself all last winter, for a reunion as soon as I got back from England. But in Princeton, for some weeks before I sailed, the atmosphere was denser than ever, and I simply could not take it. Caroline's position for years has been that if I come back and am "all right" she will be all right. I am not sure that I have been all right, but it is certain that she has not been: she cannot help the frequent reliving of the past, and as you know it all goes back to an episode of 1933. There have been wrongs done her since, but it was just as bad before they were committed. I have simply despaired of ever making it up to her. The shuttling back and forth, neither married nor unmarried, was impossible for us both. My last hope was that the threat of divorce might by force of shock (almost in the psychiatric sense) root out her accumulated grievances. At some deep, compulsive level she secretly claimed the privilege of keeping me as her husband and almost daily punishing me, meanwhile herself suffering intolerably from remorse. I am not good enough a Christian to accept this vicious circle, and the fact that I am at least three-fourths responsible for the situation does not make it easier to bear. It is all the worse in view of our age: the suffering is worse in age, and it is worse in the sense that it is little short of scandalous that at our age we cannot make it. Moreover I am tired of abortive love-affairs, which are short-lived and increase my guilt, at the same time that they do less than good to the women involved. This hasn't happened for some time, but it is a constant threat because I am dependent on women, and I cannot make a go of it living alone. I was wholly dependent on Caroline, and now that support has been replaced by a vacuum, I am up against it.

You don't need to write me about this, but I had to tell you about it. Lon [Cheney] has taken very high ground, and has virtually read me off his list. He informs me that my old friends will not view this matter as tolerantly as they did the divorce of 1945.[2] I will be sorry to lose my old friends, but I must manage the rest of my life inwardly, and take the public consequences. Lon wrote me that I ought to leave it to Caroline to make the next move. That is what I had already been doing.

I will be at Harvard again, doing the International Seminar this time, though I think it is pretty hopeless if you expect to accomplish anything. I don't know yet where I'll live but it will probably be at the same place, Farwell Place.

I have got back to a little writing and I feel encouraged about it, even in the midst of my uncertainties. But I had been away from it so long that it's like learning all over again the elementary things. I hope your work prospers. I liked the statement you sent to Moe, and I think you will get the renewal.[3] Middle-aged writers need more help than the young.

My love to Edna and the girls. If you don't want to advert to my troubles, write me a family letter—plans, etc.

Affectionately, Allen

TLS

1. Lytle dedicated *A Novel, A Novella and Four Stories* (N.Y.: McDowell, Obolensky, 1958) to Allen and Caroline Tate. 2. The Tates were divorced in January, 1946, but were remarried in April of that same year. 3. Lytle applied for and received an extension of his second Guggenheim Award.

Gainesville, Fla.
1822 NW 8th Ave.
March 22, 1959

Dear Brother:

I was awfully glad to get your letter, to know exactly where you are. I had heard from Lon that you did go to Oxford and were coming home Christmas. But I never got your college and thought maybe I'd hear when you came in. He had told me about the time of troubles, the long letters he'd got from Caroline and her condition and distress. And for some reason she made a great attack upon me, which I didn't enquire of. It's too bad, the whole thing. I don't know what to say, or how to advise you in this matter. When I dedicated the book to both of you I had hoped it would stand for a renewal of constancy, but the magic didn't work.[1] I suppose magic always deals with the illusions of things, certainly our sense of it. Sally Wood[2] is here. It was she who told me the other day about the matter of divorce. I think she feels it is almost impossible for you to live together. And of course she regrets it as must all your friends.

She brought up the matter of the Catholic world. That is a real public matter. Your dependency upon a woman, or women, will not certainly immediately be resolved by a divorce. Do you mean to marry again? It seems to me that would be a surer ground. You can still dive within yourself; and will your guilt, or sense of it, be relieved by a divorce? These are questions only you can answer. It can be only a legal severance. Can I sever the rest? Late middle years are hard. The sense of sin, fear and desire grow apace. Only the imagination and the working mind can keep you in the world, when the world's body diminishes and loses its strength. This is something the artist may hope to retain, but as Yeats said the heart grows old too. I can understand your dependency, all the more because location has never meant anything tactile, or physical to you. I wish I knew what to say. There are matters known and sensed that can't be put into words. For both of you there should be some firm resolution. No solution. That belongs to God.

I will be in Cambridge this summer, doing what you did last summer. It will be fine to have at least six weeks time together. The family isn't coming up, but I've about persuaded Edna to come up in the middle of it and spend a couple of weeks with me. I don't know whether I can lecture five days a week or not, but young [Ed] Hood wants to assist me as he did you. And both of you can advise me. I have an approach towards impressionism which, I think, will allow me to order it. I don't look for any trouble from the creative writing part.

I hope I do get the renewal of the Guggenheim. I hated to put you to the trouble of writing another letter, but money matters are pressing me here. They don't pay me enough, and I've even indirectly thrown out hints to Vanderbilt ([Harvie] Branscomb had already sort of opened the way) that I might like to come there. It would be the cheapest way to send Pamela to college. She has done awfully well at St. Mary's and has developed into a fine girl. She wants to be near the family, and I'm not sure I want her in this mongrel society here. They've been very nice to me here, but I don't think they really believe that what I'm doing deserves the full measure of pay and rank. The lectureship is temporary, although always renewed. I've sold the farm and I want a place to put the furniture. I've even thought of buying back the cabin, if I can, and maybe teaching some at Sewanee. I talked to [Monroe] Spears and [Charles T.] Harrison[3] a couple of years ago and they seemed to think it possible. But I don't know how much money they have. And it takes it now. You are right, middle years is needful in this way. I didn't mean to get off on this, when you have such real troubles.

Let me hear from you. I think you should consider mighty deep how far a divorce would do what you think it might. It seems a clean cut matter, but is there any such thing?

Always affectionately, Andrew

TLS

1. *A Novel, A Novella and Four Stories.* (New York: McDowell and Obolensky, 1958). 2. A poet and a good friend of Caroline's. 3. The editor of *The Sewanee Review* and the Chairman of the English Department at the University of the South, respectively.

All Souls College
Oxford
March 26, 1959

Dear Brother:

It did me good to get your letter. One of the most reassuring things about it is the inference I draw that I'm not crossed off your list. I simply don't know what to make of Lon's attitude. It was not so much *what* he said, but the way of saying it: it was almost a threat. I doubt, as I write you, that there will be a divorce; so the question of remarriage is not imminent. I don't deceive myself that I wouldn't try it. There's a woman you will meet this summer who would be the one I'd marry.[1] I've known her three years, and I can find very little wrong with her. But she knows my situation. I may have an apartment on Sparks St., Cambridge, and if I do live there I'm sure I could turn over to you the place I had last summer. $225.00 for the summer. And it's big enough for two, when Edna comes up—as I hope she does. I wish you would buy back the Log Cabin, and teach at Sewanee. I'd like to be there myself! But I never can. I am utterly at a loss to understand Caroline's animosity toward you. None of these hostilities are personal; they are pure projections of a conflict too deep to discern: I still don't know its source. The great thing about her fiction is atmosphere of place and the sensuous *aura*—not dramatic motivation, nor a glance at the source of action. In an ordered world she would be a great writer. I could not make that world for her. I failed. And I must face it. Any failure on her part she must face, and I do not account her a failure. I only know that I alone, unaided, cannot restore her. I must try to live at peace with myself. I hope you do have Ed Hood as your assistant. He's the best I've ever had. He has some homosexual trouble, but he is a dignified young man, and he's trying to deal with it. The news of Pamela is no more than I should have expected. She was already a fine girl two years ago. I can't see the future of Nancy's children. The boys are little Yankees. They ought to be sent to Southern schools. I'm glad you sold the farm since you can never live on it. Tom Mabry[2] is trying it too late, but he has his wife's money to carry it. Write me your news. My love to Edna and all the girls.

Affectionately, Allen

AL

1. Mrs. Robert McCormick, poetess Isabella Gardner. 2. Thomas Dabney Mabry, cousin of Caroline Gordon, was a writer who from 1935 to 1939 had been executive director of the Museum of Modern Art.

Gainesville, Fla.
1822 NW 8th Ave.
April 13, 1959

Dear Brother:

[Henry Allen] Moe came through with four thousand dollars, to free me for a semester and a summer. Of course that won't do it alone, and I as yet don't know what the university here will allow on my salary. State institutions are machines; the legislature is talking poor, and they sometimes do not allow an institution to keep its word. For example we are changing over from a twelve month basis to a ten. I've been on a ten month basis all along, though paid in twelve installments. There looks to be some confusion in this. The state may insist that the rate of installment payments would put me on a twelve month basis, in spite of the fact that the president, the dean, and the head of the department agreed (verbally) when I came here that I would never teach in the summer. The practical matter is that if I am forced to go [on] what I am already on [that] will mean a ten percent cut, which I can't see I can take. I begin the Guggenheim in the spring semester, 1960. So I don't have to do anything immediately about it. I don't know what Sewanee could or would do. Living at Monteagle or even at Sewanee would make for problems as far as the girls' society is concerned. Father Flye has a fifty acre spot with an incomplete house on it, next to St. Mary's. It overlooks the valley at Cowan and is mighty pretty. It's really a question of the cheapest way to educate the girls. We've entered Pamela at Vanderbilt. I can take two thousand from the sale of the farm and put her through one year. Vanderbilt by the grapevine has indicated that sometime they will want me there. Of course living there I could educate the girls much more inexpensively.

There's a good private school in town for Kate. At Sewanee we would only have to pay Kate's tuition at St. Mary's. Then there would be getting up the money for Pamela at Vanderbilt. Financially Vanderbilt, if I got an offer there, would be the most feasible. I think I'll write Henry [Alexander] and sound him out on it. There's [not ?] much society on the mountain for girls; too much in Nashville. So . . . you see my wheel.

And I need to get back down to work. To be where I'll be for the rest of my life. I want to stay put, and have done nothing but move every Tuesday. If I should be asked to Vanderbilt, I might try to buy the cabin back anyway and after the two girls get through their schooling there, move up to the mountain. We've got the problem of what to do with the furniture. It's still at the farm, and I don't feel like selling it.

I understood that whatever attack Caroline made on me was out of her own distress. It wouldn't worry me. And I wouldn't, if I were you, worry about Lon. He shakes his finger at me at times. It's just his way. You take your friends, as you know, as they are.

I wrote the housing people in Bill's [Elliott] office about your possibility of not taking the place you had last summer. Does it have an icebox or any kitchen facilities? I have to have coffee when I get up before anything is open, and I might want to cook a few meals, especially if Edna comes. I'm going there to save a little money, as I have to. Anyway let me know if you are going to keep it, or free it, and I'll send on the information. It's certainly a good location, and I'll have no car there.

To live at all now we have some way to try to make the world we live in, almost an impossibility. Certainly you couldn't make the world for Caroline. She's one of the finest writers in English, but with all the uprooting and destruction of the family, her world must seem strange to many readers, even in the South. It's also true that she doesn't go quite to the source of action. I don't know about dramatic motivation. Her scenes are dramatic, I think. Her chief difficulty is that of not being able sufficiently to withdraw from her private ordeal, measure it against the discretion of the world's action. She does and she doesn't. She doesn't when she is dealing with the center of the complication. We all use ourselves, but we can't rely upon what is too personal to us. Her reputation is going to stand, I feel, and grow in importance.

I'm in a crisis now. The myth of the Southern scene I've always worked with is changing for me. My future as a writer is risky and unknown. What I learned in *The Velvet Horn* may save me. If it doesn't, I guess I'll gather "sang"[1] in the mountains. I'm enclosing the piece I did for *Daedalus.*[2] You might like it. It shows how the act, and my sense now of techne[3] is working on me.

We are all pretty well. I go to Sewanee to speak this week, to Washington and Lee, and then back here the twenty-first.

Affectionately, Andrew

TLS

1. Ginseng, popularly called "sang," is an herb whose valuable root was once thought to be a cure-all, some thought it an aphrodisiac. 2. "The Working Novelist and the Mythmaking Process," *Daedalus,* 88 (Spring 1959), 326–38. 3. Lytle takes *techne* from the Greek *technē* meaning "an art or artifice."

All Souls College
Oxford
May 25, 1959

Dear Brother,

Your letter of April 13th reached me in Athens. I got back from the Continent only a week ago, so my usual procrastination was reinforced by circumstances. I have just reread "The Working Novelist and the Mythmaking Process."[1] It is a very important essay, and it will eventually become a classic. You have defined the orbit for fiction in the future. I believe I heard that you had given this essay as a lecture at Harvard last year.

About housing in Cambridge. I'm up against it. I heard about six weeks ago from my landlady of last summer that the winter tenant may stay on, and I've heard nothing further. I wrote to Maclin Guerard[2] to help me, but no word from her. So the other day I wrote to [Henry] Kissinger's office for help. What I had in mind when I wrote you fell through. So I'm a little uneasy, with only five weeks to go. I fly to NY on June 15th, and will go to Cambridge a few days later.

Caroline is blocking the divorce. I waited to see whether she would give me any human reason, not merely the reason of the Church. Could she bring herself to say that she wanted us back together again, instead of the theological line, I would have a very different view. But she is using the Church to "save" me. All this has been complicated by a new maniacal outburst of Cal Lowell's. He has had another violent breakdown, at the pitch of which he telephoned Caroline several times and urged her to save me from a Boston divorcee.[3] I like this woman, and will continue to do so, but I could no more plan to marry her than I could fly, though I am frank to say I'd like to. The lady is a cousin of Cal's and an old friend whom [he?] trusted. I am the object of his hostility. The Lowell vulgarity reached its height when he told C.[aroline] that the lady wasn't very rich—that I could look around and do better.

Caroline has a priest who tells her what to do, and of course as priest he can tell her only one thing. But people cannot be "saved for the Church" by coercion. If he would tell her that she ought to want *me,* not to save me, the whole situation would be different—as it would in the past.

I simply don't know what is going to happen. I want to talk all this over with you because there are things I can't write.

I wish to God Vanderbilt would do something about you. Branscomb[4] doesn't care a straw for what he calls the "Vanderbilt literary tradition." It doesn't even give him the kind of publicity he thinks he needs. Henry Alexander[5] ought to step in and do something. The Board of Trust takes action about the faculty only when the Chancellor wants to fire somebody.

Please let me have a line about when you'll get to Cambridge. My love to Edna and the girls.

Affly, Allen

TLS

1. *Daedalus,* 88 (Spring 1959), 326–38. 2. The wife of novelist Albert Guerard. 3. Isabella Gardner. 4. Harvie Branscomb, Chancellor of Vanderbilt. 5. A member of the Board of Trust at Vanderbilt.

May 30, 1959

Dear Sweet Allen,

I am writing this note as Andrew is not well. He was happy to receive yours this past week and will write I know as soon as he is feeling better. This has been brewing a couple of months but he finally had a sistocopic examination, kidney function etc. and he is going to have to have a prostatic operation—here probably, and soon probably. The kidney does fine; they also say there is no malignancy—everything good, except enlarged prostate—pressing on the bladder. So for a bad situation it couldn't be better and I am on the job and you are not to worry.

Your letter came happily the day of this rigorous examination 3 days ago & he has known no comfort since until just tonight. He is resting & I am waiting up for pill time and writing you. (He almost passed on out in the doctor's office following the exam. They administered oxygen & intravenous glucose & etc. & got his blood pressure back up from 60 & took him to the hospital in an ambulance for 24 hours.)

We have not yet phoned Harvard to say he cannot keep his summer school engagement, but will do this tomorrow.

My guess is he will be operated [on] in a week or ten days & they say he will be 8 weeks recovering. I send this letter from his landlord-to-be in case it may help you solve your rental problem. I am sorry you two will not have a good summer together *and* I think it would have done good for both of you. I must admit since spring, when I knew you'd be together, I had taken great consolation over the thought of his long absence . . . since he would be a while with you.

Oh yes, this landlord's letter seems incomplete. I think he must have neglected to enclose a page?

So write. He'd love to hear from you. Let me have an address and I will keep you informed how he progresses. I've already planned to move a desk in the back room and hole-up, two new lamps etc. etc. and he seems to be taking some interest and delight in this ease and this relaxing regime I tell him we will set up together. I told him how wonderful it would be for me to have him so much to myself, and needless to say I meant it [every] word . . . But this is a shock for him—and the help he is going to need is of more than one facet.

Goodnight—I write better sometimes—but you are my sweet love who will forgive and see through. And *you,* you must remember that since I love you, everything you do, or don't do, any stand, position or action you take, will have to accord not only with your ideas of the moment but also mine of you always, or else you betray unwittingly something deep and fundamental with me and with Andrew—and with others. This is a responsibility not perhaps legitimately incurred—but yours nonetheless. We love you—more soon.

Edna

AL

June 5

Dear Allen-

Your letter is just here and I will add a line & send on this letter I wrote you a week ago. I didn't ever mail it for it didn't suit me—you will see.

Thanks for your solicitude and for taking Andrew's course. He talked last Monday to Bill Elliott, said he was so sweet & just like an old mother & Andrew mentioned to him you might want to rent his apt.

Andrew's discomfort has steadily increased. We see the doctor in a few hours—as soon as he is out of surgery—and I think he will take him on to the hospital & if not I know he will real soon. This is awful and I'll be thankful when it is behind us—but we are "all right" at this point. With *best of luck,* he could be in Boston in five weeks. As you are leaving let me have an address.

Love, Edna

AL

All Souls College
Oxford
June 8, 1959

Dearest Edna,

Your two letters, along with Mr. Enstrom's, came this morning. I am quite clear about dates, but I surmise that Brother is just about now undergoing the operation; and I fear that since I leave here in five days there will not be time to get word to me about his condition. If you could just send me a card to the Princeton Club, 39th St. at Park Ave., New York 16, as soon as you get this, I would appreciate it; but I know you are harassed, so don't keep it on your mind. I will telephone you this coming Sunday. I am due in New York Saturday evening.

Brother had seemed so well in the past few years that the news has been a severe shock to me. I don't think he ought to worry about Harvard. He wrote me he needed the money, but if he goes there not completely recovered, it might be dangerous. The one good thing is that there's no malignancy. That's what we've all got to think about in middle age.

I am writing to Mr. Enstrom. His place sounds good, and if Brother is in the end able to come I can vacate it for him, and go elsewhere. I will have time and opportunity to get another place.

Andrew has been more than a brother to me, and I love you both so deeply that I am badly shaken by the news.

With love, Allen [Tate]

TLS

325 Harvard Street
Cambridge 38
July 6, 1959

Dear Brother,

I am reading "Mister MacGregor" to our class this morning, with excerpts from your "Foreword."[1] There are about 180 in the class, rag-tag-and-bob-tail, but they ought to know what they missed when you got sick.

Since classes began last week I've been run ragged. Henry Kissinger has piled on more and more extracurricular meetings, and they are more exhausting than the seminar itself.

Edna's letters were a great comfort to me. I hope you are now able to send me a few words. I, too, hope you will do *nothing* the rest of the summer. Is it likely you all will go to Monteagle before returning to

Florida? If you do, and are there after August 20th, I might get there to see you.

My own health seems to be better than it has been for some years, but otherwise I'm about the same. Some time ago you mentioned the fading out of the "Southern myth." That's part of my trouble. The concrete image is no longer there to sustain it.*

Let me hear from you. Love to Edna and the girls, and to Polly if she's nearby.

Affectionately, Allen

AL

*I've been rereading *The Fathers*. There's to be a soft-cover reprint.[2] **I can't believe I wrote it! In your terms, it's about the destruction of the Family or "enveloping action" projected *back* into the past *to one moment;* whereas, historically, the destruction was slower and later.

1. Tate is referring to Lytle's *A Novel, A Novella and Four Stories* (1958) which reprints "Mister MacGregor" and for which Lytle wrote a new introductory essay, "Foreword." 2. *The Fathers* was reprinted as a paperback with an introduction by Arthur Mizener by The Swallow Press in 1960.

1822 NW 8th Ave.
July 13, 1959

Dear Brother:—

We were more or less dismissed day before yesterday—and are resting up at home. The operation went off beautifully, but I had a secondary complication which kept me in the hospital another week. And then the rest of the two recuperating and under observation at Jane's [Hogan].[1] My strength returns, but slowly. I guess all that time on my back and the surgery accounts for this. But we are grateful all went well. The children were magnificent, especially Pamela who had the final, or rather local responsibility for them. I am ordered to take it easy three more weeks. If all goes well, I am thinking of coming up (if Edna will join me) to [the] McDowell Obolensky anniversary party Aug. 17. (Maybe we will see you there.) We hear that Caroline has consented to a divorce and that you are going to marry a Mrs. McCormick.[2] A great change. Let me hear. If you undertake this, I hope to goodness all goes as you wish it.

Just a note to re-enter the world, although I am still a kind of vegetable. It's the only way you can take the blood-letting and needles and the violation of privacy.

We all send love. Write when you can, if only a note.

Andrew

AL

1. Mrs. James Hogan, Edna's sister. 2. Isabella Gardner, the poet.

1822 NW 8th Ave.
Gainesville, Fla.
Tuesday July 22, 1959

Dear Brother-

I am glad to have your address. I sent you a note to Weld Hall (2) on our return. You never know how delayed such can be. Edna and I are getting ready to go to Jax for a check-up. She feels she doesn't want to deal with this doctor here any more, and of course she is right. I have the Nelson men's "lack of moral courage," and thought it would save his face if I let him do the small things now remaining, which I take it is to cast your water from time to time. But, of course, maybe for a while there is always the threat of more serious matters. Since Edna took charge, I will of course merely follow her wishes.

One good thing about the Sewanee anniversary[1] is to cause me to re-read not parts but the whole of your work. Of course I won't get through in time, but I am enjoying it, as well as my vegetable head will let me. Which means that I will be distressed over the small piece I'll do. I don't yet have the concentration to explore so close an intimacy over so long a time. But my strength does come back, and today I seem much stronger. But it is far from that clarity and sustained effort anything well written and explored demands.

The Jacksonville trip was somewhat tiring. I learned a good deal about such cases as mine. The infection can flare up again—I am still tender in the left testicle and must watch that for a long time, although in six months I am supposed to be well and feel well. Apparently there will remain the possibility of hazard and infection getting out of hand. However, I don't show much, and the doctor thought it was unusual so close to surgery. I see why doctors don't recommend surgery unless it needs to be done.

This lying around with the family is pleasant, but I'll be glad to get functioning again. I'm sorry you are so burdened with classes. I should have known I wouldn't be able to do anything this summer—maybe Harvard could have my part anyway and you would only have had to mess with Kissinger. Anyway the shape I was in I don't think I would have been any good in spite of the nice thing you said.

I haven't got to *The Fathers* yet. You are right. It did take longer. However, as action, that is, a particular situation, such as an individual family going down, can always happen. In this instance it merely stood for, or represented what would happen here generally, more gradually.

Let me hear something about your private dilemma. I am anxious for this to turn out well and know that there is no unravelling but a knot to cut.

All send love, Andrew [Lytle]

AL

We must see, but I don't believe Monteagle is as yet in the cards.

1. An anniversary issue of *The Sewanee Review* is being planned to honor Tate.

325 Harvard Street
August 10, 1959

Dear Brother,

It was a great relief to know that Edna had brought you back to Gainesville and that you are mending so rapidly. I am now wondering if you still plan to come to New York around the 17th. I can't get down there on that date, as my last two seminars are on the 17th and 18th, and there is a farewell dinner on the 19th. After you're through there, couldn't you come up here? That would be very fine; and Edna ought to come too. I would drive you over to Wellfleet, on the Cape, for a few days,and you could get a good rest—BOTH of you—swimming (if you are able) and sunbathing. Please think it over. For quick communication, bear in mind my telephone number: Eliot 4-3383.

Ben [Tate] and Henry Alexander have been talking to Branscomb about your coming to Vanderbilt, and Branscomb is all for it. I warned Ben and Henry that Randall Stewart would have to be approached first, and so I wrote him a strong letter, pointing out that several members of the Board of Trust and the Chancellor would cooperate. Randall's reply was discouraging, though he would obviously like to have you, simply because Walter Sullivan, who teaches the writing course and a course in the modern novel, would be put into a secondary role. Walter has been there a long time, and it would be hard to make him feel comfortable if an older and more famous man were "over" him. (I think he's pretty good, but not very good.) But there may be a way round this bottleneck. Could you think up an entirely different teaching program—one that would not encroach upon his preserves? It would be a little ridiculous for Walter to continue to teach the writing course with you there, but the main thing is to get you to Vanderbilt. Could you write me a letter about a possible program for me to turn over to Henry and Ben? Then I can write to Randall on the basis of your letter. Ben told me last week that if necessary they would get a special endowment for your salary; so you see they mean business—if we can only get Randall to think a little outside the academic groove.

My own situation—the private one—is very difficult. As the time for the divorce approaches I get more and more depressed. It may take place in the next ten days or so. I have allowed myself, in the vacuum of the past few years, to drift into a commitment to a very fine woman, Isabella Gardner (formerly Mrs. McCormick), but I am not sure that I ought to marry her. What it comes down to is this: I cannot live with Caroline but I am not sure it would be fair to Isabella to marry her as long as C. is living; and I suspect that she will outlive me. Or put otherwise, I doubt that I can be wholly commited to another woman *in marriage* while Caroline is alive. C. made the best part of what I am, or at any rate made it possible for me to realize it, and I can't repudiate this without rejecting 35 years of my life. You see the dilemma. My relation to the Church bothers me. Apart from the strictly religious problem, there is a problem of honor which the Church doesn't recognize but which counts largely in my reluctance to appear to repudiate the Church. I am very anxious to talk all this over with you; so I have an urgent personal reason for wanting you all to come here.

In any case write me as soon as you can about your plans. Friday afternoon (14th) to Sunday evening I will be at Wellfleet, Mass., % Gen. Delivery. Telephone: Wellfleet, then Fieldbrook 9-2634.

Love to you all.

Affectionately, [Allen]

TL

Wellfleet, Mass.
August 3l, 1959

Dear Brother,

We're just now recovering from the fatigue leading up to the 27th.[1] What a hectic week! But we're settled quietly for two weeks.

About Sewanee. We can't leave Cambridge before noon of the 15th, and it will take 2-l/2 days to get to Sewanee—that is, the evening of the 17th. Would that be too late for us to coincide with you all? We could stay till Sunday the 19th or perhaps Monday morning. Please let us know.

I was a week late getting this Memorandum off to Henry Alexander, but he will have it tomorrow. Second thought brought Don into the picture. There's no way to circumvent him. He's a little irritated with all of us, and he would take it ill if he thought we were conspiring with the Chancellor to pass him over. Would the arrangement I suggest in the memo suit you?

You and Edna boosted my morale tremendously. Your visit got me over the last hurdle.[2] I can't thank you all enough. The reality of my new life has yet to take shape, but it will—in time.

Isabella sends her love. My love to you all—all the girls too.

Affectionately, Allen

AL

1. Tate married Isabella Gardner on August 27, at the home of Francis Biddle in Wellfleet, Massachusetts. 2. The Lytles visited Tate following the McDowell, Obolensky anniversary party on August 17.

Box 4
Wellfleet, Mass.
Sept. 1, 1959

Dear Brother,

We have just received the fine letters from you and Edna. We are both very much warmed and reassured by them, for we *do* need the support and love of our closest friends.

We have been thinking about Sewanee, and only last night we had to make the hard decision not to come. We can't possibly leave Wellfleet before the afternoon of the 16th, and we could not reach Sewanee before night of the 18th. Two days there, and the hard drive to Minneapolis. We must allow Sewanee, some time later, at least four or five days. If Sewanee were on the direct route, it would be different. We can't have everything but this is a serious privation.

We have been resting and taking it easy. I look forward to the serenity that I had lacked for many years.

We both send love to you all.

Affectionately, Allen

AL

Gainesville, Fla.
1822 NW 8th Ave.
Sept. 4, 1959

Dear Brother:

We are going to call you about Sewanee before you will receive this. I was wondering if you had left out a sheet of the memorandum, as you sent two copies of the first page. I was wondering, since you mentioned Don. Did you mean you had written him, or included him some way in the deal:

Of course, Don can't be circumvented, but his name has an ominous ring. He hates *The Velvet Horn;* his long rambling piece, which he calls a novel, has been turned down by McDowell: the "Singing Billy"[1] piece. He doesn't believe fiction is an art, and he has an imaginary concept of what it is, just as there were no negroes on the frontier; and so what is going to happen, I'm afraid, is another one of his involutions, disguising the real meaning of his disapproval. Added to this Randall's dislike of any kind of trouble or roughening of the waters, it doesn't look so good at this moment.

Miss [Virginia] Rock's chapter on the groundwork for the publication of *I'll Take My Stand* has been read.[2] It's very interesting. After the preliminary correspondence between you and Don and others, did you note or rather did Miss Rock know what she was doing by placing Don's letter (if she did, she did it cleverly without comment) to you, ignoring all the earlier correspondence, suggesting such a book. Very strange. I mentioned to Miss Rock the meeting in which John and I confronted him over the contract, but I did it in such a way that its true nature was not disclosed. I see no reason why he should not be protected in this weakness. What it has done to his real profession is enough, and we will need charity.

In haste. I hope the moon is all honey. We'll try to get you tonight on the phone. The disparity of time is pretty great about Sewanee.

Love from all of us to you all, Andrew

TLS

1. Davidson wrote a folk opera entitled *Singin' Billy* with music by Charles Bryan, which has recently been published and a novel about a folk singer who became a Country and Western singer on the Grand Ole Opry, which is still unpublished. 2. This work is Rock's unpublished Ph.D. dissertation: "The Making and Meaning of *I'll Take My Stand:* A Study of Utopian Conservatism, 1925–39," Minnesota, 1961.

Sept. 7, 1959

Dear Edna:

How can I thank you for your letter and Andrew's, and for your coming which meant so *very* much to Allen and (both on his account and my own) to me.

The unequivocal warmth you both gave me from the start made me very happy. You can imagine how much I've heard about you both, and I know how much Andrew & Allen mean to each other.

We are sad about not being able to come South on our way back but we are both very tired. It has been a year of great strain and we feel we had best get back to Minnesota before Allen's classes begin.

I had a letter from the Dennys expressing their pleasure in meeting you & Andrew.

Today is my 44th birthday. Allen is sitting for his portrait with Marg Aiken. We have had three glorious days, bright, fresh and clear, and have canoed, and swum both in ocean & pond. People say we both look far more rested.

Thank you again for coming. Allen had been worried about Andrew and is now reassured.

Allen's love and mine to you both.

Isabella [Tate]

AL

We'll be at the Oakgrove Hotel from the 2lst or 22nd.

Wellfleet, Mass.
September 9, 1959

Dear Brother,

You know by this time we must omit the mountain. I hate this but it would have been too frustrating to stay one day and two nights.

Yours of the 4th just arrived. Very stupid of me to send *two* carbons of page 1. As to Don, I realized that he would have to be dealt with. On the missing second page, I pointed out that he had recently been reappointed for 3 years beyond retirement, and should be offered the new Professorship of Southern Literature, with the understanding that you be brought to Vanderbilt in the fall of 1960, at a salary of $10,000 and held in readiness to accede to the Prof. of Southern Lit. on Don's retirement. This adjustment seemed to me the only way of dealing with Don. He certainly doesn't believe fiction is an art: there is no "art" but folk-art. He thinks of his anti-desegregation activities as a continuation of the Agrarian Cause, to which the rest of us are traitors.

But if Branscomb has any statesmanship, he will put the new chair over. I haven't heard from Henry, but Ben liked my memo and said he would get Jesse Wills behind it too.

As to Miss Rock's[1] "placing" of Don's letter, I told her that unless she could find absolute proof, in the correspondence, that I had suggested the symposium, she should give Don credit for it. I agree that he must be protected. The priority in suggesting the book is of no importance to me.

Maybe we can come to Florida next winter, say round Christmas time. Would there be a place nearby where Isabell's son [Dan] could boat, fish, and swim? Please think about it. (He's nearly 15.)

Love to you all. I doubt you'll get this before you start for Tennessee.

Affectionately, Allen

AL

1. Virginia Rock.

Gainesville, Fla.
1822 NW 8th Ave.
Sept. 22, 1959

Dear Brother:

I got your letter on my return from Tennessee. Edna told me more or less what she had written you. Of course what I am looking for is a place to settle down, with decent pay, so that I can educate the girls on a professor's salary. I'd rather they didn't go here. To begin with there's a fine school (day school) for Kate in Nashville, if we could get her in which I think maybe we can. What I'm saying is the honor of the chair doesn't mean too much to me. In a subsidiary calling I don't want to lose sight of its actual meaning, which is utilitarian, bread and meat and other necessities.

The politics in a university would make professional politicians look like amateurs. When I took Pamela to Vanderbilt, [Randall] Stewart saw me and came over, but not until he began to think fast. I waved to him, but he pretended not to see me. When he did come over, he asked in a rather gruff way what I was doing there. I introduced him to Pamela and put him on the defensive. We talked pleasantly enough, but made eyes all along. His interest is just as selfish as mine. On no grounds can he pretend that his position is for the good of the school. I just thought I'd throw this out for what it was worth.

[David] Patterson, a friend of mine in Nashville, said that Branscomb was only interested in money. Ben made the same point. I take it this might be a good sign, so much money for a chair given without his effort. However, it has been known that promises are never kept in University circles. What I'm saying is that you can't apparently count on any statesmanship. It is money that makes that horse run.

I think, perhaps, you have interpreted rightly the procedure; and after all Don has been there for a long time, is the distinguished professor and should have had recognition long before this. The fault is partly his own. They hate him in Rutherford county, because of the people he has allied himself with up there. I tried to warn him in this, and he gave me a little lecture. I think, however, he is withdrawing from these activities. Sometimes in my weaker and less Christian moments, I resent his high moral tone, that Puritanical display of ego, of speaking with the tongues of angels . . . but at such moments I hesitate to look behind it, for what is really there, and so learn again the value of Christian charity and humility.

Let us know how things go out there. Maybe now you can get back to work, be comforted and taken care of. I thought I'd get this off before going to class and hope things turn out for the best.

We send love, and remember that nobody ever really died of love.

Affectionately, Andrew

TLS

Oak Grove Hotel
230 Oak Grove St.
Sept. 26, 1959

Dear Brother,

Isabella is writing to Edna about coming to Florida for Christmas. We both think it's a wonderful idea. We would plan to drive down so that these Yankee girls, both I[sabella] and her daughter Rose, could see some of the Southern country.

Your conversation with Randall Stewart doesn't surprise me. You see what we're up against. Money is the key to the solution. If his departmental budget isn't threatened, he may be *forced* to accept the plan. But it all depends on whether Henry and Ben can find the money; not *all*, keckafas,[1] because Don's attitude is unpredictable. That's why I deemed it absolutely necessary to offer him the grandiose title first. I know you don't care anything about that; but if we're going to put it over, it must be separate, in a way, from the English Department, with funds that are not drawn from the English budget. The grandiose plan, in other words, would be easier to put over than just a new job *in* the English Department.

Randall has not answered my second letter in which I suggested the Professorship of Southern Literature. We stopped at Gambier; I told John Ransom about the plan and he predicted, before I could tell him about Randall's attitude, that we would have more opposition from him than from Don. John thinks it's a wonderful project, and you're exactly the right man for it.

Your operation and the end of a stage in your work have brought about a critical situation similar to the crisis I've been facing—the end of which, for me, is in sight if I have the reserve creative strength to allow my good fortune to have its way. Every day with Isabella gives me courage and determination to go forward and resume the poem I began and had to let lapse in my critical period. Edna's letter to me is one of the great letters of a dedicated woman. We are both lucky as we enter old age.

For the present I am leaving Christmas plans to our ladies.

We think we've found a house to buy—a large, ugly bulk that nobody but people like us would want and that can be bought cheap. For the interval we have a large apartment in this hotel and are already fairly well settled.

We're looking forward to Christmas. It will mean a great deal to me for us to be together at this particular time.

Love to you all.

Affectionately, Brother

AL

1. Slang for *keck*—"to feel or show great disgust."

Gainesville, Fla.
1822 NW 8th Ave.
Oct. 5, 1959

Dear Brother:

Have been meaning to write you, but the fall illnesses have gone through the family, with Edna in bed for a week, very unusual, and golden pellets for cure. Now we are mending. Your letters arrived today. Looks good. Very interesting. By the way, I also got in the mail a letter from the Ford Foundation people, offering in effect one of their fellowships, a poet or novelist to spend six months with a theatre, at home or abroad, but a year's fellowship.[1] Seventy-five hundred plus possible travel and other mysterious expenses. It might be no bad strategy to take it and put them off at Vanderbilt for a year. In other words the Guggenheim goes through September. This would begin in the fall and run until next September. Maybe we can go to Greece after all, or something like that. Of course it hasn't absolutely been settled, but I guess pretty much so or they would not have written.

We are going to have a fine time Christmas. Edna is working on a place to stay. The motor courts are pretty expensive. I always hate to buy food or lodging. There are several possibilities. She will write Isabella. We are going to Santabel Island this week or next to explore it. It is near Fort Myers and will be warm. The greatest place for sea shells short of the Great Barrier Reef. This part of Florida is really South Georgia, and may be cold as hell by Christmas. But we can arrange at least for fishing, Gulf or lakes. The water skiing I don't know about, but I have students that do. Edna will write soon.

After reading the prospectus and the letter to you, it might just be a good thing to go on this Ford business, if it really comes through, saying yes, I would love to, but I can't this year. . . .

Love to all of you, Andrew

TLS

1. Lytle accepted the nomination later in October but not without conditions—first, that he could not set date and, second, that he could not accept award unless it included travel expenses for his family. Probably because of these stipulations, the fellowship was granted to someone else.

Oak Grove Hotel
230 Oak Grove Street
Minneapolis, Minn.
October 9, 1959

Dear Brother,

Poor Edna. A virus has laid most people low here—except us (so far).

That Ford money sounds fine, but don't do anything definite about it till we get the next report from Vanderbilt, *provided* it's not too long in coming. How long can you put Ford off? If I don't hear from Randall in two weeks I'll write him; I'm making a note on my calendar to do this. Meanwhile I'll write to Henry Alexander.

Maybe Santabel Island is the place for us; you will know by the time this reaches you. We have friends here who have a house on Captiva Island. We are lunching with them day after tomorrow, and they can give us all the information. I don't know just where it is but I believe it's in the warm belt.

Back to the Vanderbilt thing. If you delayed a year going there, Randall and Don might cool off and make complications. That's why I suggest holding Ford off for a while. The plan has gone over so well up to now that we mustn't allow them any pretext to back away.

As soon as we have some information about Captiva, Isabella will write to Edna. I hope Edna is on her feet again. The strain of the summer no doubt aided the work of the virus

Love to you all.

Affly, Allen

AL

Gainesville, Fla.
1822 NW 8th Ave.
Oct. 13, 1959

Dear Brother:

You are absolutely right. I had lost for the moment a view of the darker aspects of the scene. As a matter of fact the announcement for the Ford fellowships comes in Feb. I don't have to have my acceptance of the nomination in until the 26th of this month. The final acceptance, I should imagine, would be in Feb.

Captiva is next to Santabel. You might prefer the Atlantic Coast. It would be more expensive over here, I should imagine. Do you suppose your friends would offer you their house on Captiva? A student of mine is writing his father-in-law, who has a boat and may run us down there from St. Petersburg this weekend. We will know more by then. We ought to have a good time. There will be young married couples, students of mine, and some few bachelors, I think, for Rose. There is always fishing here. It will be too cold in this area for water-skiing. Maybe down in the warm area around the islands or over on the Atlantic it would still be possible.

In haste, our love. It's a comfort to know you won't freeze in that weather this coming winter.

Andrew

TLS

Oak Grove Hotel
October 19, 1959

Dear Brother:

The other day Monroe [Spears] sent me an advance copy of the birthday issue, and I've been lost in a Narcississtitic daze.[1] (The prolongation of

N——was accidental, but not irrelevant.) Curiously enough the only piece that seems to be very *close* to me besides yours is by a foreigner, Herbert Read. I have read yours at least twenty times,[2] with more pleasure every time, and a great feeling of communion. What you say about the relation of friendship to time is brilliant and profound; and your definition of my "subject" is the only sharp one in the symposium. But I am grateful to the others, especially to John and Don. (If we could keep Don within the Mode of Nostalgia he would love us completely.) I know you are talking about me, but most of the others I feel are talking about somebody disguised as me. No matter. I feel both embarrassment and consternation, mingled with perplexity and pride.

Isabella is writing to Edna. Our letter to Captiva went astray, and it will be a week before we hear. The hotel we have a line on sounds cheap and perhaps you all would go there with us, at least the day after Christmas. It's called Tween Waters and [is] run by a Virginia lady.

If I don't hear again from Randall Stewart by the end of this week, I'll write him, and also Ben and Henry.

Love to you all.

Affectionately, Allen
TLS

1. The autumn 1959 issue of *The Sewanee Review* honored Tate on his sixtieth birthday and contained tributes by Lytle, Ransom, Davidson, T. S. Eliot, and Herbert Read. 2. Read's essay was entitled "Our Cousin, Mr. Tate," 572–575; Lytle's was "Allen Tate: Upon the Occasion of His Sixtieth Birthday," 542–544.

Gainesville, Fla.
1822 NW 8th Ave.
Nov. 21, 1959

Dear Brother,

I've been trying to write you for days, but David McDowell is pushing me for a foreword to the *Forrest* which he wants to bring out in Feb.[1] I just can't do it. It's a gap of thirty years, and yet I feel I ought to be able to say something. So————

I'm glad you liked the little I did. I didn't have everything about me. It was the first act of will after my recovery. I'm of course glad it came out as well as it did. I think the issue is a fine one. I've read everything but [Howard] Nemerov—[R. P.] Blackmur was at his best or worst,[2] as you see it. It was so confused, as to be meaningless. I've decided what's the matter with [him]. He always uses an abstract adjective or a general one with an abstract noun. So he can always be evasive. You see what that is: it's the state of chaos before the creative Word. I haven't read enough of him, and so maybe I do him an injustice—but I just can't see him.

Time draws nigh when we will see you. We can make it all right—with quarters here at no cost. Make sallies into Florida, depending upon the weather. I wrote Don about his poem[3] and got a nice letter in return. He mentioned the chair and seemed very agreeable but said if it can be worked out. From what I hear they are resigned to it or happy about it openly & officially, even though it is not of course mentioned yet. They are apparently preparing some kind of ground for it.

More later. By the way, I thought Spears did a nice introduction to the whole. I'll write him about it. Love to both of you.

Andrew

AL

1. McDowell, Obolensky brought out a "new edition," actually a fifth printing of *Bedford Forrest* in 1960 for which Lytle wrote an introduction (pp. i–xvii). 2. Nemerov's contribution to the issue honoring Tate was "The Current of the Frozen Stream: An Essay on the Poetry of Allen Tate," 585–97; Blackmur's was "San Giovanni in Venere: Allen Tate as a Man of Letters," 614–31. 3. Davidson wrote a poem entitled "Lines Written for Allen Tate on His Sixtieth Anniversary" for the Tate issue.

After Dec. 5th:
2019 Irving Avenue South
Minneapolis 5
December 1, 1959

Dear Brother:

Before I get to your letter, look at the carbon of my letter of today to Henry Alexander,[1] My chief worry is that since last summer both Henry and Ben may have put the whole project in the back of their heads, not out of indifference but because they are under daily pressure of their own sort. The money will have to be raised. Branscomb will not finance the new job out of his regular budget. I wonder if you've heard from Henry?

We've changed our minds so many times about the Florida plans since Isabella last wrote to Edna that I hesitate to tell you the latest—which is to go to Captiva after all. We *think* we've found an inn, the Gulf View Inn, which has reasonable rates; and we tentatively plan to *drive* down, leaving here the 20th or 21st, and arriving the day before Christmas. We'd stay till about the 31st. A long gruelling drive, but we would be heading towards warm weather; and Isabella sort of likes the idea of driving through the lower South, where she's never been. I believe the problematical weather in northeast Florida has given us more pause than anything else. But we would like to feel that a condition of our going to Captiva is your coming there too, as you seemed willing to do at first. Is this still possible? We would like to hear from you at once about this. I should add that another consideration is Rosie, whom we hesitate to take to a town where she is not acquainted, whereas at Captiva she could swim and lie on the beach daily, and not miss the Chicago life. She is also in a very mixed-up state, and we hesitate to bring her to Gainesville; and moreover she is a little more than we are perfectly certain we can handle.

I agree with you about Dick Blackmur's article. I scarcely see why he wanted to write it. It is certainly not about me. And I don't quite like the little workout on San Giovanni in Venere. Nemerov is a little heavy and solemn (he wrote the piece years ago),[2] but I like what he does. Your piece is closer to me than any of the others, though I find John's very moving.

It's too bad you have to write a preface to *Forrest* after all these years. The Michigan Press got my *Jackson* out in paperback,[3] but luckily for me didn't ask for a preface.

One way or another we'll be seeing you in a little more than two weeks. Love to all the girls.

Affectionately, Allen

TLS

Isabella feels mighty bad about the possible change. She wants to see you all very much indeed, and sends love.

1. See Appendix J. 2. Nemerov's piece first appeared in *Furioso,* 3 (February 1948), 50–61. 3. *Stonewall Jackson, the Good Soldier: A Narrative* was brought out by Ann Arbor Paperbacks in 1957.

IV

1960–1968

The letters of the final section are dominated by personal narrative. Although in 1961 Lytle resumes editorship of *The Sewanee Review* and, as a consequence, many of the exchanges between him and Tate deal almost exclusively with the business of publication—particularly as regards Tate's guest editing of the special Eliot issue in 1966, the greater part of the correspondence in this sequence, and certainly the most memorable, centers on their private ordeals.

This is especially true for Lytle. Not long after the sequence opens, a letter comes from Lytle in Memphis informing Tate that Edna has lung cancer and is to have surgery. Once the operation appears successful, Lytle decides to leave Gainesville and move his family back to the Log Cabin at Monteagle. Involved in fixing up the Log Cabin for winter and concerned for Edna, Lytle's letters at this point typically alternate between describing a particular stage of repair and reporting on Edna's health. Time passes, and though she rallies, eventually Edna's condition worsens. By the first of 1963 her cancer returns, and in April, after several months of suffering, she dies. Not quite a year after her death, Lytle has to undergo another painful operation himself. Learning about the experience from a letter, Tate in Minneapolis writes in return, "It is a relief to know that you are back at the Log Cabin. . . . The ordeal of the past four years topped by your illness, has been too much for any novelist."

Although his trouble is of a different nature, Tate's letters also show a man harassed by a series of personal problems. Most of these, at least initially, are created by his two step-children. First, it is the daughter's wedding that is cancelled because the reputation of her fiancé, a bullfighter, prevents him from getting a visa. Next, it is the strain caused by the irresponsibility of the son who refuses to attend college. Then it is the mulatto whom the daughter finally chooses to marry. But ultimately it is the marriage of Tate and Isabella itself. Tate writes Lytle from London concerning the relationship in July 1965 and reveals plans to return to Minneapolis and then Tennessee. Although Lytle's answer has not been found, he must have responded as friend and confidante because Tate closes his next letter thanking him for all his "kindnesses" and naming the Log Cabin as "both a haven and a renewal." By February of the next year, Tate reports that the divorce is scheduled to take place in March.

Although there are no letters in the file to tell the story of their wedding, by the close of the sequence, Tate has married Helen Heinz, is building a house at Sewanee close to Lytle at Monteagle, and is the father of twin boys. In the final letter dated February 9, 1968, Lytle looks forward to the Dallas Literary Festival which is to honor the Nashville Agrarians in April. The correspondence ends with this letter, for soon afterwards, Tate moves to his house in Sewanee where he and Lytle see each other almost every day.

University of Minnesota
January 11, 1960

Dear Brother,

We've been in touch in such a rush since we got back ten days ago that I'm just now getting down to writing letters. It was a fine visit, but of course not enough time. If we can get you to Tennessee you will be much nearer both morally and geographically. I thought the girls were very fine, and Edna in excellent condition in spite of her ordeal last summer; you too seemed in top form, if a little fatigued. I wish we could be together more, and maybe we will in the near future.

I enclose, belatedly, two letters pertaining to the Vanderbilt situation. There ought to be more news after January 28th. I am writing to Jackson Mathews a detailed description of the project.

I am trying to get to work again, but it's tough; so I just get to my desk every morning so as to be in position if anything comes. Isabella is feeling a little let down and tired after her labors of the fall and of the trip, but she is better than she was a week ago.

I'll keep you informed of progress. Let me know how it goes with you all. Love to everybody.

Affly, Allen

TLS

Love to the [Bea and George] Foxes.

Gainesville, Fla.
1822 NW 8th Ave.
Jan. 31, 1960

Dear Brother:

We've got a little winter here today, twenty-six or so, which must be the breath of spring to you out there. But it justifies a good fire. I just can't keep from burning wood when I've got it—there's no luxury like burning a fire and keeping the door open—and your Cousin Edna is in there with it and Langdon recovering from a little virus. I give the woman one of them quilted robes for Christmas to favor my eye, but she says it keeps her warm, as well. And here I am beginning the day by writing you.

The situation about Vanderbilt doesn't look too bad. It's certainly been a chore to you. Maybe we can bring it to some kind of an end before too long, or maybe it has reached a situation where you can't push too hard. You will know about this better than I do. If nothing comes of the Commonwealth business, it looks like old Ben needs to be prodded some way. These matters are hard to cipher. Although I'm awfully proud at the way you are working on this, and then too it's almost as good that Ben spoke right out as he did. And Henry, too, would like it. Well, anyway the future holds its own.

It was a little hectic arriving with four women in a car, but we had a good visit, if a short one and Isabella's children are fine, and maybe Rosy will work everything out to some good end. Pamela turned up with a fine young man, but too far involved to suit me right now. It certainly took us by surprise. But as well as I could make out, he's all right. I'm just thinking of the most extreme possibilities. She's only a freshman and he is her first love, but they can get married, you know. He teaches Latin and Greek at St. Andrew's, I rather think as a kind of curative business. He was four months on the front lines in Korea without relief and wounded twice. He is receiving money from the government, but he seems all right except for shrapnel in his head. I don't like this disability business, but anyway I think he is finding that the crier of the Holy Cross is not all goodness and harmony either. I don't know what is going to come of this. But he's a real man, and so.

Keep at it. You bound to find it tough getting back to work after not working for several days. It's awful but I think you got to do it. You married a young woman and they ain't anything else for you to do but git to work. I've sort of got down to it. I'm going to do this little memoir with the fable of instructing the three girls as to who they are.[1] I will be the narrator, not the central actor, sort of like David Copperfield. I think this will do to get me back into the habit. I had all my shots or most of them for Mexico and I'll go down there in the middle of Feb. for two weeks. By then I ought to have the first chapter or so done and maybe like old Ford write while I go about there looking things over. It is coming too easily and that frightens me, but maybe this kind of writing is easy. By the way I thought *Time* mag was very respectful in the review of the essays,[2] something very unusual. Maybe there is a turnover of staff and young men are coming on who understand a little better. By the way I think he was right about that self-deprecation. It's become now almost a convention with you in the beginning [of] anything critical. It doesn't seem any longer ironical. I've been meaning to call it to your attention.

Well, no more now. All these conferences at the tail end of the semester are on me. Let me hear, and keep at it.

Our love to you both.

Andrew

TLS

1. Lytle is beginning plans for *A Wake for the Living: A Family Chronicle* (New York: Crown Publishers, Inc., 1975). 2. The review is of Tate's *Collected Essays* (Denver: Swallow Press, 1959).

Gainesville, Fla.
1822 NW 8th Ave.
Jan. 31, 1960

Dear Brother:

I've been thinking since that last hurried note to you. We are going to have to set a limit to the time you put in on this Vanderbilt matter. After all we are not trying to sell a bill of goods. It could get embarrassing for both of us. There was some preparation over the years in Nashville; that is certain of our old friends there have mentioned that it would be a good thing, and with your vigorous campaign—if nothing comes soon, maybe we had just better sort of drop it. You can only force these fateful matters so far. It may be it's not in the cards, which doesn't make me not feel with real warmth Henry and Ben's attitude, particularly Ben's. Of course with you it's beyond gratitude.

We've been in some turmoil. I've been taking the shots to go to Mexico for a look-around. Edna has not wanted me to go alone, but with a young child it's hard for her to get off. Maybe I won't go. I told her I wouldn't this morning, and the whole round was opened again. Pamela is getting awfully serious with this young man. . . .

Well, no more, Brother. I just thought that since the Commonwealth has met, the business grew fresh in my mind, and I thought I ought to write you this note.

Our love to you both,

Andrew

TLS

2019 Irving Avenue South
Minneapolis, Minnesota
February 2, 1960

Dear Brother,

I appreciate your feelings about my small part in the Vanderbilt matter,[1] and I feel very keenly your own embarrassment. Since I wrote you there has been a favorable reaction on the part of the Bollingen Foundation, to the extent that they want to have an interview with me when I am in NY on Feb. 24–25. So don't be depressed yet by the situation. It always takes a long time to put these things through. The only way to get them done quickly is for some individual to step forward with the money. It's the kind of thing that Branscomb wouldn't mind having, but he would not divert one penny from his general funds to get it. I have an idea that if Ben and/or Henry came forward with the cash, Branscomb might well argue them out of it and say that the Social Sciences needed it more. If I can get a foundation to donate it, we can have it ear-marked, and Branscomb can't touch it. I have a sort of liking for Branscomb, but I wouldn't trust him out of sight.

I can't have an opinion about Mexico. You'd plan[ned] to take the whole family for the summer. I just heard today that you're going to Oregon for two weeks in June. How news do get around.

I've had a little flu in the guts, but am mending; and Isabella is well. We send love to you all. Ain't a thing you can do about the young man if Pamela's a mind to take him.

Affectionately, Allen

TLS

1. Tate has tried for some time to get Lytle a position at Vanderbilt. See Appendixes K through M.

Gainesville, Fla.
1822 NW 8th Ave.
Feb. 9, 1960

Dear Brother:

You'll have to tell your Cousin Edna that I think she's reconciled. We got since I wrote a special from Pamela saying they were going to marry in June, and she hoped at St. Mary's chapel on the mountain.[1] Why don't you all come by Sewanee on the way to the cape. It's a shock for both of us. He's a real man, with only ten percent disability from his Korean wounds. He said total when he was here, but I must have misunderstood. He was a hundred and fifteen days on the front line without relief and twice wounded, and his godfather sent him to teach Latin at St. Andrew's to recover. To recover is your Cousin Edna's interpretation. I wrote Pamela I had to know about this disability; it became ten percent. I guess I was just hard of hearing. He certainly don't look disabled. And we are very pleased at her choice, but since this is her first love, maybe they will quarrel and break up. And so keep it quiet, not that anybody in Minnesota would be interested.

That's good news about the Bollingen Foundation. We'll just wait and see then. And maybe it is best to move slowly. Anyway you can't push it faster than it, or anything, will move, I guess. Let me hear. I may be in Mexico for a few weeks looking around for a place for us to stay in the summer. Your cousin Edna has given me a lot of trouble on this point. It's not flattering any more. She just don't want me to git out of her sight. And I tell her I have to do these things. Where does she think the extra money comes from? Anyway all the pleasure is out of it when I set out. I was offered fifteen hundred dollars for those eight lectures in Oregon. I just couldn't see turning it down, without tempting fate. We'll need this extra money for the marrying. Anyway, this is the condition of our plans: they are very fluid.

The trouble is the savor of things is getting mighty flat. Did I tell you I started that little memoir McDowell wanted me to do. I think I have the tone right and the point of view, which is merely a voice called mine. Like David Copperfield's. Which means I can limit it as I please, to show the nature of the Old West's inheritance. Of course it will be anecdotal. With the three girls to limit its form, their varying ages, etc. (it is written presumably to tell them who they are). I can do almost anything, even to putting a fairy story in it.

We send love. It will be wonderful to see you all at the mountain, if

Isabella feels like going that far out of the way, and the timing works good.

Aff., Andrew

TLS

1. Pamela married James W. Law June 11, 1960.

Gainesville, Fla.
1822 NW 8th Ave.
March 4, 1960

Dear Brother:

I tried to make it to Boston, but I just couldn't face another group of people, and as it turned out, I really didn't get done in N.Y. until Sunday afternoon. I hope I did a little good, but you never know. I avoided the abyss of motives; dealt only with the formalities which I hoped defined them. If they want to sink their sorrows and fears and desires into a fresh amity, my coming on the scene could have helped. Otherwise, things are far along towards ruin.

Isabella, tell her, looked very beautiful and distinguished, and her friends made a chorus. I felt a little sad about Malcolm [Cowley] but especially his wife.[1] He in a way is now at his best as a man. It seemed to me so—in a resounding Pathos. The world is staling a little for me, but if I can withdraw and get to work, I'll be all right. The young I meet lack "bottom" as we used to say of horses. I wonder if they will make any kind of decent and substantial life for our children here.

Well, hope things went well all around.

Our love, Andrew

AL

1. Cowley's second wife, Muriel Maurer. Cowley is, indeed, at a peak; in 1960 he taught a talented class at Stanford whose students have since produced more than seventy volumes.

2019 Irving Avenue South
Minneapolis, Minnesota
March 15, 1960

Dear Brother,

I too was very sorry you couldn't make it to Boston, but we understood the pressure you were under.

While I am waiting to hear the final word from the Bollingen Foundation, I have written to Ben to see if he will take some sort of action. I have some hope of this, but will not go into it in detail till I hear from him. Some weeks ago I mentioned the possible new chair in a letter to Red. He replied that it would be fine, but offered no help.

We're going to Arizona with the two children for the spring vacation—leaving day after tomorrow and returning the 27th. It will be pleasant, but it is distracting and a waste of money and time. It will take me a year to show Isabella that this sort of thing isn't necessary for the well-being of Dan, and that if she didn't have the money to do it, a simpler way would seem just as good. Our address will be Circle Z Ranch, Patagonia, Arizona.

Have you and Cousin Edna made further plans for the mountain and the marryin'? We can get there by June 16th, but will have to leave by the 25th. If the Woods go there then, and get a large cottage, we will rent a room from them; otherwise, we can stay at Clara's motel in Sewanee.[1] Please let us know.

I hope Edna is feeling better about the wedding. She will find Pamela will be a greater joy to her afterwards than she has ever been before! Our love to you all.

Affly, Allen
TLS

1. Clara Shumate's Claramont.

2019 Irving Avenue South
Minneapolis,Minnesota
April 1, 1960

Dear Brother,

We were back from Arizona just two days when yours of March 28th arrived. Well, it's all moving apace. I've been looking at my schedule, and I believe we can make it to the wedding on June 11th. My one examination is on the 9th, and I'll have my assistant air-mail the papers to me. I'm allowed four days to get the grades in. We would hope to leave here on the 6th or 7th and arrive on the mountain in the evening of the 8th or 9th.

The big problem is where to stay. If you get a house at Monteagle you will be full up with family. I still don't know whether the Woods will be there, and I won't know till the last minute: you know how they are. So I'm writing Monroe [Spears] and also to Margaret Myers. We could stay at Clara's motel, but I imagine she will have all her rooms engaged for the Sewanee Commencement. Margaret is too old to keep us a week without servants, and she too may be full up with family. But it will work out somehow. I'd much rather be at Monteagle, and make forays into Sewanee. I'll let you know how it works out.

I reckon Langdon is settled down again, and I hope Miss Edna isn't too upset by the attempt to run away from home. All children at one time or another have that fantasy. The wedding is going to be rough on you both, but you can take it. Edna can't quite know, as yet, what a great improvement it will effect in the relations of mother and daughter.

Love to you all.

Affly, Allen

TLS

P.S. No word yet from my present attempt to get money for the chair. But soon, I'm sure.

2019 Irving Avenue South
Minneapolis, Minnesota
May 1, 1960

Dear Brother,

We're back a week from ten days in Washington and Virginia, and I'm in a rat-race. This month will be tough and I welcome the day we drive towards Tennessee—which ought to be June 6th. I've got to make three trips out of Mpls. in May—Duluth, St. Louis, and Lexington, Ky.

The latest report on the Chair at Vanderbilt is not encouraging. The Bollingen Foundation finally answered, but not hopefully, though the door isn't closed. Try again next year, etc. But time in this thing is of the essence. My next move was really disheartening. I decided to put it up to Ben, and asked him if he and/or Louise couldn't manage it. I suggested that if Louise did it, the Chair could be called the Benjamin E. Tate Professor of Southern Literature after Ben's death. No word for a month. Then Ben wrote me that *he* couldn't afford to do it now, and that Louise *wouldn't* do it. She preferred to give $475,000 to a hospital this year. The state of mind of a woman like Louise is to me impenetrable. I think Ben was genuinely sorry, and maybe he couldn't give that much money all at once. As a further sidelight on the rich, uprooted society that they represent, I will explain what happened a few days ago. I am going to Lexington on the 30th to get an honorary Litt. D. from the University of Ky. I wrote Ben that I might be able to come by Cincinnati a couple of days in advance, and would he and/or Louise be able to go to Lexington (90 miles) for the ceremony—I'd like some member of my family there, etc. They telephoned us the moment they got my letter. Not one word about the degree, congratulations or otherwise. I asked Ben if he could go to Lexington. "No," he said—just that one word. He went on to say that they wanted to give us a party. Louise got Isabella on the line and said there were some Boston people in Cincinnati, and she wanted to have a big party for us. She has learned that Isabella is what she would call "Boston society." No further comment necessary, except that we told them we couldn't come.

We shall have to think of other ways to endow the Chair. I haven't by any means given up. It is going to take us longer than we had expected, but we will do it.

I've heard nothing from Monroe since I wrote to say that we would like to have their house. But we can find a place without too much trouble. Commencement will be over and the mountain deserted.

Well, Brother, life is tough, but we've been through it so far, and we can take more. Love to you all. Exactly when do you all expect to arrive on the mountain?

Affectionately, Allen

TLS

1822 NW 8th Ave.
Gainesville, Fla
May 6, 1960

Dear Brother:

We are just back from Tennessee to arrange for the wedding; two trips to Sewanee, I hopped over to Missouri to make a talk and pay for the trip. It was exhausting; Pamela looks purple from fatigue, but after an initial breakdown Edna got on her feet and the two of them did well. The Spears spoke of your having their house; so you will hear, I'm sure. We didn't go to see Betty,[1] as we went through the place like Sherman through Georgia.

Don't worry about this chair. I'm sure that Ben was genuinely sorry, but you can't expect Louise or people who deal in big money to think much of learning. She can see what good comes from a hospital, because she's had a pain. I expect they were somewhat embarrassed by the whole thing and that's why they didn't want to come to Kentucky. I wouldn't hold that against Ben or Louise either. Maybe you ought to have let her give you a party. I don't know. Ben would have done it if he was able or knew how to locate the money. I might sort of talk to Henry sometime when it's proper. You can't do this sort of thing so well for yourself, but I think I might risk it in this instance. It's too late now except under special circumstances to make a change for this coming year. Granted this place would replace me, which I doubt, it would be too late to find anybody else.

I've got to go to the dentist; so I'll close. Love to both of you. We go to the mountain the end of this month; have rented the Maney cottage, at the bottom of that first egg-shaped drive as you come in. It used to be Mrs. Scott's house from Murfreesboro, but then that was after your time. I'm on a trade, trying to buy my house back. I don't know what will come of it, because the ladies are going to be greedy. I practically gave it to them. I've got to find some place to put that furniture.

Affectionately, Andrew

TLS

I'm sure Isabella will like the mountain and the people will like her. We are awaiting your advance.

1. Probably Betty Chitty.

Friday

Dear Brother:

Our Mexican trip was rather disastrous. Almost as soon as we got there, Edna came down with pneumonia.[1] We were in a fishing village and by the time we found a real doctor who could speak English, we were pretty desperate. He cured her fever and told me to get her out of the country, the quickest way. I finally was able to fly her and Langdon out and followed with the car.

I won't go into it all, but we have her here in the hospital (the Baptist Memorial) taking cobalt treatment. The University hospital in Gainesville advised taking out the whole right lung, but Dr. Carr hopes to get by with only the middle & lower lobes.

She is in good spirits and otherwise in good health so we are hopeful. They do the best they can, say she has the slowest-growing kind but actually they never know how it will go.

We are all very hopeful, and her care is the best in the Southeast, and that's how it stands now. We don't quite know where she will be operated on. Pamela & Jim are staying with the children. Jim's school opens 20th of Sept. and after that I can let my assistant and his wife stay with them. We do not know about time—as the radiologist determines that. At present they mean to reserve a fourth of the treatment for after the operation.

Our love to you and Isabella. I will write again when there is anything to write.

Room 805 GLB-9515 Baptist Memorial Hospital. I am staying at

Jane's, 175 W. Chickasaw Parkway, Memphis. Edna says she will write you herself soon.

Andrew

AL

1. They discovered she really had cancer of the lung.

Memphis, Tenn
175 W Chickasaw Parkway
Sept. 9, 1960

Brother -

I wrote you at Wellfleet. They should have forwarded the letter. In case it went astray I must tell you our news is not too good. Edna has cancer of the lung. We brought her here on several counts. Now she is taking that strong cobalt ray before the operation. The doctor feels he can leave the upper right lobe and left side is o.k. Which will make her more comfortable. We just don't know. Cobalt has done great things. He can find no evidence yet of its spreading. Her spirit is good. She has gained weight and is taking the treatment without too much hardship.

Our love to you both.

Andrew

AL

Memphis 11, Tenn.
175 W. Chickasaw Pkway
Sept. 11, 1960

Dear Brother and Isabella-

Jane told me of your call, and the flowers came, were here when I brought Edna back from Jane's. The doctor doesn't give her cobalt on Sunday, and sometimes she feels like going out. Her spirits are good, except that every now and then she breaks down. She is very tired, but if she has nausea from the cobalt, she is keeping it to herself. All in all she is making a gallant effort. We have strong hope that she may live several years and with luck much longer.

I am going to see the children this week and arrange for somebody to stay with them when Pamela has to go back. It will be at least ten days before she is given another broncostomy, which will precede the operation. The flowers were elegant, and she was delighted to see them. She is going to try to write. I expect after I leave. Thank you, brother, for offering to come. But there's nothing now to do but wait until we know the score better. She will enjoy Monteagle; and if all goes well, we may have good times. And you all will have to spend some time then.

We both send love.

Andrew

AL

2019 Irving Ave. So.
Minneapolis 5
Oct. 2, 1960

Dear Brother,

I was mighty relieved to get yours of the 28th. Last Sunday—a week ago—we telephoned the hospital in Memphis, and were informed that Edna was not there; and the Hogan's didn't answer their telephone; so we were at sea.

I am no judge of these things, but your report does sound encouraging. The bad thing now for you both is the waiting. Will you take Edna back to Memphis for the x-ray pictures? It's to compare very small things to very serious ones to mention that I have a skin cancer which will be removed tomorrow. It's on my right cheek. It's the third I've had in five years. The doctor says this doesn't mean a general tendency to cancer; its a peculiarity of the skin.

I have a strong feeling that Edna will get through this crisis and be with us the normal span of life. I take it as a virtual certainty. Why all this suffering for her and for the rest of you, we shall never know.

We've got to go to NY on Oct. 28th–31st. I suppose nothing will be taking you there then.

I will write to David McDowell for more specific information. Does this mean that McDowell-Obolensky is breaking up?

Our love to you all—more particularly to Edna, who is in my morning prayers daily.

Affectionately, Allen

TLS

P.S. Have you heard that Monroe Spears is resigning from *The Sewanee Review*? Effective next summer.

[Undated]

Brother:

We will be back in Memphis when you and Isabella are in New York. About that time the doctor means to operate. Like a good tactician he is feeling "the rhythm" of the disease. However, we scarcely can look for no operation, as the cobalt is most effective on new cells, not established ones. However, this is the most metaphysical of diseases. Prayer, the spirit, the action of the mind, all have to do with it. The way her spirit and her general well-being supporting it are working, we have high hopes. I just sent in the last money, a large commitment of my reserves, as a pledge of confidence to the normal span of life you speak of, for the closing of the Monteagle deal.[1] We must have a reunion there. I will have the furniture moved up from the farm in May, the place got ready, and so forth. I've written Charles Harrison to ask if he got any solid response to having me teach there.[2] I also wrote Monroe. Nine years is long enough. He was a gifted writer and ought to get back at it. David McDowell, among other things, might like to be editor and run the press, I think sort of like a New Directions. However, I don't think he would really like to leave New York. He has fought Madison Ave., and I rather suspect they are making him feel it now. I thought you knew about his eviction by Obolensky. It's a long story I'll tell you sometime, if you don't come upon it.

I use A-fil, rub it on your face and it protects you from the sun. It's better than most. I've actually had it reduce a sun-growth on my nose. It's not gone, however.

Our love to you both.

Affectionately, Andrew

TLS

1. Lytle bought back the Log Cabin from the Monteagle Woman's Association. 2. Chairman of The English Department at the University of the South.

Gainesville, Fla.
1822 NW 8th Ave.
Nov. 15, 1960

Dear Brother:

It is almost miraculous, Edna's rapid recovery. It's a clear case of prayers, as well as her will and the doctor's skill. You've been awfully sustaining through this, you and Isabella. Edna enjoyed her good and long letter and she will write her after we get home. We'll leave the end of this week, stop over at Polly's, and go slowly south. I don't know how much juggling she can take in a day. She has adequate capacity in the lung that is left. The cavity has now filled up three-fourths with blood and fluid, which apparently solidifies and may show a slight depression in time. Her greatest trouble now is coughing. She hasn't much to cough up, but she feels she'll choke to death if she doesn't; so it is partially a nervous reaction. I guess I've got a real nursing job for the next six months, as at times she grows awfully discouraged. The awareness of what has happened to her comes over her and leaves her in despair. But she pulls out of it. It's going to be hard. I think Monteagle next summer will help a lot, and you all must come up. Peter Taylor has bought the old Lincoln cottage you know. I wish it could be that we could spend a year there in quietitude and work, but that must be in the future, I guess.

There's not much to say, except to tell you how your love sustained us. It's been right long of a vigil, but the worst is over, and we can get down to living again. The girls have behaved mighty well during this whole business, and I hope we don't have to leave them again soon. Langdon is growing apace and needs parental guidance and discipline. My assistant and his wife are in the house, and they are kind gentle young people. We have a servant who is very expensive and dramatic. She loves to bring Edna trays and has had her church pray for her, but it's hard for her to get the other work done. I think she would have hoped for Edna gradually to worsen so that she could nurse her. Well, write us.

Our Love, Andrew

TLS

2019 Irving Avenue South
Minneapolis 5, Minnesota
March 13, 1961

Dear Brother,

I take it no news is at least not bad news. I have been so beat-down by laryngitis for nearly two months (better now) that I've scarcely been able to get to the University. But there's little time now before we leave, which will be on the 26th; and we sail on the Liberté on April 5th.

We're going to settle in Urbino for about six weeks, and I hope the climate and the boredom will make it easier to do a little work. We go to London first, for about two weeks, then Paris for a few days, and Italy around April 28th. Our address will be American Express Co., Florence.

Please write us how Edna is, and give her our love.

I'm going to Lexington on Thursday of this week to pick up a little money, and then to Salem College in N.C. for the same purpose. I'll be back here on the 21st. I hope to have the weekend at Smyrna with the Cheneys.

Love to you all. I'm just praying that Edna is out of pain by this time.

Affly., Brother [Allen Tate]

TLS

Gainesville, Fla.
1822 NW Ave.
May 4, 1961

Dear Brother:

Well, you and Isabella should about be in Italy now. I had meant to have a letter awaiting you there, but alas I have been fretted with affairs and trading in a selfish and vulgar world, and moving up and down the country, and now we are painting and talking with movers and uprooting ourselves in all those ways you have to, when you leave a place. I'm taking a year's leave of absence to edit *The Sewanee Review*[1] at ten thousand a year. One class. I hope it is the right move, and I expect we'll be going there for good. The little girls are not saying much, but they don't like the idea. This after all is home to them. Kate came here in diapers and Langdon had her long fight with the cord in the local hospital. It's very curious, now that I'm leaving, the head says it will ruin his department (I'm the third in two years); so it's not too personal, but the others realize I've brought them their best graduate students. Well, anyway, we'll have a year up there, to see how all goes. Kate will be ready for Sister Christobel,[2] and Langdon will love the mountain children, I hope. The chore of driving will be something, but we've plans for fixing up the cottage permanently, with furnace [making] the whole lower floor into one long room. Maybe that not right away. (I'll have to wait until I sell this place: we've rented it I think to a doctor coming in to the new hospital. We are going to sign the lease today. Real estate is off here, and it may be better in another year. That is the gamble.)

This is the time for you to finish, by the help of Her Ladyship, the poem; so that I can print the whole of it in the *Review*. And maybe Isabella is doing something too. And if you hear of any good essay or any good man over there who has something, bespeak it.

Lon and I went to the Catholic Renascence Society. I didn't realize what a perfect mask the nun's habit is. Sister Bernetta was on the program and I tried to find her to congratulate her, but from the back you can't distinguish anything, and even from the front it's bad. The priests have the faint suggestion of being eunuchs. There is this terrible distance even among themselves. The things they say in public, the smiles they give are meaningless, because it is no more than a bare convention without real meaning. I saw, I think, exactly the weakness of the Church: it views itself as another church, not The Church. Some priest congratulated the assembly in having two protestants there, me and another (I didn't tell I'm an old Christian, no protestant); it was done in such a way, in a provincial way, not as if everybody was still in the church but sinning in a flagrant way. It was a veiled partisan attitude. Well . . .

Lon writes that Katherine Anne was at the Vanderbilt symposium. And took the show, even to giving down at a cocktail party and having to be carried to the doctor (a bad foot this time). She as you may know is to be in residence at the University of Texas, with nothing to do but be on the campus for nine months: pay twelve thousand. Well, she's earned it.

I don't know any other news much. Edna has good and bad days, but on the whole what I reported in Smyrna still holds, please God. She is mending, and the shortness of breath may improve. She sometimes drinks too much, but I've been on her about it. I don't think it's good for her; it makes her cough.

Our love to you both. Write us.

Brother

TLS

1. This began Lytle's second time to serve as editor of *The Sewanee Review,* though the first time he was officially managing editor. This editorship began with the Autumn 1961 issue and concluded with the one for Autumn 1973. 2. In the Episcopal school at Sewanee.

Pensione Annalena
via Romana, 34
Florence
May 14, 1961

Dear Brother,

Yours of the 4th awaited on return yesterday from a long tour, a week exactly, to Rome, Assisi, Urbino, Arezzo, and Perugia. I can't look at pictures again for a while. We've at last come to roost, after six weeks of travel, and hope to do a little work. We're established in a comfortable pensione across from the gate to the Boboli Garden;[1] we have a few friends here, and we expect to have quiet enjoyment.

Your news of Edna is very encouraging, and the whole tone of your letter is the most cheerful I've had since Edna's operation. I shall light a candle for her the next time I go into a church.

I had heard from Monroe that you were taking the SR over. Why not do it indefinitely? Where could Ned McCrady[2] do better? You belong there. If I *can* finish the poem this summer you shall have a large part of it.

Beginning in London on April 13th I've given eight lectures and readings. I'm a little tired, but I feel fine, and so does Isabella. I have never enjoyed Europe so much.

I don't know whether K.A.P. has *earned* $12,000, but I agree she ought *to have* it!

We're counting on seeing you all on the mountain come September. No more for the moment. I must attend to business. When do you leave for the mountain? Isabella sends love to you all, as I do.

Affly, Brother

TLS

[Note around edges of letter, added by Isabella:]

Wonderful to know Edna is feeling more herself and good to think of you going to Sewanee. Allen has been doing a great deal of walking which seems to agree with him wonderfully. Now we settle down to some *working* which would have begun sooner but for Allen's scattered lecture engagements. We look forward to Sept. To Edna and you much love.

Isabella

AL

1. The garden is behind the Pitti Palace, home of the Medicis. 2. Edward McCrady, Vice-Chancellor and President of University of the South.

Box 761
Wellfleet, Mass
Thurs. June 29, 1961

Dear Brother,

Here we are. We landed a week ago today; I went to Washington for one day; both to Boston; and finally here on Monday. Very complicated. But we both were improved by the trip, and I feel that I can now do some real work. I hope Isabella can too.

Doubtless you all are settled in the Log Cabin. It's where you ought to be. When do you take over the S.R.?

Please write us how Edna is. She is constantly in our thoughts. I pray the improvement reported in your last letter continues.

We are settled in a delightful house on a different pond—but there's no hot water: like *old* Monteagle.

We still plan to come down in early September—I alone in the car, and Isabella flying to Chattanooga.

Nancy and Percy are coming here on July 15th for two weeks. Will be my longest visit with them since 1954.

Our love to you all. Please write.

Affly, Brother [Allen Tate]

P.S. Just got the announcement of George Myers' death. I am more moved by it than I could have imagined being. A landmark is gone.

P.P.S. On the boat we met an old friend of yours—Hutch Sullivan[1]—and found him very good company.

1. Actually only an acquaintance. He was a friend of Abbott Martin.

July 15, 1961

Dear Brother:

Thanks for your note. We are looking forward to your coming. It's been rather hectic. Only yesterday did I get the furniture from the farm, and I've another load yet to go. We are going to put a kitchen and bath in that back room, the one without a fireplace. I've got to get it ready for winter, too. I've barely looked in here,[1] but in another week, I'll put my mind on it. There is some backlog. You'll have to help me out some, but I'd rather it would be in an issue entirely mine. If you know anybody who is good, in any way, let me know. Edna is bearing up pretty well. Love to Isabella and yourself.

Andrew

AL

1. *The Sewanee Review* office.

The Sewanee Review
July 31, 1961

Dear Brother:

I hate to write these hasty notes, but I've turned into a contractor, taking the back room and making of it a kitchen and bath. Finding my way around, paying by the hour, adding to Edna's strain, hating this kind of detail; but I vaguely see the end of it. I can postpone the insulation and weather-stripping until late in August. I've been half-crazy, trying to get over here and keep some things going, although I'm not on the payroll until Sept.

I think that's a fine piece on the "Four Seasons"[1] and I want to try to publish it. It is too long. It ought to be reduced to forty or forty-five pages which will make twenty-five or thirty pages in the magazine. He has critical mannerisms which you noticed, and I noticed others. I think he means tone at times when he says style. I would like for him to sharpen that. Style inhabits the entire poem [essay?]. I take it to be the definition of the whole which is form and content. I think he could take out his opinion, that is the phrases around his "I" and go on to his critical judgment. That would tighten it up considerably. Would you like to write him? I will of course; but I think he needs a little direction in this. He's got to bring it to its own end, not the one involving his dissertation, I think. I also think he can take the people Hock etc., reduce them to their essential statements and proceed. Five or six pages could be cut here.

I had to turn back Red's novel.[2] For the one time there is no short story in it, which will make an organic whole, or rather dramatic whole. I hated to do this; he was so generous as to think of the *Review*.

Love to you all. Be sure to come by. More later

A

TLS

1. R. K. Meiners, "The End of History: Allen Tate's 'Seasons of the Soul,'" *Sewanee* Review, 70 (Winter 1962), 34–74. 2. Lytle is probably referring to *Wilderness* (New York: Random House, 1961).

Box 761
Wellfleet, Mass.
August 30, 1961

Dear Brother,

We are very depressed and have been for a week, knowing that we can't make it to the mountain. I won't go over the details. But since mid-July, when the Woods came for two weeks, we have been under terrific pressure, and we are both so tired that we can't undertake a long, 3,000 mile trip. We've got a graduate student to drive the car to Minnesota, and we are going by train. Nancy's visit was the longest and best I've had with her since 1954, and I got to know the children for the first time since they were infants. This was followed by plans for Rosie's wedding to the bullfighter: I believe I wrote you about that. Elaborate social plans were made—two large parties here at hotels, and arrangements for putting up the large Garner clan, who had all clenched their teeth and decided to see it through. But at the last minute the bull-fighter couldn't get a visa. An investigation followed, undertaken by a man in the Embassy who is a friend of Isabella's sister Kitty. The report said that he had been married and divorced quickly about five times, and was notorious for exploiting well-to-do young American women; his name was already in the Embassy files as a person of shady reputation. The result is that Rosie pulled out, and has been here for nearly three weeks. Isabella is absolutely exhausted. Maybe we can dash down from Mpls [Minneapolis] by air some time in the fall.

In Italy we had got into a rhythm of work which continued here for a while. Part of the exhaustion is in frustrated hopes of accomplishing something. But we've got to take it, and we'll recover once we're in our house.

I had a good letter from Peter [Taylor] the other day. Please save me writing him at present by passing on our sad news. We had been looking forward to seeing you all for six months. And this is another frustration.

Love to Edna and the girls.

Affly, Allen [Tate]

TLS

The Sewanee Review
Sept. 5, 1961

Dear Brother:

We tried to phone you a week ago, but you seemed to have none. I meant to write you to phone us. Strange things in the changing world at Monteagle, although it's still about as it was, we have a phone. You may want the number. WA (Wabash) 4-2433. Of course we wanted to know when you would be here, and then your letter disappointing us came. You've had, of course, an exhausting summer with company and kin and the disappointing wedding, but still all of you were well out of that. And certainly Rosie must know it and will probably be more circumspect from now on. But do try to fly down here later on. You know how beautiful October can be.

I've done nothing but try to get the house in shape for winter, and it has been hard on all of us. I had old Mr. Wells eighty-two, his sixty-odd son-in-law, a deaf plumber named Farmer. Neither liked the other. Old man Wells would sit in the chair in the hall and sulk until Farmer got out. His work still leaks a little. When he would finish anything hard, he would open his hands and arms, as if saying—"Look at my master stroke," or "such is beyond any repair." I had to watch them every minute, make decisions I didn't know how to make. Once I left the bathroom where the boy was laying tile, so well and so fast I thought he would do it. He turned eight sheets upside down, and it took a half a day to tear it out and put more in. I won't go on with such, except to say I couldn't get over here at the *Review* office and get well under way. The mss. pile high, and school will soon begin. Pamela has been here a month and Jim comes this week to stay a few days and take her back. She's been awfully sweet and helpful. Edna has had a bad spell. I think the paint from painting the porch started it off. She still coughs; she is worried about herself, and does not have enough breath. Jimmie, her brother-in-law, is coming up for an Episcopal meeting, and we will let him see what he thinks. This move has been terrible on her and all of us, because we don't know what it entails. And could have no peace this summer because of renovation. Now, with just a little to do, we can pull it all together before cold weather. I hope and pray that Edna's disability is the exhaustion from all we've been through these last months.

We are putting in electric heat, insulating, etc. That's on its way to being done. Franklin Taylor is so erratic, but he does come. If I can get him to run the wires under the floor this week, we can bring in the weatherproofing men. We took that back room and made a bath and kitchen out of it. You'll like it, I think. Nothing modern, a bath with tile inside a kitchen. Nowhere but Monteagle would you get that. The cabin looks good, but we suffer from the loss of that back room. If I have any money left, I'm going to put a study under the house. The ladies tore it all out.

Well, our love to Isabella in her hard summer. And to you, always from us. The young man who did the piece on you [R. K. Meiners] won't have it revised until the winter issue. By the way, I have this idea. I feel that both Peter Taylor and Flannery [O'Connor] have reached that stage where they need a concentrated appraisal. Say two or three pieces on them. But not only that. Let them give me something, a story or piece of fiction, to go with the criticism. I think this will lighten somewhat, without lessening, the heavy effect which criticism makes in a quarterly.[1] Peter has agreed, and I've written Flannery. You wouldn't want to do something on Peter, would you? It wouldn't come out until the winter or spring issue. And could you help me with suggestions as to who might be good to do this. I've written Caroline to do something on Flannery. And I wrote Eudora Welty. I thought I'd later practice the same strategy on her work. She hasn't done anything for a long time really, and needs a different kind of an appraisal. When you get back, let me hear from you. I'll be out sometime. [Reed] Whittemore is going to bring about twenty editors to his school for a conference. It's not set when.

Aff., Andrew

TLS

1. As a consequence of Lytle's plan, the 1962 Summer issue highlighted the work of Flannery O'Connor. Accompanying a new novella, "The Lame Shall Enter First," 337–379, were two critical essays about her work—Robert Fitzgerald's "The Countryside and the True Country," 380–394, and John Hawks' "Flannery O'Connor's Devil," 395–407. Similarly, the 1962 Autumn issue highlighted the work of Peter Taylor. Taylor contributed a new work, "At the Drugstore," 528–558, which was followed by three critical pieces: Morgan Blum's "Peter Taylor: Self-Limitation in Fiction," 559–587; Brainard Cheney's "Peter Taylor's Plays," 579–587; and Ashley Brown's "The Early Fiction of Peter Taylor," 588–602.

The Sewanee Review
October 3, 1961

Dear Brother:

Thanks for your note. I would be delighted to stay of course with you all when I come out to the editors' meeting. Edna would like to come but I don't think we can afford it. I have spent far too much money doing over the Monteagle cottage. It has silver paper underneath the floors, stuff blown in overhead, all the doors weather stripped, and electric heat plus our four fireplaces. We hope to keep warm and be permanently situated at not too great an expense. Don't give up the idea of flying here some time this fall, you and Isabella. You all are so much more affluent than we.

Edna seems to mend, but yesterday she had severe pain most of the day. I think she must have twisted something. Evidently the cavity is not yet all closed up. Maybe the heart or lung shifted over.

Meiners has cut his piece on you from seventy-one to forty-seven pages. It came in too late for this issue but I mean to run it for the winter one. I haven't read the revision but I rather think it is going to be much more suitable. You know it would be awfully nice if you had part of the long poem you are working on to go with it. What about this?

I have written John Wade to ask him to review Don's recent book[1] but I rather expect a refusal. Who should I get to do this? You have got to help me out with such things. The fall issue I think is going to be a good one. Partly by accident and partly by design it makes a kind of whole.

I know what you mean about Flannery's reputation. But she is good, and the wrong kind of thing that is being written about her must be corrected and this *Review* is the place to do it. By the way, what is Robert Fitzgerald's most recent address?

The girls are making the adjustment pretty well. Langdon's measure is heroic. She refuses to speak of or think about her friends in Gainesville. Kate, the child of divine unrest, is doing awfully well and is about to become some help to me.

No more now. Love to you both.

Brother

TLS

1. Davidson's *The Long Street* (Nashville: Vanderbilt University Press, 1961).

2019 Irving Avenue South
Minneapolis 5, Minnesota
October 10, 1961

Dear Brother,

I talked to Reed Whittemore last night, and it seems the conference will last two days, Fri. and Sat., Nov. 10th and 11th. We hope you will arrive on Thursday and leave not before Sunday. We plan a cocktail party on Saturday.

There's a great deal to talk about, private as well as literary. I will try to get a poem to you for the winter issue. Rosie is making so much trouble that I may come to the mountain for a week the day after Christmas for about a week. This is strictly between you and Edna and me. It is so complicated that I can't go into it in a letter.

I am sending a very fine essay by an English philosopher-friend of mine. This pamphlet as I see it does not constitute real publication. It is simply local routine for an inaugural lecture. It is just about the best statement I know anywhere on the difference between philosophical and poetic truth.

I am looking forward to your visit, and I hope you *will* arrive on Thursday so that we can have a visit before the conference begins. And we both hope that Edna can so arrange for the girls that she can come too. Love to you all.

Affly, Brother [Allen Tate]

AL

The Sewanee Review
Oct. 19, 1961

Dear Brother: —

I would have written sooner, but the pressures seem never to let up. About two weeks ago Edna had great pain in back & front. I hardly could get her out of bed to see Henry [Kirby-Smith].[1] Fortunately it seems to be nothing serious. Some sudden motion did something inside, but there seems no evidence of a return. Part of it was fright and hysteria, I think. She is very hoarse. It may be nothing—but it is occasion for speculation. She's much better and it looks now as if I can come. I'll have to find somebody to stay with her and the children. I'll try to get in Thurs.

The first issue ought to be out in two weeks.[2] It's longer than it should be, but I was so anxious to get an issue I miscalculated. It has a kind of design. It would be wonderful if you could have a poem ready for winter. The piece by that boy would go well with it. I think we need somebody in England better than [Bonamy] Dobree. [E.] Lucas [Myers] suggests his friend, Ted Hughes. What do you think? Tell Isabella her volume[3] came in all right. It looks good, and I am now considering where to send it for review. Thanks for the address, and your friend's piece. I haven't had a chance to read it yet. I hope to achieve some kind of leisure & peace before too long.

I'm looking forward to a good visit. Keeping fingers crossed. Our love.

Aff., Brother

AL

1. A surgeon from Sewanee. 2. Lytle's inaugural essay appeared in the Autumn issue, 1961, pp. 711–12. 3. Lytle is referring to Gardner's collection of poems entitled *The Looking Glass* (Chicago: University of Chicago Press, 1961).

2019 Irving Avenue South
Minneapolis 5, Minnesota
October 21, 1961

Dear Brother,

Evidently Edna's attack was not a relapse, or "return"; and that's to be thankful for. Give her our love. We fervently hope you can come here, but if you can't we'll certainly understand why. Thursday will be fine. That would give us a whole day for visiting, as the conference doesn't begin till dinner time on Friday.

I can't promise the poem, but I will try hard, God knows.

Dobree is a fine man (I know him well) but he is getting a little tired. I don't know how good a critic Ted Hughes is, but I am convinced that Frank Kermode is the best critic, especially of fiction, in England. Why not try him? He has been writing a monthly article in *Encounter*. You could probably get him to do an article twice a year, or maybe oftener. Address: Frank Kermode, Dept. of English, The University, Manchester, Eng.

Love to you all.

Brother [Allen Tate]

AL

P.S. I'd be interested to know if Lucas has finished his novel.

The Sewanee Review
Nov. 20, 1961

Dear Brother & Isabella—

I had such a good time the glow is only now wearing off. I wanted to sit down as soon as I got back and tell you this, but I was caught up—maybe I'll learn to order my life and affairs while there is energy left to make the most of them. Edna asked many good questions, showed a little sorrow that she was not along. Jane stayed with her until Sunday. So she really didn't miss me much. Friends of hers came from Memphis to see [a] Southwestern play. Langdon got a letter from her little oriental friend and she fell into tears and homesickness, but the birthday soon after helped out, and a little collie puppy who kept us awake for thirty-six hours—the runt whose mother tried to kill him. What sold him was style—you never saw a peacock carry his tail so nobly. He no longer cries in his sleep. Love has cured him. So we go. It is thirty this morning. I made up the fire at a little after five to help the electric heat. It is wonderful to be at Monteagle, in winter, and warm.

Scribner wrote after your note giving permission.[1] Ellen Webb[2] had written too. I wrote John Logan asking him to review Isabella's book.[3] Haven't heard yet; but if I don't, I have probably the wrong address.

Pull yourself together and finish the poem. It will make all the difference in the effect of the issue. New and old between criticism.[4] The first of December will do. Even if it isn't perfect—you can work on it later. It doesn't have to be what you might think of as finished—versions have their uniqueness. Herbert Read sent in a long poem which I'll include in this issue.[5] I want to keep the poetry pretty down this time, so that it may be savored better.

Our love, Aff. Brother

AL

I forgot to pay for the whiskey. Enclosed may be enough.

1. The permission was to reprint Tate's poem "Seasons of the Soul" along with Meiners' article. 2. The Business Manager of *The Sewanee Review*. 3. Logan's review, "The Poetry of Isabella Gardner," appeared in the 1962 Spring issue, 250–53. 4. That is, the new poem Lytle is urging Tate to finish plus the reprinting of "Seasons of the Soul." 5. Read's poem was "Daphne" which appeared in the 1962 Winter issue, 1–7.

2019 Irving Avenue South
Minneapolis 5, Minnesota
November 24, 1961

Dear Brother:

I'm sending a copy of my poems to make sure that the right version of "Seasons" is available.

We've been a little anxious lest you returned to find Edna not too well. I hope all is quiet.

Your visit was a great pleasure for us. When you get a breathing spell drop a line.

Love to Edna & the girls.

Affly. Brother [Allen Tate]

AL

Why not put the poem in *very small* type at the end of the article?

Had just sealed this when your letter arrived. I have spent 2 hours looking at that section of the poem.[1] Brother, I just can't do it! There are some 25 lines which are still *very wrong*. I'm sorry to let you down, but I must refrain.

Good news that Edna was, and is, in good shape.

That whisky was a stirrup cup—not to be paid for except, on the mountain, in kind!

1. Tate is referring to the new poem Lytle has urged him to finish.

Nov. 30, 1961

Dear Brother—

The book came,[1] and I took it home to Edna. We are mighty proud to have it, and we will re-read these long winter nights the lines we know, that stay with you and enlarge their meaning in time, as if they drew time in and made it a suffusing mirror. This boy's piece has just come in, and it is good. I could wish you would put pressure on yourself and still try to finish the poem. I know it's always a question of how much pressure; but then you've always worked under it. I hear the brilliant students say here that you are the only one in English who can do well the terza rima.

John Logan was glad to review Isabella's book. I thought we might do it alone. I also took three poems of his which I thought were good.[2] He was slow to write because I addressed him to the English Dept. He apparently is not honored at home, a thing too often repeated.

Edna has had a spell, but she is recovering. Thanksgiving was too much for her. John came up and spent the night with us,[3] and she enjoyed him immensely, although she told me she could hardly sit in the chair. I never know when she is putting up a good front and when maybe her psyche is taking over. Sometimes we think we made a mistake going to Monteagle. For Langdon's sake we probably should have taken a house here [at Sewanee]. You never know.

Well, this is just a note. I'm trying to pull together the winter issue. Christmas is not long away, and we are looking forward to seeing you whenever you can come.

We send love to both.

Aff., Andrew

AL

1. Tate's *Poems* (New York: Charles Scribner's Sons, 1960). The volume contains poems included in *Poems: 1922–1947,* among them the four parts of "Seasons of the Soul," plus two poems not previously collected, "The Swimmers" and "The Buried Lake." 2. Logan's "Monologues of the Son of Saul," a poem in three parts, appeared in the 1962 Winter issue, pp. 8–11. 3. Ransom was a Visiting Professor of English at Vanderbilt during the fall semester of 1961.

Jan. 16 [1962]

Dear Isabella and Allen,

Thank you so much for the delicious Dutch cheese. It was a happy addition to our holiday and enjoyed so much by ourselves and our guests. We were so happy you thought of us and only kept wishing we'd hear you were coming to see us—as mentioned. I should have written or phoned but things were strenuous and I kept waiting for some order to resume. Pamela and Jim spent about ten days with us and their visit just made Christmas for us. The little girls were so happy to have Pamela again and Andrew enjoyed having a companion in Jim instead of running about and doing things all by himself. There is a slight chance they will return to this part of the country to teach, which would be wonderful for all, to share the trials and pleasures ahead. The problem is that he can so much more readily do graduate studies in N.Y. He has only a B.A.—did a little work last summer and is going to take a couple of courses this coming semester.

After the New Year my sister Jane and Jimmy spent a week with us and the day they left the snow began again, temperature below zero all week, as low as 12 below; water froze, drains froze, car gave up and had to be towed to Tracy City; schools closed. So we have all felt very gay the past few days since the thaw though it is still cold; 20 degrees this morning.

I was reading the new *S.R.* last night and think it is a very good whole. Claude Koch's story[1] holds up well on rereading, but some of the local gentry are not going to like the "goddamns" etc. in Charlie Rose's story[2]—a bit. [Note in margin: These people make themselves so vocal and it worries Andrew.] Also a few misspellings and printer's errors I could have so easily have caught if I'd put a little time on it. Maybe next issue I keep hoping I'll be more capable—I do very well but my strength is certainly limited.

Keep us in your plans—maybe you could come in the spring or June? You will almost have to do the travelling as so far my moving out has been a trip to the county seat once—not that I couldn't have done more but someone has to stay home with the workmen, or the fire, or thieves; no safe way yet to lock this place. It has been difficult, for us all, but Andrew is certainly happier. He's the only man I ever saw who enjoyed thawing out a frozen faucet.

Isabella, I'm no poetry critic but I want to say how much I enjoyed your verse—an individual touch, so all your own it seems to me; strong lines, altogether delightful. Much love.

Edna

AL

1. A Matter of Family," 70 (Winter 1962), 93–136. 2. "By the Waters," 70 (Winter 1962), 14–33.

The Sewanee Review
March 7, 1962

Brother:

I don't know how in the hell I'm going to keep at this thing. Just business. We telephoned to have Don's book airmailed you. Get it in as soon as you can. It's holding us up.[1]

I can't publish the whole of Logan's piece on Isabella. I haven't got the money. I've been running over my budget, but that's not the only reason. I'm featuring the "Arts and Letters," since Peter Taylor's story didn't get in on time to plan. And he has to do something to it, too. I'm pleased in a way about Logan's praise, but the whole is awfully discursive and should have been better. I wish now I had asked Jim Dickey who did a like piece on Logan himself.[2] I told him to cut down his excessive use of the first person, and he did and his performance was much better. A real piece of writing.

When you come in in April. Try to juggle it. I've got to be at a festival in Converse College the twentieth, that is Thursday, Friday, Saturday noon.[3] You won't be in Nashville until the following Monday, but Lucas says you had planned to be here on the 20th. Are you going to the ALMA[4] thing in New York? I think I am. I am planning to. I wish you could be there.

I wake up with mss. raining down and smothering me. I can't keep this up forever and yet I am about to cut my bridges with Florida.

Our love, Edna is taking heart and doing better. To you both.

Brother

TLS

1. *The Long Street* (Nashville: Vanderbilt University Press, 1961). Tate later reviewed it in "The Gaze Past, The Glance Present," *Sewanee Review,* 70 (Autumn 1962), 671–72. 2. Lytle is referring to Dickey's "A Note on the Poetry of John Logan," 70 (Spring 1962), 257–60. 3. The Southern Literary Festival held at Converse College in Spartanburg, S.C.—Eudora Welty and Cleanth Brooks were among the guests. 4. Association of Literary Magazines of America.

March 31, 1962

Dear Brother,

I am sorry to have let you down—and Don too—about that review. For your eye alone: my ulcer has returned and I have been knocked flat by it. I am now on a strict regimen of rest and diet and will continue to be for some weeks. I may have to cut Nashville[1] as well as Sewanee; but I want to wait till the last minute to see how I am. It's not a serious ulcer, but it could be if I neglect it.

Affly, Brother [Allen Tate]

AL

1. Tate was to participate in Vanderbilt's annual literary symposium beginning April 25th.

The Sewanee Review
April 15, 1962

Dear Brother-

I've been worried about this business of ulcers, at many levels, but if you are going to make it down here, you must be better. I can't bear to think of you on a diet of mush and milk—and nothing to drink. There's only one thing left to do.

Do the review on Francis [Fergusson]. It's too late for Don's—we made an emphasis with John & John Wade this spring issue;[1] you were to have given the final notice. I'm sorry it didn't work out, but if you are sick, you are sick. We'll try to get down to Smyrna but maybe not until Tuesday. I'll just be back from Spartanburg and may have to rest a little. I think Edna will be able to make it. I rather doubt us spending the night. It will depend on what she's up to at the moment.

I don't want to see any of those people at Nashville. You would have thought they might have invited us down, not as paid guests, but out of courtesy. I told Lon this morning I didn't care to see them—not that it makes any real difference; but they [were] funny the last time you were there and Edna and I came up for Pamela's affairs.

We send love. Awfully glad you are better and we will see you, God willing.

Brother

AL

1. Both men contributed reviews of Davidson's *The Long Street* to the 1962 Spring issue. Ransom's essay was entitled "The Most Southern Poet," 202–207; and Wade's, "Oasis," 208–11.

The Sewanee Review
May 29, 1962

Brother:

When are you going to Europe? Will you do this summer Fergusson's review? There is a very brilliant boy here who has done a critical piece for Charles Harrison on rhetoric. He admires you tremendously and apparently has in this piece on Longinus put you in. Charles would like to send it to you to see.

Love from us, Brother

AL

The Sewanee Review
September 24, 1962

Dear Brother: [2019 Irving Avenue, South,
Minneapolis 5, Minnesota]

I hate to impose on you, but I am sending a few poems entered for the Mary Rugeley Ferguson Civil War Contest.[1] The prize is $250.00. There have not been very many good poems. These few I am sending you are the best. Will you look at them and see if any one is worth the prize. If not, I can call it off or postpone it; but if I postpone it we will have to write around and request entries of better people.

I am glad you all are safely back. I will write you very soon.

Affectionately, Andrew Lytle

TLS

P. S. Only have about a week to decide on this, as we are at the press.

1. This contest was for the best poem concerning the Centennial of the Civil War. The editors of *The Sewanee Review* were to be the final judges and the announcement was to appear in the 1962 Autumn issue.

The Sewanee Review
October 4, 1962

Dear Brother:

All summer I have meant to write you. I was thrown off by your stay in the French Alps. I didn't know whether to write you there where you seemed to think you might stay on, or write you in Italy. I think our news is fairly good. You know how Monteagle is; the social pace in summer is extreme, and it's not always fun. I can't quite say what the hairdresser at Sewanee says about the Sewanee social life: she says it's just like Paris. Edna has had her ups and downs, but she looks better really, that is, than she has in a long time. However, she doesn't have much voice. Whether that is psychosomatic or whether it is something more gravely to consider I don't know. However, I do think that a complication has set in—the usual complication of women, her time of life. I would like to get her to go to the doctor to have a check-up, but she refuses. Our really good news came recently. It is two-fold, I suppose both of them are good. Pamela's going to have a baby, we think in April, and Jim is going to enter the priesthood. Of course, we couldn't try to dissuade him, even if we wanted to; but I did write him to the effect that this is a secular world, and that most of the priests—liberals, extreme liberals—are at least sociologists (of course not all of them), and that if he was going to be a priest he would find himself with his traditional interests and beliefs somewhat at a disadvantage in the priestly world. However, this is their business. I haven't lived my life to my satisfaction, and I'm certainly not going to advise anybody else about theirs.

I've at last got around to digging out under the house for a study. You know I haven't unpacked my books since I've been here, and I haven't done any real work. I'm doing for *Daedalus* something on the recent impressionist novelists.[1] It's already due in, and I only hope that it'll be a decent performance. It takes a long time to get back into work. The

Review, I think, is pretty much under control. All my office force has changed. Betty Chitty is the new Business Manager,[2] and she is doing awfully well. If I have luck this year maybe I won't go at the frenzied pace I felt I had to go for the last two or three years. I hope to find the leisure in this new study and the atmosphere to consider doing some creative work. I am awfully glad to hear that you all are well. I wish I could go to Greece sometime, but I don't think much we'll ever get off the mountain again. We went to Murfreesboro for supper at John's, and Edna dreaded it for a week, and it took her four or five days to recover. I can't see how that trip could have caused her all that distress. The children are growing apace. Langdon is learning to paint, and Kate is doing a little of it too, and is pretty good. Langdon is also developing a sense of humor. All of the girls are passionate and extremely voluble in their human relationships. But we seem to be making out.

Write me your news about how things are going as soon as it slows up there. Thanks for reading the poems so fast. I didn't think any of them would do, and I was surprised at [Edgar] Bowers. I don't think he put his mind on it. I don't know whether to call it off or to postpone it and try to get somebody who is good to write a few poems.[3] What do you think? I can certainly postpone it till the winter issue, but if I do, I'll have to come up with something I think. Our love to all of you, and look after yourselves, and don't wait so long to write.

Affectionately, Brother

TLS

1. "Impressionism, The Ego, and The First Person," *Daedalus,* 92 (Spring 1963), 281–296. 2. Elizabeth N. Chitty replaced Ellen F. Webb with the Fall issue of 1962. 3. The contest was postponed. Although Bowers' poem, "Autumn Shade," did not win the prize, it was later announced as one of the finalists and published in the 1964 Fall issue, p. 668.

The Sewanee Review
Nov. 13, 1962

Dear Brother:

I needed an obituary on Faulkner. This will be the very thing. It's just right. Is that an English journal? Will you arrange permission to print, or shall we?[1] Advise. I was afraid [Morgan] Blum was in trouble. I'm sorry, although I never knew him.

My study is almost finished, twice what I had figured. Obolensky owes me $900 and I can't get a peep out of him, after [a] telephone call & two letters. This is that continuing option on *A Name for Evil,* by movies.

Edna coughs a good deal; is up and down in performance and spirit. I hope all is well. She ordered clothes the other day, but she won't drive a car any more. Are you going to be in this country in July? Converse

College needs a partner with me for three days, summing up a summer program at Tryon, pleasant place & people. I tried to get to [the] Library of Congress to have a visit, but it looked to be a full schedule, and when the invitation read first come, first served, it seemed a little too formidable. What about that review on Fr. Fergusson?

No more now. We send love.

Aff., Brother

AL

How is this poetry I'm publishing?

1. Lytle is arranging to reprint Tate's "William Faulkner 1897–1962," an essay first published by *New Statesman* (London).

2019 Irving Avenue South
Minneapolis 5, Minnesota
November 21, 1962

Dear Brother,

Glad you want to use the obituary. You don't need permission. Just run a footnote: Reprinted from the *New Statesman* (London) by permission of the Editor. I will clear it with him.

You ought to sue Obolensky. And what is David McDowell doing since the salary from ALMA has ceased?

Of your recent poets, Wheelock and Roethke are fine.[1] The others good.

I have been under the weather recently—bad stomach and fatigue. Isabella is well but also tired. I suppose your report of Edna's condition is something we must expect. I wish we could get down to see you, but I see no immediate prospect.

Our love to you all.

Affly., Brother [Allen Tate]

AL

1. John Hall Wheelock's poem "The Part Called Age" had appeared in the 1962 Fall issue, 603–607; and Theodore Roethke's "The Far Field" had appeared in the same number, 609–12.

The Sewanee Review
Dec. 2, 1962

Dear Brother:—

We enjoyed your Christmas notes. Tell Isabella I'm sorry she don't feel like writing on that fellow, because he's in a great hurry to be a great poet and noted figure. But tell her to send me some verse instead.

Edna's losing, I'm afraid. She coughed up blood for ten days. This has stopped and I think we are returning to Memphis Sunday for a series of tests which she dreads. It can be something else. It's a long chance maybe worth it. She is weak, but we say that may be the menopause.

I'll let you [know] after we get down there, if we go.

Love, A

AL

2019 Irving Avenue South
Minneapolis 5, Minnesota
January 2, 1963

Dear Brother,

Since just before Christmas we have been in such confusion that I haven't been able to write any sort of letter. Rosie was here a week, and kept her mother up all night, night after night, talking. Dan has caused strain too; but he is registering at the University today (after doing virtually nothing since September) and we hope his problem is at least temporarily solved.

Your report of Edna's condition has been much on our minds. That blood sounds really serious. But I take it that things have not gone worse with her since your letter, or we should have heard. She looked so well last spring that I couldn't have believed that she had ever been ill. I suppose she must expect setbacks and recoveries all along. I wish we could be with you. Give her our love.

Isabella sends her love too. We never cease to miss you. Maybe next summer we can have a good visit, in addition to the meeting at Tryon [N.C.].

Affly., Brother [Allen Tate]

TLS

The Sewanee Review
Jan. 3, 1963

Dear Brother:

Our news is not good. I am back here, putting Kate in school. Edna is taking cobalt in Memphis. The cancer, as we feared, returned; this time in the esophagus, which means cobalt to lessen it, else she would starve to death. It presses on a nerve and makes her voice bad. Another pressure droops her eye. The lung & windpipe seem clear. They do not expect her to get well, but they are variable as to time. If it is only where it shows, her time will be prolonged.

Langdon is still in Memphis and I'll kind of commute. I doubt if they'll keep her longer than two more weeks.

Well, our love.

A.

AL

2019 Irving Avenue South
Minneapolis 5, Minnesota
January 11, 1963

Dear Brother,

Your letter of the 3rd came the morning we left for New York; and since we got back, on the 8th, it has been lying before me on my desk. I suppose the cobalt treatments will have to continue indefinitely, though doubtless that depends upon the person and the location of the cancer. We have a friend here who after a year of cobalt was pronounced "cured," at least for several years. I pray this may be the case with Edna. Will she be able to come back to the mountain without having to be taken to Memphis at intervals? This would be very hard on both of you. Henry [Kirby-Smith] surely can give cobalt. This entire crisis, for all of you, depresses me beyond any gloom I have felt for many years. And in this kind of ultimate crisis one's closest friends feel helpless.

I thought I might fly down for a weekend soon, and stay at Clara's,[1] or in spring vacation come for a week. But then I would be one more person for you to have on your mind. Let's see how you feel after a week or so. Love to you all,

Allen [Tate]

TLS

I wish we knew whether Edna is in that hospital or staying with Jane.

1. Clara Shumate's inn, Claramont.

The Sewanee Review
Jan. 30, 1963

Dear Brother:

I haven't written, because I've been nearly a month in Memphis, coming back here twice to catch up on the accruing work. In the hospital, with the progressing crisis, it's not possible to do anything. I would try to read or study and I would always fall asleep. We got back last night, after a harrowing departure, the hospital drugstore keeping us waiting for two hours while they got up the medicines. We had to make a scene to get out. Then I left my bag and had to go back down, another half hour. But we got here and a student who was feeding the dog had a fire going. She is now sleeping.

They gave her a great deal of cobalt; they promise nothing but hope it will make her more comfortable. It works about two months after they stop giving it, and for three weeks it will be very painful to swallow, as the rays have irritated everything in the area and especially that large blood vessel which drains the head and upper regions. For a while her face was round and red, and this was humiliating. But there is always a chance of a miracle. If we hadn't gone there, they only gave her a month or two. I finally told her that. She's been awfully fine about drinking and eating through pain (they don't give too much dope) but she is weak and feels bad. They told us that seventy-five percent of lung operations gave the patient only a year and a half. Well, it's been well over two years now and with this respite we look forward maybe to as much again, that is I do. She doesn't know about the odds. It's going to be hard on all of us, but Kate has matured well and will be of help. Langdon is awfully cute and growing but suffered under the best of conditions her exile from home.

No more now, as I'm sort of up in the air. I'm glad you think so well of the *Review*. I think it's good, too; and I'm glad you like Ed Moore's piece.[1] He is a brilliant boy and a great admirer of yours, as you see. Charles Harrison and I thought of keeping him in mind for the editorship here in five or six or more years. Of course that is planning too far ahead, but he could do it. He is in France now and goes to Harvard on a Woodrow Wilson next fall. Did I write you Pamela is going to have a baby in April? Her husband is one of those being looked over for the headmastership at Webb School. Bill Elliott got this started. It would be wonderful to have them so near, but I don't know how it would turn out. He is going to be an Episcopal priest, and I'm afraid this stands in his way. I'll try to see several of the members and talk with them if I can get away.

I'm thinking about printing a large part of Miss Raine's Bollingen lecture on Blake for the piece de resistance in the summer issue.[2] We thought we would do that and some poetry. You ain't got nothing done yet? Or has Isabella? It ought to be choice and good verse. Of course we can put some that is gifted, but we've got to have one or two poets as well. We've got a right good fiction number coming up for the spring, nearly all of them unpublished and young writers.[3]

Well, no more brother, our love.

A

TLS

I think later on a weekend here would be the the very thing. I've got two cars and can lend you one.

1. Edward M. Moore wrote an article concerning the Torchbook reissue (1962) of *I'll Take My Stand* entitled "TheNineteen-Thirty Agrarians" which appeared in the 1963 Winter issue, 133–42.. 2. Raine's paper which she delivered at the National Gallery of Art in Washington City as one of the A. W. Mellon Lectures was entitled "Blake's Debt to Antiquity." It appeared in *The Sewanee Review,* 71 (Summer 1963), 352–450. 3. The fiction writers who appear in the 1963 Spring issue are Helen Hudson, Madison Jones, Smith Kirkpatrick, James McConkey, Harry Crews, Fred Chappell, and Andre Dubus.

2019 Irving Ave. So.
Minneapolis 5, Minn.
March 2, 1963

Dear Brother,

Much time has passed since your last letter, but we assume that no change has occurred, or we should have heard about it. Sudden death brings a shock, but slow dying is worse since it means daily, even hourly attrition of the mind and body for the dying and for the living as well. We have reached the age at which these things will happen more and more. But Edna is too young for it, and that upsets nature as we live in it.

We have been rather upset too, but less grievously. Dan decided that he would not continue in the University. He ran off to Omaha, but we located him and finally caught up with him in Chicago. Isabella insisted that he come back here for a few days to clean up the mess he had left in his apartment; he came; and then went off again to Chicago where we presume he still is. Isabella agreed to give him an allowance, so that he will not be a bum or impose on his and her friends; but the allowance will be cut off in June unless he decides to back to school. After June 15th, if he has not made a decision, he will be on his own. We are completely baffled as to what is wrong, though we do see the surface trouble. He thinks he doesn't need an education, and though he is gifted as an artist he isn't even committed to that. We both feel that he will pull through, but we can't be complacent about it. We simply can't get through to him. For example, he read this winter *The Portrait of the Artist,* and identified himself with Stephen Dedalus. I reminded him that when Dedalus, at the end of the book, left to "forge the conscience of his race," he knew Latin and Greek, and six modern languages. This made no impression at all.

We are going East on the 19th, first to Boston, then back to NY, and then several days in Princeton for a good visit with the Woods. This winter quarter, plus the anxiety about Dan, has just about thrown us, but with warmer weather and a vacation we expect to improve. We now plan to go by Tennessee on our way East in June. If a crisis comes on suddenly I will of course come sooner—in fact, at any time.

Let us know how things are going. I hear from Don occasionally but he doesn't seem to know what you are doing. I wrote a tribute to JCR for *Shenandoah.*[1] I suppose you wrote one too.

Our love to you all.

Brother [Allen Tate]

TLS

1. "For John Ransom at Seventy-Five," *Shenandoah,* 14 (Spring 1963), 5–8. Lytle did not write an essay.

The Sewanee Review
March 7, 1963

Dear Brother:

I was glad to hear from you and sorry you've been having trouble with Dan. I think, it's none of my business, that with a boy you force him to be responsible for himself. If he throws himself away, then he does it. Not having any, I can say this. It looks as if the situation is being handled all right. You are giving him time to come to himself, and maybe all boys need this.

The cobalt gives Edna high fever, and she is weak but gallant. She even gets up and stumbles about the house, trying to set it in order. Or seeing things to be done. She loves to have letters; so why don't you write. She knows the dangers, the peril; but she also hopes that the cobalt will prolong her life, particularly in the day time. At night she wakes me up and her conversation is otherwise. She feels at time as if she will explode: this must be the cobalt, and she can be eased with pain-killers. The other night the dog howled right out her window as they do for death, and she said, "Collin is very proud of his voice." It passed us by and killed the potter in Miss McGee's old stone house on the bluff, back of Sunset Rock. You remember it.

Thanks for the recommendations. I'll get it. We have the Ramsey book.[1] The spring issue will have seven pieces of fiction, (four of them former students) and for the summer we are printing Miss Raine's Mellon lectures as the piece de resistance. How should I call them? Should the Bollingen people be named along with the Mellon? I suppose they must be partly patrons, as they originally sent it to me. I can't get any communication out of them, though.

I can't do anything but the work at hand. I rush home as soon as I can, and with broken sleep some of my days are dull as a teacher and editor. She doesn't want a strange face about her. One of her eyes droops, and her voice is hoarse. That is alarming. I did a piece for *Daedalus,* on the recent impressionists (these useless names) I wanted to call it "The Hero with the Private Parts," but that was a little strong for them. If all is well I'll give it at Vanderbilt when I go down there in April.[2]

We'll be looking forward to your stop-over in June, and I hope nothing interrupts the meeting in July at Converse.

Our love to you both.

Brother

TLS

1. Paul Ramsey's book *The Lively and the Just* (Tuscaloosa: University of Alabama Press, 1962) was reviewed by Peter Swiggart in an essay entitled "Neo-Classic as Truth" in the 1963 Fall issue, 687–89. 2. Just minutes before he was to deliver this address at Vanderbilt he learned of his wife's imminent death. He insisted on fulfilling his obligation because the audience was already assembled. The tears in his eyes and the break in his voice were obvious as he was speaking.

WESTERN UNION TELEGRAM
Sewanee, Tenn.
April 26, 1963
2:36 PM CST

Allen Tate [2019 Irving Ave South MPLS]

MRS. ANDREW LYTLE PASSED AWAY 9:30 THIS MORNING. FUNERAL ARRANGEMENTS INCOMPLETE.

Secretary the Sewanee Review

The Sewanee Review
May 18, 1963

Dear Brother:

I've been meaning to write you and thank you and Isabella, but all I've been feeling and going through requires the language of art and I don't have it now. Poor Jane says she always has her with her, in the mind. But that's not so, or it's not worth anything. No matter how many people are about, the house is always empty. But I see sharp images of her and this is the substance of eternity, I guess. She was a passionate and, at times, a difficult woman. To be so long dying perfected her. Gradually everything but her essential spirit died away, and that was left. So it is that nobody has the right to relieve or refuse a person his death. Even when I went to Nashville towards the last, she for once didn't complain, and when I came back late the night she was dying, she told me she didn't call me back, that Henry [Kirby-Smith] did, and that he always did the right thing. It really undid me, this fight between us, at last resolved in such a way at such a time. I've really been sort of sick recently. I get up when I wake, three-thirty or four or five. Langdon is beginning to feel it and often I have to sleep with her. I sent both the girls yesterday to their niece's christening,[1] which is today. They came back Monday. I couldn't afford it, but it was the thing to do. I don't see how we are going to work out the mechanics of bringing the girls to the Cape. Flying is right expensive, and I'm doing the summer things to catch up on my expenses. It doesn't make sense to spend the money otherwise. There is only a day or so between Kentucky and Converse, and a day to fly to Cambridge. If you will keep the invitation open, maybe we can do it later. It looks as if Pamela and Jim will move in with us, and he may do no more than a little coaching at St. Andrew's, going full time at the seminary here. He has that young man's pride, saying Pamela can't have two husbands. But he doesn't think of what it is worth to me, even economically, to have them there to run the house and give the girls a home. I think we will work it out all right. I got a nice note from Henry Alexander and a remarkable letter from Ward [Dorrance?], whom you wrote. Of course he had to ruin by prefacing it with hurt feelings, saying he was on the periphery. You can't write everybody at that time. And I'm glad you did.

Well, no more now. Thank Isabella again for her letters and thoughts and everything.

Love to you both, Brother

TLS

P.S. Who is George Whalley? I. A. Richards, in refusing to do reviews on Coleridge books, suggested him.

1. Pamela's daughter.

2019 Irving Avenue South
Minneapolis 5, Minnesota
June 7, 1963

Dear Brother,

Your letter has been before me for several weeks, and even now I can't properly answer it. This has been a bad spring. We've had too many visitors. Last weekend John Ransom was here, and we had a fine reunion, but the result is nervous exhaustion. Isabella's troubles have got worse, and may have to get even worse than that, before they can get better. Rosie married that mulatto in Chicago. It was predictable, but that doesn't make it any easier to bear. We have refused to invite them here before we leave; but Isabella is going to Chicago on Sunday for one day because she feels obligated to meet him. They are going to Europe, and I hope they stay there. So does Isabella. I am appalled at what Rosie's grandfather did for her when she was 21. No member of the Gardner family had been irresponsible about money; so he set up a trust but gave her free access to the capital. This is about $260,000. The girl is a moral idiot, and she will go through it in about five years, and will then bounce back on her mother with several mulatto children. *Sunt lacrimae rerum.*[1]

I hope by this time that Jim and Pamela are established in the Log Cabin. Jim will realize that his authority will not be infringed upon. I know how you feel about being in an empty house. For very different reasons I frequently feel the same way. You can't be married to a woman 36 years and pretend she was never there, whatever your life may have since become.

I want you to marry again. And I think Edna would want you to.

We leave on the 16th, and will arrive at Wellfleet around the 22nd. Of course we will get together at Tryon [N.C.] on July 11th. John Ransom says he will be at Richmond, Ky., with you, and that you plan to come to Cambridge to attend the Bill Elliott celebration.[2] Wouldn't that be the time to come to the Cape to see us? Please think about it.

Our love to the girls and to yourself.

Affly., Brother [Allen Tate]

TLS

1. "Here are tears for human things (or sufferings)." This plus the rest of the line from Vergil—*et mentem mortalia tangunt,* "and mortal woes touch the heart"—was translated by Matthew Arnold as "the sense of tears in mortal things." 2. Elliot was going to Washington to advise the President.

The Sewanee Review
June 19, 1963

Dear Brother:

Just a note to say that I'll try to get up for a few days to see you and Isabella after Bill Elliott's celebration. You are leaving the 29th, I believe, so I'll calculate the time so as not to get in the way of departure.

Pamela comes the first week in July, Jim not until the first week in August, as he will be teaching summer school.

Of course this is an appalling thing that has come about with Rosie, and please tell Isabella I am mighty sorry about it. But I've got to the point where I don't know or understand the aims or ends of things too well. Maybe some good will come out of it. I liked your Civil War piece[1] and am wondering if you're ever going to get that review done on Francis Fergusson's poems.[2]

Did you know that Eileen Ransom[3] died suddenly of cancer in Nashville? I'm trying to get the girls off to Florida to stay with Edna's friend, Virginia Rappenecker, there for ten days or two weeks. My love to you both.

Affectionately, Brother

TLS

1. "The Battle of Gettysburg: Why It Was Fought," *Carleton Miscelleny,* 4 (Summer 1963), 32–45. 2. Despite Lytle's repeated proddings, Tate never published an essay on Fergusson's work. 3. John Crowe Ransom's sister, Ellene, died on June 6th.

Wellfleet, Mass
June 24, 1963

Dear Brother,

Arrived yesterday to find your letter. That's mighty good—you'll come here after the Elliott celebration. I'm to be chairman of the meeting at which you are to speak. That's July 24th; so we can come to Wellfleet that evening or next morning.

Since you're coming up here I'm thinking of backing out of Tryon. I can't stand these exhausting trips. But I'll try to think of a substitute.

It seems that the killer of [Medgar] Evers is a Yerger cousin of Elizabeth Moss. My God!

See you either Tryon or here. Love from both.

Brother [Allen Tate]

AL

The Sewanee Review
June 29, 1963

Dear Brother:

I got your note yesterday. Two things: I do wish you would come and sustain me in Tryon. It won't be too bad really, and they are certainly counting on you. If you don't, I'll be thrown with that sort of second-rate person from Georgia, who I'm afraid is on the make. I've had to return everything he's sent us. You are a big feather in their cap, and they are awfully kind and generous at Converse—more than any place I have been . . . so for goodness sake, you all come on. You frighten me when you say I'm supposed to speak at Harvard on the 24th. Nobody else has told me that. I was told I was to swell a scene or two in the discussion. I haven't got anything proper. John is supposed to speak.

The girls have been in Florida a week and ought to be back in another week. Langdon writes and asks me how the weather is on the mountain. Love to you both.

Affectionately, Brother

TLS

The Sewanee Review
July 6, 1963

Dear Brother:

Just a note, so that you can arrange the visits. I can't possibly come before Harvard as I don't get out of Kentucky until Saturday. Why don't you do this—if Isabella's sister can more conveniently come after we get through with Harvard, I can forego the visit this time and come some other time; or maybe you all could stop over after your return from Europe. You're leaving the 29th; so it is not a good time anyway for a visit. You'll have to be packing and finishing those articles.

Pamela comes Monday with her baby. Jim will be teaching summer school; so he won't get in until the middle of August, I guess. It will work all right, I hope; and I mean to see that it does. The main thing is for them to counsel and advise the children but not take over. In that way the children would lose both parents.

I've got to make a Confederate talk this afternoon, and it's raining, in Miss Medora's [Cheatham] front yard. The hundredth anniversary of the battle of Sewanee. Love to you both.

Brother [Andrew]

TLS

The Sewanee Review
October 4, 1963

Dear Brother,

I've just managed to get your address from Nancy. This is to urge you before you go to Italy to see [T. S.] Eliot and those people who will give us a statement. We'd like to get it into the Christmas number, which goes to press in a month.

Your grandson, Petie,[1] is here. I've seen him once, and he seems to be a nice boy. We'll get together when he is less busy with personal affairs. He is a young man with definite ideas. He wants Kappa Sigma instead of SAE or Phi, and it is a very good chapter here. Love to you both.

Affectionately, Brother [Andrew]

TLS

1. Peter Wood and his brother Allen are at Sewanee.

44 Marsham Court
Marsham Street
London S.W. 1
November 16, 1963

Dear Brother,

I reckon you think I let you down about those testimonials for the winter issue of the *Review*. I wanted to start with T. S. E[liot], but he has been very ill, and I hated to ask him. We've seen him only twice. They leave for Nassau in about ten days. I will ask his wife about it: she might be able to write something from dictation. And I will get after the others on the list. Could you use the blurbs in the spring issue? A letter from Nancy yesterday. She says Pete is ecstatic about Sewanee, and that Allen thinks Webb[1] is "great." You can imagine how pleased I am. Apparently Pete adheres to some Yankee ideas of race, but Allen does not, being deficient in abstract idealism like his Grandpa. It's going to do those boys good to be among real people during their higher education. Doubtless the boys will call them Yankees for a while because [of] their accent; but that won't last very long. Pete is a born conformist, and for the run of mankind I see nothing wrong with that. I hope Pete has called on Margaret Myers. If you think of it, won't you please ask him to do so? Nancy says he attends your writing seminar.

We were a month in Florence,[2] and had a wonderful time; but that was the trouble—too many people turned up who expected us to drop everything and show them around. I came back here on the 7th; Isabella five days later. My work stopped in Florence; I'm just getting back to it, and have only a month before we leave for NY and Mpls. I've accomplished only about one-third of what I had hoped to do. Only distraction came about as the result of Dan's—Isabella's son's—return to Minneapolis. He begged to go back and get a job, pending his reentry into the University in January. Our colleagues there became indignant. Weren't we getting rid of him so that we could pursue, unharassed, our affluent hedonism in Europe? They've quieted down a little now; but I'm more or less permanently sour about them. The latent hostility and jealousy they've felt for me over many years came to the surface. When they don't ignore whatever reputation I've brought the Department, they positively dislike it. It's an old story in the academic world. You felt it in Florida.

We land in NY on Dec. 19th. That evening there's to be [a] joint reading by JCR, Red, and me (the three of us introduced by Cal), in honor of John's 75th year.[3] Wish you could be there.

My love to all in the Log Cabin. How I wish I could see you all. Isabella sends her love too.

Affly., Brother [Allen Tate]

TLS

1. Possibly John Webb, Dean of Students. 2. Tate is abroad on his 1963 Fellowship Award from the Academy of American Poets. 3. Ransom was being honored by the Academy of American Poets.

The Sewanee Review
January 24, 1964

Dear Brother:

These are the poems for the Contest.[1] Choose one for the prize. You might indicate which is second and which is third. I've sent three of Scarbrough's[2] for you to choose the best, which I intended to publish anyway. He's a young man who began to write a few years ago, fell into abeyance, then started again. I think he's mighty fresh, although I am not sure he always does what he thinks he does.

Sorry you've had bronchitis; once it was flu. The dead season is hard on all of us. I've not been too well. Love to you both.

Affectionately, Brother [Andrew]

TLS

1. This is the continuation of the contest held in memory of Mary Rugeley Ferguson. The award, not given in 1962 as announced because no poems submitted justified it, was doubled to $500 and the restrictions on subject matter removed. 2. George Scarbrough won the award with his poem "Return: August Afternoon" which was published in the 1964 Spring issue, 175–77. Another of his poems, "Summer Revival: Brush Arbor" appeared earlier in the Winter issue, p. 91.

The Sewanee Review
March 14, 1964

Dear Brother:

Henry [Kirby-Smith] sent me home yesterday, after three weeks in hospital. I am weak and the butt takes some handling, since I'm never off it. I'm working on the real problem of control. One method is to take an enema every morning. I'm trying first to see how well I can manage something more normal. Jim has been a real son through this. It is a painful operation. For fourteen seconds the pain was so exquisite it turned into a flame before my eyes and so I could bear it. After it was over Henry sat down on the bed and shook my hand, he groaned too. The head nurse looked away. My nurse presented the comic element with the oldest platitude, "Isn't it a pleasant day?" she said. Henry replied, "No, Mrs. Medford, it isn't." Well, I'm thankful to be home and mending. I don't know how long it's going to take. I'm grateful [for] prayers & kind thoughts. I made myself [empty?][1] like the Emperor of Japan, and it worked.

Thank Isabella for the flowers and you both for loving thoughts.

Aff., Andrew

AL

1. Although the handwriting makes this word uncertain, it's possible that Lytle is referring to the Emperor's claim of divinity, hence his indestructibility.

2019 Irving Avenue South
Minneapolis 5, Minnesota
March 18, 1964

Dear Brother,

It is a relief to know that you are back in the Log Cabin. I fear you'll have to lie low for a considerable spell, but maybe that won't be too bad, if you're not in pain, because you'll be able to let ideas boil up from below, and you may start writing again. That's what you ought to do. The ordeal of the past four years, topped by your illness, has been too much for any novelist. I want another novel, or at any rate some stories to get you going again.

We've been pretty well. But I get more and more afraid of this climate, which is not bad but simply too cold for me to breathe the air. I wish I could retire at 65, but circumstances won't allow it. A year from next fall, Sept. 1965, I will be at the Univ. of Kentucky as Visiting Professor during their hundredth anniversary. That's a milder climate but it's a long time off.

I know that Pamela and Jim and the girls have rallied nobly. Give them my love. Isabella joins in love to you.

Affly., Brother [Allen Tate]

TLS

The Sewanee Review
April 10, 1964

Dear Brother: [2019 Irving Avenue, South,
Minneapolis, Minnesota]

I'm delighted you will be here in May. We have a good, comfortable bed for you. I see no point in your staying in a tourist court unless you need a special kind of privacy.

Would you look at these two poems by Hobart Myers? They don't seem to me to have enough point to print, but I'd like to get judgment.[1]

As ever, Andrew Lytle

TLS

[Your letter] said you were coming the 1st of May? Did you change your mind. Any time will delight us. I'm mending but slowly.

1. Myers' poem "Seemed No More Important" appeared in the 1965 Winter issue, 97–98.

2019 Irving Avenue South
Minneapolis 5, Minnesota
April 14, 1964

Dear Brother,

Hobart sent me the same poems, but I haven't got round to writing him. They are not without merit, but they seem to me loose and without centre. I shouldn't think he's ready for the S.R.

About my trip. Would May 8–11 be all right? There's something here on May 1st I can't get out of.

I was supposed to go yesterday to Louisville, then on to Philadelphia for two days, and Kenyon on Thursday. I came down with flu three days ago, and am leaving out all but Kenyon where I hope to be able to go day after tomorrow.

I accept gratefully the offer of that nice bed in the Log Cabin. Give Pamela my thanks and love.

Love to you all,

Brother [Allen Tate]

AL

University of Minnesota
Minneapolis, Minnesota 55405
June 6, 1964

Dear Brother,

We've been on a treadmill ever since I got back from the mountain. And now we're trying to get the house in order for the summer tenants and to pack for the trip, as well as all those papers and exams I have to read by next Thursday.

You know what a fine time I had at the Log Cabin. But you must take it easy all summer. I'm worried about your going out to Utah which I believe you will do in a few days.

The other day I met a young banker named [Philip] Harder who showed me these poems. I think they are very good indeed—direct and economical. Maybe you'll want to print them, or some of them.

We're hoping to see you in September. Love to all the family.

Affly., Brother [Allen Tate]

TLS

P.S. I hope the package of trinkets for the girls arrived.

Box 359
Wellfleet, Mass
August 26, 1964

Dear Brother,

I hope all is going well, and that Kate's wedding wasn't too arduous. We sent her a small silver present from Florence direct from the shop, about a month ahead. We hope that it arrived.

We got here on August 10th, and we have the best house we've ever had. Couldn't you come up for a week or so? We will be here till about September 20th.

Last week we had our annual dinner with Bro. Ben and Louise (at a restaurant), to which they brought Janet Alexander. Janet informed us at once that she and Henry were getting divorced. But you have probably heard this. Poor woman. Yet it would be impossible to imagine a more amiable and more stupid woman anywhere.

A young man, Jonathan Aaron, who sent you some poems last year, is sending you another in a few days. We have seen it, and think it absolutely first-rate. I call attention to this with the hope that you will give the poem a second look. Your summer issue is one of the two or three best you've ever had.

I have heard nothing from Vanderbilt. Is there any news on that front?

I hope to get down there to see you before too long. I am going to Hollins College in October, and if I can include a weekend I want to come by Sewanee. Love to Pamela, Jim, and Langdon. Isabella sends love too.

Affly., Brother [Allen Tate]

TLS

The Sewanee Review
Aug. 27, 1964

Dear Brother:

By now you all are back at Wellfleet and the wedding is over.[1] It was a good wedding, the chapel now is a perfect place for it. They had a nuptial mass, with the Bishop of La. giving the blessing. They all, the whole bridal party, looked like beautiful children. We have some awfully well-featured children in our family, and the Louisiana people looked good too. She was a beautiful bride and handled most of the wedding herself with Edna's efficiency. Pamela sort of went to pieces and hindered instead of helping, but don't say anything about this. She's a fine girl and has too much, too soon, to do here.

The silver shaker was mighty pretty and thank Isabella for its selection. I finally got all the presents off to Louisiana, and then got knocked out with a chest cold and have been in bed for two days—a needed rest I guess. For all of this has made me sad, too. I looked at the young man and thought he was too sober-minded to marry in college. He outfigured me and told me they could together go through school at L.S.U. on what he spent at Sewanee. He had no intention of letting her get loose with all those boys at Vanderbilt. They'll make a good marriage, I hope. I like the family—it's a real one—and they will cherish her, I think.

I've got a long poem that looks good but I don't understand it, more than the literal sense. I'll send it to you, if you've got time to read it. We are bought up for a year, but I thought it needed more than I could give it.

No more now. My love to you both.

A

TLS

1. Katherine Anne Lytle had married Talbot Wilson.

The Sewanee Review
Labor Day

Dear Brother:

Our letters must have crossed. I'll look for Aaron's poem. I've forgotten about the others he sent. If you all think this is a good one, I'll be glad to print it.[1] I could only take one of the young banker's[2] as we are so full up. I have let myself get over-bought on everything and will have to slow down. I don't want to be more than a year behind. You have to have more than just enough, to make decision flexible. It's a fine point, I guess.

I wish I could see you all and come up. I don't see how I can quite. School opens here the sixteenth of September. My living habits now are special, with a private bath each morning for an hour, and I notice if I go away on a trip for a short while, it throws my habits off. There is a faint possibility of having to go to N.Y. on business, but the time is so short, although I wish I could. Aren't you going to Kentucky for a semester. I didn't know about Hollins. How long will you be there, and when? I see now it is October. Try to make it by here. [Paul] Ramsey is taking

[Monroe] Spears' place, and he sends his regards. I rather like what I've seen of him, but he seems rather self-assured on short acquaintance. I am enclosing one of Kate's newspaper pictures. I don't know how this wedding got so large and expensive. I wanted to do it right; I didn't want it to do me in. I'll be pore all fall. You can't have an in between wedding at Sewanee. It's hard just to keep it to the immediate families.

Well, try to get by and give Isabella my love.

Affectionately, A

TLS

Nothing on Vanderbilt. The Bishop here is working on some project. V.[anderbilt] hasn't even got a head of department yet.[3]

1. Two poems by Jonathan Aaron appeared in the 1965 Spring issue, 281–84, "Grecian Attitudes" and "The Traveller in Plaster." 2. Philip M. Harder's poem "Get Thee Hence" appeared in the 1954 Winter issue, p. 57. 3. After the death of Randall Stewart, Edgar Duncan served as acting head while the committee looked at candidates. Russell Fraser was hired and served for a brief period; then Thomas Daniel Young took over.

The Sewanee Review
Nov. 23, 1964

Dear Brother:

Just a note to find out where you are and what you are doing. Are you at Kentucky now? Or is it the spring semester? I was asked to give the Founders' Day address this year, and they printed it up.[1] Since it is the only hard work I've done in so long, I'm sending it on. And I wouldn't have got this done but for my concupiscent past. A widow woman (she was married then) I knew thirty years ago called me up at one-thirty one in the morning and said, "This is Goldsby." I said, "Goldsby who?" and then I woke. She was just back from the Carribean where she'd been sunning herself and eating well on the ship. And she only weighs now a hundred pounds, and she's younger than ever. She has an apartment in Knoxville and anything else I need. It was too sad, but since my operation, I've lost my nature. I didn't tell her that. It looked like I was so far behind her. Anyway I couldn't go back to sleep; so I got up and finished the middle part of the speech. A body don't know when he's sinning.

My love to Isabella and you.

Brother

TLS

1. *A Christian University and The Word* (Sewanee: The University of the South, 1964). The address was delivered October 10, 1964.

2019 Irving Avenue South
Minneapolis, Minnesota 55405
November 30, 1964

Dear Brother,

Seems like I heard tell of Goldsby. More'n thirty years ago. Effen she weighs only a 100, she ain't got much nature left either; ain't no reason why you need to hesitate. Go right on up to Knoxville or get her to the Log Cabin. Effen she et well on the boat, she's eaten well on dry land. Let her furnish the victuals and you furnish the literary character.

The Founders' Day Address is very fine. I wish it could be printed so that it would get around more widely than the brochure. Why not in the SR? The conclusion (Thos. Dabney and Jay Gould) is perfect.[1] I'm wondering how the local audience received it.

We don't go to Kentucky till next September. It's their centennial, 1865–1965. Of course it's a carpetbag university: United We Stand, Divided We Fall. But I expect to enjoy myself—if Isabella can retrain her abolitionist heritage. She promises to.

I might get down to see you for a few days between Christmas and New Year's day. Will you be on the mountain? Isabella will have Dan and Rosie here.

Love to all the children and you from us both.

Affly., Brother [Allen Tate]

AL

1. Lytle contrasts the attitude of the two men toward honor. While the old Civil War veteran, Colonel Dabney, worked the last years of his life to pay off a war-inflated debt and so make good his name, Gould was relieved when his failure to corner the gold market cost him nothing but his reputation.

WESTERN UNION TELEGRAM
Sewanee, Tenn.
January 12, 1965

Allen Tate [2019 Irving Ave South MPLA]

260 PAGES FINE. WONDERFUL IDEA. IT WILL BE A GREAT PERFORMANCE.[1]

Love, Brother

1. As the subsequent letters reveal, this telegram expresses Lytle's enthusiasm about having Tate edit a special issue of *The Sewanee Review* as a tribute to T. S. Eliot.

The Sewanee Review
January 13, 1965

Dear Brother:

I sent you a telegram yesterday. This is merely to amplify it a good bit. The 260 pages, more or less, will be fine; so, go ahead and invite the people you want to. I would think that tactically this would be desirable: to make of *The Review* the final homage to Eliot. Nobody else can do it like you and nobody else knows the proper people. If you would like to, wire all or some of them, and send the bill to us. We can discuss this further when you come in March.

I am going to New York the end of January for several days. Is Jackson Matthews still there? If so, would you send me his address? And, is there anybody I ought to see and try to get an essay, story, or verse out of for *The Review?* My acquaintance is limited, as you know.

My love to Isabella.

Affectionately yours, Brother

TLS

2019 Irving Avenue South
Minneapolis, Minnesota 55405
January 20, 1965

Dear Brother,

Just back from East to find your telegram and letter of Jan. 13th.—260 pages will do it: many thanks. Will get all the letters off this weekend.[1] No cables necessary.

Jackson Matthews address: Frenchtown, New Jersey. Office: The Bollingen Foundation, 140 East 62nd St., N.Y.C.

More later. Swamped with unanswered letters.

Affly., Brother [Allen Tate]

AL

1. The special edition of *The Sewanee Review* in honor of T. S. Eliot. It was later published as *T. S. Eliot, The Man and His Work: A Critical Evaluation by Twenty-Six Distinguished Writers* (New York: New American Library, 1968).

The Sewanee Review
January 26, 1965

Dear Brother:

The names look good. We are going to try to give them more money than the usual *Sewanee Review* fee. I am not sure this can be managed, in which case we will just have to pay the regular.

Although your chin is fairly greasy these days, we are going to manage something worthy of your gifts.

I am off to New York and will see Katherine Anne,[1] I think, on my way back. Do you think, by any chance, you ought to invite her?

Love to Isabella.

Affectionately, Andrew

TLS

1. Having achieved financial independence with *Ship of Fools* (1962), Porter was living in Washington, D.C.

The Sewanee Review
February 16, 1965

Dear Brother:

We have a piece here on Eliot by David Hirsch[1] at Brown University. Of course, we can't take anything now over the counter because of the Issue. I told him to send it to you in case you wanted to consider it. I hope things are going well in this matter.

I saw Red in New York recently, and I am not sure how he is going to respond.[2]

We are anxiously looking forward to your visit in March. In the meantime, my love to you and Isabella.

Haste, Brother

TLS

1. The essay by Hirsch was not used. 2. Warren did not submit an essay for the Eliot issue.

2019 Irving Avenue South
Minneapolis, Minnesota 55405
February 22, 1965

Dear Brother:

I was mighty pleased to get yours of the 16th and to know you had survived the ordeal of the trip East.

Of the thirty or thirty-two people I've asked to contribute to the Issue, 16 have definitely accepted and 6 more tentatively. It looks as if we're going to have a fine issue. I will be glad to see David Hirsch's essay though I hesitate to commit myself however good it may be, until I hear from all of Eliot's friends of the older generation. I was very plesed to hear yesterday from John Ransom who says he will be extremely glad to write an essay. He seems to have changed his mind about Uncle Tom after all these years, and I'm sure he will treat the subject sympathetically.[1]

If it's convenient for you and my niece Pamela, I will arrive on the mountain from Houston on March 23rd. I expect to arrive in the Nashville airport about mid-afternoon and drive a Hertz car directly to Sewanee, arriving about 5:00. If it is convenient, I can stay until Friday, the 26th. By that time the Eliot issue ought to be in final form, even if only a few of the manuscripts are in.

I'm going to ask Miss Katherine Anne[2] to write a piece for us if several of Uncle Tom's old friends let me down. I put off asking her because, first, she was not a friend of his and, second, she is not a "critic," but she would do something very charming, nevertheless.

In view of your trials and tribulations, I reckon I ought not to complain about a misery I've had in my left leg the last month. I'm depressed by the fact that my innards ain't as calm as they mought be while those parts north of them are right serene.

Love to all the folks at the Log Cabin.

Affectionately, Brother [Allen Tate]

TLS

P.S. Nancy may join me on the mountain. Of this more later. In which case we'll stay at Clara's.

1. As it turned out, Ransom's essay, "Gerontion," arrived too late to be included in the Eliot issue and so appeared as the main piece in the following one, *The Sewanee Review,* 74 (Spring 1966), 389–420. 2. Apparently they received a sufficient number of essays from critics and Eliot's old friends without having to invite Porter to contribute to the issue.

The Sewanee Review
March 6, 1965

Dear Brother:

Thank you for your letter. You've got a very impressive list of contributors. I could hope that three or four others who are uncertain might still come through. But even so, it's mighty fine.

We are looking forward to your visit very much, and we hope that Nancy will stop over. I suppose you will phone me from the Cheneys' if you don't come right up.

My love to Isabella.

Affectionately yours, In haste, Brother

TLS

Mpls, March 19, 1965

Dear Brother,

Leaving tomorrow for Houston. Arriving Nashville airport on Tuesday 23rd at 6:53 P.M. So I will spend that night with the Cheneys and drive to the mountain next morning.

Affly., Brother [Allen Tate]

AL

The Sewanee Review
April 20, 1965

Dear Brother,

Thank you for your kind words about the Hemingway.[1] They please me very much.

I went down Sunday to Lon's wake for Teilhard.[2] It was a motley group—two Catholic priests with Irish names. One of them was a "jumping" priest[3] who stood at the back and read from Teilhard. It soured the drinks in everybody's bellies. At the most moving portion, Isabel Howell, who sat just beyond me, began to snore. Somebody asked me to describe Monteagle. I touched on its governing council, numbering the protestant sects which composed it and said, looking about me, that neither Catholic nor Jews were allowed to own property there. And suddenly I discovered I was talking to two Jews. You know what a good cook Fanny [Cheney] is. She showed her disapproval in a very subtle way: her food was terrible. I represented our household: nobody else felt up to going down.

I don't believe we've got the final statement of names for the Eliot issue. I want to announce the names in the Summer issue.

Give my love to Isabella.

Affectionately, Brother

TLS

1. Review of *A Moveable Feast, The Sewanee Review,* 73 (Spring 1965), 339–343. 2. Pierre Teilhard de Chardin (1881–1955) was a Jesuit Father and a distinguished paleontologist whose metaphysical books about the Christian meaning of evolution became widely popular after his death. 3. A priest who shows his approval by leaning forward on his tiptoes as he reads, like a "shouting" Methodist says "Amen" when he agrees with a point the preacher makes.

The Sewanee Review
May 15, 1965

Dear Brother:

I think "The Marquis and the Crocodile"[1] is a mighty fine thing, and I would like to print it. It's mighty long, but right now I don't see how it can be cut much. I will study it carefully. If you will send the address, I will communicate with Mr. Brewster.

If it can be arranged, we ought to print, by all means, Frank Kermode's piece.[2] Could you arrange it with *The New Statesman?* After all, this is your choice.

I have been on a speaking tour to Purdue and to Chattanooga, and so haven't had a chance to read the two pieces you sent. I think, with you, that we ought to get nearly all of them in before you try to have anybody cut.

I have written to Chatto and Windus,[3] sending the list of contributors and saying that there's a good chance to print the issue on this side too.

I hope Francis Fergusson does something. He hasn't responded much to the *Review* in several years. I almost feel like he has lost interest and ought to be dropped from the Masthead.[4]

I should think that [W. H.] Auden might feel a poem goes beyond the specific mourning.

I would like to do this up handsomely. Do you suppose Bollingen or any small foundation might give us from $3–5,000 to help finance the issue? You know these people so much better than I.

It would be fine if you all could come to Kenyon. I am having a student drive Polly and me up. The dates are Saturday and Sunday, the 29th and 30th.[5] We are staying at Robert Daniel's.[6]

I have just looked into this fellow Stewart's book.[7] He certainly means well, but it makes you doubt all historical scholarship in it. There's nothing like an earnest, second-rate mind (with the best sympathy in the world) for distortion and losing the essence of what took place.

I hope you got Pamela's letter. She liked the blouse, but found it awfully hard to get the letter mailed.

Affectionately, Brother

TLS

This letter is staccato. Shows you how pressed I am.

1. This story by Harry C. Brewster, his first to be published, appeared in the 1965 Fall issue, 535–86. 2. A short version of Kermode's "A Babylonish Dialect" was published in London's *New Statesman* (1965); it appeared in the 1966 Winter issue, 225–37, in an expanded form. 3. An English publishing firm. Lytle and Tate are making plans to have the Tate issue published as a book. 4. Francis Fergusson, along with Allen Tate and Monroe Spears, appeared as an Advisory Editor of the *Review*. 5. Lytle is going to Kenyon in order to receive an honorary D. Litt. degree. 6. A Ph.D. from Yale who was for years chairman of the English department at Kenyon. 7. John L. Stewart's *The Burden of Time: The Fugitives and Agrarians* (Princeton: Princeton University Press, 1965).

University of Minnesota
Minneapolis, Minnesota 55405
June 5, 1965

Dear Brother,

I am outraged by that stupid book by John L. Stewart. I enclose a copy of a letter I wrote him,[1] and a copy of a letter to Willard Thorp.[2] I agree with Louis Rubin that Cleanth [Brooks] has a duty to review it. If he won't, then Joe Bryant would do a good job.

I am outraged too by his stupid treatment of you. The man is a humorless and pompous prig. He likes Red better than the rest of us but he is no better about him. And he [is] very bad on Don.

I won't go into detail. Just read the enclosures.

For ten years this man wrote me mealy-mouthed letters of flattery, and I succumbed by letting him see my papers. Never again, while I live.

I reckon the boys will all call you Doctor Lytle now, if they haven't already. Wish we could have been there.

Affly., Brother [Allen Tate]

TLS

1. See Appendix N for the letter to Stewart; the letter to Thorp is missing. 2. Stewart's book grew out of a dissertation he did at Princeton where Thorp was a professor and a member of the Committee of the Princeton University Press; hence, Tate was calling his friend to account.

University of Minnesota
Minneapolis, Minnesota 55405
June 10, 1965

Dear Brother,

I think this is an excellent story. Mrs. DeMenles is the best writer I have had since I came here fourteen years ago.[1]

Affly., Brother [Allen Tate]

AL

1. This story does not appear. Sometimes Lytle accepted enough fiction to run the magazine for two years; then he wouldn't accept any for a while. If this is true, he probably telephoned Tate to explain why he couldn't accept.

The Sewanee Review
June 14, 1965

Dear Brother:

This is just a note to say I'll write later. I think the letter to Stewart was fine. I'm not sure he is sensitive enough to get all the reproof you give him. John is answering him himself in a small magazine in California.[1] I guess this is all right. Before I try Cleanth who is so involved over there, I'm thinking of Walker Percy.[2] I don't know whether he would be interested, but he has a real mind. He may not be sufficiently aware of those involved.

I'm putting the essays together to read soon. I don't understand how I get so busy, but the transition to our present staff is still going on. By the way Sam Lawrence and the paperback which supports him has offered a five thousand dollar advance to publish in this country the Eliot. We are also in touch with Chatto and Windus. He offers me a five thousand dollar advance on my next book and twenty-five hundred for an anthology of *Sewanee Review* fiction.[3] I had thought that concentrating on fiction might make a better book; the general collection of *The Hudson* failed financially.

The impact would seem to me to be surer. [Louis] Rubin has asked me to make a collection of my essays for the La. Press.[4] He wondered if he or you might not make an introduction. I told him as editor of the series he should not; that you might if you would; or I've got that introduction to *The Novel, Novella etc.,* which might do. I don't know how I'm going to get all this done, but the one lecturing thing I was to do is off; so I plan to settle down this summer, although there are three weddings which take several days apiece. Polly's Mary marries this weekend.

Don't go nowhere without giving me your address. You must make some kind of introduction to the issue, anything of course you think is right for it.[5] It doesn't have to be long unless you want that. I thought out of the five thousand advance, give the contributors a hundred dollars apiece; and maybe half or a fourth of anything that goes over that. If the English firm comes through, this will add to their initial fee too. We are going to need this twenty-five hundred dollars to bring out the issue. I am going to try to get a little gift money somewhere, but you can never tell about that. Usually these small foundations are willing to pitch in. What about Jack Thompson's. If you know the address, I might write him. I've decided to take that other story. To bring a sainted ghost to life is reason enough, although I don't like that story as well as the other.

This is very inchoate, but everything is in here I wanted to say to you. I'm just back from the Swann Ball in Nashville, where I went with a beautiful widow woman, who snuggled up right close. It's too bad that Henry Kirby-Smith in saving my life taken hit away.

Love to Isabella and to you. Don't forget to keep me informed of your movements.

Aff., Brother

TLS

1. There is no record of such a response by Ransom. 2. Brewster Ghiselin finally reviewed Stewart's book for *The Sewanee Review* in the 1966 Spring issue, 527–40. 3. *Craft and Vision: The Best Fiction from The Sewanee Review,* ed. Andrew Lytle (New York: Delacorte Press, A Seymour Lawrence Book, 1971). 4. *The Hero with the Private Parts: Essays by Andrew Lytle* (Baton Rouge: Louisiana State University Press, 1966). 5. Tate added a short essay to the end of the Eliot issue entitled, "Postscript by Allen Tate," the Guest Editor, 383–87.

20 Chesham Place
Belgrave Square, London S.W. 1
July 1, 1965

Dear Brother,

Yours of June 14th reached me a few days ago in Italy. I arrived here only last night. Isabella is in Florence acting as guide for her parents, and will arrive here Monday.

Trouble has developed between us, *largely because of my character,* which you know better than anybody else. I have betrayed her for the same reason I betrayed C.[aroline]—as an escape from pressures which most men could take but which I can't. She knows what I have done. On my side I feel as if her whole past were present daily—her husband, her early lovers; and all this is present through her children. I am blamed for Dan's aberrations because I couldn't do for him what she was not able to do. My *flight* was brought about by her insistence that I meet, and my refusal, *Dan's father's first wife.*

I tell you this because I may return at once to Mpls. and then drive to Tennessee, for the rest of the summer.

If I don't return I will answer you in a few days about the details of the Eliot issue.

Affly., Brother [Allen Tate]

AL

Oak Grove Hotel
Minneapolis 55403
July 29, 1965

Dear Brother,

I arrived last night, having left the car in St. Louis instead of driving back to Nashville. The car will arrive tonight. I found a driving agency. It was tough driving, Nashville, Louisville, St. Louis in two days. But I found the—or rather—*a* graveyard, the first Allen graveyard, but was told there was another about 10 miles away. Nevertheless I took about 20 pictures, and I am pleased with the results of my pilgrimage.

I haven't seen the young lady.[1] I was too late last night, and she went to work at 7 this morning. So I don't know what the schedule is: telephone conversation must be guarded. If it goes off as planned I will return Monday by air, and have the car driven.

Thank you, Brother, for all your kindness. The Log Cabin is both a haven and a renewal.

Love to all.

Affly., Brother [Allen Tate]

AL

Please seal and mail the enclosed.

1. Helen Heinz, a student of Tate's from St. Paul, who served as a head nurse in a Minneapolis hospital.

The Sewanee Review
Smyrna, August 19, 1965

Dear Brother,

Damn it, I don't see how I can get back before Monday afternoon.

Attached is a list of the firm contributors, along with a list we may count on. All these names can be announced with at the bottom "and others."

I've made an estimate of the word count, and get only a few pages short of an average issue; so in any case expansion will be necessary.

As to the teaser, I should think the form you've used will do, with the addition of something like:

Critical Essays, Reminiscences, and Tributes
to his Memory. And then list the names.

I'm so inexperienced about subscription cards, or at least very rusty, that I don't quite know what to suggest. Perhaps it ought to be said that a new subscription beginning with the Eliot issue will give the subscriber *five* issues, the Eliot issue free and bait to the prospective subscriber. Wouldn't you come out ahead with this plan?

There's a cloud over Florence. I'll tell you about it. But it may be no bigger than Hamlet's cloud.

Affly., Brother [Allen Tate]
TLS

P.S. I gave up the idea of copy-editing. I've forgotten the signs and your manual of style.

Trinity College
Hartford 6, Connecticut
c/o Prof. Stephen Minot
Oct. 12, 1965

Dear Brother,

Here's a letter from Valerie Eliot. So that's cleared. I wrote to Farrar, Straus, and Giroux for permission for the quotations from the work they published; but I haven't written to Harcourt, Brace and World. Maybe that should be done right away. To Robert Giroux I emphasized the fact that only lines, not complete poems, are quoted, and only sentences and short paragraphs from the prose.

I expect to arrive in Nashville at 11:30 Saturday morning, and will drive to the mountain at once. I am refusing to go to New York, and I hope I can sustain that resolution. Just as Isabella would yield nothing in the past, she is now willing to yield everything. But that, too, is wrong.

I am sure that from now on you will not have to tell more lies in my behalf. I have forbidden her to telephone you again.

In spite of the strain, I still feel well. This college is splendid—a close

New England twin of Sewanee. The boys have fine manners, and the faculty are humanists. If I had to teach in the East, Trinity would be my choice.

Affly., Brother [Allen Tate]

AL

P.S. Please tell Jim[1] that I can't reach his brother: the telephone is "temporarily out of service."

1. Probably Jim Law, Pamela's husband.

The Sewanee Review
Jan. 20, 1966

Dear Brother:

I'm wondering how you are making out, and how the divorce[1] is proceeding. Today all of the Eliot issue ought to be off the press. It looks like a lot of his friends talked a heap about themselves, but such can't really hurt it much. It's going to be a distinguished thing. All my budget for the year is gone, but there will be the advances and some back issue sale to tide us over. This is my gamble, that we could do it out of itself.

I got a nice note from Helen.[2] She said one class seemed to be right hard work for you. I know those signs. Just make out it's the winter weather, and don't get *flu* or *poisoned*.

I lifted something and found "The Mediterranean" and the inscription. I thank you. I turned and read "Anabasis." That's a mighty moving poem, aside from my special feeling in the matter.

Well, no more. Keep me informed.

Affectionately, Brother

TLS

1. Tate and Isabella Gardner are obtaining a divorce. It becomes final March 28, 1966. 2. Helen Heinz, whom Tate marries on July 30, 1966.

University of Minnesota
230 Oak Grove St.
Minneapolis 55403
February 2, 1966

Dear Brother,

At last I've done the Introduction (2000 words),[1] and my assistant is copying today. It will go to the La. Press tomorrow. I'm sorry about the delay but under the circumstances it seemed inevitable.

I'm on leave next year (without pay) and I have two jobs. I'm going to Greensboro for the first semester, to Vanderbilt for the second. Princeton asked me too, but it's too complicated there. Walter Sullivan had said many times they wanted me to come. I wrote him that was the time; and they came through. I'll have to come back here for 1967–68, unless I'm willing to forfeit some of my retirement fund, and I can't afford it.

I'm expecting the Jan. issue any day.

The "situation" remains the same as at my last writing.

Affly., Brother [Allen Tate]

1. "Foreword" to *The Hero with the Private Parts,* xiii–xvii.

The Sewanee Review
Feb. 7, 1966

Dear Brother,

We've been frozen in off and on with ten below zero. Both fires in the hall going. I've been meaning to write and thank you for the letter to the Rockefellers. I hope it will come through and with funds enough to allow me to take off. I noticed the highest was $14,000 for the colored man.

Now that the issue is joined you are bound at first to suffer the break—but you will return to the reasons for it and that will bring the necessary comfort. Let me know how it is going along and when you will be free to not be free. Peter Taylor sent me his play to read and reported you would take a semester there next year.[1] Are you coming here in the summer to look about for a house? I'll keep my eye open.

Everybody here seems pleased with the Eliot issue. The press did mighty well, I think. Ned [McCrady] asked me to thank you—not formally—he merely showed pleasantly his thanks. That fellow [G. Wilson] Knight is a nuisance; said his whole piece was ruined for a wrong letter. He wanted to thank Mrs. Eliot by himself. We already had to unlock the press to change a lot for him. I never saw such vanity for one of the poorer pieces in the issue.[2]

No more now. I've got to get to work. Pay my respects to Helen.

Affectionately, Brother

AL

1. Taylor taught at the University of North Carolina at Greensboro from 1946–1967. The play Lytle mentions receiving is probably *A Stand in the Mountains.* 2. Knight's contribution to the Eliot issue ws "T. S. Eliot: Some Literary Impressions," 239–56.

Oak Grove Hotel
Minneapolis 55403
Feb. 13, 1966

Dear Brother,

I been so pestered in my mind I haven't been able to write you a proper letter. I'm still pestered, but I'm a little more at ease.

The Eliot issue is extremely good,[1] I think, the one really weak essay being that of Wilson Knight. I'm now sorry I invited him, but once his piece was in it was not possible to reject it. So my original mistaken judgment in inviting him is to blame. Some of the pieces towards the end are not quite first-rate, but they are modest in intent, and do not disgrace us. I'm inclined to think that of the reminiscences, [Herbert] Read's is the best.[2]

The front cover is perfect: no contributors' names, nothing to clutter up the aims of the symposium. The press indeed did a good job. There may be a few printer's errors but none that are serious. I'm proud of the job, and proud that you asked me to do it.

Isabella leaves tomorrow for a month in Mexico. The divorce is scheduled for March 28th; she expects to return the day before. The situation is unbelievably difficult. Every conceivable sort of pressure is being put upon me by colleagues and friends out in town, to cancel the whole thing. Since Christmas I have realized for the first time her complete dependence upon me, or at any rate upon our marriage—even though she would not sacrifice an iota of her "past" as an acknowledgement of the dependence. The poor girl tells everybody that she loves me and can never love anybody else, and that she has no pride that will prevent her from saying so. I simply don't know what to do about *that*. I shall probably become a part of her past that she can't give up, and so take my place with the others. It is just possible that she may call everything off before March 28th. If she does, I don't know how to oppose her. Meanwhile Miss H[einz] is getting uneasy and even restive. Who can blame her?

I'm worried about John Ransom. I wrote him a few weeks ago, but no reply. He may be going the way of Brother Ben. He's two years older than Ben.

Yes, please do look for a house for me. I may have to teach the first summer session here, but it is over on July 16th; so I could arrive on the mountain around the 20th, to stay till the middle of September. If it could be a house that I could consider buying, all the better; but if not, I could use it this summer while I'm looking around.

Love to the family.

Affly., Brother [Allen Tate]

TLS

P.S. Please say to the Rev.[3] that I am quite aware of his noble efforts in the Eliot issue.

1. This issue appeared as the 1966 Winter number. 2. "T.S.E.—A Memoir," 31–57. 3. Reverend William H. Ralston, Jr., had been Associate Editor of *The Sewanee Review* since Summer, 1965.

University of Minnesota
Feb. 15, 1966

Dear Brother,

I wrote you a letter Sunday morning but lost it at the airport where I had gone to meet Brewster Ghiselin between planes. I hope somebody picked it up and mailed it. I'll wait to see before I repeat what I said.

I have a letter from Seymour Lawrence and the carbon of his letter to you. It's a favorable sign that our publisher is enthusiastic.[1] But why shouldn't he be? It's really a superb issue. Some of the points he makes:

1. If the type hasn't been distributed why couldn't plates be made from it? He could pay the *Review* for the type-setting, and save money himself, and save you some.

2. I'm much in favor of an insert of photographs. I've sent him some made in 1948 in Washington.

3. I can move my Postscript to the front, adding a paragraph of thanks to Valerie Eliot and to the contributors.

4. I suspect that if we want to use Eliot's own essay we'll have to negotiate for it again, on either a royalty or a fee basis, with both Farrar, Straus and Giroux, and Faber & Faber. Lawrence should be consulted about this, and I will handle it.

Isabella left yesterday for Mexico, and will later go on a reading tour of California. I wish you could get a good review of her book.[2] It *is* a fine book, and under the circumstances such a review would do a lot of good.

In haste,

Affly., Brother [Allen Tate]

TLS

1. The Eliot issue of *The Sewanee Review* was published as *T.S. Eliot, The Man and His Work: A Critical Evaluation by Twenty-Six Distinguished Writers,* ed. Allen Tate (New York: Delacorte Press, 1966). 2. *West of Childhood* (1965).

The Sewanee Review
Feb. 16, 1966

Dear Brother:

I got your letter this morning. She [Isabella] is the vortex and her letters and expostulations the round whirling. If she backs out, then you've got to apply for a divorce. After all you can't lie in the bed with a woman who audibly dreams of past husbands. Of course she is dependent upon you, the vortex is always dependent upon what it can suck in. It's never been a marriage; it's been a long arrangement, complicated by legality.

You've got to sweat it out, and it's going to be hard for you; but it will ruin you if you give in now. This is trial for Helen [Heinz]; it will also clarify her feelings. In such matters everybody has to pay his part and, as you know, we always pay twice, in the coin of the realm and by sorrow.

I don't want you to undo yourself, or to get involved in the repercussions. It's mighty easy for those around you to solve your problems; they don't have to live with them.

More later. I thought I would sit down and tell you this.

[Stephen] Spender is out of the country. He lectures here and the committee wants to know what to say about him. I told them I would ask you.

Love from all of us, Brother

TLS

University of Minnesota
February 21, 1966

Dear Brother,

I appreciate your letter. The situation *is* tough, but I seem to be making out. I may have written you that Isabella has gone to Mexico—went a week ago today—and she plans to return a few days before the hearing, which will be on March 28th. My financial future has been clouded by Ben's loss of memory. There has been a tricky arrangement by which I have been receiving annually enough to pay Caroline's alimony: tricky because secret, and there's no record of it, for a record would have meant a considerable loss in taxes. Now that Ben is *non compos mentis,* no change in his will is possible. I have consulted my lawyer, who says there is no possible way to correct matters short of exposing what has been going on since 1959. So, whether I can undertake and finance another marriage is very doubtful; and at present I don't know how to explain it to the young lady; for there is no tangible evidence of the situation that I can show. What has been happening is that annually, in four installments, I have received a *gift* amounting to Caroline's alimony. That ceased on last October 1st.

But as long as I can have these visiting professor jobs I'll be all right. I'll have to gamble on this.

I hope some arrangement can be worked out so that the SR type can be used for the book publication. It is a very handsome page, and this plan would save everybody money.

I don't know what to tell you about Stephen except what you will find in the British *Who's Who.* He may be in the American also. He has resigned from *Encounter,* and is for this year Consultant in Poetry at the Library of Congress. He also has some sort of part-time job at North-western University. He is writing a long, autobiographical poem parts of which I have seen; it is his most impressive piece of work.

Let me know how matters go with Seymour Lawrence. I hope to get down there toward the end of March.

Love to all.

Affly., Brother [Allen Tate]

TLS

University of Minnesota
March 10, 1966

Dear Brother,

Here's a story by a graduate student in French history who happens to be taking my course in writing—which he doesn't need. It's the most talented story I've ever had here.

Affly., Brother [Allen Tate]

AL

The Sewanee Review
March 18, 1966

Brother-

I thank you for that record.[1] It makes you sound almost in the next room. I'm awful glad to have it. I would have written sooner, but I've been in bed with flu. Bring any correspondence [about] Harcourt Brace rights when you come.

All send love, A

AL

1. Tate recorded some of his poems for the Yale Series of Recorded Poets, ed. Cleanth Brooks, New Haven: Carillon Records, 1960.

Oak Grove Hotel
230 Oak Grove Street
Minneapolis, Minn. 55403
May 2, 1966

Dear Brother,

Here's what I consider a very fine essay on Conrad Aiken. I hope you will like it. Conrad and JCR are the last of their generation, and I'd like to see something done for Conrad by the SR. I don't think the SR has ever had a full-length essay on him. This essay is too long. Miss Aldrich could cut it to less than thirty pages, by omitting some quotations.[1] It's the best thing on the subject I've seen except perhaps a piece by Kathleen Raine in the *Times Literary Supplement* a few years ago.

I talked to Nancy yesterday and they are greatly excited by the prospect of a week on the mountain. We all expect to arrive on Friday June 3rd. Allen [Wood] has been accepted by Sewanee; I hope he doesn't get accepted elsewhere because I want him to go to Sewanee. He'll like it once he's there.

Love to all, Brother [Allen Tate]

TLS

1. Jennifer Aldrich's essay "The Deciphered Heart: Conrad Aiken's Poetry and Prose Fiction" appeared in *The Sewanee Review,* 75 (Summer 1967), 485–520.

The Sewanee Review
Oct. 6, 1966

Bro:

The board hasn't met. I talked to Ned [McCrady] & Sollace [Freeman]. Ned said there was no reason to delay this. I've been going over family grave yards & documents, copying etc.[1] I don't quite know when I'll get up. Maybe not before November.

You have two copies of the essays, but I noticed they were sent to him. Can you write out there and have them forwarded? They did, I think, a good job.

Love to Helen, regards to others.

Affec., Bro. [Andrew]

AL

1. Lytle is gathering genealogical materials for his next book.

The Sewanee Review
May 8, 1967

Dear Brother:

Here's for the whiskey. Sorry we didn't get down. Jack[1] and I went to meet Pamela & Polly, but the plane did not get in until after two. Then it was too late for me to drive back down. I thought of staying with Lon, but thought better of it, as some of us were arriving & some leaving. See you soon.

Affec., Brother [Andrew]

AL

1. Maybe one of his students. He always had a student around to drive him.

The Sewanee Review
Oct. 19, 1967

Dear Brother:

I've been thinking about you all considerably. Now that Michael is there, it's going to be doubled up, the work.[1] I think, if you can find a good one, a practical nurse is absolutely necessary. I imagine a poor one would only add to Helen's trouble. It's good you don't have too much work. Usually you ain't much help in the house, but maybe you'll have to bestir yourself now. Just think of those little boys, growing up in front of your eyes. There seem to be a lot of workmen about your house.[2] I haven't had time to go in, but Eleanor[3] says they've done a lot inside. I can't see much changing outside. I gather they think they will be done in November.

No news here, except I am slowly doing some work on the memoirs,[4] but I'll declare the work increases here. We've had beautiful weather, and it is now changing to a deep chill. I wrote [Leonard] Unger and he accepted.

Let us know when you come in and we'll get fresh sheets on the bed.

Love to Helen.

Aff., Brother

TLS

1. On August 20, 1967, Helen Heinz Tate gave birth to twins—John Allen and Michael Paul. Michael was killed in July of the next year in a nursery accident. 2. Tate was having a house built in Sewanee to move into after his retirement from Minnesota in June 1968. 3. Wife of Charles Harrison, head of the English department. 4. Published as *A Wake for the Living* (New York: Crown Publishers, 1975).

The Sewanee Review
October 31, 1967

Dear Brother,

I went by your house yesterday and they're pretty far along. Everything is nearly done inside. However, it is my experience that it takes a long time to finish a lot of small things, but maybe the architect will see to this. I hope the practical nurse is working out because you all sounded pretty desperate.

I can't seem to get what I have to do done, although I'm moving slowly on the memoir. I don't think the good Father [Ralston] and I can make it to Knoxville as he has been away too much and that is the time of his seminar. I'll see you when you get here. Just drive on out to the house. I have to be in Louisville the 18th, to speak to the Descendants of the Mayflower Compact and visit with the children. By the way, did Tom

Landess write you about staying over for the questioning and setting straight certain historic matters concerning the movement?[1] He seemed to think that the Foundation would be more interested with Red there. By this I take him to mean that Red's liberalism might betray an attitude which foundations might like. You might drop Red a note, since the fee is large. Red did not give him a firm answer to the Festival itself. He had not been able to get a response from John Ransom. Do you suppose he is ill? Maybe he and Robb[2] are so deaf they can't hear the phone.

We are enclosing this letter from this crazy woman and returning her money. Somewhere Ralston has misplaced Anthony Hecht's address. I should have written him earlier. Our love.

Affectionately, Brother [Andrew]

TLS

I can't find that spy's account of Lee's entry into Chambersburg. I've looked in *Battles & Leaders* where could it be? I'd like to use it soon.

1. Lytle is referring to the Southern Literary Festival held at the University of Dallas in April 1968. The festival celebrated the Nashville Agrarians and among those present were Ransom, Tate, Lytle, and Warren. Davidson was too ill to attend. 2. Ransom's wife.

The Sewanee Review
Feb. 9, 1968

Dear Brother:

I liked this young lady's poems, all but these two I am returning. She misses the point about *The Secret Sharer*, but of course all she needed to do was have it set her going. However, I don't think that [it] is up to the others; nor do I quite think Anger is realized. There is too much in it which hides its center. If you like it and see things I don't I would be glad to add this to the other poems, since as you know we are now trying to print more poems and fewer poets in each issue. This is hard to make work.

I'm sorry about your heat bill at the house, but nobody can get the key. Eleanor [Harrison] doesn't feel like keeping on asking the man. I will say, however, that we've had some cold weather, the house is empty, and there may need adjustments to the heating apparatus. It seems high. Of course my bills, being electric, are higher still. For Jan. it is some eighty dollars. I'll be glad when you get here, with wife and twins, all in the expansion of a new day, a new house, to hell with time and those things that afflict the rest of us.

I'm over the flu and am working on my Joyce piece for Dallas.[1] The last two days it has gone well, and I think I will have a good reading of that; then back to the memoirs. I may have to go to New York for business, and

I hate the thought. By the way did they elect you? There's not much to say here. I get lonely in spite of a growing grandson, who is a delight and fine children to keep house for me. It's a good thing Henry didn't tell me the full powers of his knife. Langdon is making good grades but wants to come home. I told her she couldn't and explained it to her. With maturity beyond her years she has reached an attitude. She hates the school (she says) but she has made up her mind to do her best and endure it. We'll see about next year.

Give Helen my love and to yourself and offsprings love too.

Aff., Brother

TLS

1. "A Reading of Joyce's 'The Dead,'" which he gave at the reunion of The Agrarians at the University of Dallas. Later printed in *Sewanee Review*, 77 (Spring 1969), 70–85.

Appendixes

APPENDIX A

(Accompanies Tate's letter of November 3, 1929)

MESSAGE FROM ABROAD

Paris, November 1929
(To Andrew Lytle)

"Their faces are cut sharp . . . are very florid despite that their forebears nigh two hundred years inhabited the miasmal banks of tidal rivers where malarial fevers make men gaunt, and dosing with quinine shaketh them as with a palsy."
—Traveller to America (1799).

I

What years . . . what centuries
Broken, divided up and claimed?
A few here, a few there—in vigilance
Ceaseless and stale, to keep us unashamed
And fearless, not worried as the hare
Scurrying without memory:

Provence,
The Renascence, the age of Pericles—
Each a broad rich-carpeted stair
To pride, with manhood now the cost,
For the ways taken are all notorious
Lettered, sculptured and rhymed.
Those others, incuriously complete, lost,
Not by poetry and statues timed
Battered by sunlight and the impartial sleet.
What years . . . what centuries . . .

Only

The bent eaves and the windows
Cracked, and the thin grass; the hollow
Pine that screams in the new storm—
These we have seen at length

And the man, red-faced and tall, leaning
In the day of his strength
Not as a pine but the stiff form
Against the east pillar,
Hearing the ox-cart in the street,
His shadow gliding, a long nigger
Gliding at his feet.

II

Voyagers to the west, voyagers east:
I followed the cold northern track
Hung over the stern-rail
And the sleet sprinkled the sea
While the dim foam held back
The night . . . steadily
Steadily, steadily the sea.

At dawn the gull perched on the crest
Stared at the spray fell asleep
Over the picked bones the white face
Of the leaning man drowned deep,

The red-faced man, ceased wandering,
Never came to the boulevards
Nor spat covertly in the sawdust
Sunk in his collar
Shuffling the cards,

The man with the red face the stiff back
I cannot see in the rainfall
Down Saint Michel by the quays,
At the corner the wind speaking
Destiny—the four ways.

III

I cannot see you
The incorruptibles
Yours was a secret fate
The stiff-backed liars the dupes;
The universal blue
Of heaven rots,
Your anger is out of date:

What did you say mornings
What, evenings?
The bent eaves
On the cracked house
That ghost of a hound . . .
The men tall and red-faced
Cast no shadow
From the province of the drowned.
Allen Tate

APPENDIX B

(Accompanies Tate's Letter of July 31, 1931)

Route 6
Clarksville, Tenn.
July 28, 1931

John:

I thought I'd better write this to let him know I'm not too angry to write him. It is, of course, more hard-boiled than any public reply I could make. Hope you're writing one.

A.T.

Dear Edmund [Wilson]:

. . . *The New Republic* arrived punctually as usual yesterday morning, which was Monday, and tearing off the envelope with my accustomed eagerness, I felt rewarded for my long partiality to that journal's intelligence and disinterestedness, by the announcement of an article entitled "Tennessee Agrarians." Before I turned the pages, I said: Here at last is a full, able, and responsible discussion of our symposium, perhaps composed of arguments refuting our position, but at least informed where other critics have not even read the book; conscientious in its presentation of the facts; courageous in its desire to examine a position opposed to that of the *New Republic,* and all the more eager to do this because of the detached viewpoint of the editors, perhaps not least because most of the editors and many of our contributors are friends.

Instead of this, I find a slick piece of journalese which falsifies everything we stand for. I am unable to recognize your Cousin Charles; what I see there I am not in sympathy with. This is followed by the renovation of the family mansion, by marrying or rather by coming home to marry the Southern girl, by day-dreaming of Southern heroes. Not a single item of your impressionistic picture of an "agrarian" is true, and the whole is naturally false.

It seems to me, Edmund, that you have very lightly betrayed the *New Republic* and us. Hard words; but they are true.

Can you really with such unblushing glibness reduce our position to *ancestor worship?* You simply have not read the book. I challenge you to say whether you have.

I won't go into detail, but there are some leading points that I want to make. In the first place, if I held, as you seem to hold, so doctrinaire a position as a belief in Planned Economy, short of Communism, I should not quickly patronize others for lack of realism. It simply isn't nice, my dear Edmund. There is in your article a tone of superior wisdom that is not supported by evidence on your part of superior insight into the bad state of national affairs. Now if you can see no further into our position than your article shows, can we be certain that you are perfectly responsible when you deal with Henry Ford or the West Virginia miners? I'm afraid we can't.

You like to think that we are wistful boys mooning over the past. I will not go into that, except to say that we don't care a damn for the past as such; it is simply that our situation makes impossible for us to discuss the present [except?] in terms of the past; and I think you would be a hell of a lot better off if you could. There is one true statement in your article: we believe that the North got us into a mess. But first of all it got itself and is still getting itself into a worse mess. You resent our desire to get into it as deeply as you have; so you pretend that we are in as deep. Neither is this nice of you. And in you, Edmund, it simply isn't intelligent; for it represents the imperialistic impulse of Northern capitalism towards the South. If you are repudiating capitalism, you must repudiate the defense mechanisms which permitted the capitalists to pretend that the South need not be taken seriously, that anti-industrial is ancestor-worship and sentimentality.

Contrary to your suspicions, I admire greatly your moral fervor, but I think you ought to feel a little more responsibility towards it. You, in your turn, when the realism of opinion comes up, must remember that the N.R. boys, rather like Cowley's sex boys, are the Liberal Boys in a Balloon—which is hardly better than ancestor-worship, if we did that. There are, in our book, arguments of some seriousness and dignity representing the latent or avowed convictions, social and economic, of a vast number of people. Has the *New Republic* such a constituency? I doubt if it has a constituency at all in that sense. However, instead of examining our position, and perhaps finding it, as set forth, inadequate, instead of saying: Let's see what may come of it—you glance at the book superciliously in an occasional editorial and at last do it off in an ill-informed piece of gentle satire.

I think we must conclude inevitably that only some remnant of crank New Englandism can be taken seriously by you people—Planned Economy seems to worship an ancestor somewhere near Brook Farm—for we suffer terribly in your attention as compared to your recent friend Borsodi. In fact, you have no ear for a doctrine which does not confess that things are as bad as you find them in the North and East. We draw this moral: you are socially and spiritually bankrupt, and you won't have it that other people aren't—people who still see some hope of building on what they have, without throwing up the sponge and falling into the arms of a super-committee.

You have never answered your own question: Why is a Big Engineer better than a Little Engineer in planning where the engine is to run? My God, Edmund, what a plight you people are in, to put your faith in engineers. This is the most astounding religious faith I have ever seen.

There is another moral, but I merely touch it. Is there not some connection between the spiritual bankruptcy that I speak of and the irresponsibility of your opinions of us? I leave it at that.

Curiously enough your article made me think of you as a modern Orestes—driven by your curse of industrialism, hating it, but still cherishing it as if it were decreed in heaven. Whom the gods destroy they first make mad.

I must be very explicit, and subscribe myself.

Ever affectionately yours,
[Allen Tate]
TL

APPENDIX C

(Accompanies Tate's Letter of June 9, 1932)

THE SECRET OF THE CAPTAIN
(The Night before the Re-union)

People, people of my own kind, today
Home-folks, but strange with a new light
In the face; and the streets hard with motion,
And the hard eyes that look one way.
I am here with a secret in the night;
I am here because the dead wear gray.

It is a privilege to be dead.
You cannot know what absence is
Nor what the odor of pure distance is
Until—like me slowly dying in the head—
All sights and sounds of the moment, all
The life of sweet intimacy shall fall
Like a swift at dusk, and the heart of time,
Being time's, is bled.
There is no time. My secret
Is damnation; where have they, the new citizens, all
Come from? They were not born in my father's
House, nor in their fathers': on a street-corner
By motion sired, not born; by rest dismayed.

When I was a boy there was no cessation
Of the bright course of blood along the vein;
I moved, an old dog by me, to field and stream
In the pellucid ease of summer rain.

When I was a boy the light on the hills
Was there because I could see it, not because
Some special gift of God had put it there.
Men expect too much, do too little,
And have no skill in the interior mind
To fashion dignity with shapes of air.
Where have they come from?
                                        My father said
That everything but kin was less than kind.
The young men, like hogs, argue for a rind,
A flimsy shell to put their weakness in,
Will-less, ruled by what they cannot see;
Crouched like savages in a hollow tree,
They wait for the thunder to speak: Union,
That joins their hearts in fear.
                                        I fought
But did not care: well may war be
Terrible to those who have nothing to gain
For the satisfaction of the sense;
When the peace is a column of figures
Life, grown bloodless and immense,
Lusts after immunity to pain.
There is no civilization without death;
There's now only the wind for breath.

Waken, lords and ladies gay, we cried,
And marched to Cedar Run and Malvern Hill;
In the far distance, in the smoke, they died,
Our fathers, guardians of the iron will.

Waken, we shouted, lords and ladies gay!
We go to win that precinct of delight
That rears the bright center of the day. . .
We won it but they forfeited our right,

They, the young men who watch us from the kerbs,
They have the ease of wonder in their stare:
Our crooked backs, the hands like gnarled herbs,
The fixed eyes, gray face, the foreign hair.

March on, soldiers, we shall not fight again
Yankees, with our guns well-aimed and rammed,
For all are Yankees of the race of men
And this too, now, the country of the damned. . .

Poor bodies crowding round us, white of face,
Eyeless with eyesight only; shifts of power;

Stricken sublimities of time and space—
They are the fragments of an ancient tower

That stood in easy strength upon the land
Pouring its long white light into the mind,—
Damned souls, running the way of sand
Into the destination of the wind!
Allen Tate

APPENDIX D

(Accompanies Tate's Letter of June 17, 1932)

TO THE LACEDEMONIANS...

The old Confederate on the night before
the Re-union speaks partly to himself,
partly to imaginary comrades:

People, people of my own kind—today
Home-folks, but strange with a new light
In the face; and the streets hard with motion
And the hard eyes that look one way.
I am here with a secret in the night;
I am here because the dead wear gray.

It is a privilege to be dead. You
Cannot know what absence is nor what
The odor of pure distance is, until
From you—slowly dying in the head—
All sights and sounds of the moment, all
The life of sweet intimacy shall fall
Like a swift at dusk, and the heart of time,
The lightning pulse, is bled. . .
My secret, gentlemen, is
Damnation: where have they, the citizens, all
Come from? They were not born in my father's
House, nor in their fathers': on a street-corner
By motion sired, not born; by rest dismayed.
I have watched it, and endured it, I have delayed
Judgment; it wasn't in my time, by God, so
That the mere breed absorbed the generation:
When I was a boy there was no cessation
Of the bright course of blood along the vein,
I moved, an old dog by me, to field and stream
In the pellucid ease of summer rain:

When I was a boy the light on the hills
Was there because I could see it, not because
Some special gift of God had put it there.
Men expect too much, do too little,
Put the contraption before the accomplishment,
And have no skill in the interior mind
To fashion dignity with shapes of air.

Where have they come from?
(Go and tell them
That we their servants, well-trained, gray coated
And haired, whether foot or horse, or in
The grave, them obey . . . obey them,
What commands?)

My father said
That everything but kin was less than kind.
The young men, like hogs, argue for a rind,
A flimsy shell to put their weakness in,
Will-less, ruled by what they cannot see;
Crouched like savages in a rotten tree
They wait for the thunder to speak: Union,
That joins their hearts in fear.
I fought
But did not care: well may war be
Terrible to those who have nothing to gain
For the illumination of the sense:
When the peace is a column of figures
Life, grown sullen and immense,
Lusts after immunity to pain.
There is no civilization without death;
There is now the wind for breath.

Waken, lords and ladies gay, we cried,
And marched to Cedar Run and Malvern Hill—
His black stallion reeled in the smoke; he died,
My father, captain of the iron will.

Waken, we shouted, lords and ladies gay!
We go to win the precincts of the light,
Shadowless eternity of our day;
We won it, but they forfeited that right,

They, the young men who watch us from the kerbs,
They hold the glaze of wonder in their stare:
Our crooked backs, hands fetid as old herbs,
The fixed eyes, tallow face, the foreign hair.

Soldiers, march! We shall not fight again
The Yankees with our guns well-aimed and rammed,
For all are Yankees of the race of men
And this too, now, the country of the damned. . .

Poor bodies crowding around us, white of face,
Eyeless with eyesight only; bones of power;
Stricken sublimities of time and space—
They are the fragments of an ancient tower

That stood in easy strength upon the land
Pouring its long white ray into the mind,—
Damned souls, running the way of sand
Into the destination of the wind!

Allen Tate

APPENDIX E

(Accompanies Tate's Letter of November 2, 1932)

c/o Guaranty Trust Co.
4 Place de la Concorde
Paris
December 22, 1932

Robert Penn Warren, Esq.
Benfolly Tenn.

Dear Uncle Penn:

I send you herewith the only story that Tate has ever written, and something about it tells me that he will never write another one. I hope you will tell me all that is wrong with it. And when you're through, send it on to Andrew. I enclose a self-addressed envelope for the purpose . . . I fear the machinery in the story creaks and groans something awful. But there it is.

In haste, but Merry Christmas.

Yrs., Allen

APPENDIX F

(Accompanies Tate's Letter of November 2, 1932)

PICNIC AT CASSIS

Quem das finem, rex magne, laborum?

Where we went in the boat was a long bay
A sling-shot wide walled in by towering stone,

The air feckless dissolved the easy spray
Washed the white shadows, the sun's skeleton:

Where we went in the small ship the sea-weed
Parted and gave us up the murmuring shore
And we made feast and in our secret need
Devoured the very plates the hero bore:

When you O Trojans shall see through the dim light
The green coast where you thunder-tossed would win,
Drop sail and hastening to drink all night
Eat dish and bowl—to take that sweet land in!

Where we feated and caroused on the sandless
Pebbles, affecting our day of piracy,
What prophecy of eaten plates we landless
Wanderers fulfilled by the ancient son?

We for that time might taste the famous age
Eternal here yet hidden from our eyes
When lust of power undid its stuffless rage
And, in a wineskin, bore earth's paradise:

Let us once more lie down by the breathing side
Of ocean where our live forefathers sleep
As if the Known Sea still were a month wide—
Atlantic howls but is no longer steep!

What country shall we conquer, what fair place
Unman our power and locate our blood. . .
We have swallowed the world, run through the race
Of men. From the Gates of Hercules we flood

Westward, westward till the barbarous brine
Whelms us to the tired world where ripening corn,
Fat beans, grapes sweeter than muscadine,
Rot in the field: in that land were we born.

Allen Tate

APPENDIX F

(Accompanies Tate's Letter of November 2, 1932)

THE MEANING OF LIFE

Think about it at will: there is that
Which is the commentary and that other
Thing which may be named the immaculate

Conception of its essence in itself.
It is necessary to distinguish the weights
Of the two methods lest the first smother
The second; the second be speechless without the first.
I was saying this more briefly the other day
But one must be explicit as well as brief.
When I was a small boy I had my home
For nine years in that part of Old Kaintuck
Where the mountains fringe the Blue Grass;
The old men shot at one another for luck.
It made me think I was like none of them:
At twelve I was determined to shoot only
For honor; at thirty not to shoot at all;
I know at thirty-three that one must shoot
As often as one gets the rare chance—
There's more in killing than mere commentary:
Our sense of the proper decoration alters
But there's a kind of lust feeds on itself
Unspoken to, unspeaking; subterranean
As a black river full of eyeless fish
Heavy with spawn; with a passion for time
Longer than the arteries of a cave.

APPENDIX G

(Accompanies Lytle's Letter of Thursday [June 1936])

1531 Forrest Avenue
Memphis, Tenn.
June 27, 1936

Dear Mr. Chambers:

I have been away in Louisiana, and I've just read your letters. Here is something to use.

The Long Night, by Andrew Lytle, is at once the most powerful and the richest in substance of all contemporary novels about the South. There is in the book enough material for twenty novels.

Here is an alternative suggestion. If you'd rather have me review the book in a New York journal, I should be delighted to do so; but in that case I doubt if a blurb by me ought to appear.

Since you are general in this campaign, I shall await your orders.

Sincerely yours,
(Signed) Allen Tate

D. L. Chambers, Esq.
Bobbs-Merrill Co.
Indianapolis, Ind.

APPENDIX G2

(Accompanies Tate's letter of May 1937)

AN OPEN LETTER

Chancellor James H. Kirkland
Vanderbilt University
Nashville, Tennessee

My dear Sir:

This letter will reach you as the intrusion of a stranger, yet I hope without impropriety. I am an alumnus of Vanderbilt and I take interest in her affairs.

It is now common knowledge that Mr. John Crowe Ransom is about to leave Vanderbilt to join the faculty of a college in Ohio. I know nothing of the reasons that may prompt Mr. Ransom to go, after twenty-five years at his Alma Mater, to another institution. If he goes it will be a calamity from which Vanderbilt will not soon recover.

Mr. Ransom is, I fear, a little more famous internationally than locally. He is one of the most distinguished men of letters in the world today. Where Vanderbilt is known outside her Alumni Associations and similar groups of persons whose enlightenment of interest is not quite perfect, she is known as the institution where John Crowe Ransom profoundly influences, through his teaching and writing, the course of modern literature. I need not cite any of his more brilliant achievements, but I should like to bring to your attention two recent incidents that illustrate the far-reaching character of his reputation. The Lowell family of Boston and Harvard University has just sent one of its sons to Nashville to study poetry with Mr. Ransom—I do not say Vanderbilt, because young Mr. Lowell will follow Mr. Ransom to Ohio. In the past few months a correspondent of mine at Cambridge, England, has informed me that his fellow students repeatedly express a wish to study under John Crowe Ransom.

I am sure that you have applauded the notable revival of letters in the South and that you have felt in it a proprietary interest, since the center of this revival has been Vanderbilt University. I can only ask you to imagine Harvard University, at the height of the New England revival, letting Charles Eliot Norton go to a small college in the Middle West.

I know that college officials labor under peculiar difficulties. Occupied as they must be with organization and finance, they are infrequently in a position to judge the value of certain members of their faculties. If this is true of the officials, it is even truer of boards of trustees, which, I believe, are as a rule composed of business men who tend to look upon professors of even the first distinction as mere employes. If you are not aware of Mr. Ransom's distinction, which is of the very first order, the sources of your information have been faulty, and I am sure that you will see it as your duty, in view of the gravity of the occasion, to correct them. But if you, as the head of a great university, are indifferent to the grounds of this expostulation, then I can only pity you, and meditate upon emotions that I shall not easily get my own consent to express. The literary historians of the future will express them for me.

Very truly yours,
Allen Tate

APPENDIX H

(Accompanies Tate's Letter of February 17, 1942)

William Roth
The Colt Press
615 Commercial St.
St. Francisco, Calif.
[Aboard the San Francisco Overland Limited] Feb. 13 [1942]

Dear Mr. Tate:

Please excuse this short and messy note. The train bounces and the typewriter is terrible. Thank you very much for sending me "Alchemy" to read. I thought that it was a very exciting piece of work and something that our press could very well do—in a small edition and attractively done. I am through trying to put out short works like that as inexpensive trade books, people are not impressed by concentrated value. But I think we can get away with it charging slightly more (three dollars or so for a short book) and really spend time on the design and printing, etc.

I left before I could discuss the project over thoroughly with my partner, but have asked her to write me what she thinks and I can then get in touch with Lytle.

I hope to be in Princeton for a day, and should like to call on you if you are there.

Best,
Bill Roth

APPENDIX I

(Accompanies Lytle's Letter of July 31, 1957)

Critical Comment on
THE VELVET HORN
by Andrew Lytle

"Andrew Lytle has something that I am tempted to call genius. I don't know of any other way to account for his achievements. He breaks most of the rules and emerges with a novel which is beautiful and terrible and utterly his own. I suspect that it is a landmark in American fiction. I do not know any other novel like it."

—Caroline Gordon

Taken from the back of the dust jacket of
A Novel, A Novella, and Four Stories

APPENDIX J

(Accompanies Tate's Letter of December 1, 1959)

University of Minnesota
December 1, 1959

Mr. Henry C. Alexander
Morgan Guaranty Trust Company
140 Broadway
New York 15, New York

Dear Henry:

Some weeks ago Harvie Branscomb was up here for the Vanderbilt-Minnesota game, and I talked to him a little about the financing of the proposed chair of Southern Literature. He seemed to have nothing definite in view, though he was still very much interested.

Shortly after his visit I made an indirect approach, through a friend in Washington, to the Old Dominion Foundation. This Foundation is one of Paul Mellon's institutions, and although there is a possibility, I am not too optimistic, as Paul Mellon is primarily interested in Yale; so I am just wondering whether you and Ben have had any ideas on the subject.

The English Department at Vanderbilt is completely enthusiastic, as evidenced in a memorandum of Randall Stewart's to the Chancellor back in October, copy of which Stewart sent to me. That hurdle of academic politics has been jumped.

I was enormously pleased by the great Alexander spread in *Time* magazine.

Ever yours, Allen Tate
TL

APPENDIX K

(Accompanies Tate's Letter of February 2, 1960)

NATIONAL GALLERY OF ART
Washington 25, D.C.
Smithsonian Institution
December 14, 1959

Dear Allen:

I discussed your little problem with Ernie Brooks, the President of Old Dominion, when I was in New York last week. Ernie said that you had already written to Jack Matthews about the problem and he will try to bring it up at the next meeting of the Trustees of the Foundation which will be about January 28th. Jack has promised to fill him in on any details he may need.

I hope you will be coming East this winter. All the best,

Ever,
Huntington [Cairns]
TLS

Professor Allen Tate
University of Minnesota
Department of English
Minneapolis 14, Minnesota

APPENDIX L

(Accompanies Tate's Letter of February 2, 1960)

MEMORANDUM

Wellfleet, Mass.
August 29, 1959

To: Henry C. Alexander
Benjamin E. Tate
From: Allen Tate

Following our recent conversations at Chatham, Mass., I propose to recapitulate some of the ideas we discussed concerning a possible Professorship of Southern Literature at Vanderbilt University.

I believe we were agreed that Vanderbilt would be the most appropriate university in the entire South for the location of such a chair. Although the recent Southern Renaissance was not confined to Vanderbilt, it was nevertheless at Vanderbilt that the Fugitive group appeared, and these men are increasingly held to have been the most important literary group to appear in America since the New England Transcendentalists. It would seem, then, that Vanderbilt has what amounts almost to an obligation to recognize the part it played in the recent past and to do further service to Southern Literature through the foundation of a chair in this field.

The practical steps to be taken must, of course, be left to the joint action of the Chancellor, the Board of Trust, and the Department of English. The following possibilities, however, occur to me:

1. The new chair would be administered by the Department of English, and its scope confined to the teaching of Southern Literature, with the supervision of projects in creative writing at the graduate level. This would be the traditional way of setting it up, and a satisfactory way.

2. A different method would make possible a broader range of interests; that is, the inclusion of history, philosophy, and literature; so that the chair might be called the Professorship of Southern Civilization. A program for majors in this

broad field could be coordinated with the Departments of History, English, and Philosophy. I do not know whether there is an administrative precedent at Vanderbilt for this kind of chair. There are precedents elsewhere: the University Professorships at Rutgers University, and the professors who comprise the Committee on Social Thought at the University of Chicago. These professors cooperate with the various departments but are not "in" a department. They are directly responsible to the Chancellor or President.

APPENDIX M

(Accompanies Tate's Letter of February 2, 1960)

140 Broadway
New York 15
December 3, 1959

From: Henry C. Alexander

Dear Allen:

Thank you for your letter of December 1 about Vanderbilt, its English Department and Andrew.

No, I haven't really done anything more about pushing the subject with the Chancellor and I suppose the matter now comes down to money. I saw Randall Stewart's memorandum to the Chancellor or Ben told me about it. Anyway, I do have the impression, as you do, that the hurdle of academic politics has been crossed. I should think that money is the only remaining hurdle and whenever the Chancellor, with his many duties and interests, can get around to it I should think that he would find the money some place. It was good of you to approach the Old Dominion Foundation. I am not familiar with its interests or purposes. I hope to see Ben some time in the near future and he and I will talk about other approaches that we might make.

Thank you for your reference to the spread in *TIME* magazine. It was rather horrifying to me. I didn't recognize the man they talked so much about but some day I have hopes of meeting him.

With my best,

As ever, Henry
TLS

Mr. Allen Tate
Department of English
University of Minnesota
College of Science, Literature and the Arts
Minneapolis 14, Minnesota

APPENDIX N

(Accompanies Tate's Letter of June 5, 1965)

May 28, 1965

Dear Mr. Stewart,

I was away when your book and your letter of May 19th arrived; so I received them at the same time.

I have read all the two chapters about me, and much of the parts on Ransom and Warren, as well as a great deal of the preliminary matter on the Fugitives and Agrarians. I am surprised to see that you do not, as a scholar, use earlier criticism of us in your "analyses" of our poems. Would not some of the things you misunderstand, or simply misread, have been made plain? This applies to your commentaries on Ransom and Warren as well as to myself.

Many things in your chapters on me are perplexing. Why, for example, do you give six or seven pages to the early version of my "Ode to the Confederate Dead," and ignore the existence of my three published poems in *terza rima:* "The Maimed Man," "The Swimmers," and "The Buried Lake"? The inference is almost irresistible that you had not looked at *Poems* (1960), even though you refer to it in a footnote. ("The Maimed Man" could have been found in an issue of *Partisan Review* in 1952.) This is all the more puzzling when one observes the scholarly zeal with which you tracked down my *juvenilia*. I might point out that the "Swinburnian" lines that you quote are clumsy attempts at Laforgian irony, and likewise the poem "Lycambes Talks to John," and not "serious" poems. The poem "William Blake" was a deliberate joke. I contemplate your animadversions on my youthful manners with as much serenity as I am capable of.

I detect in your method throughout a passion for connecting everything with everything else, by means of inference, not of evidence. Because Hart Crane was living in the house with my wife and myself at the time I wrote "Ignis Fatuus" you assume that the poem was influenced by him and even about him. Hart had nothing whatever to do with the poem. I wrote it deliberately as a companion piece to Tennyson's "The Gleam" and Poe's "El Dorado": a poet's creed. Hart, alas, had no "latinity" whatever. I was placing myself in the perspective of Mediterranean classicism. This is analyzed by Miss Lillian Feder in an essay which you do not refer to, published in 1960, entitled "Allen Tate's Use of Classical Literature." You have reversed the roles of Hart and myself. I admired him greatly, but he had no influence on me whatever. Influence cannot be proved by geographical propinquity; it can be established only by the comparison of texts.

The inference you draw from my "Mother and Son" about the character of my mother I find disconcerting. Even had she been a "dominating woman," I do not see how this would in any way aid the critic in elucidating the poem: the poem speaks for itself. Moreover, when you come to "A Dream" and "A Vision," you say that my mother was "proud of her ties with this group"—presumably antebellum Virginia. What, sir, is your authority for this statement? She simply took her family and its connections for granted; and there was no "group." Again I do not see how this statement throws any light on the two poems. Historical scholarship further misleads you when you assume that "The Oath" is "about" the dead of the Old South. How the poem came to be written is as follows: I had for years been impressed by W. W. Jacobs' story "The Monkey's Paw." I wished in my poems to dramatize a supernatural intuition which cannot be reduced to language: Are the living really living, or are they [the] supposed dead the actual living? This is a question universal in any Christian society, and it has nothing specifically to do with the South. The only way such a question can be actualized is in its *effect* upon people who are aware of it. In Jacobs' story we do not see the dead son knocking at the door; we see the *effect* on the mother and father. Here again is a mistaken application of historical inference.

You have spent more than ten years writing this book, and it is a formidable achievement. I seem to see in your book the charge against historical scholarship made years ago by Irving Babbitt: the combination of Baconian positivism and impressionistic criticism. The critic who can say of Ransom's "The Equilibrists" that it "wanders and gropes" is not a good reader of poetry: he is a person who either over-reads or misreads. You seem to like Warren better than either Ransom or myself. I too like Warren better than myself; but that is beside the point. The first three or four pages on Warren's background are simply wrong: you don't get it.

The failure to consult other critics and the humorless elaboration of trivial matters have resulted in a book of doubtful value. I am sorry to say these harsh things. I do not see how I can possibly be proud of my record as you set it forth in your book.

Sincerely yours,
(Signed: Allen Tate)

Professor John L. Stewart

Index